ONMYOJI

19

STORY & ART
YOSHIAKI SUKENO

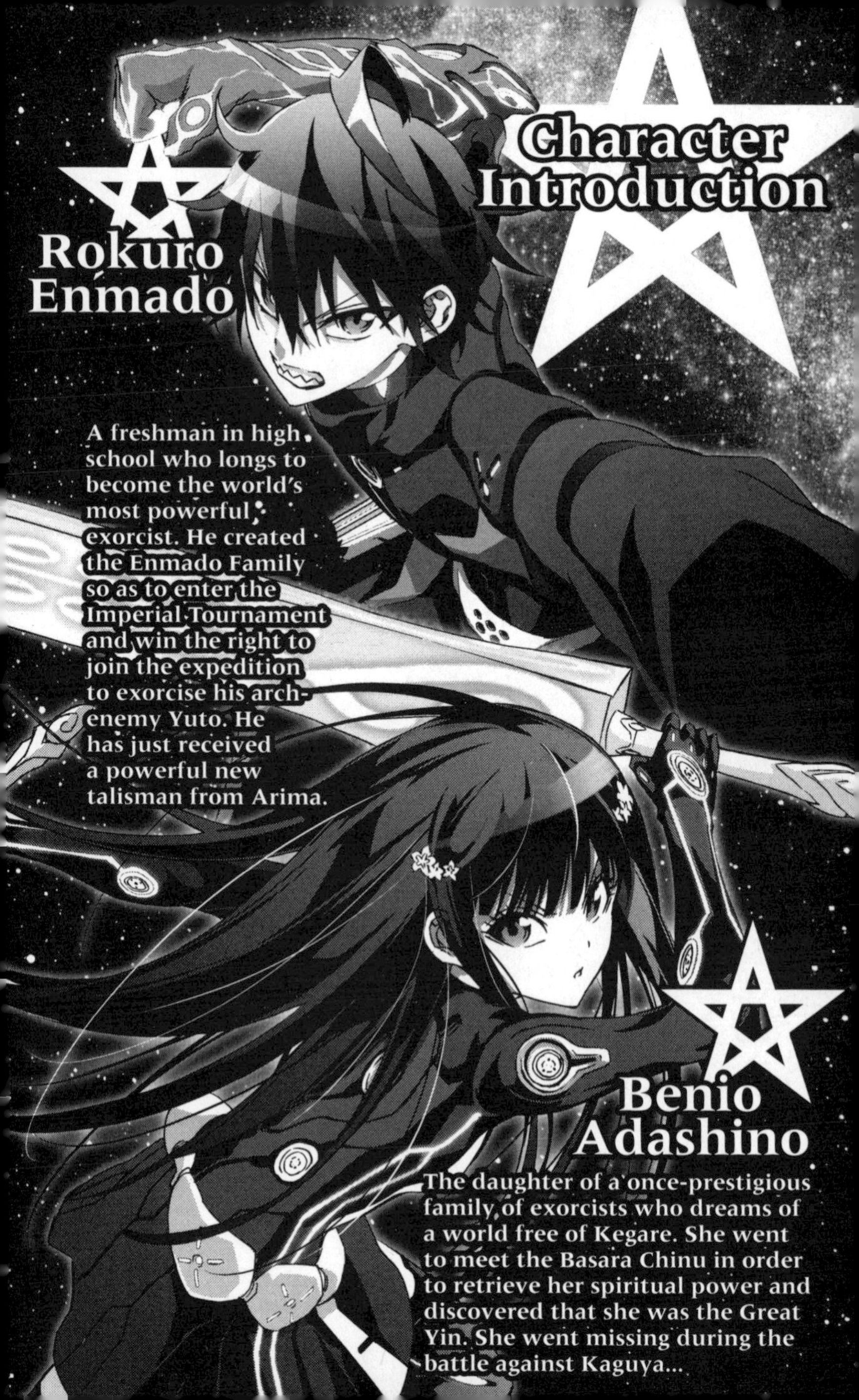

Character Introduction

Rokuro Enmado

A freshman in high school who longs to become the world's most powerful exorcist. He created the Enmado Family so as to enter the Imperial Tournament and win the right to join the expedition to exorcise his arch-enemy Yuto. He has just received a powerful new talisman from Arima.

Benio Adashino

The daughter of a once-prestigious family of exorcists who dreams of a world free of Kegare. She went to meet the Basara Chinu in order to retrieve her spiritual power and discovered that she was the Great Yin. She went missing during the battle against Kaguya...

Twin Star Exorcists

ONMYOJI

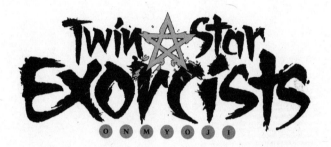

Arimori Tsuchimikado

The Chief Exorcist of the Association of Unified Exorcists, the organization that presides over all exorcists. Before dying in battle with Sakanashi, he gave Rokuro a powerful new talisman to fight with.

Yuto Ijika

Benio's twin brother. He was the perpetrator of the Hinatsuki Tragedy, and has now joined forces with the Basara to destroy Tsuchimikado Island.

Tenma Unomiya

Twelve Guardian member God of the In-Between. Head of the Unomiya Family and said to be the most powerful exorcist. He was under house arrest following the Imperial Tournament, but has now joined Rokuro's battle against Yuto.

Mayura Otomi

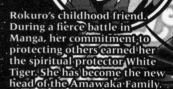

Rokuro's childhood friend. During a fierce battle in Manga, her commitment to protecting others earned her the spiritual protector White Tiger. She has become the new head of the Amawaka Family.

Story Thus Far...

Kegare are creatures from Magano, the underworld, and it is the duty of an exorcist to hunt, exorcise and purify them. Rokuro and Benio are the Twin Star Exorcists, fated to bear the Prophesied Child who will defeat the Kegare. Their goal was to go to Tsuchimikado Island to get revenge on Yuto, the mastermind behind the Hinatsuki Tragedy and Benio's brother. After two years, Rokuro qualifies to go to the island, but Benio loses her spiritual power in battle. Rokuro heads down to the island without Benio to train for a showdown with Yuto Ijika.

However, before the exorcists manage to organize their expedition, Yuto joins several other Basara to launch a coordinated simultaneous attack on five locations inside Magano! The force field that separates the two worlds is breeched, and the Association of Unified Exorcists is in grave danger. Before meeting his fate, Arima manages to defeat Sakanashi and lift the seal he had cast upon Rokuro to both bind his powers and enable him to store up a massive amount of energy over time. Arima's dying hope is that his sacrifice will hasten the end of the everlasting battle between the exorcists and the Kegare. Now, together with Tenma, Rokuro must face his archenemy Yuto under less than ideal circumstances...

Twin Star Exorcists

ONMYOJI

EXORCISMS

19

ONMYOJI have worked for the Imperial Court since the Heian era. In addition to exorcising evil spirits, as civil servants they performed a variety of roles, including advising nobles by foretelling the future, creating the calendar, observing the movements of the stars, measuring time...

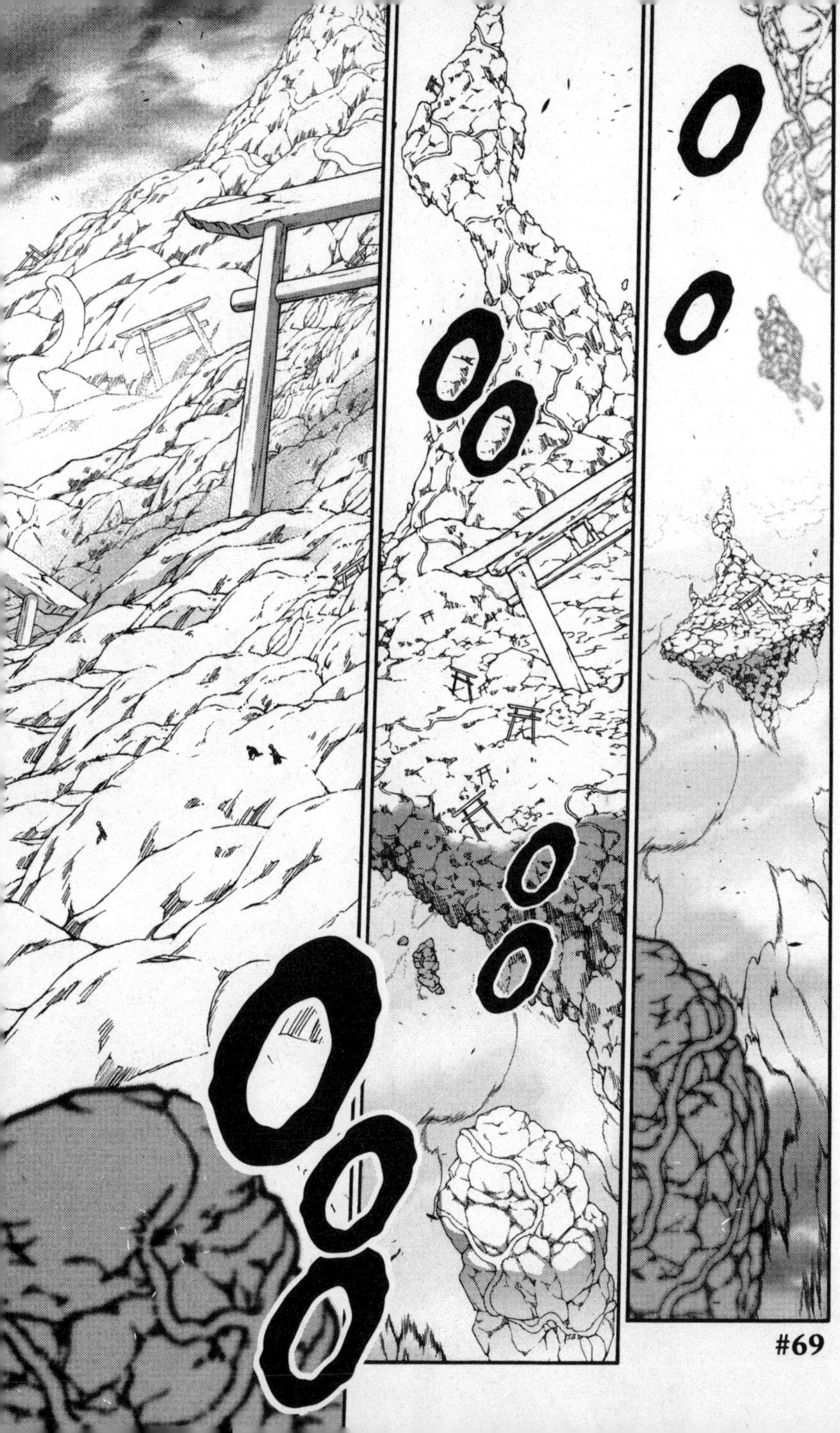
OO
OOOO
OOO

#69

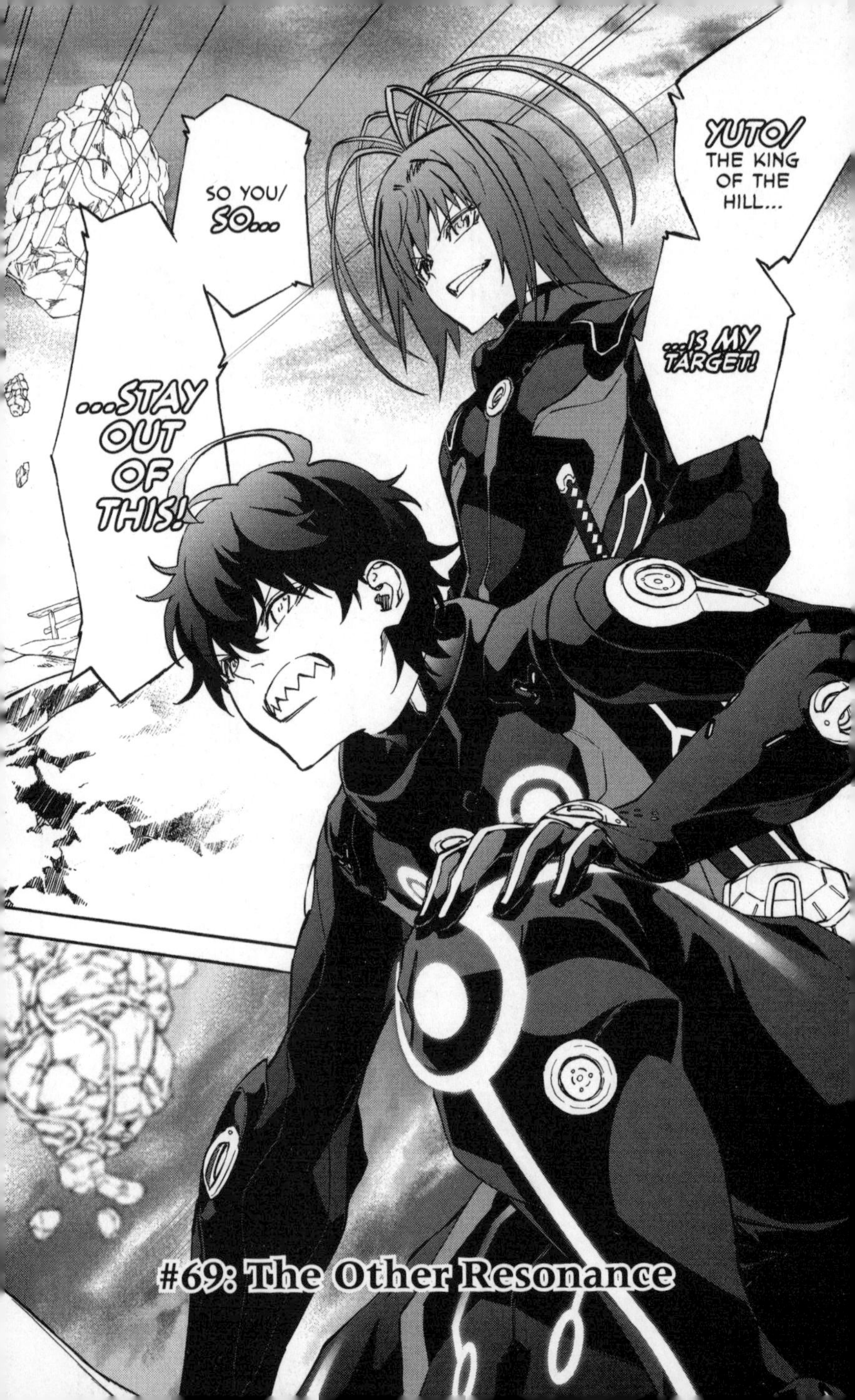
YUTO/
THE KING OF THE HILL...
...IS MY TARGET!
SO YOU/ SO...
...STAY OUT OF THIS!

#69: The Other Resonance

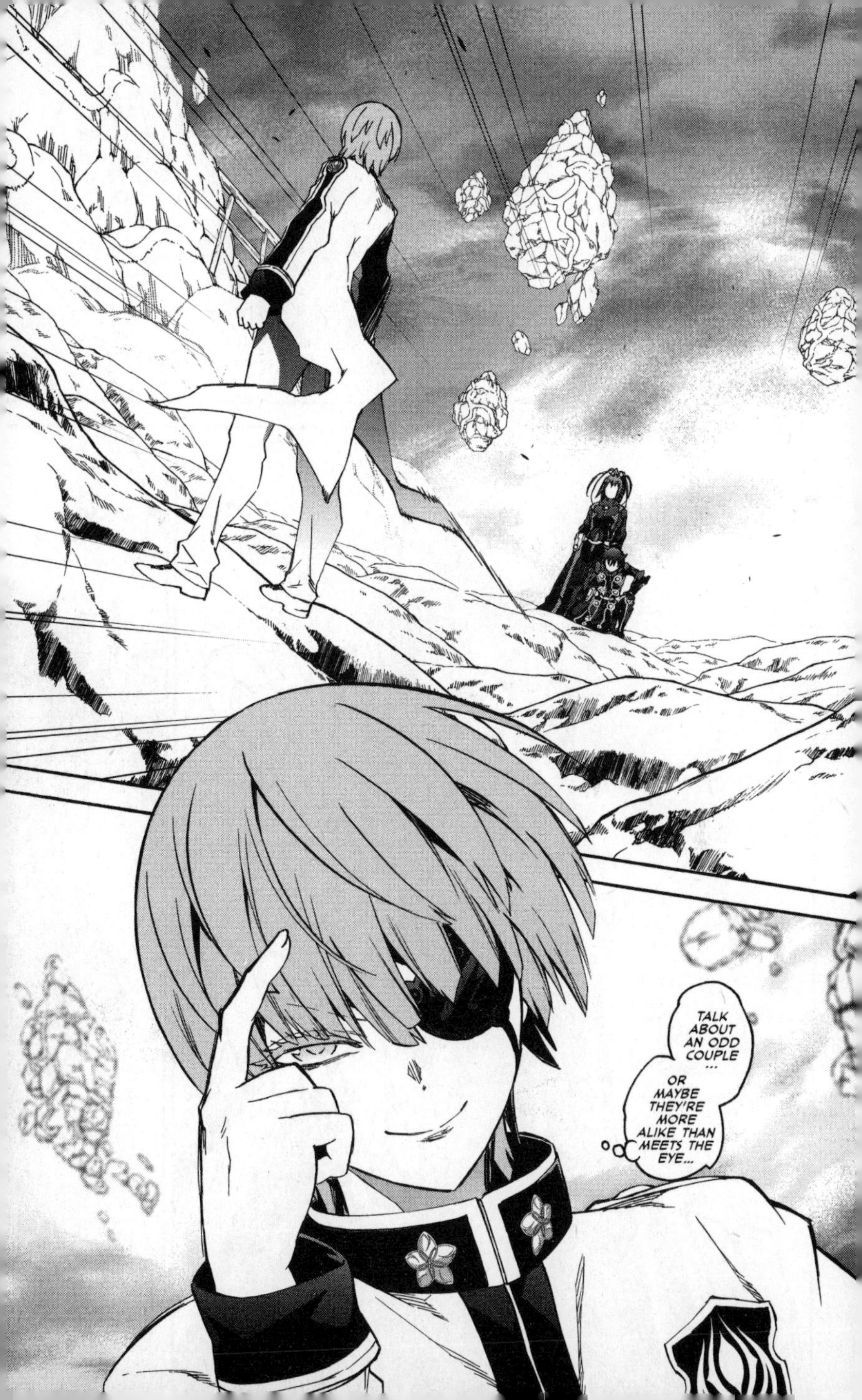
TALK ABOUT AN ODD COUPLE...
OR MAYBE THEY'RE MORE ALIKE THAN MEETS THE EYE...

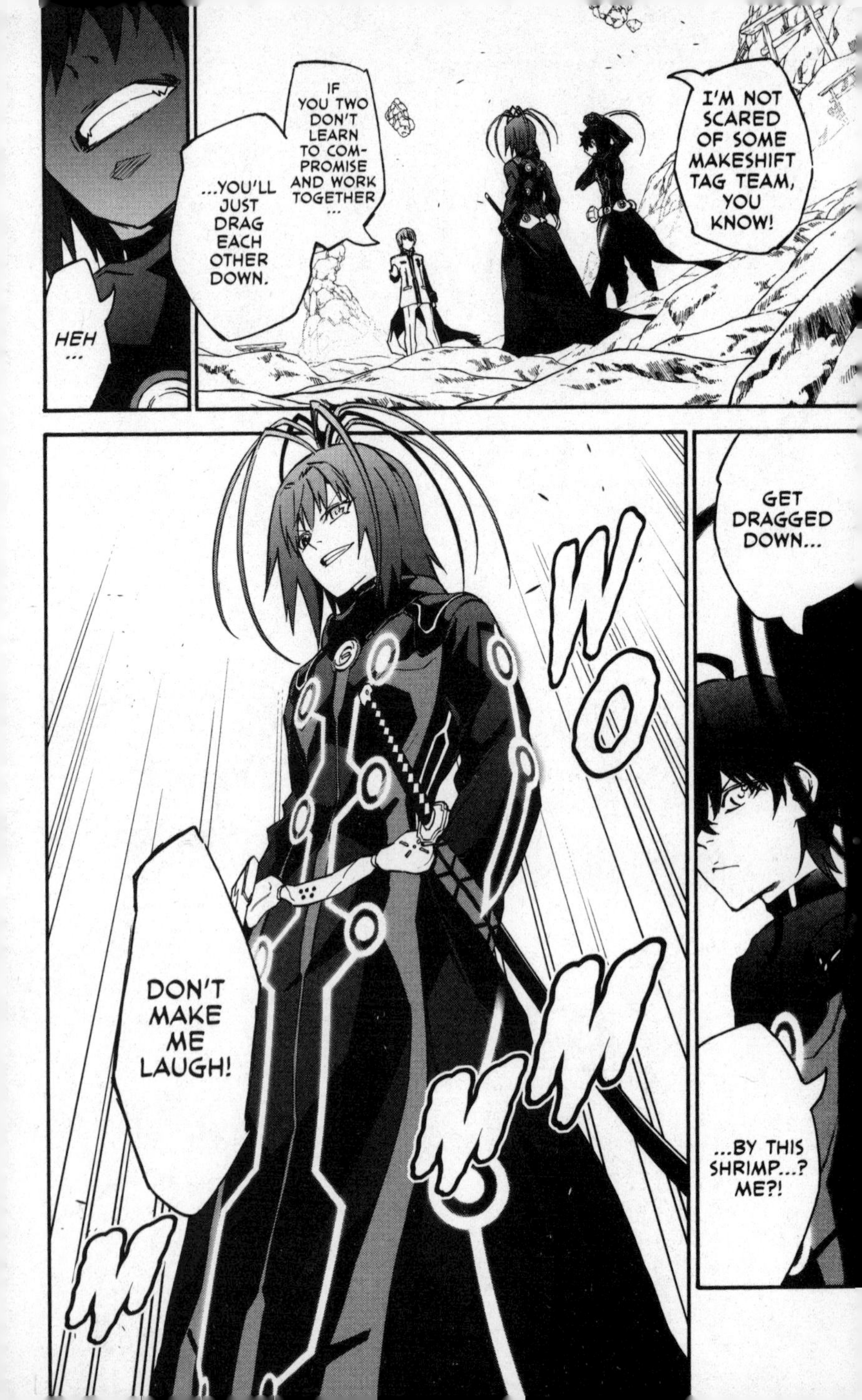
I'M NOT SCARED OF SOME MAKESHIFT TAG TEAM, YOU KNOW!
IF YOU TWO DON'T LEARN TO COMPROMISE AND WORK TOGETHER...
...YOU'LL JUST DRAG EACH OTHER DOWN.
HEH...
GET DRAGGED DOWN...
...BY THIS SHRIMP...? ME?!
WOMMM
DON'T MAKE ME LAUGH!

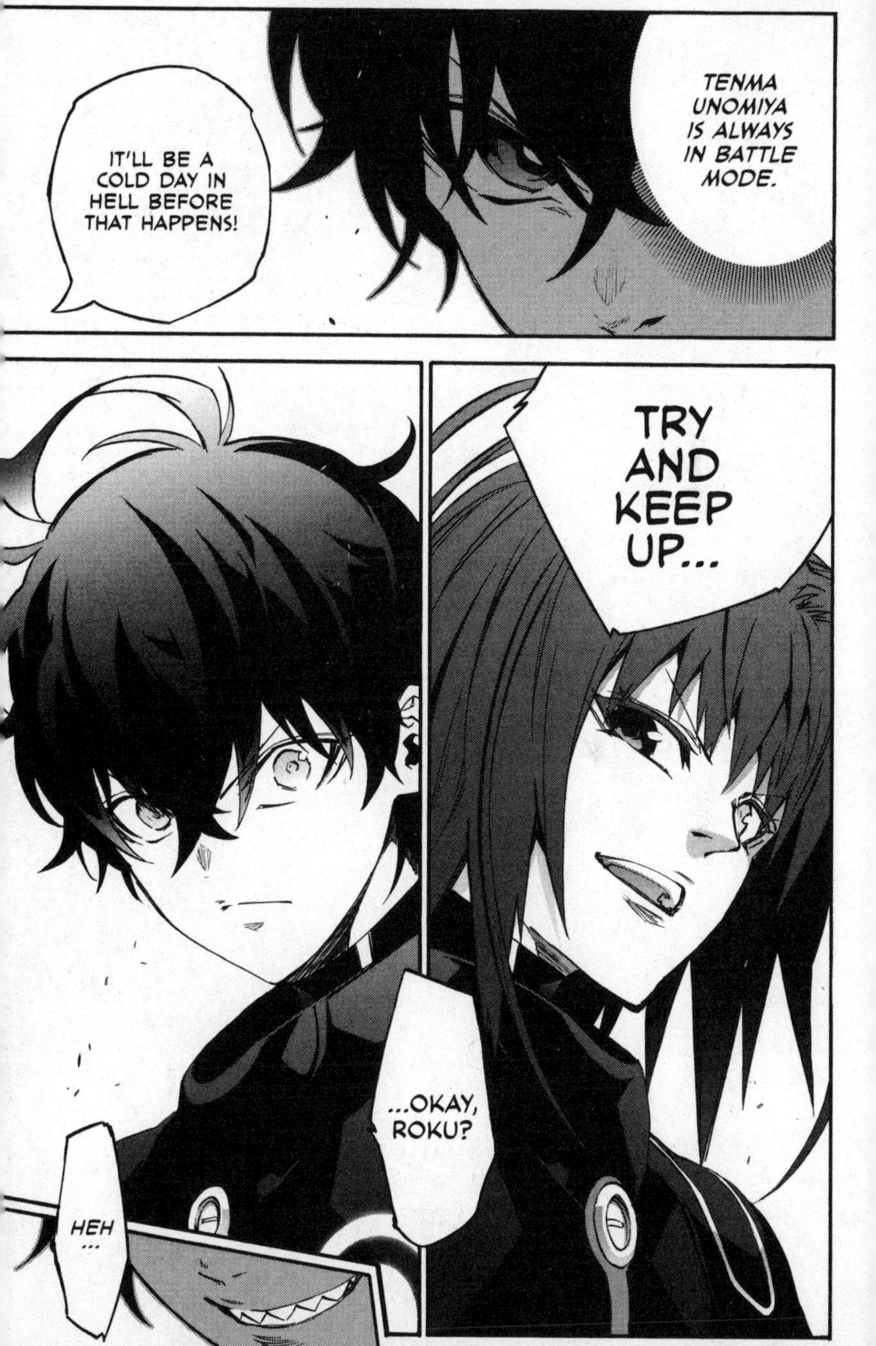
TENMA UNOMIYA IS ALWAYS IN BATTLE MODE.
IT'LL BE A COLD DAY IN HELL BEFORE THAT HAPPENS!
TRY AND KEEP UP...
...OKAY, ROKU?
HEH...

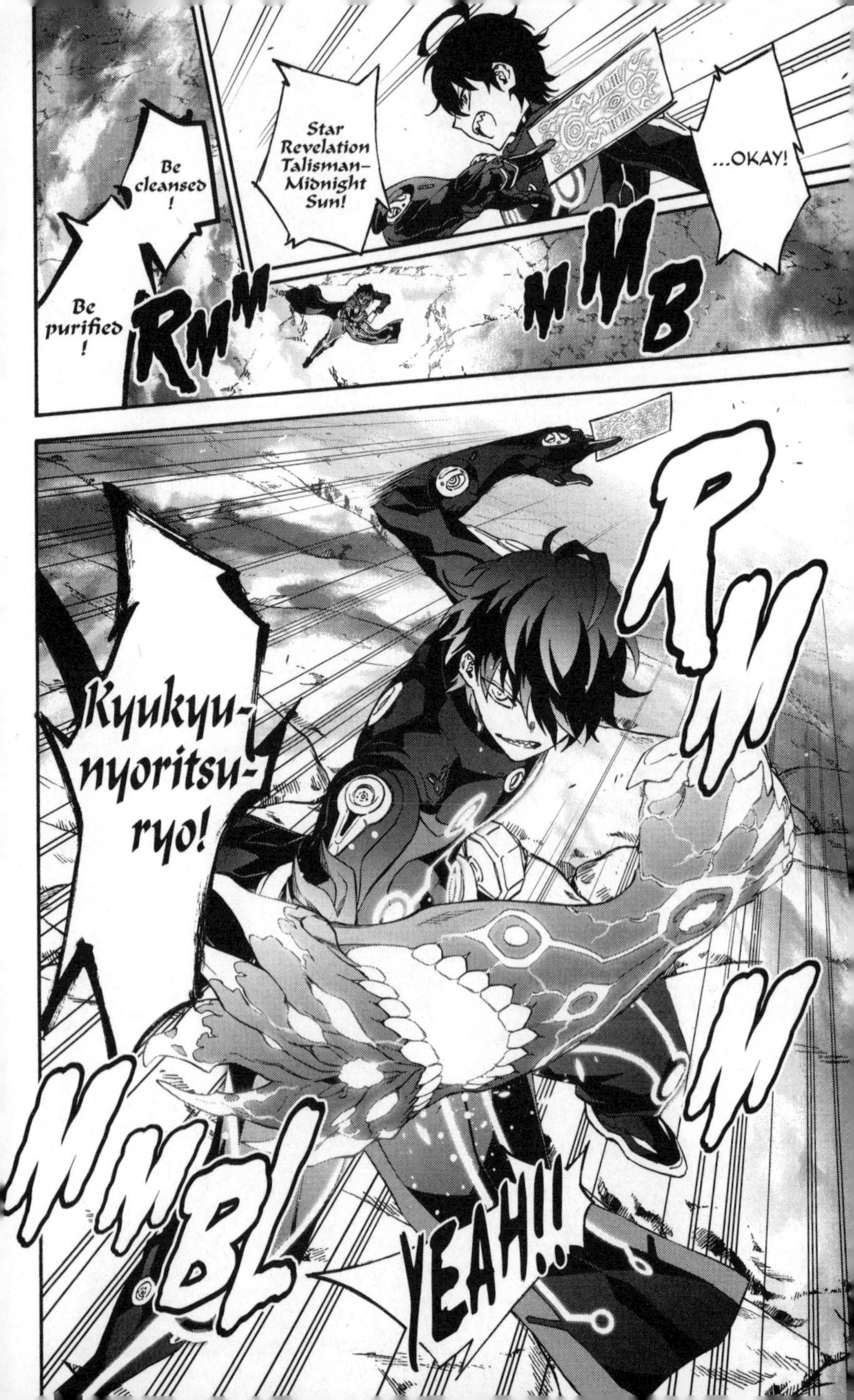
...OKAY!
Star Revelation Talisman— Midnight Sun!
Be cleansed!
Be purified!
RMM
MMMB
RMM
M
Kyukyu-nyoritsu-ryo!
YEAH!!
MMBL!

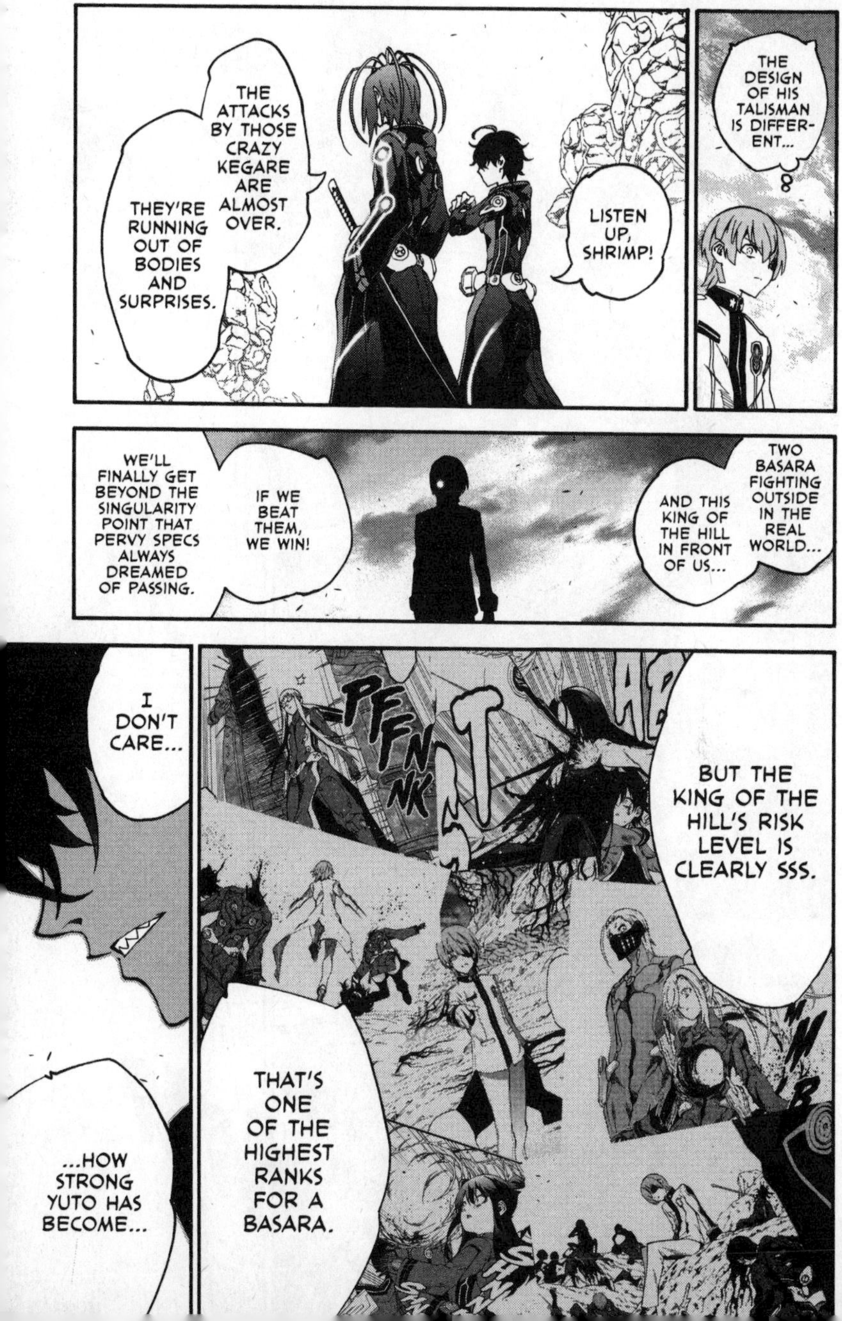
THE DESIGN OF HIS TALISMAN IS DIFFERENT...
LISTEN UP, SHRIMP!
THE ATTACKS BY THOSE CRAZY KEGARE ARE ALMOST OVER.
THEY'RE RUNNING OUT OF BODIES AND SURPRISES.
TWO BASARA FIGHTING OUTSIDE IN THE REAL WORLD...
AND THIS KING OF THE HILL IN FRONT OF US...
IF WE BEAT THEM, WE WIN!
WE'LL FINALLY GET BEYOND THE SINGULARITY POINT THAT PERVY SPECS ALWAYS DREAMED OF PASSING.
BUT THE KING OF THE HILL'S RISK LEVEL IS CLEARLY SSS.
THAT'S ONE OF THE HIGHEST RANKS FOR A BASARA.
I DON'T CARE...
...HOW STRONG YUTO HAS BECOME...

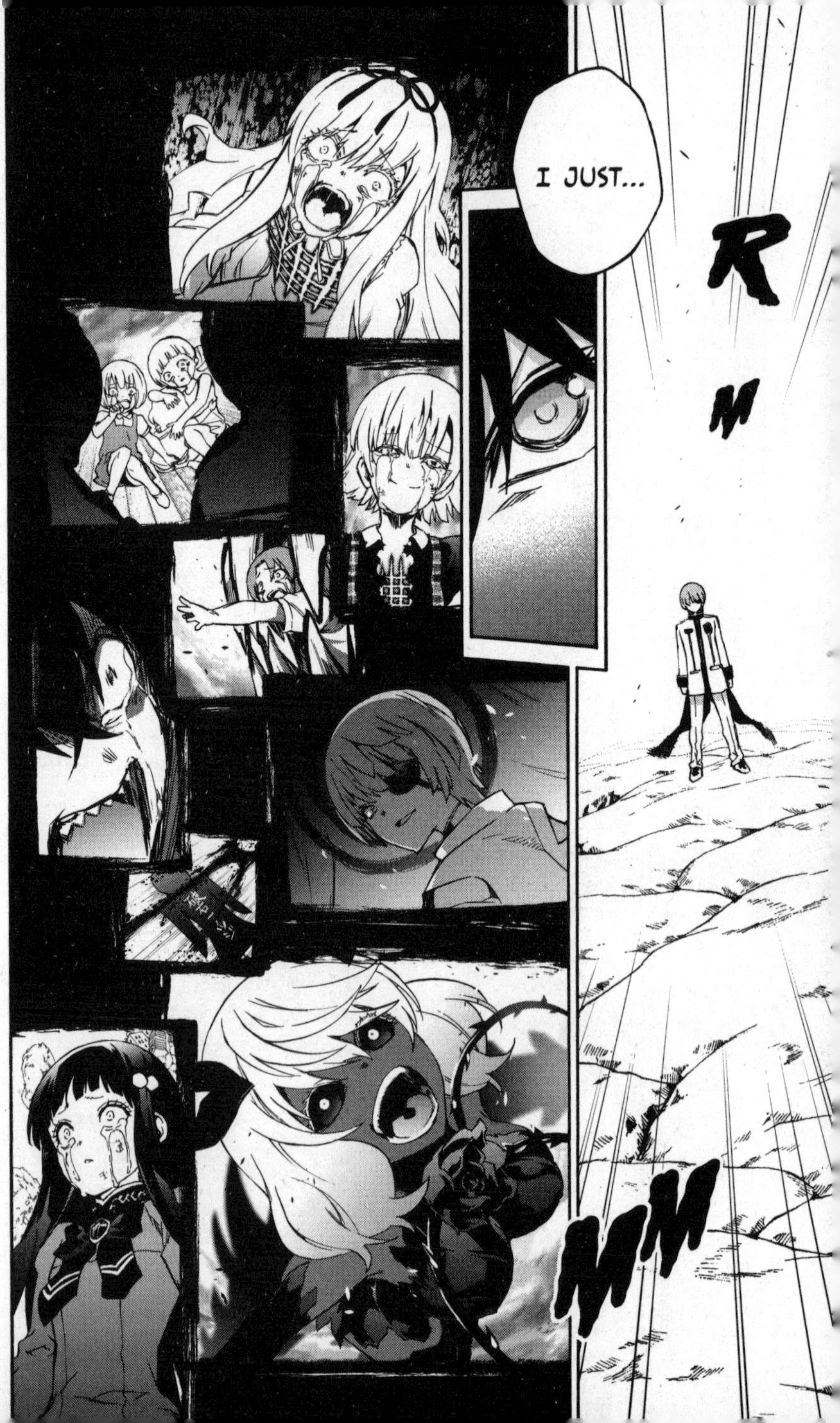
I JUST...
RMMM

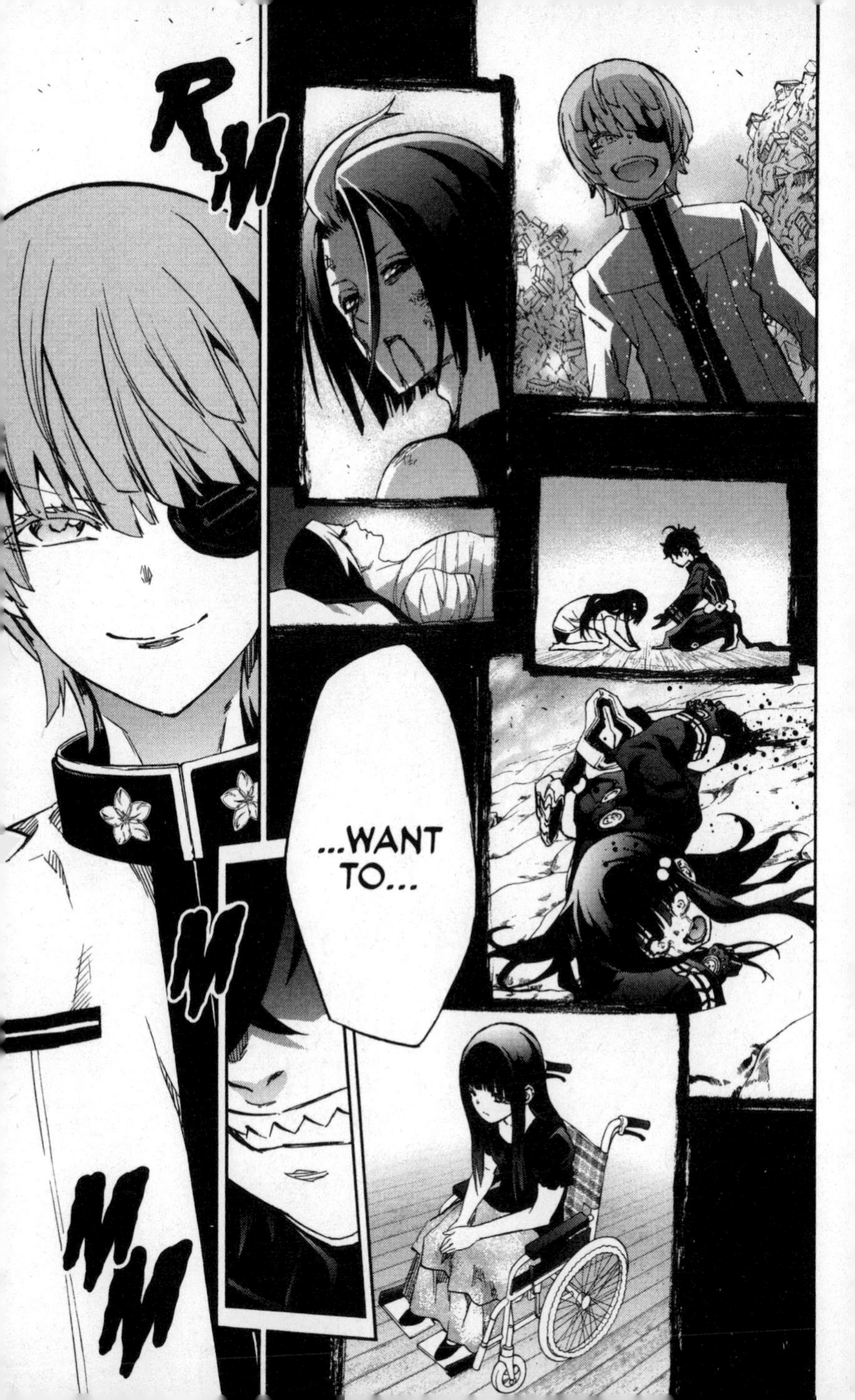
RMMMM
...WANT TO...

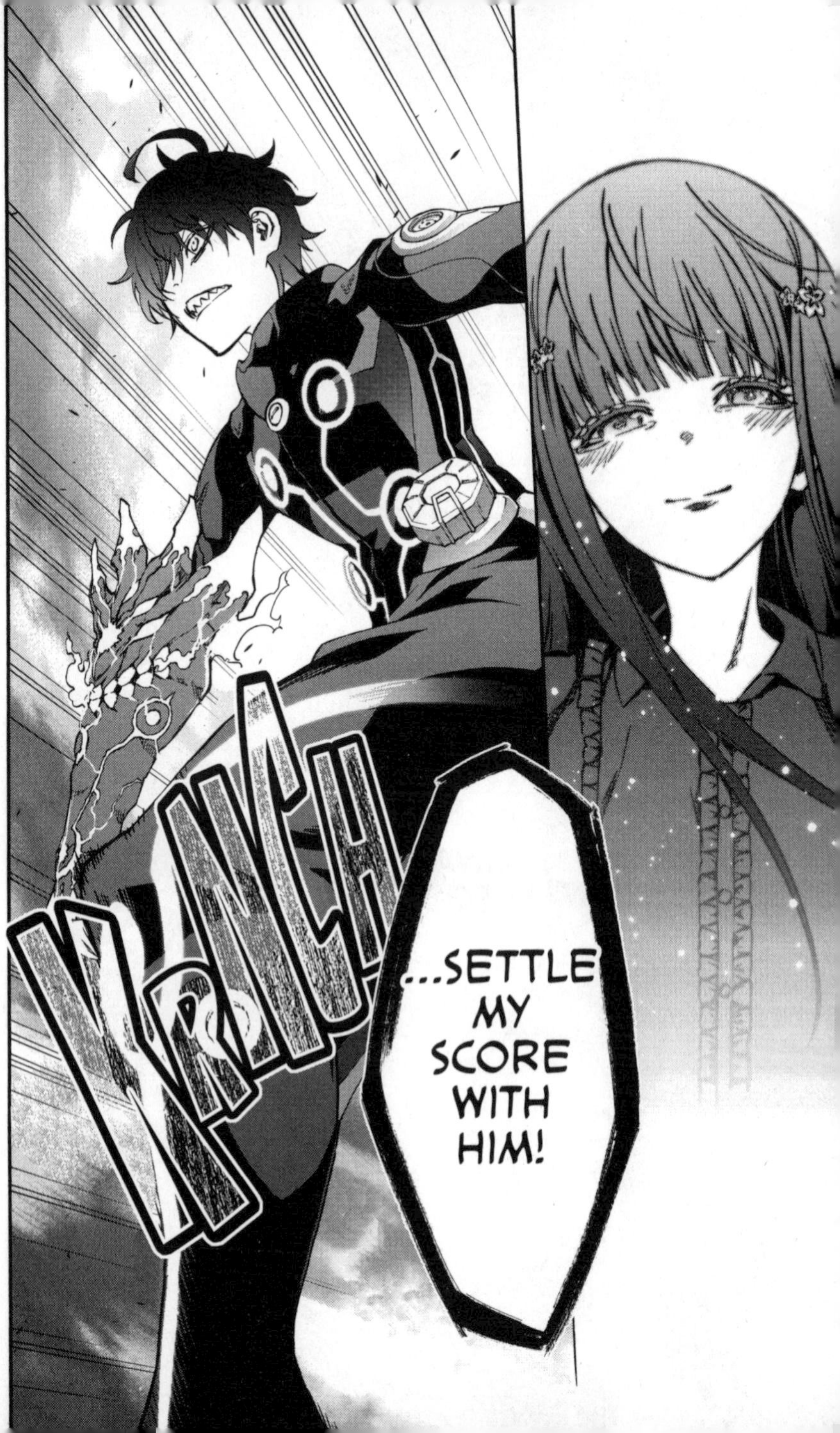
...SETTLE MY SCORE WITH HIM!

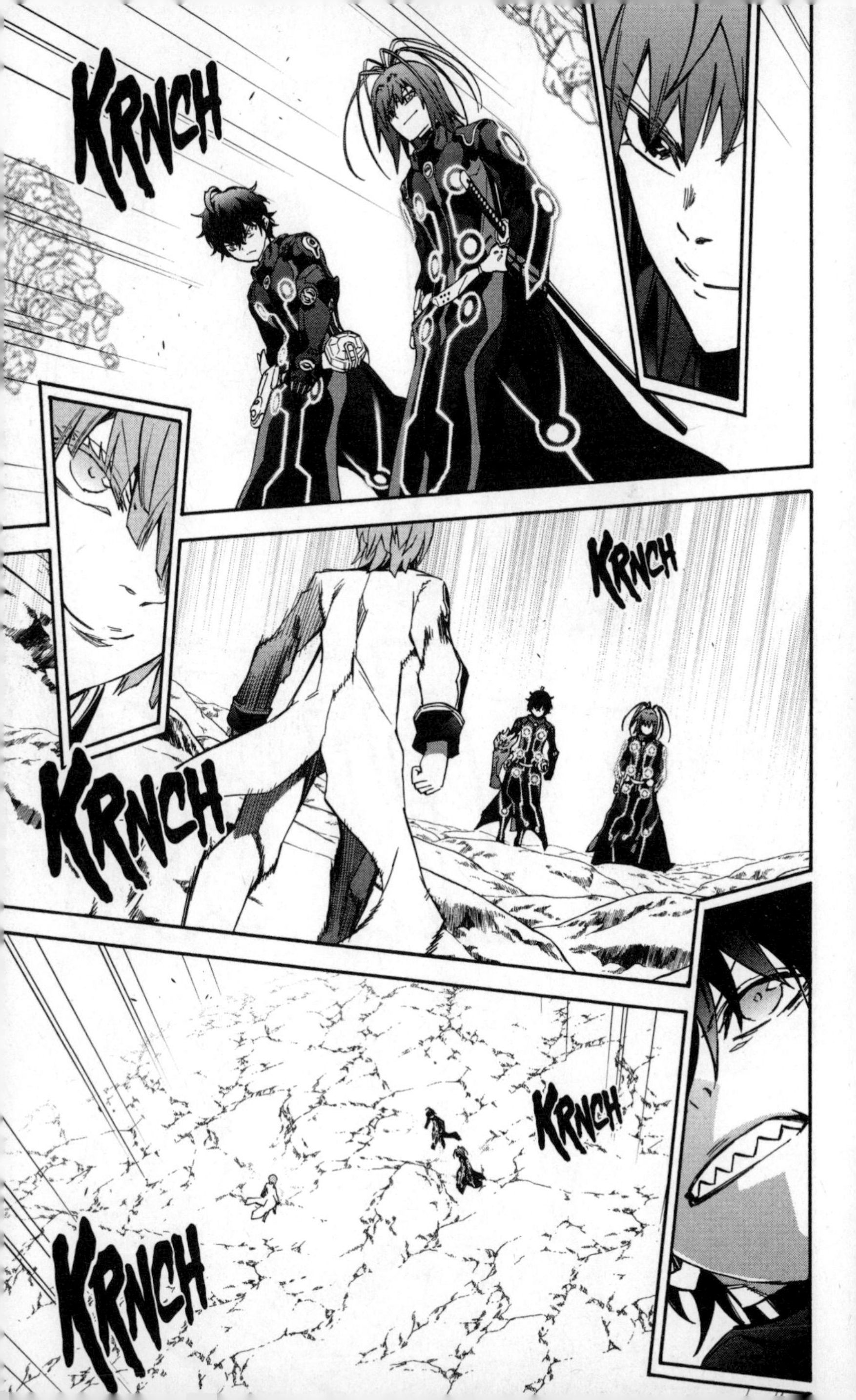
KRNCH
KRNCH
KRNCH
KRNCH
KRNCH

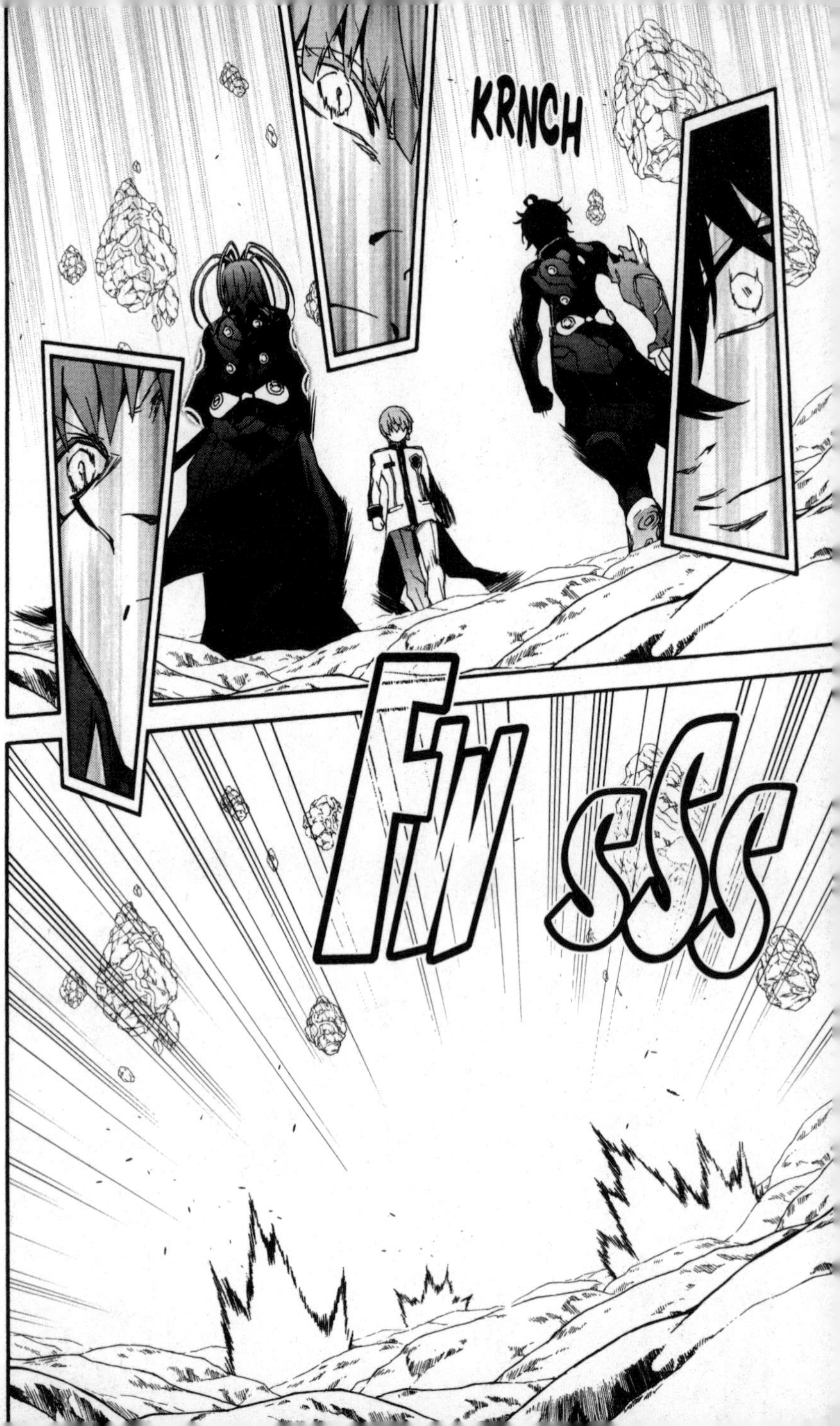
KRNCH
FW sSS

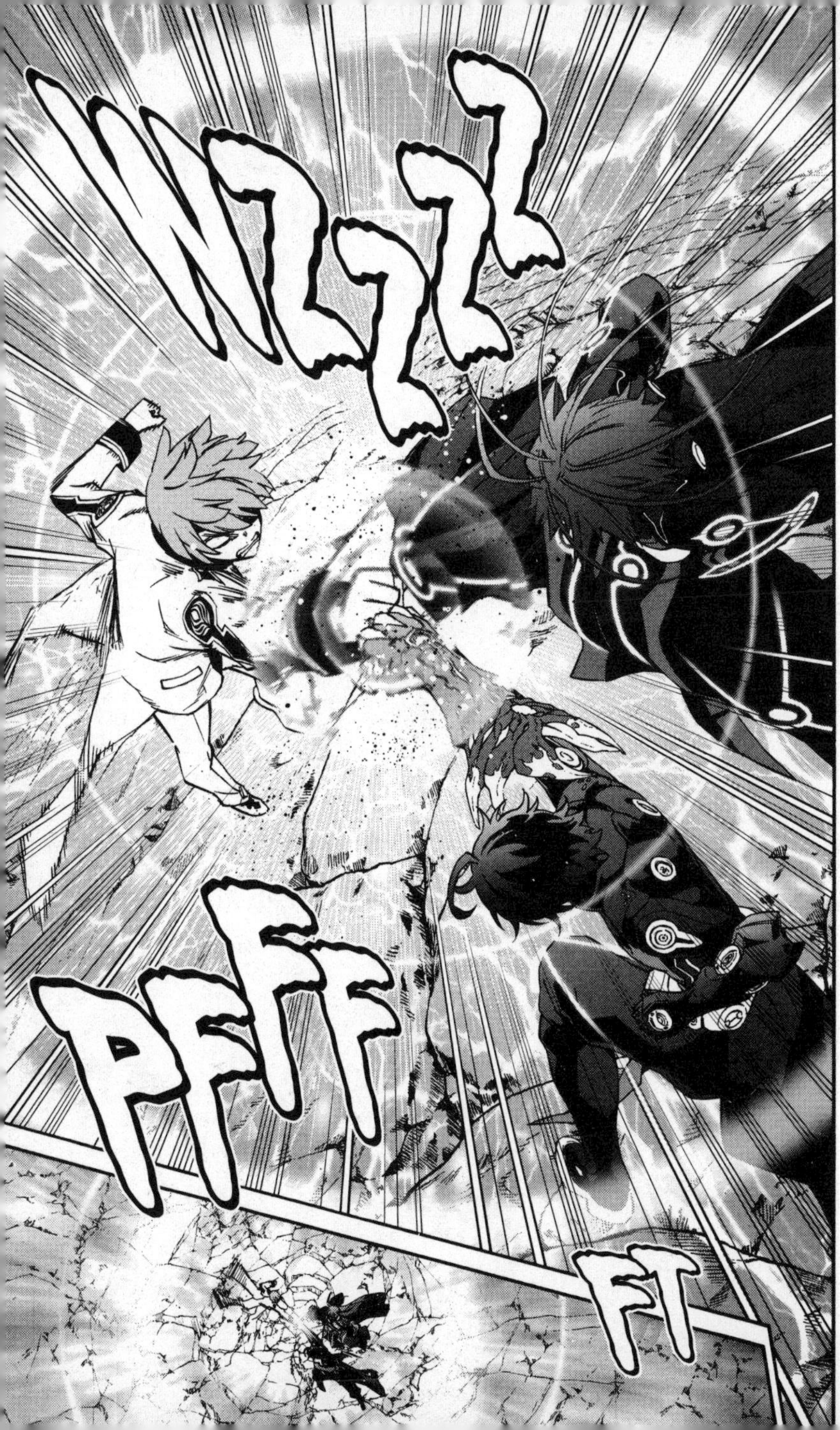
WZZZZ
PFFF
FT

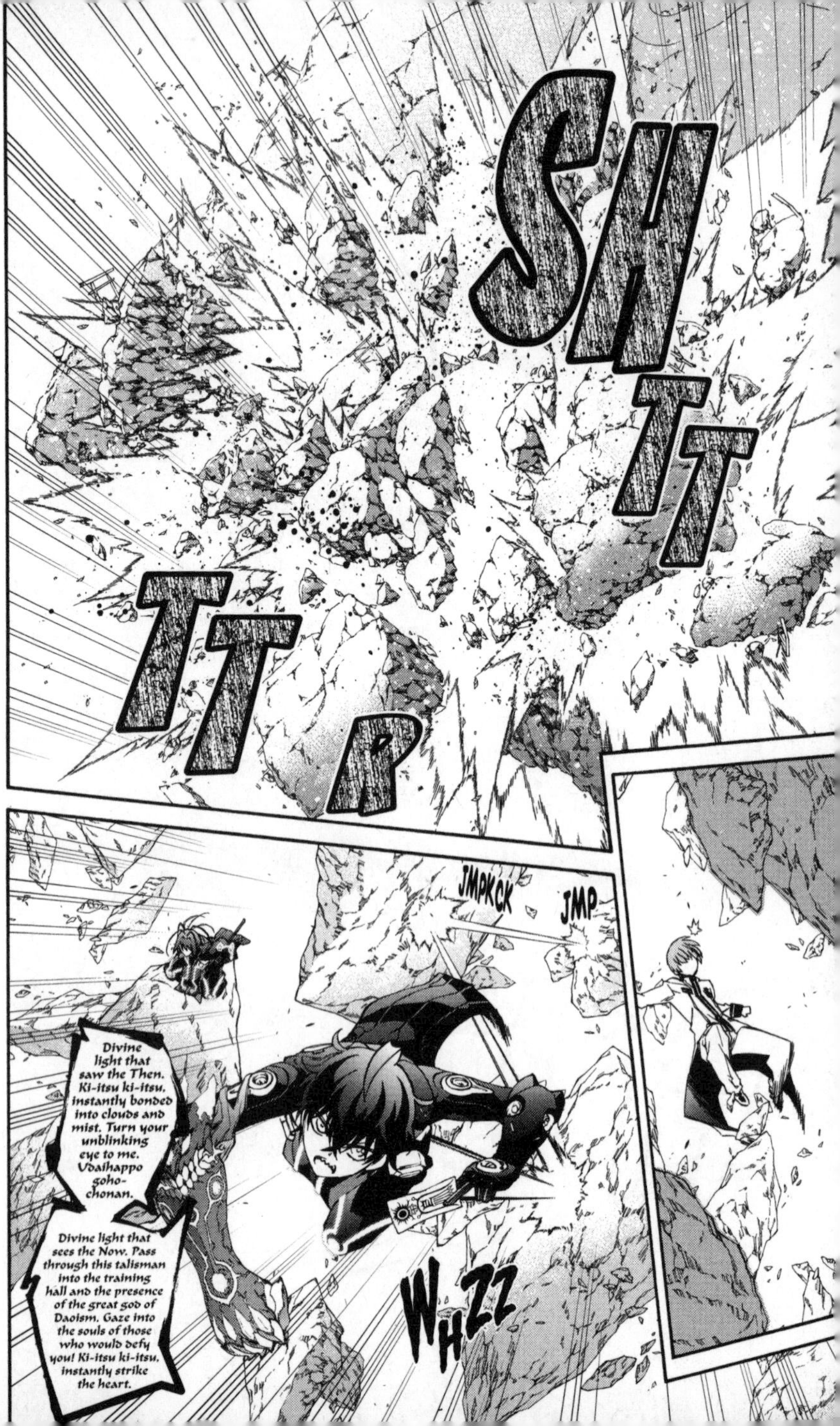
SHTTTTR
JMP
JMPKCK
Divine light that saw the Then. Ki-itsu ki-itsu, instantly bonded into clouds and mist. Turn your unblinking eye to me. Udaihappo goho-chonan.
Divine light that sees the Now. Pass through this talisman into the training hall and the presence of the great god of Daoism. Gaze into the souls of those who would defy you! Ki-itsu ki-itsu, instantly strike the heart.
WHZZ

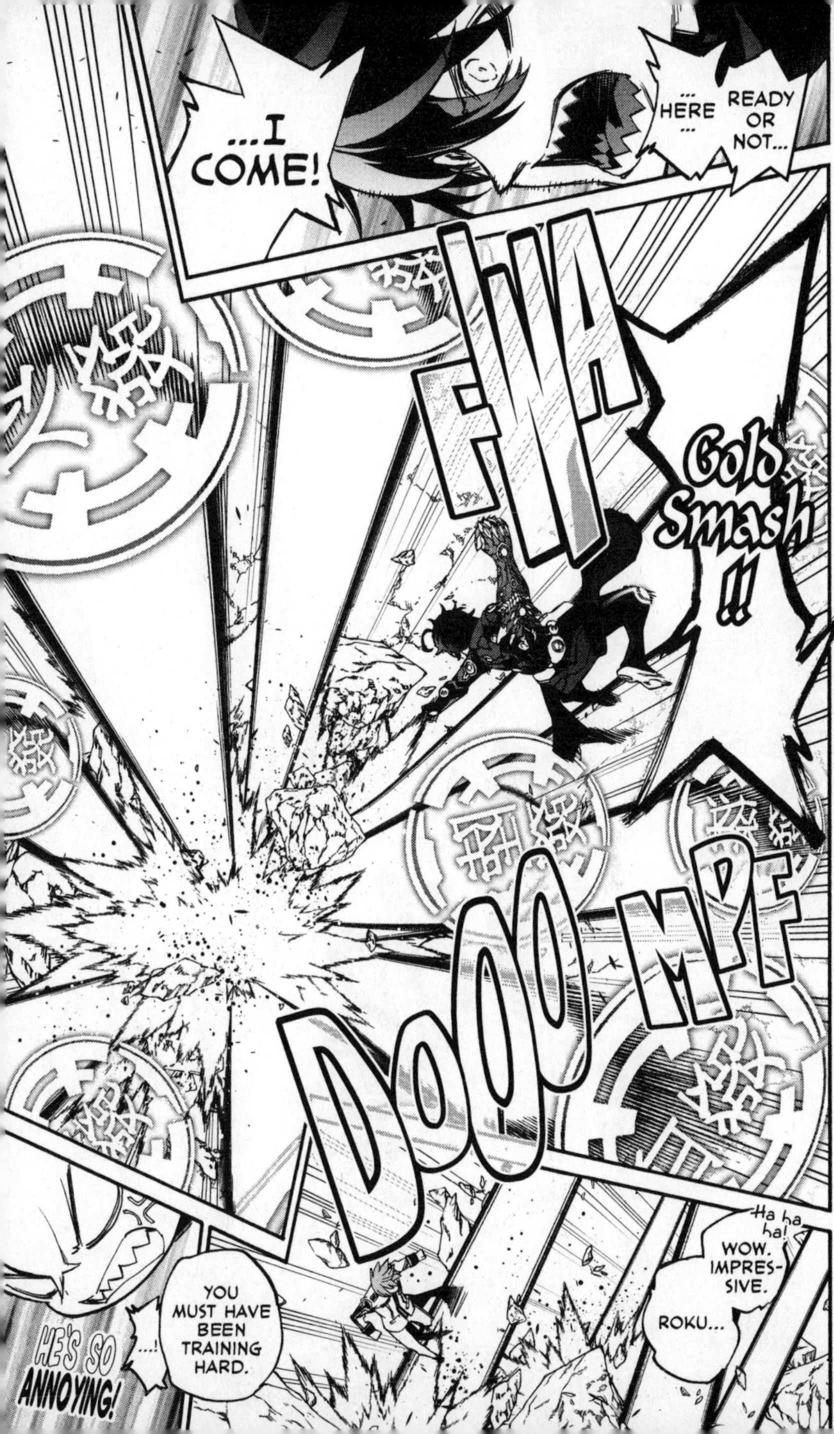
READY OR NOT...
...HERE...
...I COME!
FWA
Gold Smash!!
DOOOMPF
Ha ha ha!
WOW. IMPRES-SIVE.
ROKU...
YOU MUST HAVE BEEN TRAINING HARD.
...!
HE'S SO ANNOYING!

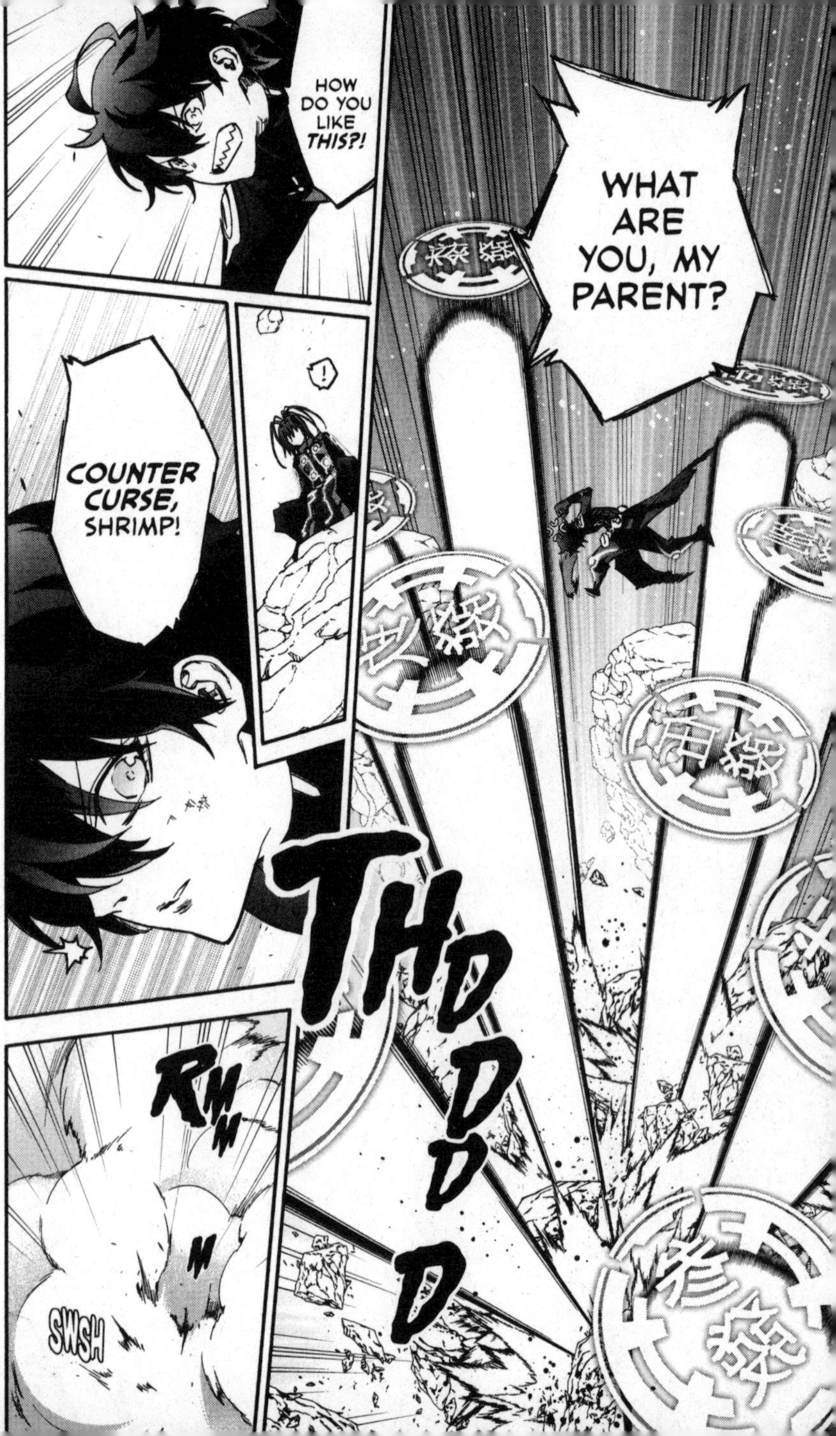

WHAT ARE YOU, MY PARENT?
THDDDD
HOW DO YOU LIKE THIS?!
!
COUNTER CURSE, SHRIMP!
RMMM
SWSH

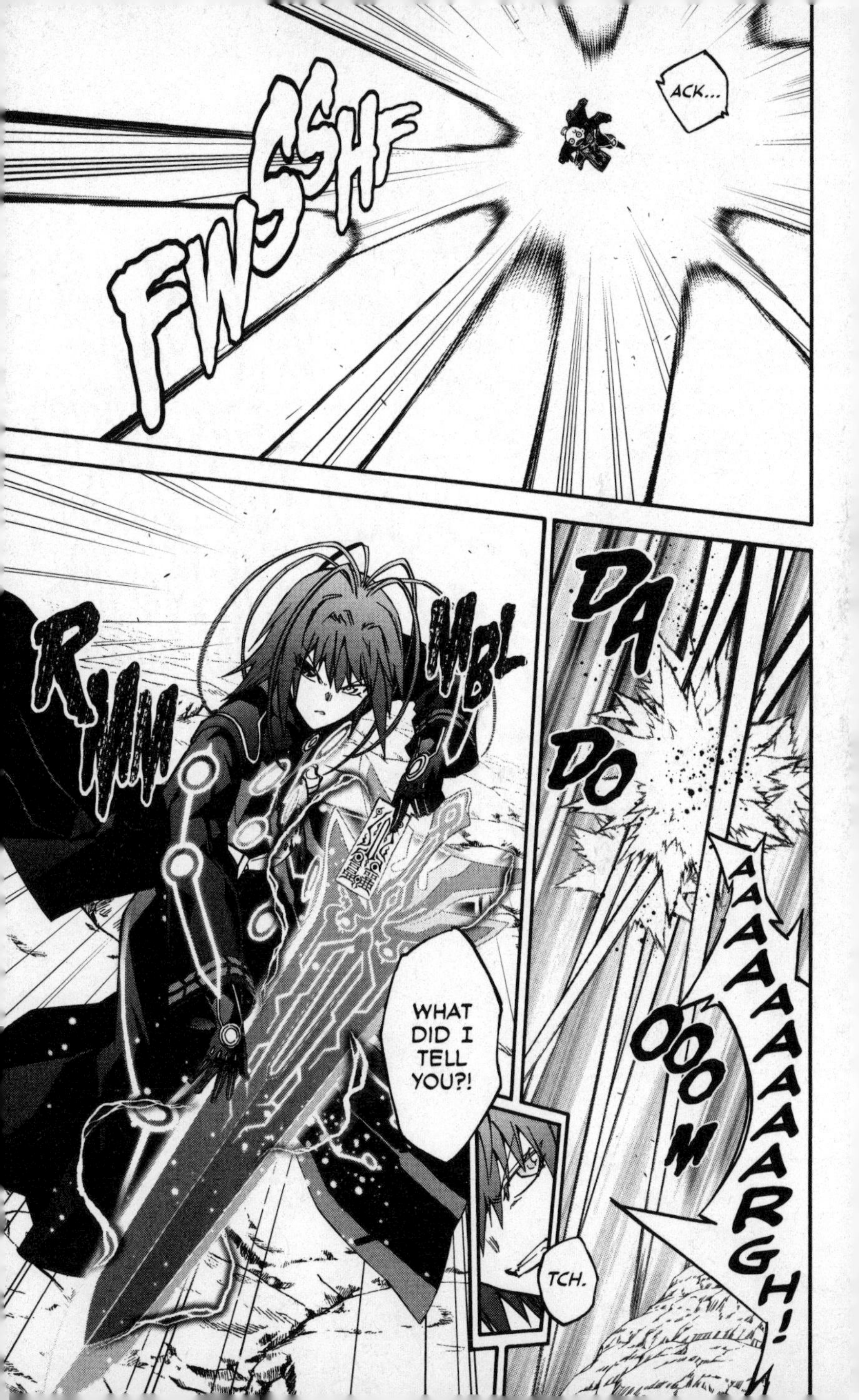
ACK...
FWSSHF
DA
DO
OOOM
AAAAAAAAARGH!
TCH.
RMMMBL
WHAT DID I TELL YOU?!

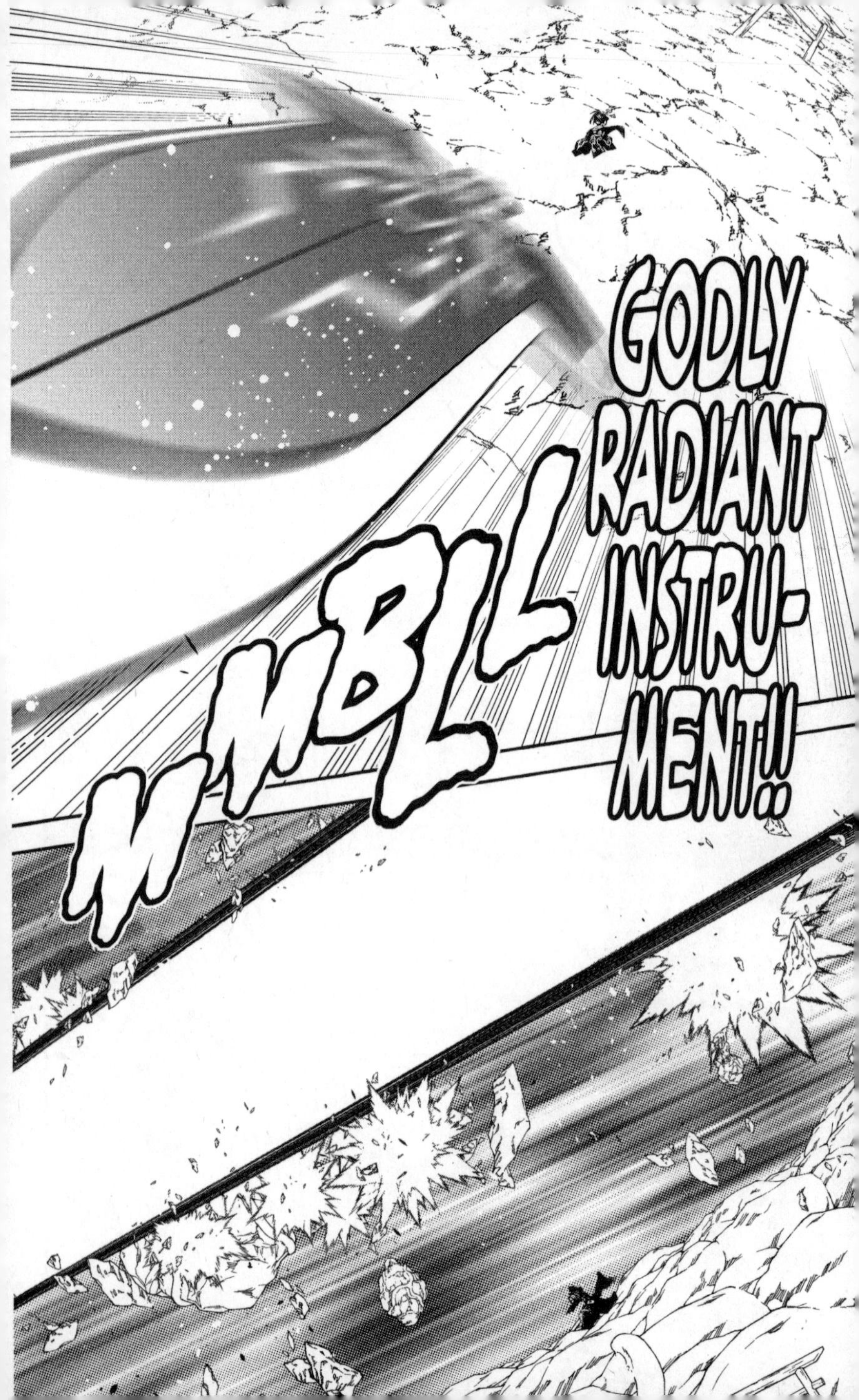
GODLY RADIANT INSTRU-MENT!!

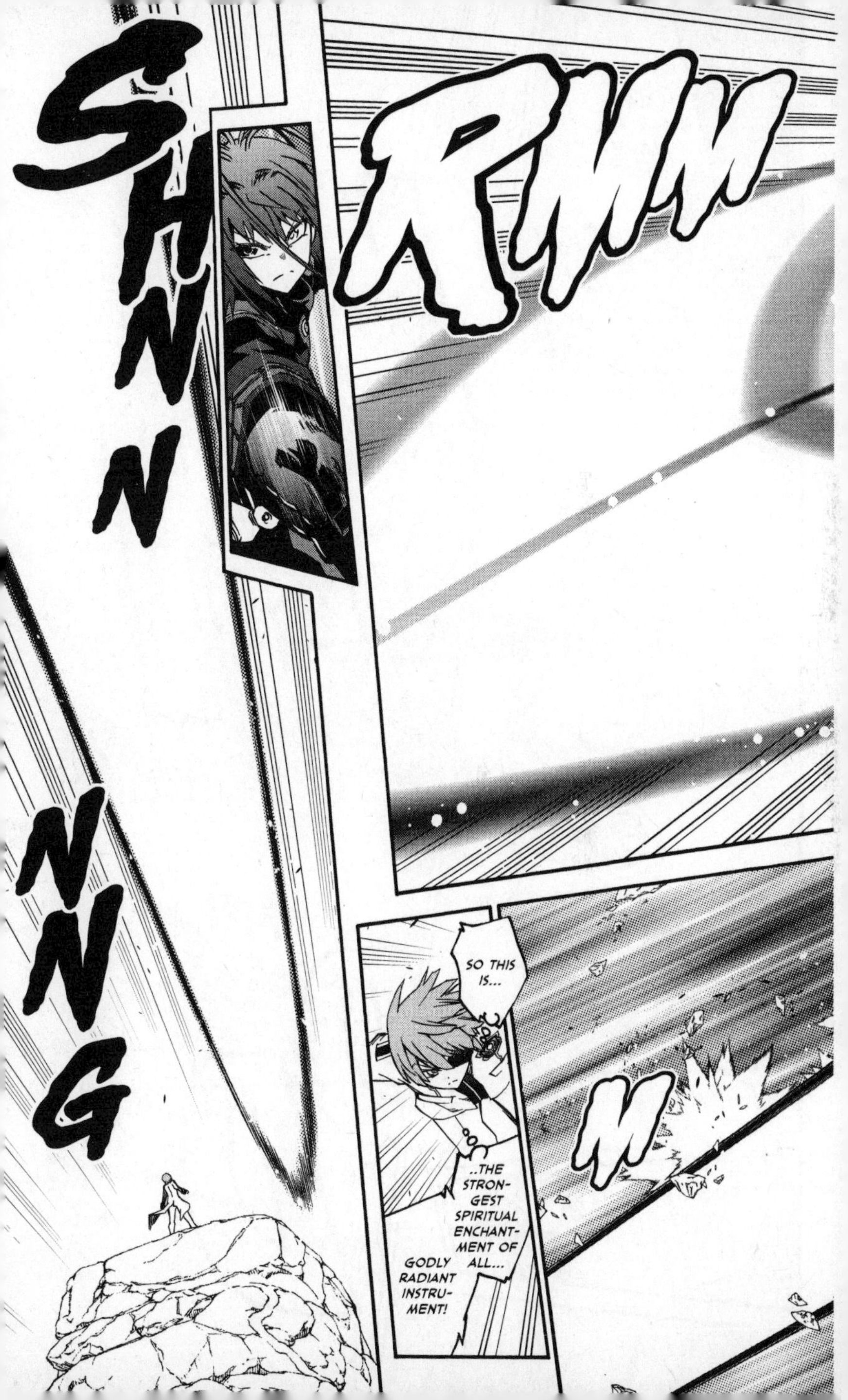
SHNNN
RMM
NNNG
SO THIS IS...
...THE STRONGEST SPIRITUAL ENCHANTMENT OF ALL...
GODLY RADIANT INSTRUMENT!
M

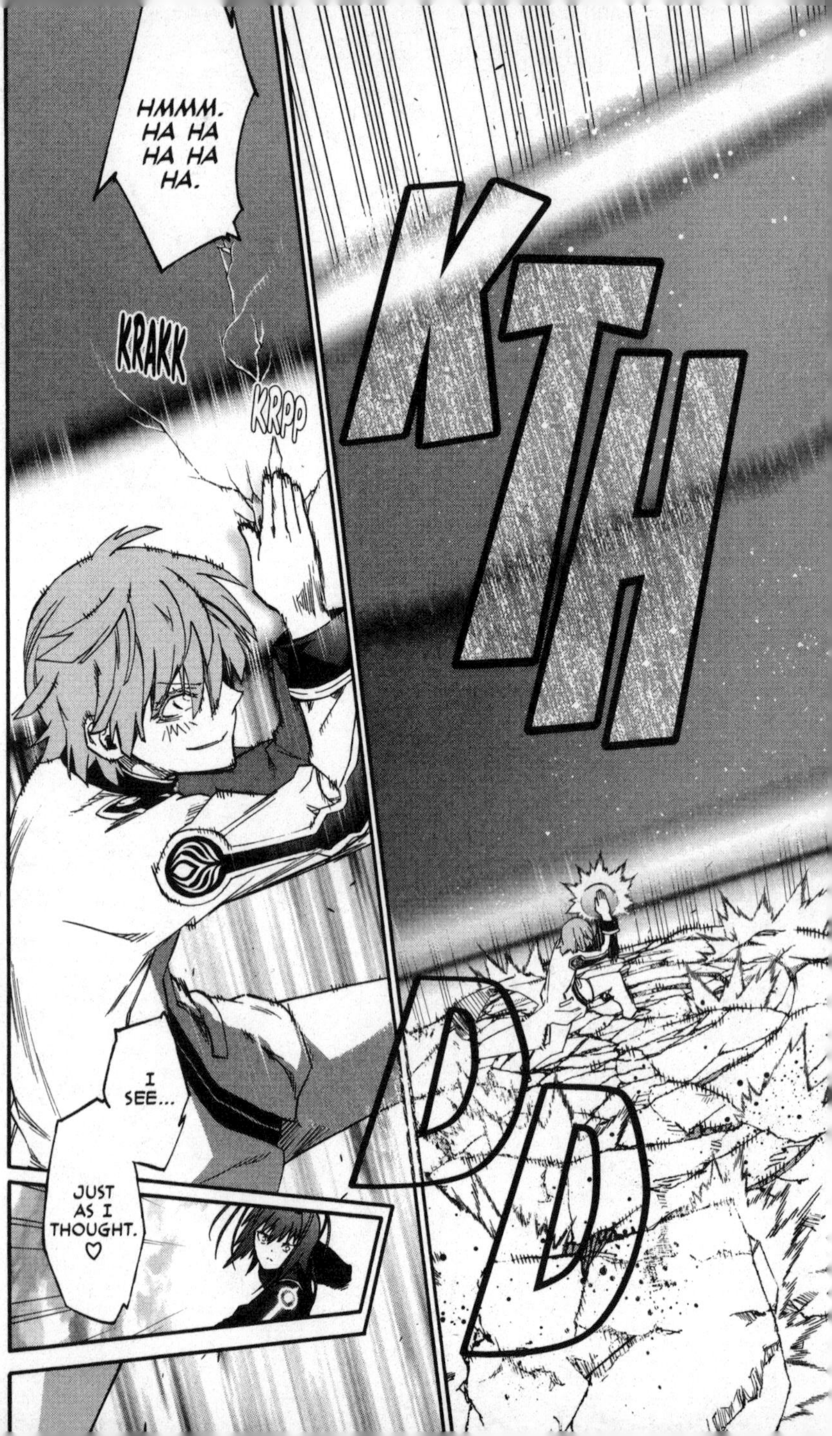
KTHDDD
HMMM. HA HA HA HA HA.
KRAKK
KRPP
I SEE...
JUST AS I THOUGHT. ♡

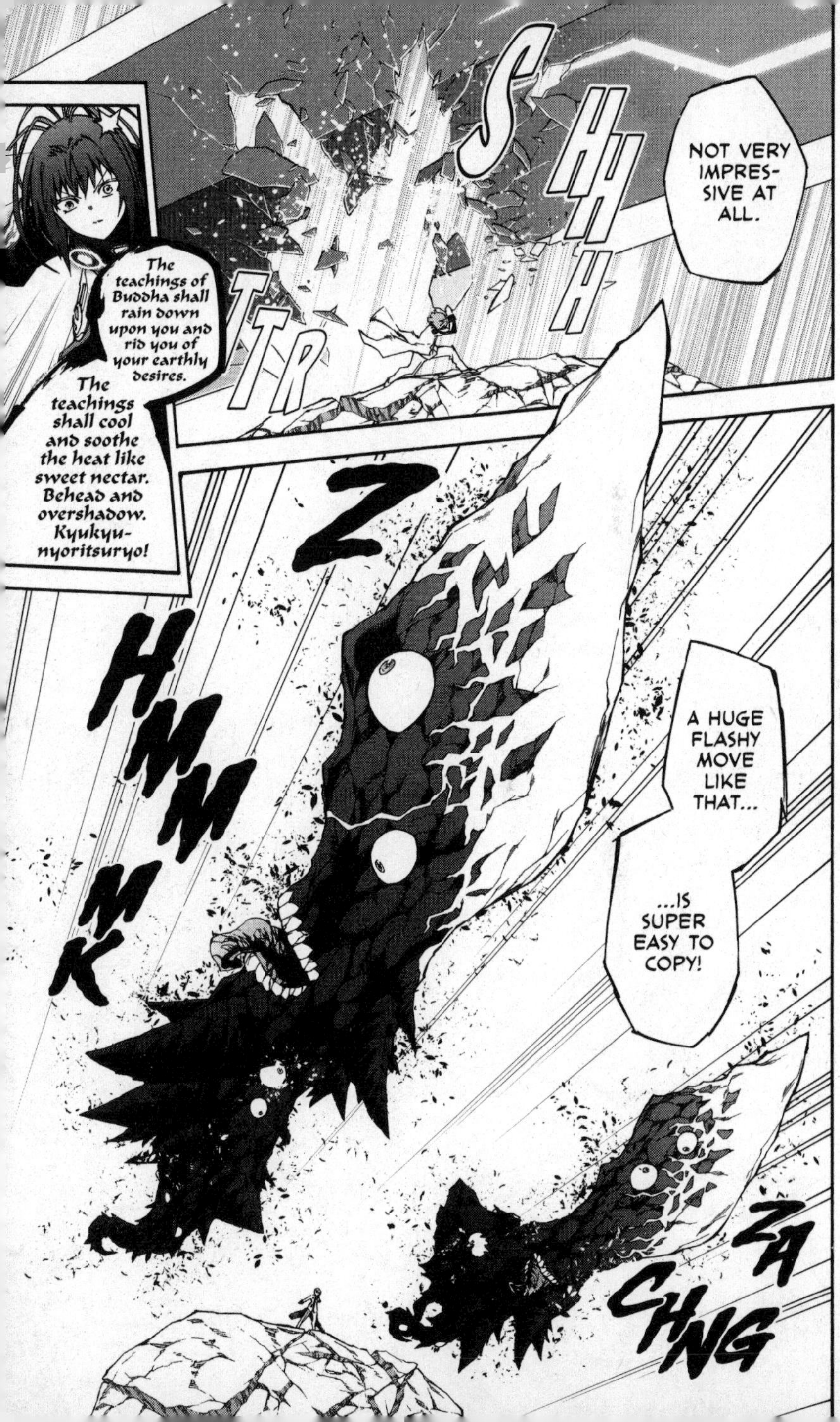
NOT VERY IMPRES-SIVE AT ALL.
SHHHHH
TTR
The teachings of Buddha shall rain down upon you and rid you of your earthly desires.
The teachings shall cool and soothe the heat like sweet nectar. Behead and overshadow. Kyukyu-nyoritsuryo!
ZHMMMK
A HUGE FLASHY MOVE LIKE THAT...
...IS SUPER EASY TO COPY!
ZACHNG

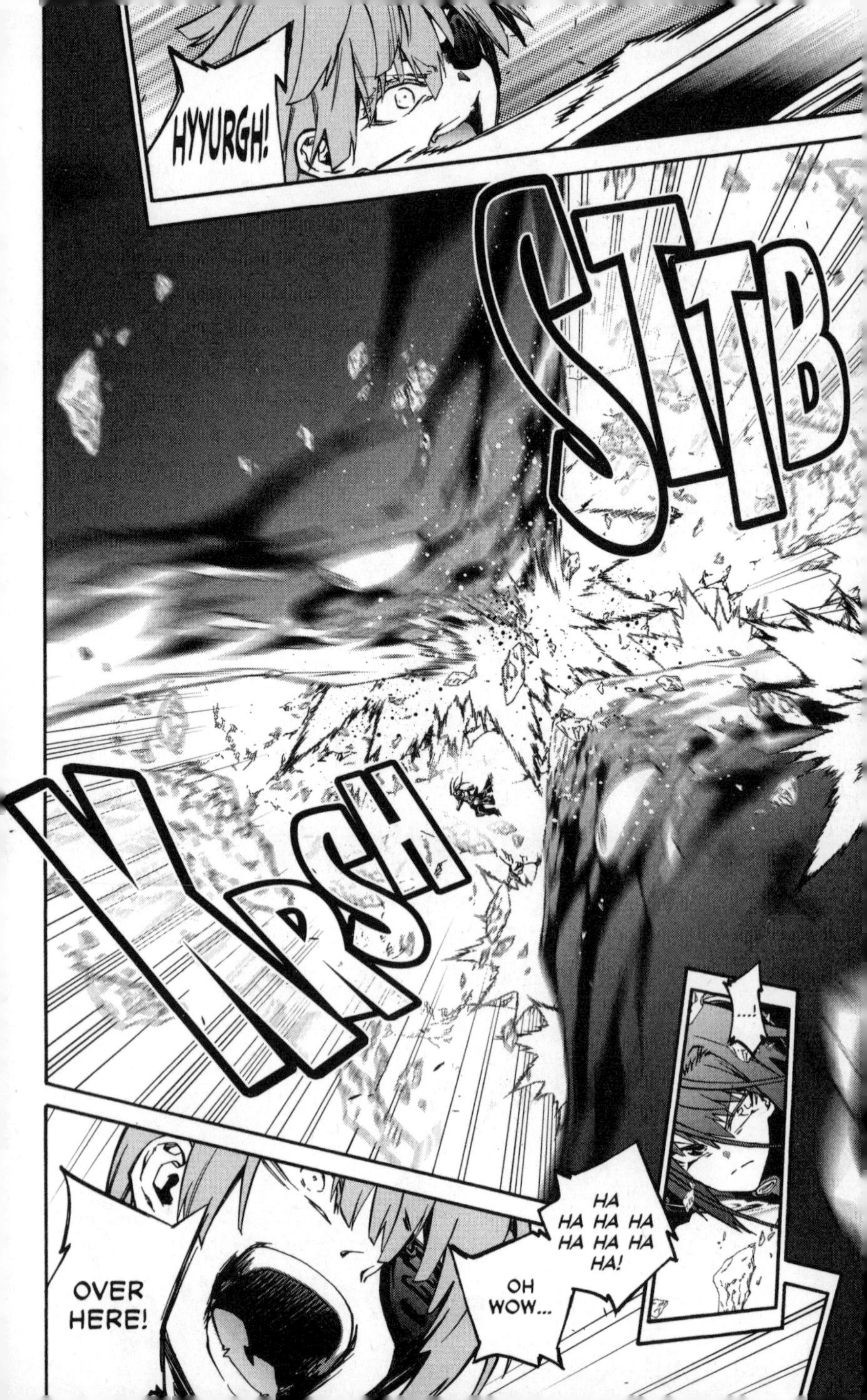
HYYURGH!
...!
HA HA HA HA HA HA HA HA!
OH WOW...
OVER HERE!

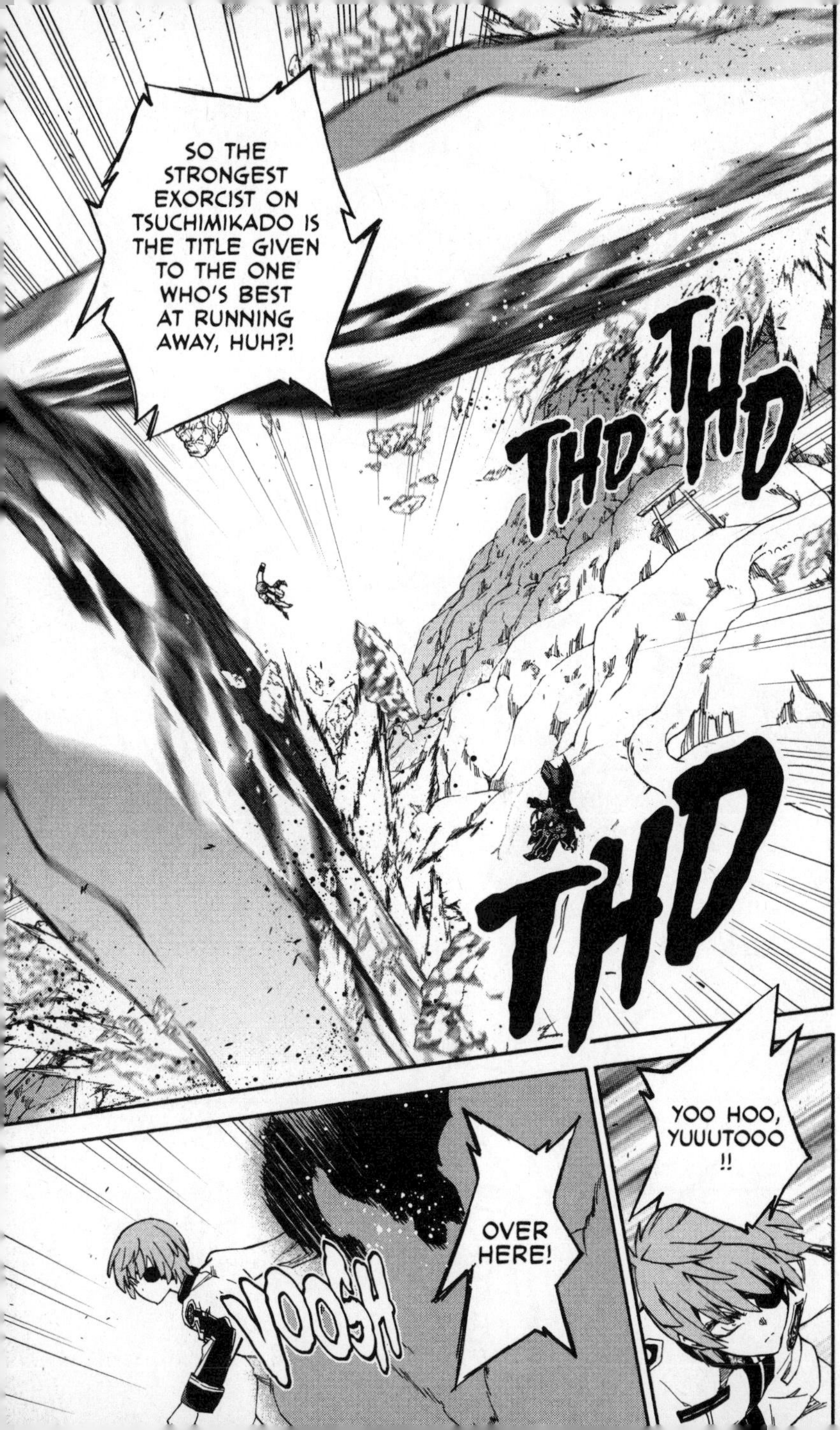
SO THE STRONGEST EXORCIST ON TSUCHIMIKADO IS THE TITLE GIVEN TO THE ONE WHO'S BEST AT RUNNING AWAY, HUH?!
THD THD
THD
YOO HOO, YUUUTOOO !!
OVER HERE!
VOOSH

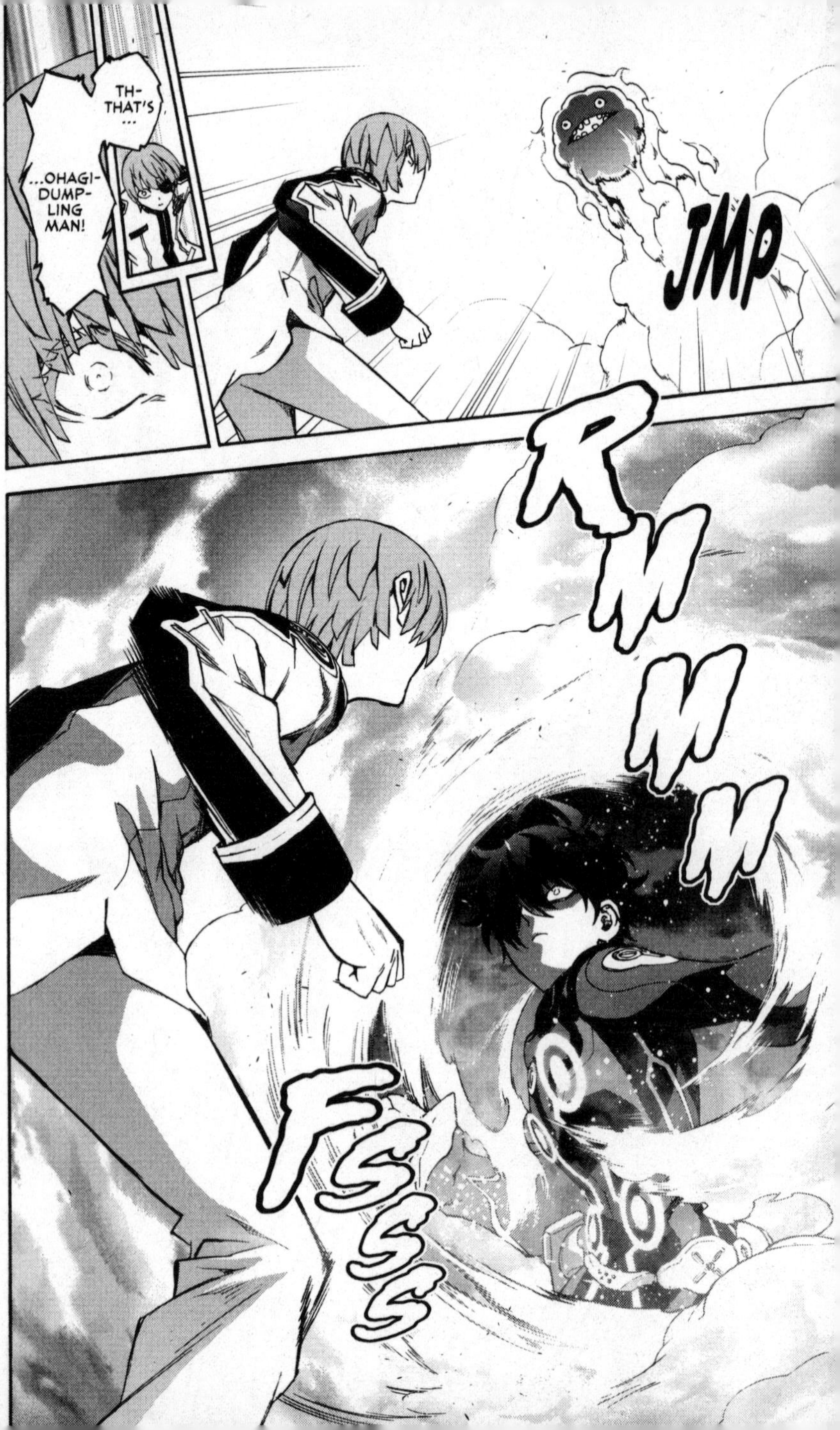
JMP
TH-THAT'S ...
...OHAGI-DUMPLING MAN!
RMMMM
FSSS

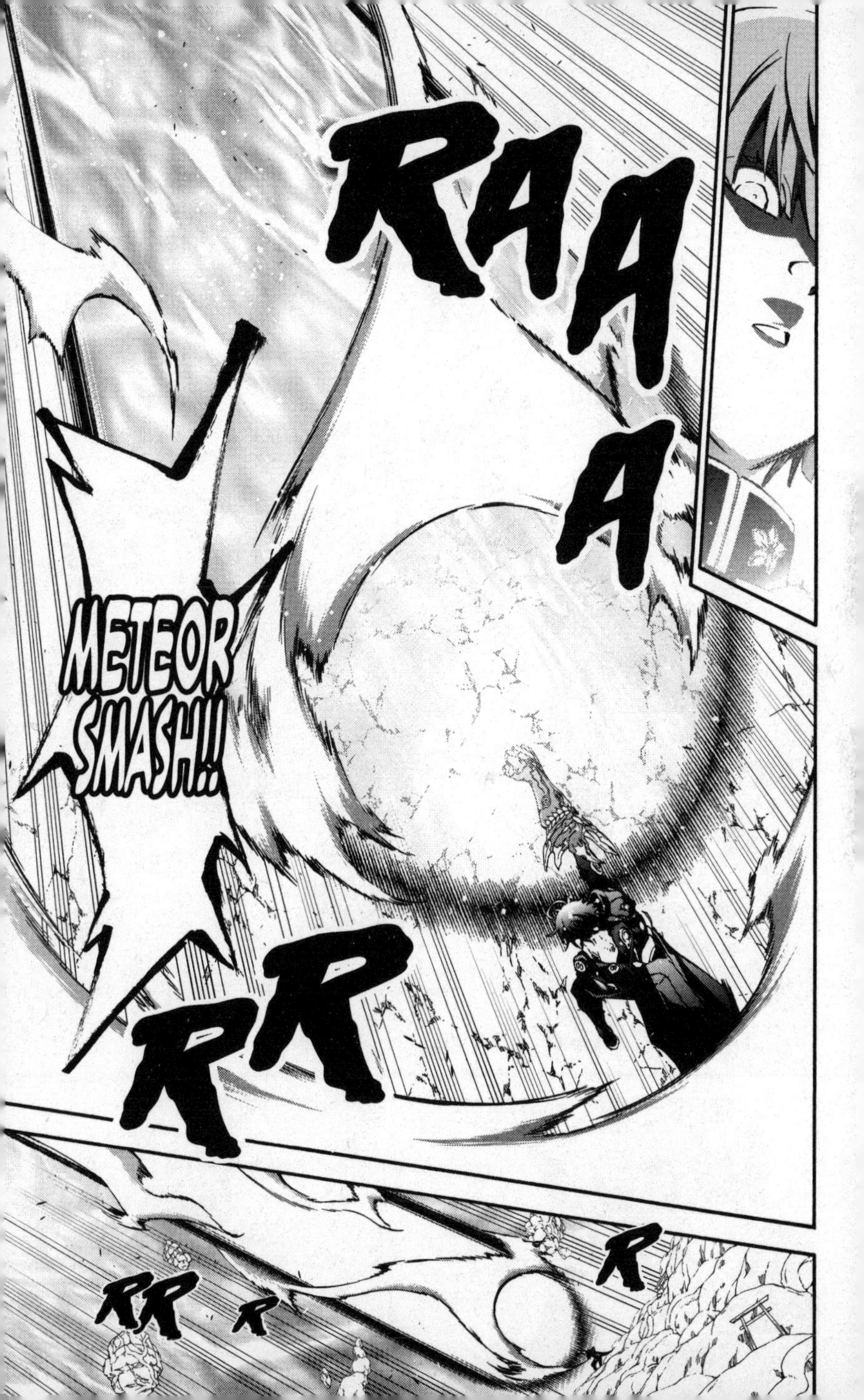
RAAA
METEOR SMASH!!
RRR
R
R
RR

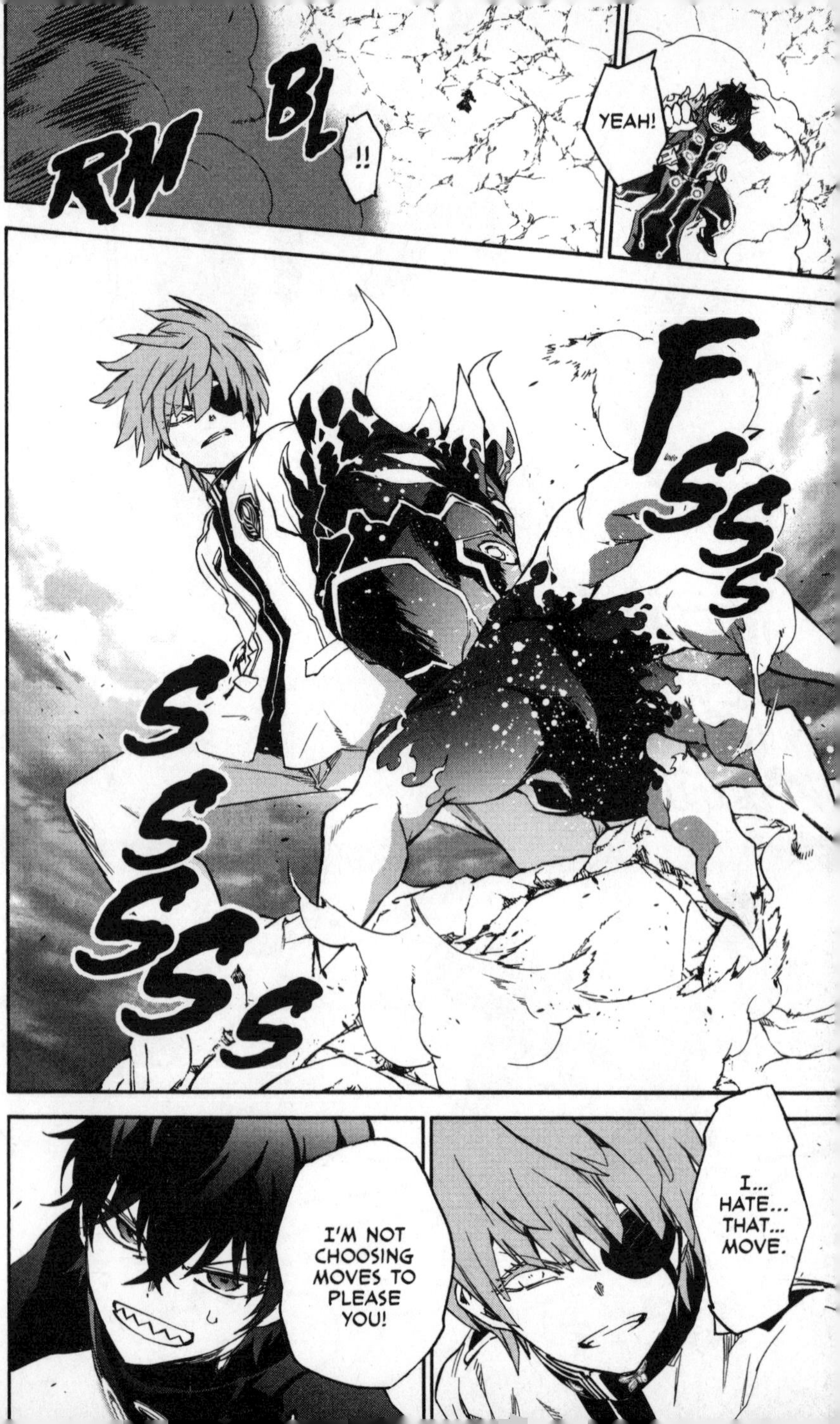
YEAH!
RMBL
!!
FSSS
SSSSSS
I... HATE... THAT... MOVE.
I'M NOT CHOOSING MOVES TO PLEASE YOU!

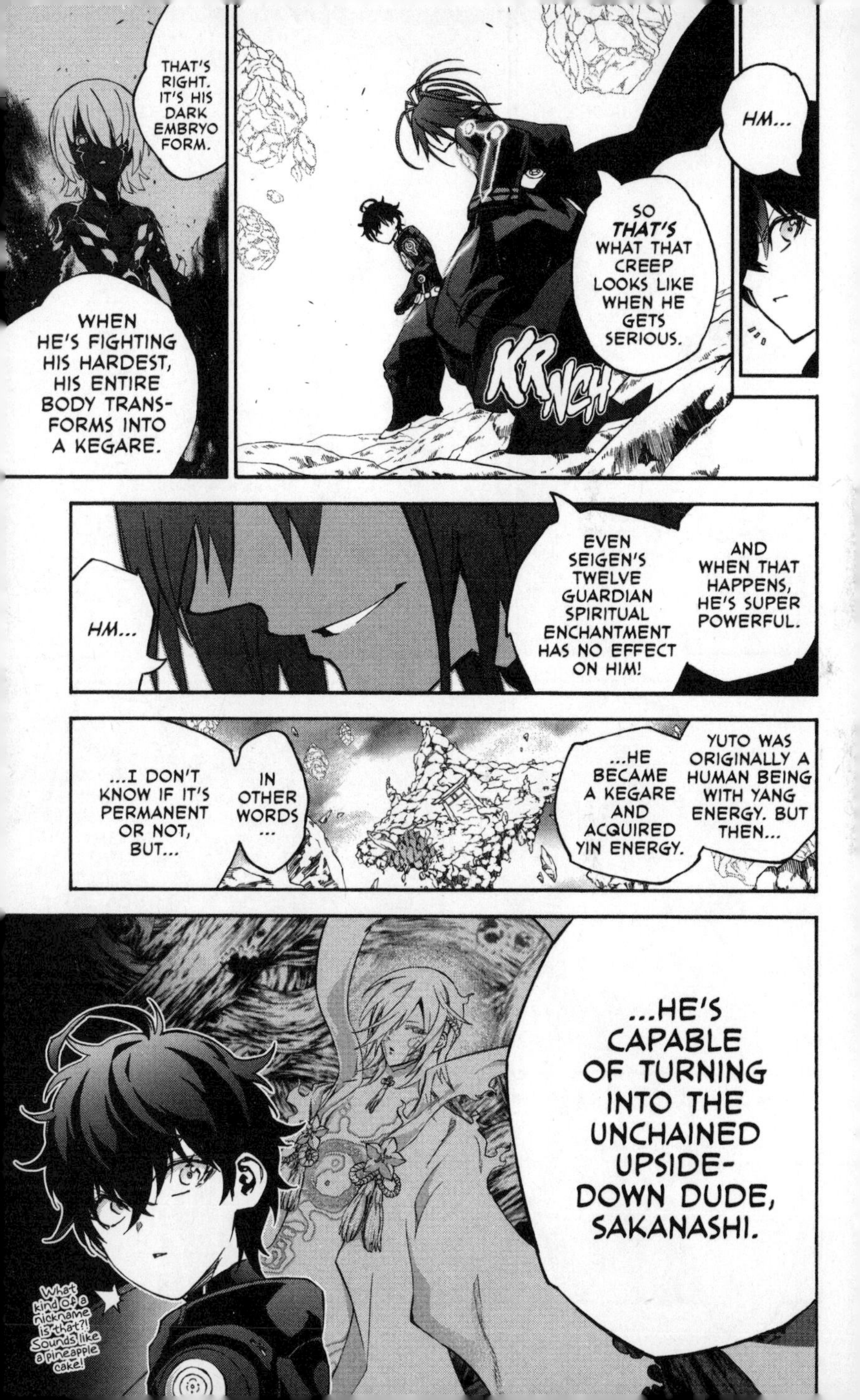
HM...
SO *THAT'S* WHAT THAT CREEP LOOKS LIKE WHEN HE GETS SERIOUS.
KRNCH
THAT'S RIGHT. IT'S HIS DARK EMBRYO FORM.
WHEN HE'S FIGHTING HIS HARDEST, HIS ENTIRE BODY TRANS-FORMS INTO A KEGARE.
AND WHEN THAT HAPPENS, HE'S SUPER POWERFUL.
EVEN SEIGEN'S TWELVE GUARDIAN SPIRITUAL ENCHANTMENT HAS NO EFFECT ON HIM!
HM...
YUTO WAS ORIGINALLY A HUMAN BEING WITH YANG ENERGY. BUT THEN...
...HE BECAME A KEGARE AND ACQUIRED YIN ENERGY.
IN OTHER WORDS...
...I DON'T KNOW IF IT'S PERMANENT OR NOT, BUT...
...HE'S CAPABLE OF TURNING INTO THE UNCHAINED UPSIDE-DOWN DUDE, SAKANASHI.
What kind of a nickname is that?! Sounds like a pineapple cake!

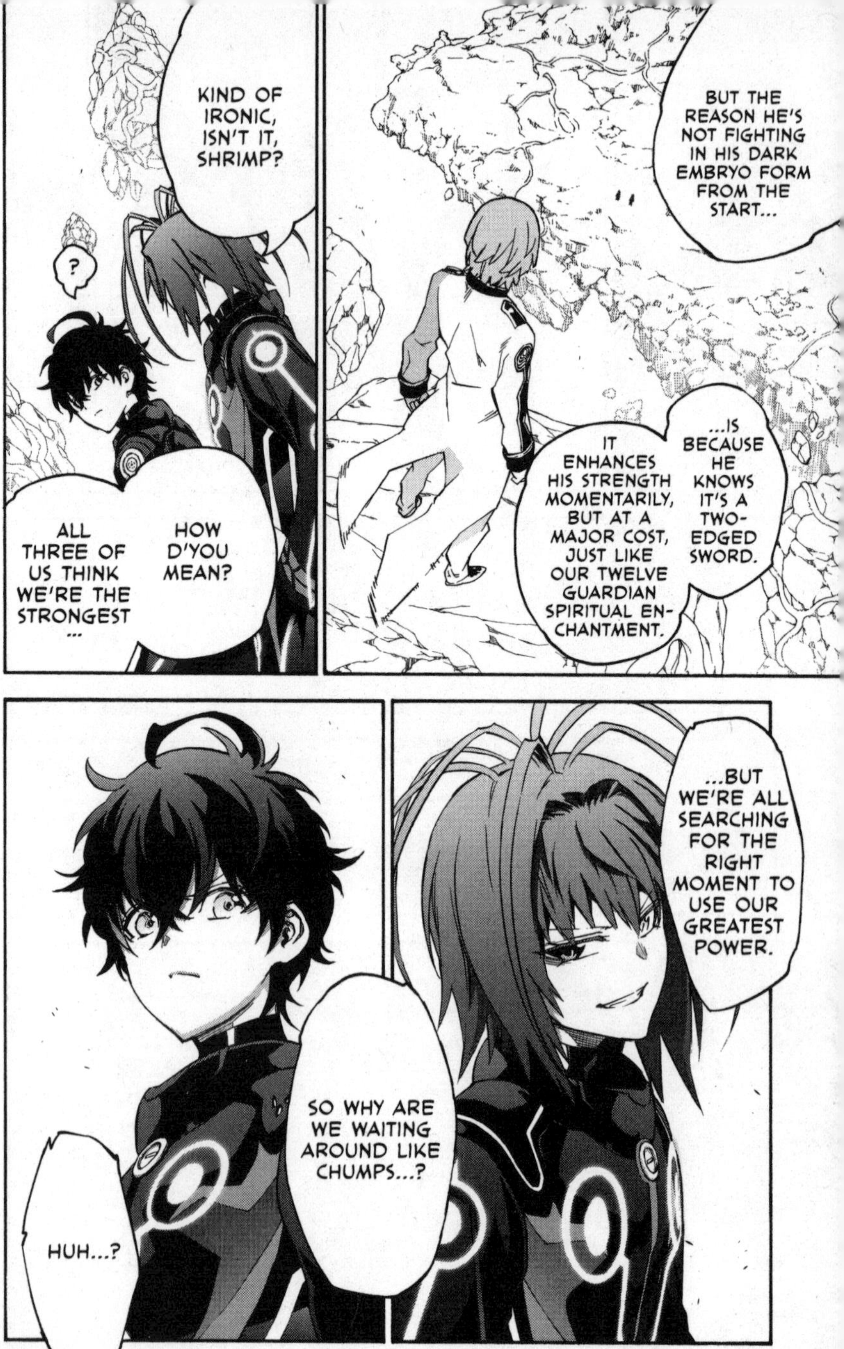
BUT THE REASON HE'S NOT FIGHTING IN HIS DARK EMBRYO FORM FROM THE START...
...IS BECAUSE HE KNOWS IT'S A TWO-EDGED SWORD.
IT ENHANCES HIS STRENGTH MOMENTARILY, BUT AT A MAJOR COST, JUST LIKE OUR TWELVE GUARDIAN SPIRITUAL EN-CHANTMENT.
KIND OF IRONIC, ISN'T IT, SHRIMP?
?
HOW D'YOU MEAN?
ALL THREE OF US THINK WE'RE THE STRONGEST ...
...BUT WE'RE ALL SEARCHING FOR THE RIGHT MOMENT TO USE OUR GREATEST POWER.
SO WHY ARE WE WAITING AROUND LIKE CHUMPS...?
HUH...?

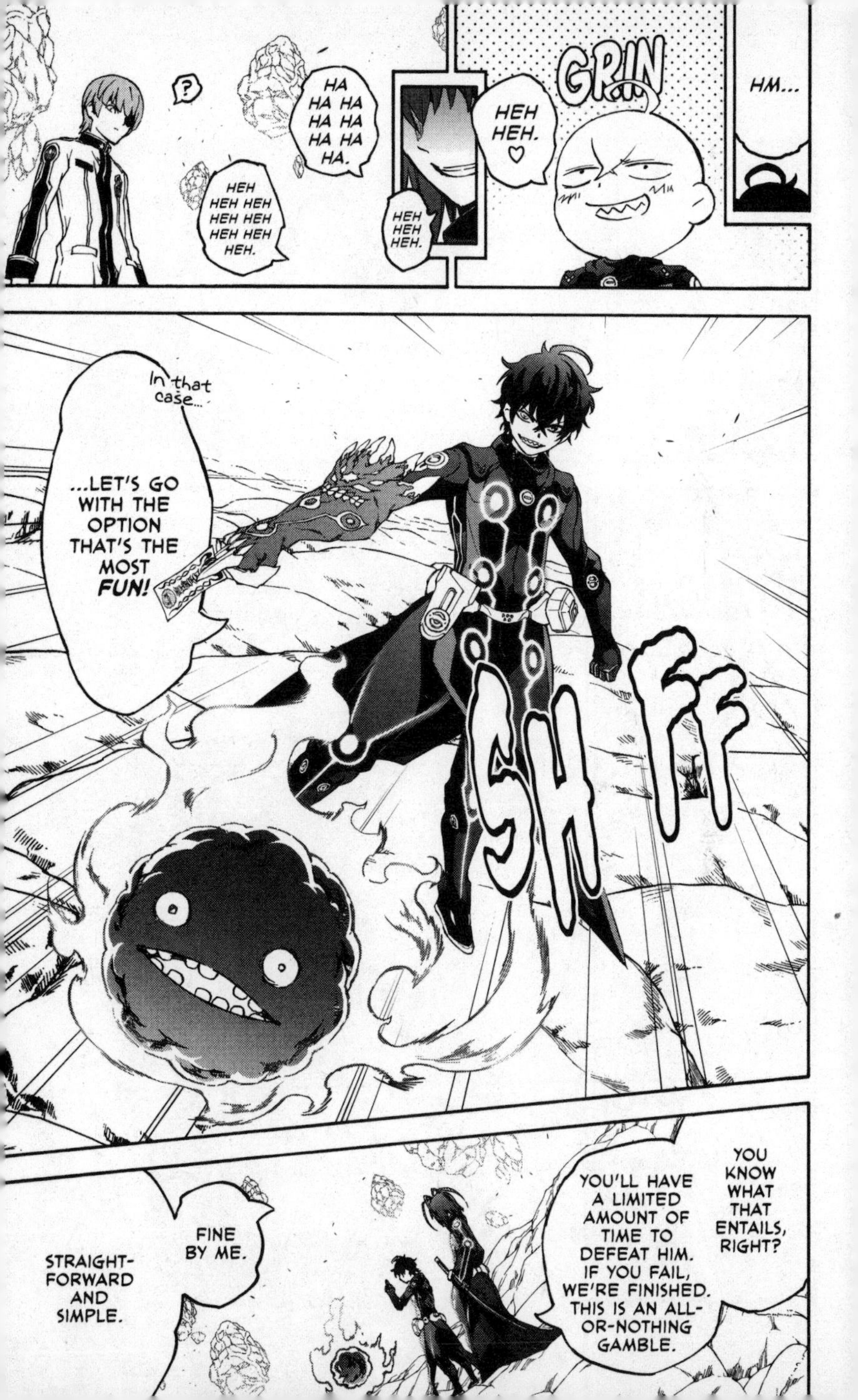
HM...
GRIN
HEH HEH. ♡
HEH HEH HEH.
HA HA HA HA HA HA HA HA.
HEH HEH HEH HEH HEH HEH HEH HEH.
?
In that case...
...LET'S GO WITH THE OPTION THAT'S THE MOST *FUN!*
SHFF
YOU KNOW WHAT THAT ENTAILS, RIGHT?
YOU'LL HAVE A LIMITED AMOUNT OF TIME TO DEFEAT HIM. IF YOU FAIL, WE'RE FINISHED. THIS IS AN ALL-OR-NOTHING GAMBLE.
FINE BY ME.
STRAIGHT-FORWARD AND SIMPLE.

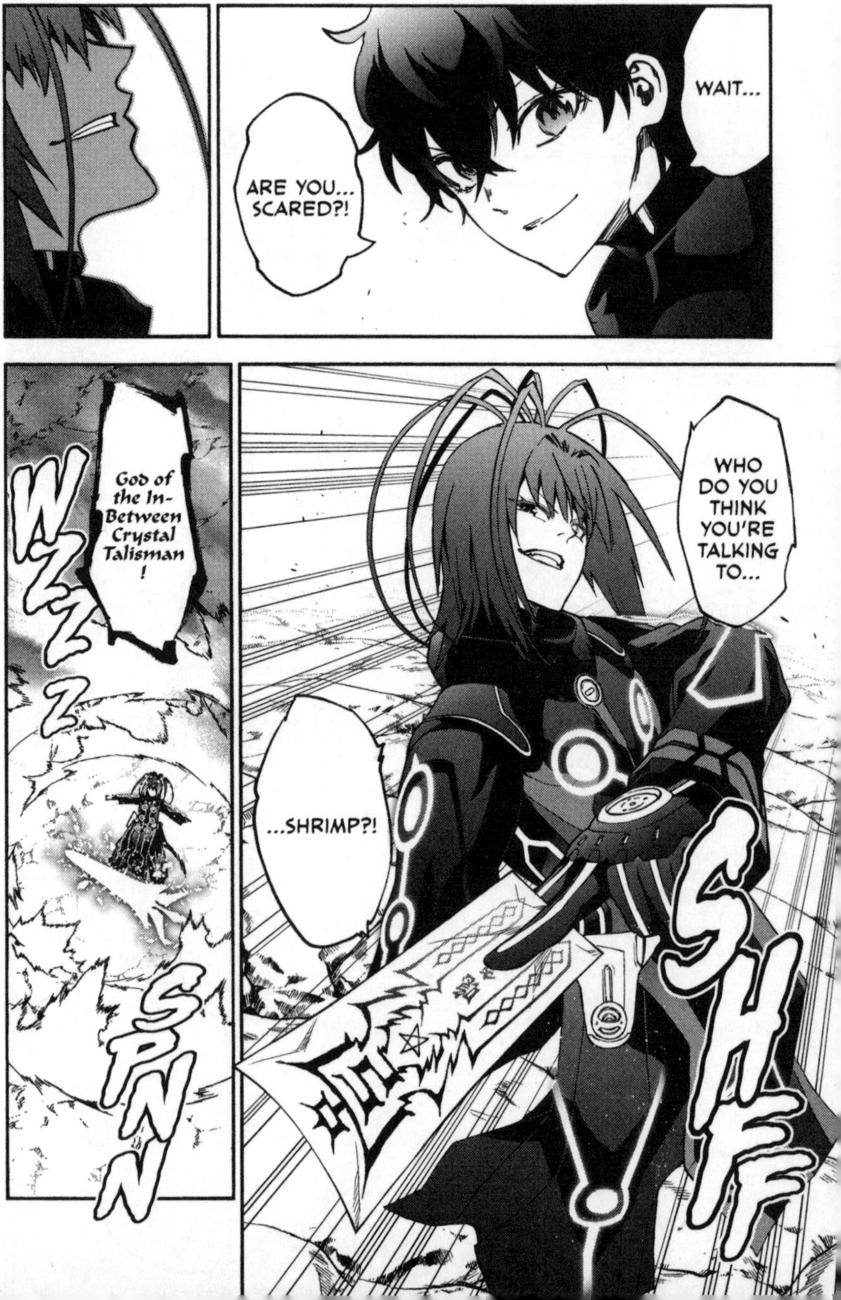
WAIT...
ARE YOU... SCARED?!
WHO DO YOU THINK YOU'RE TALKING TO...
...SHRIMP?!
SHFF
God of the In-Between Crystal Talisman!
WZZZ
SPNN

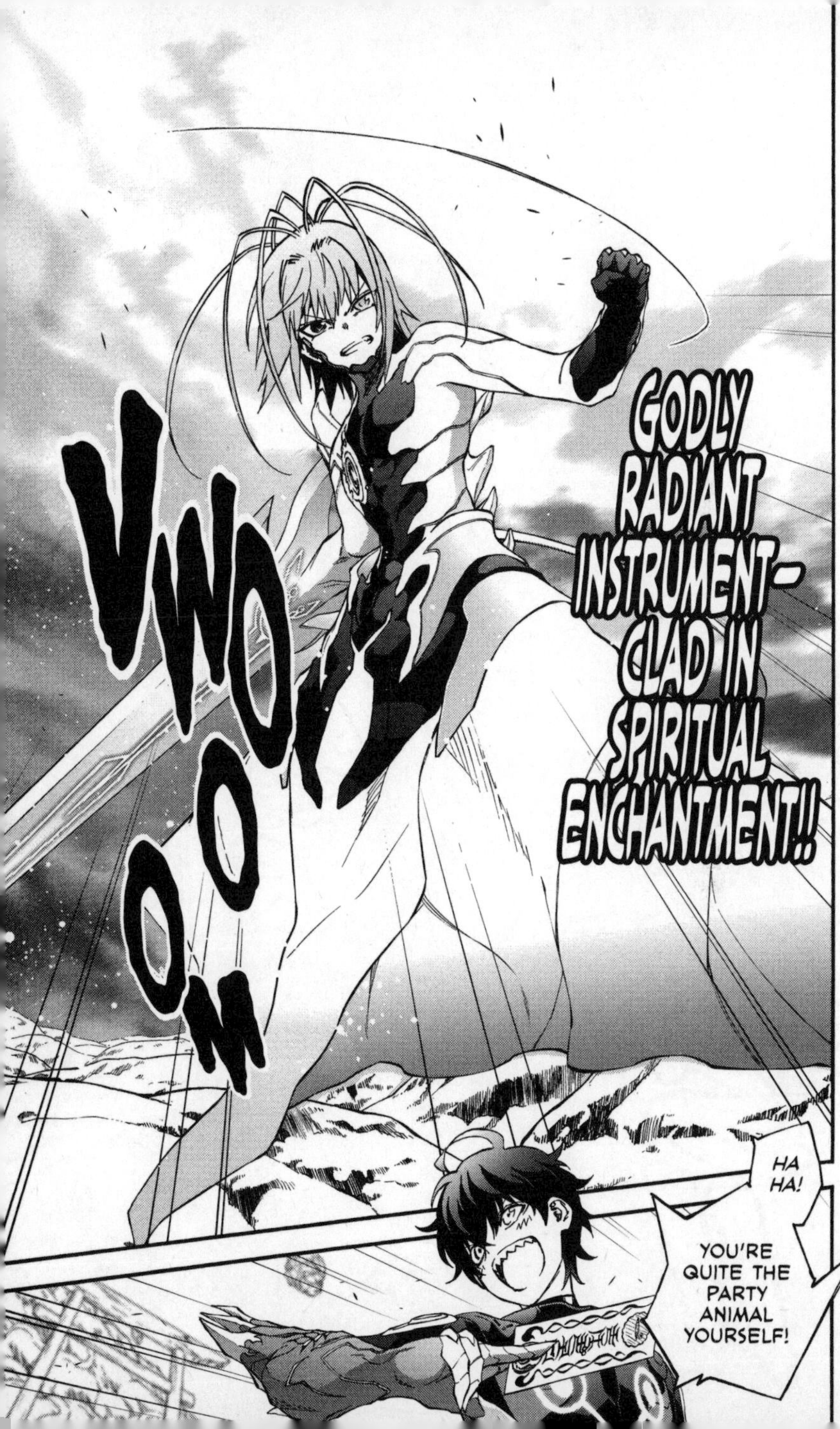
GODLY RADIANT INSTRUMENT-CLAD IN SPIRITUAL ENCHANTMENT!!
VWOOOM
HA HA!
YOU'RE QUITE THE PARTY ANIMAL YOURSELF!

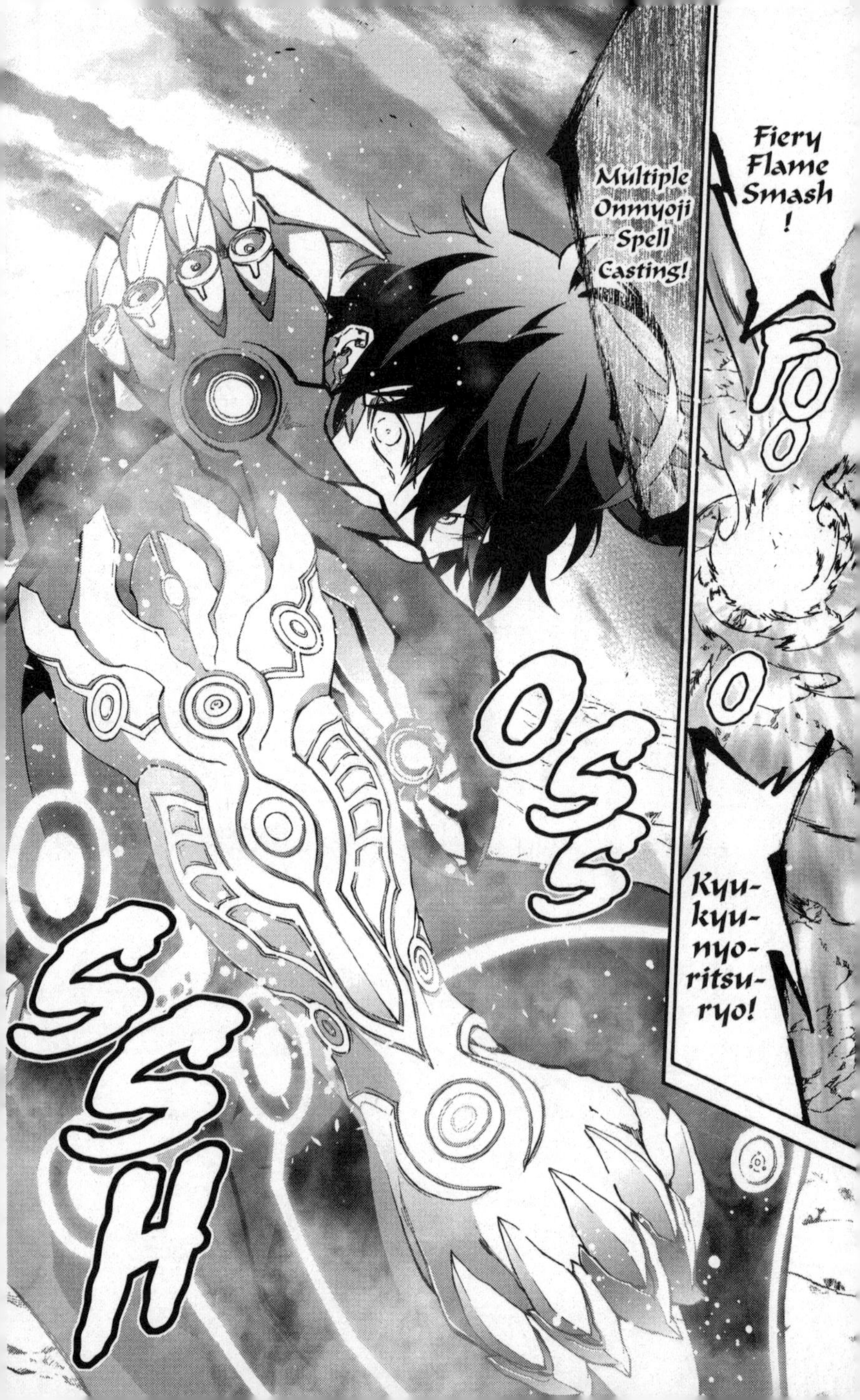
Fiery Flame Smash!
FOOOO
Kyu-kyu-nyo-ritsu-ryo!
Multiple Onmyoji Spell Casting!
OSSS
SSSH

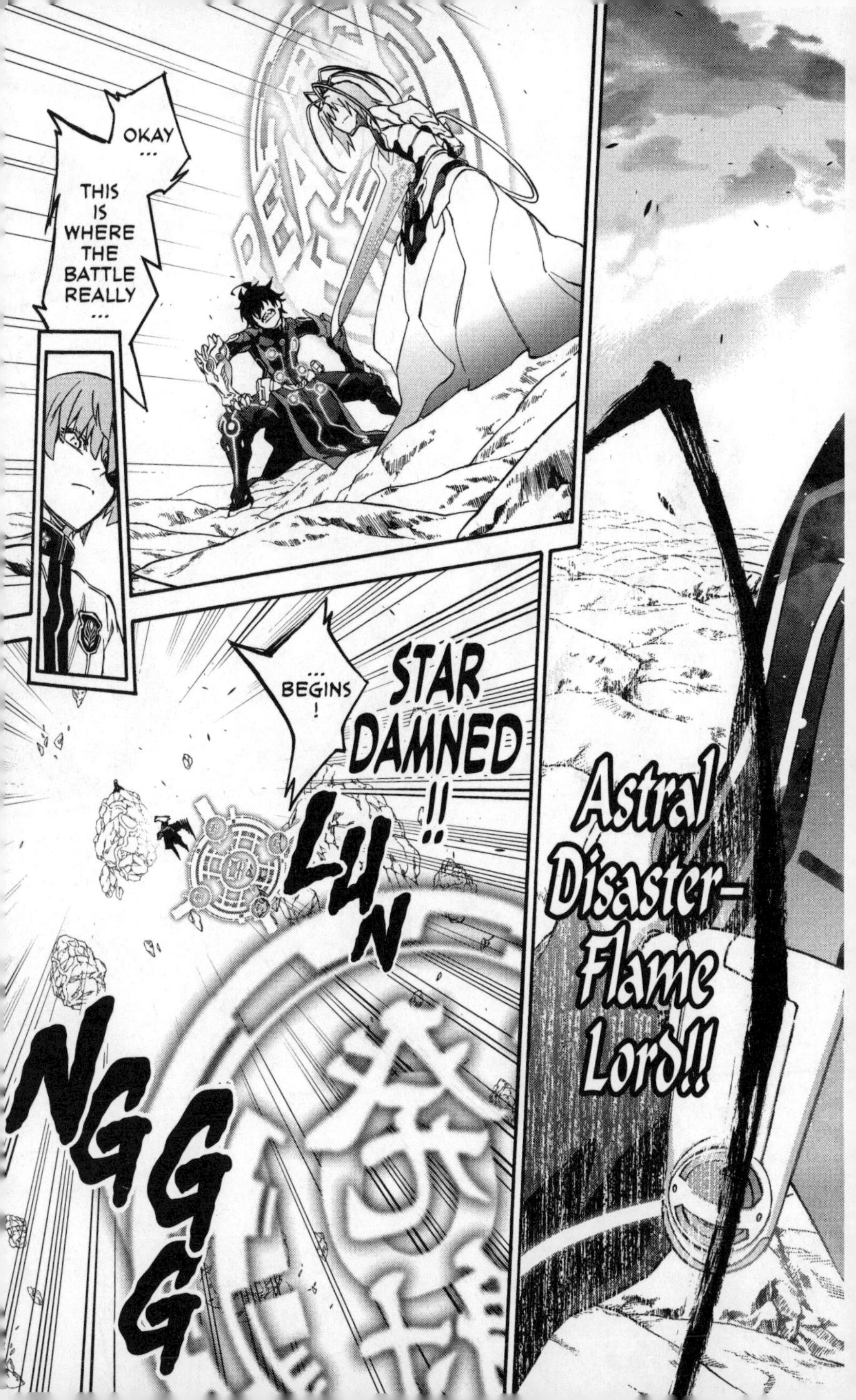
Astral Disaster-Flame Lord!!
OKAY... THIS IS WHERE THE BATTLE REALLY...
...BEGINS!
STAR DAMNED!!
LUNNGGG

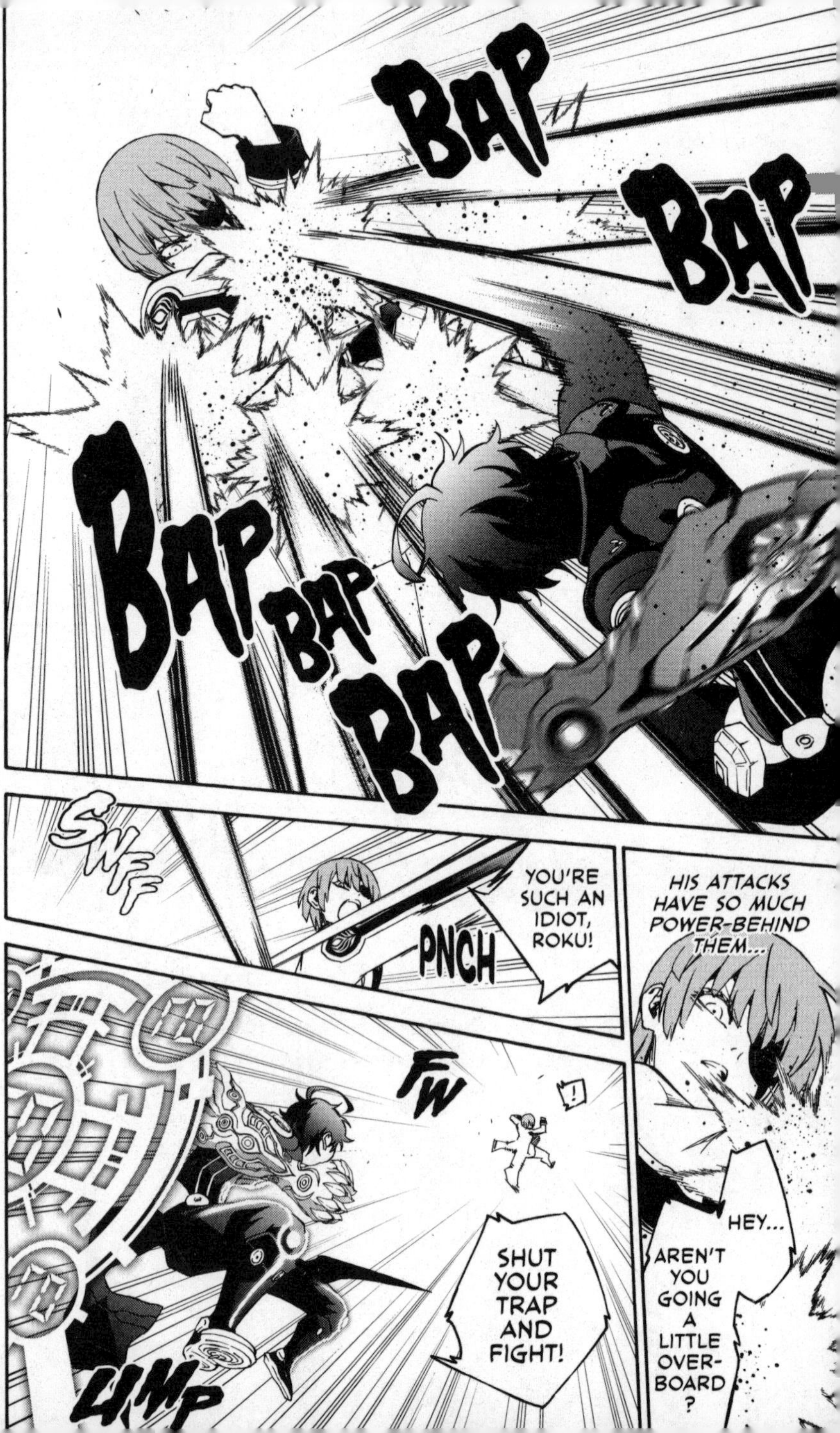
BAP
BAP
BAP BAP BAP
HIS ATTACKS HAVE SO MUCH POWER BEHIND THEM...
HEY...
AREN'T YOU GOING A LITTLE OVER-BOARD?
SNFF
YOU'RE SUCH AN IDIOT, ROKU!
PNCH
FW
!
SHUT YOUR TRAP AND FIGHT!
LIMP

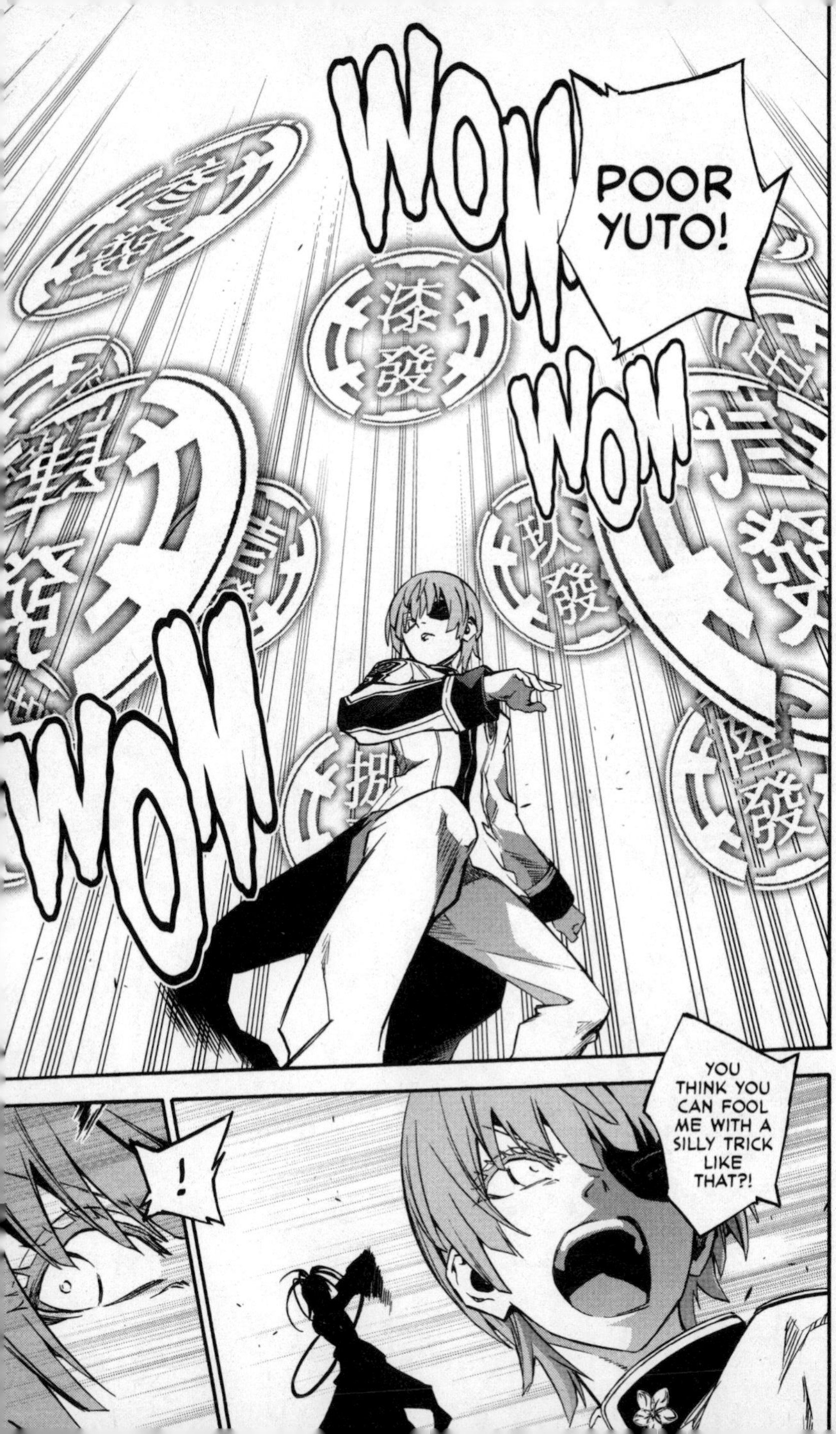
WOM
POOR YUTO!
WOM
WOM
YOU THINK YOU CAN FOOL ME WITH A SILLY TRICK LIKE THAT?!
!

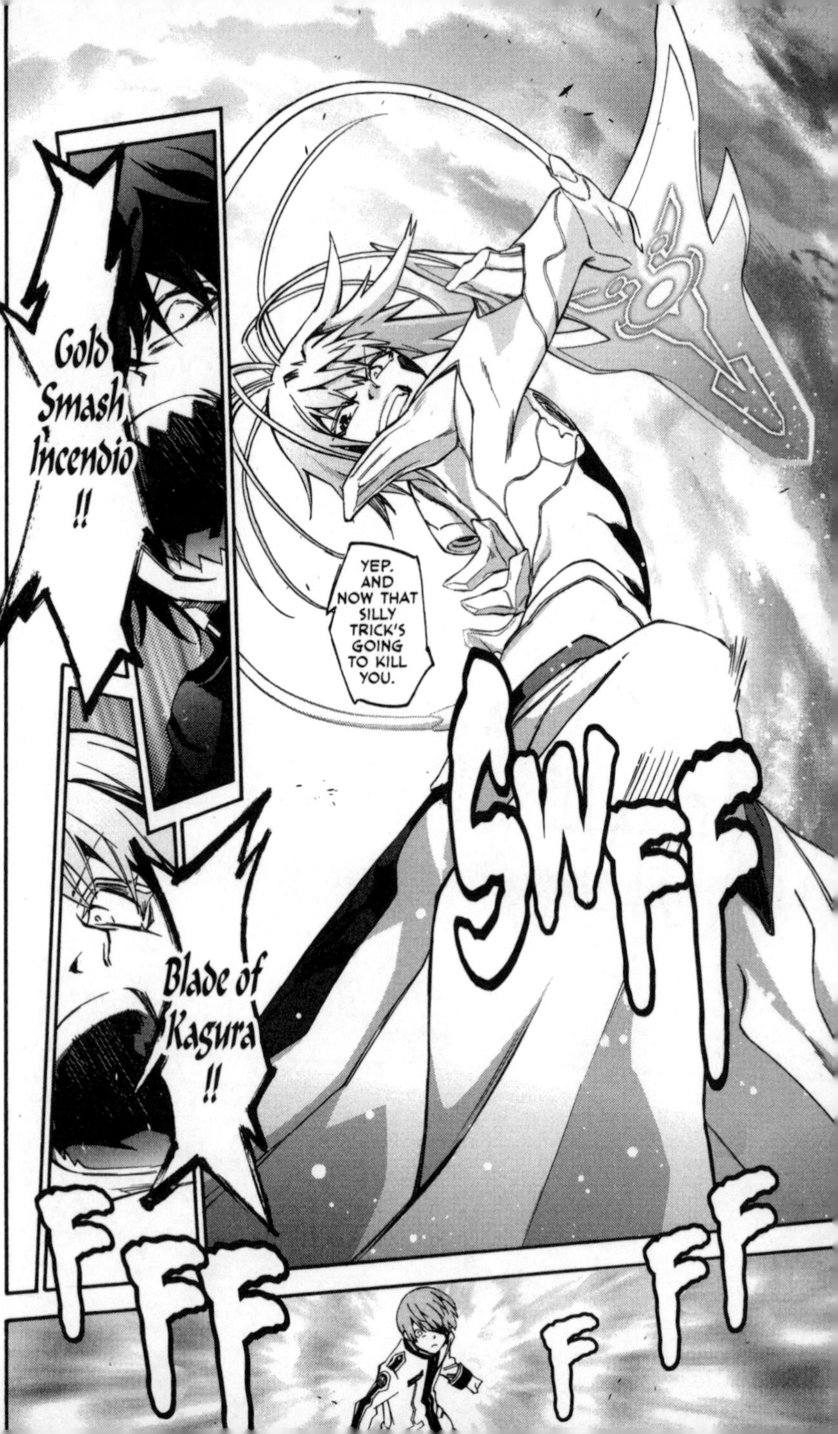
YEP. AND NOW THAT SILLY TRICK'S GOING TO KILL YOU.
SWFF
Gold Smash Incendio !!
Blade of Kagura !!
FFF
FFF
F

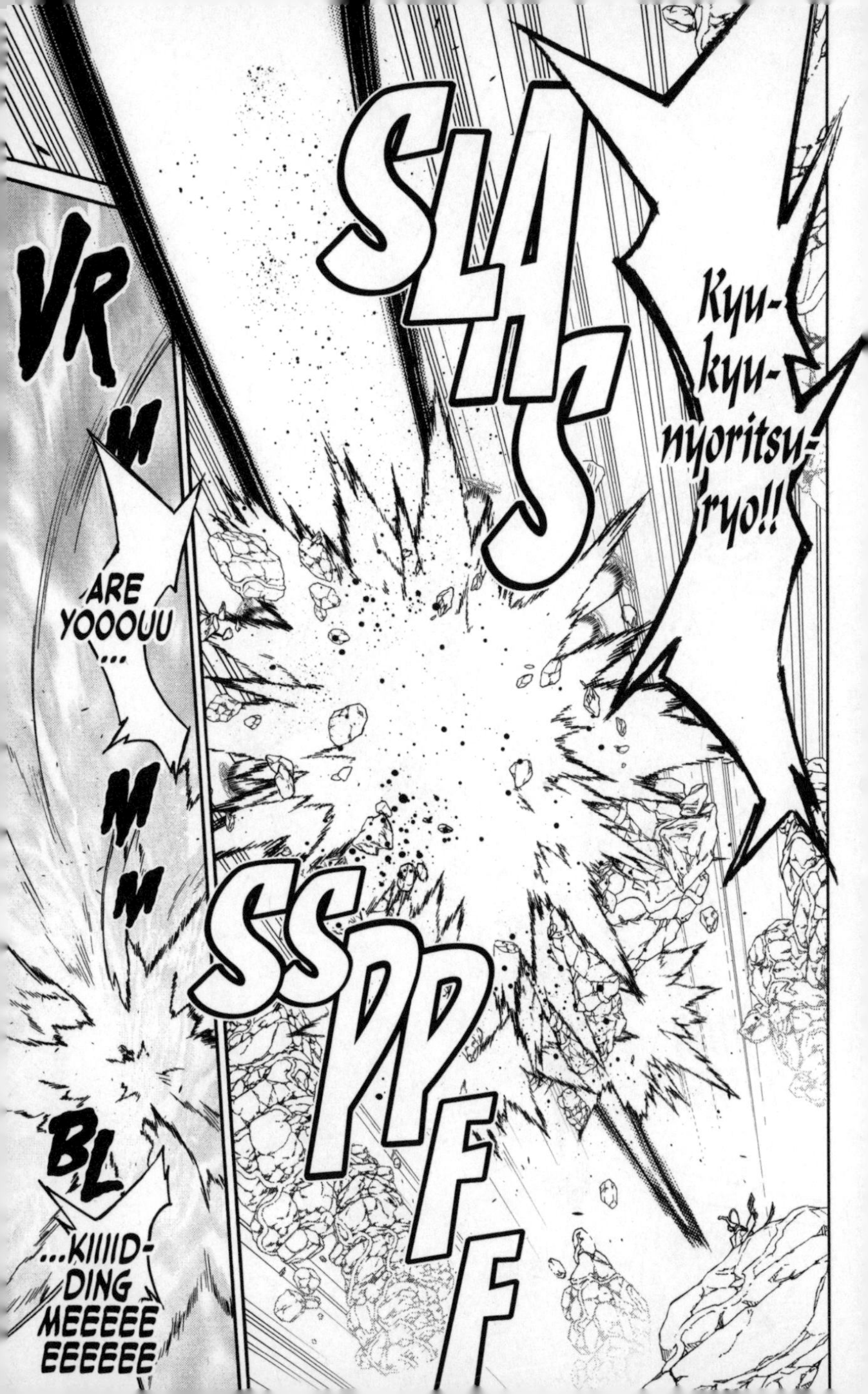
Kyu-kyu-nyoritsu-ryo!!
SLASS
SSPPFF
VRMMMM
ARE YOOOUU...
BL
...KIIIID-DING MEEEEEE EEEEEE

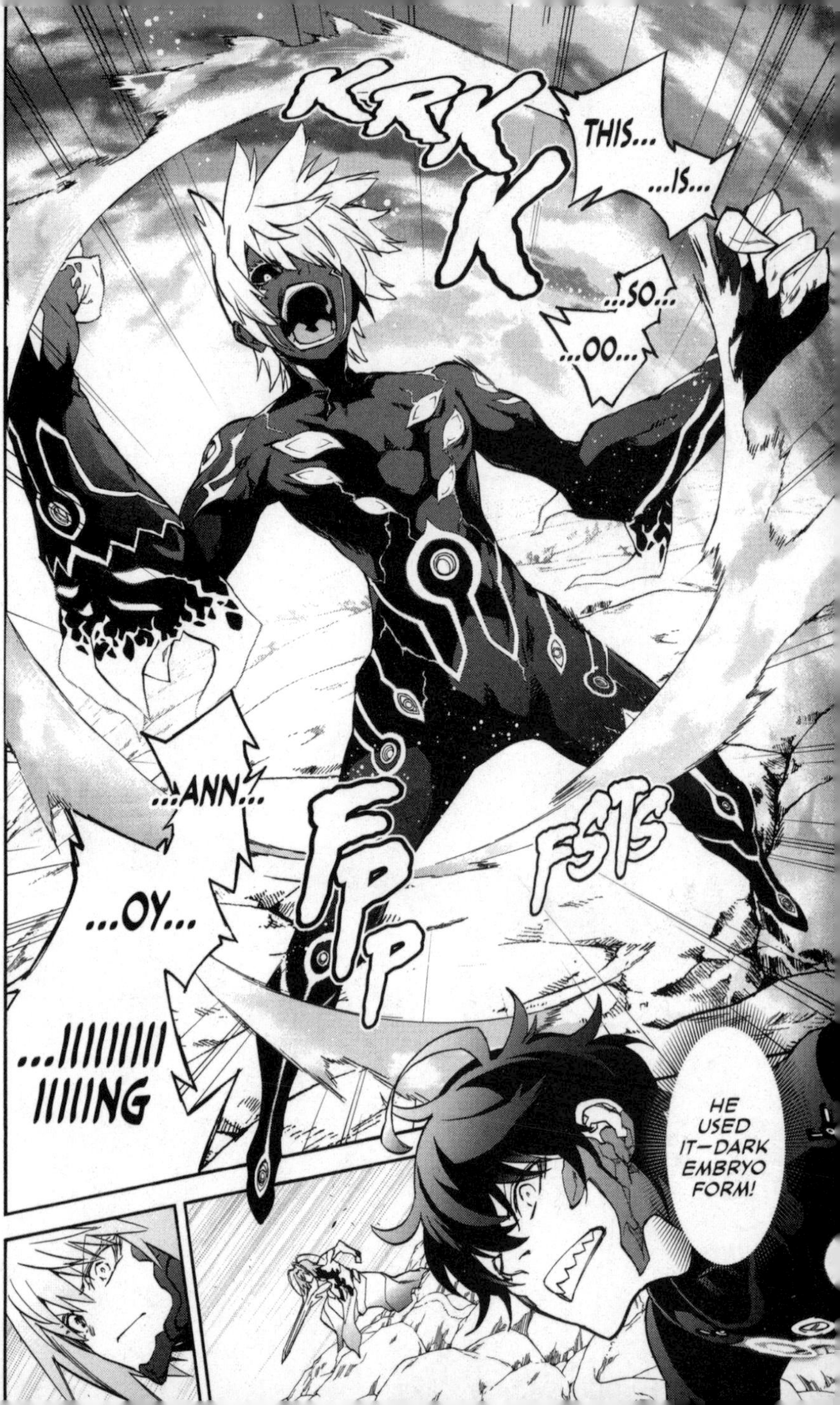
KRKK
THIS...
...IS...
...SO...
...OO...
...ANN...
...OY...
...IIIIIIII
IIIIING
FP
FSTS
HE USED IT—DARK EMBRYO FORM!

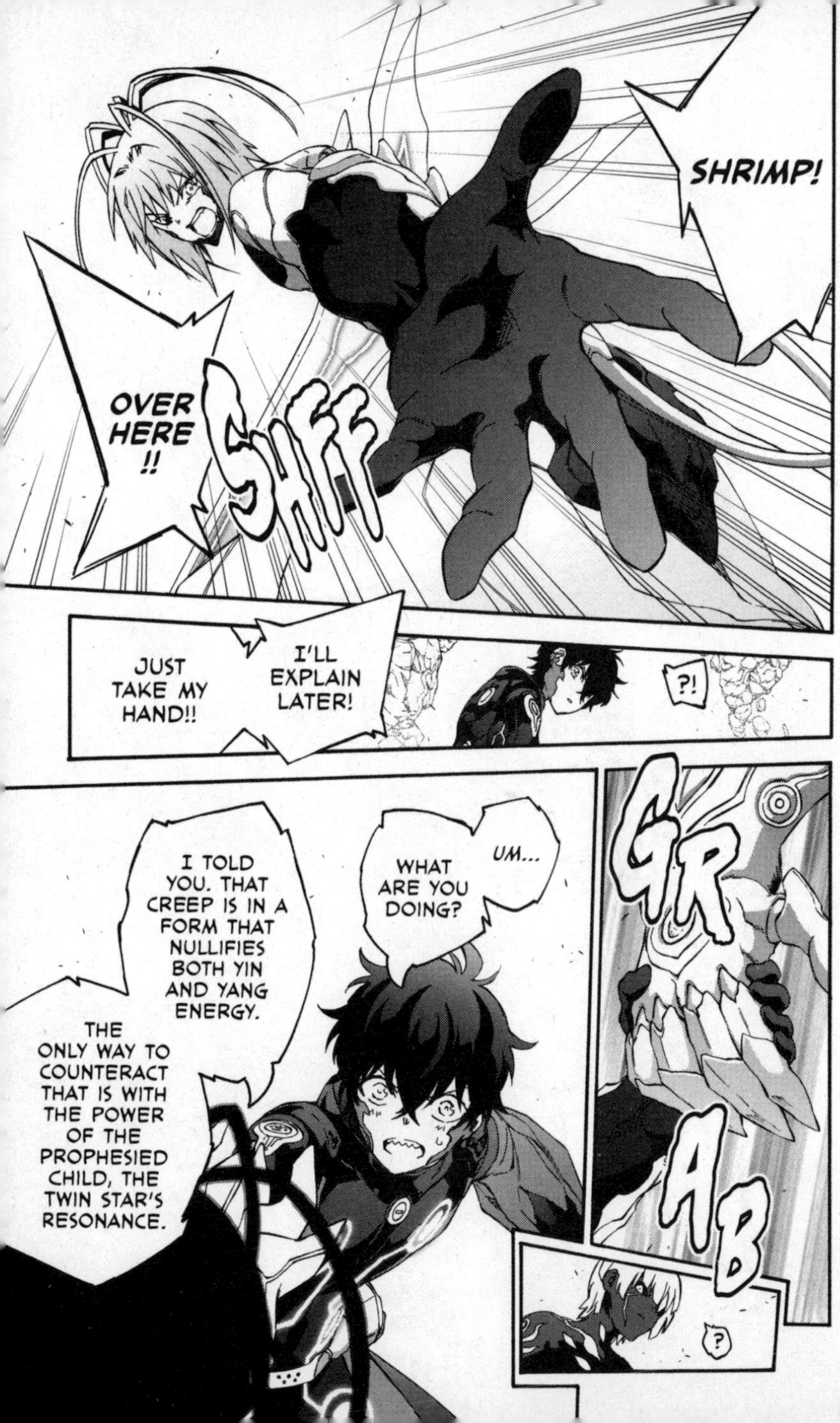
SHRIMP!
OVER HERE!!
SHFF
?!
I'LL EXPLAIN LATER!
JUST TAKE MY HAND!!
GRAB
?
UM...
WHAT ARE YOU DOING?
I TOLD YOU. THAT CREEP IS IN A FORM THAT NULLIFIES BOTH YIN AND YANG ENERGY.
THE ONLY WAY TO COUNTERACT THAT IS WITH THE POWER OF THE PROPHESIED CHILD, THE TWIN STAR'S RESONANCE.

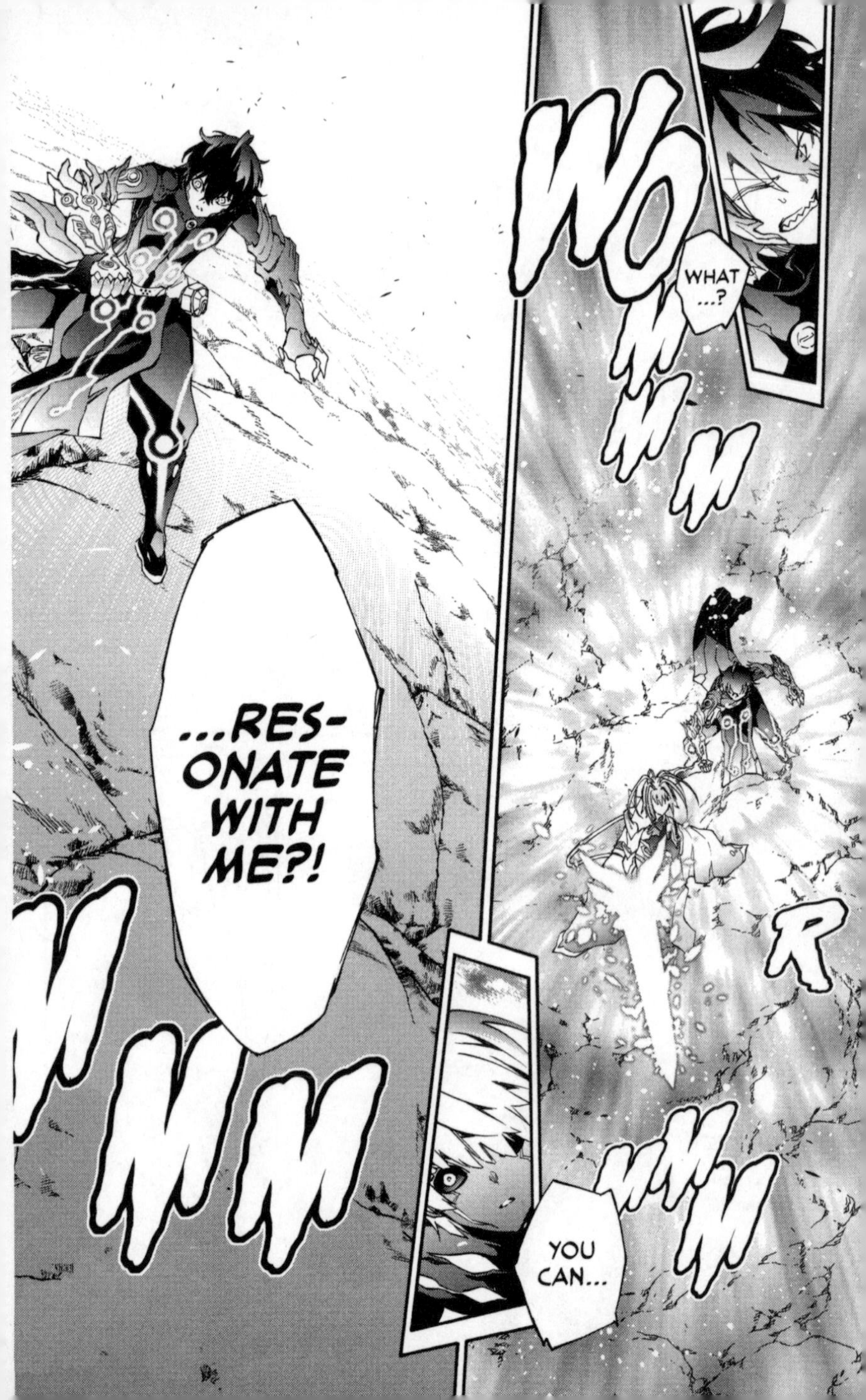
WHAT ...?
YOU CAN...
...RES- ONATE WITH ME?!

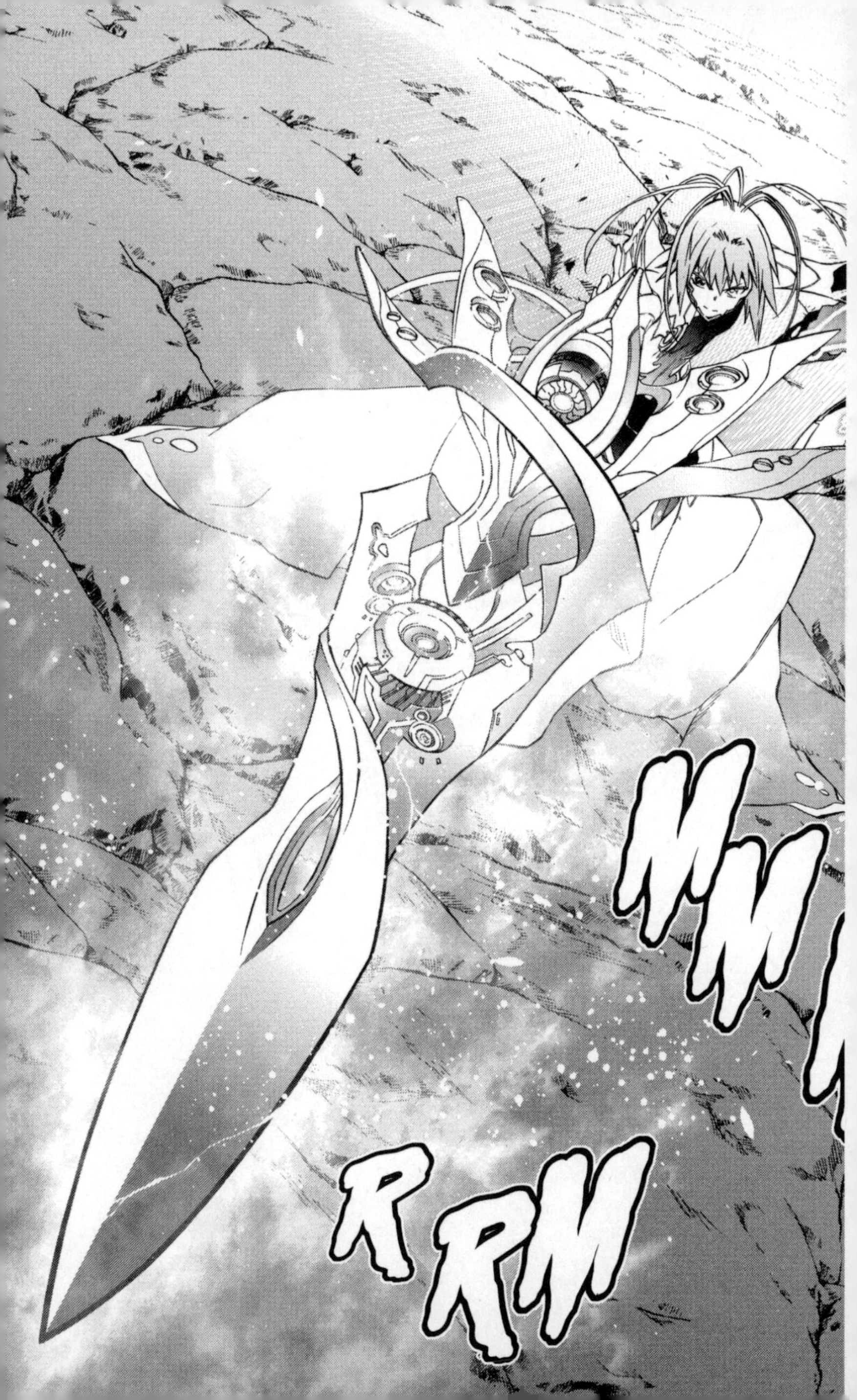
RRMMMM

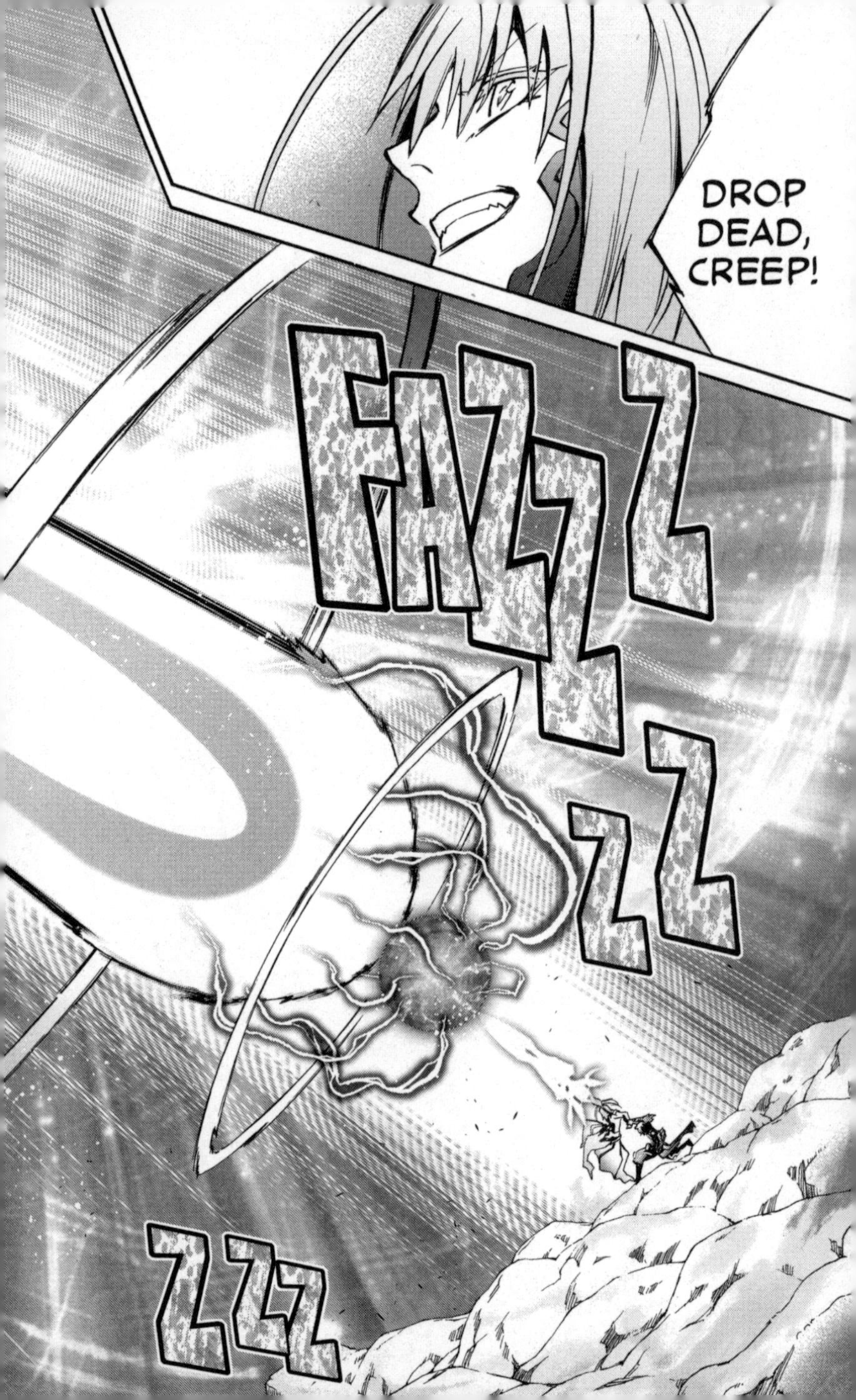
DROP DEAD, CREEP!
FAZZZ
ZZ
ZZZ

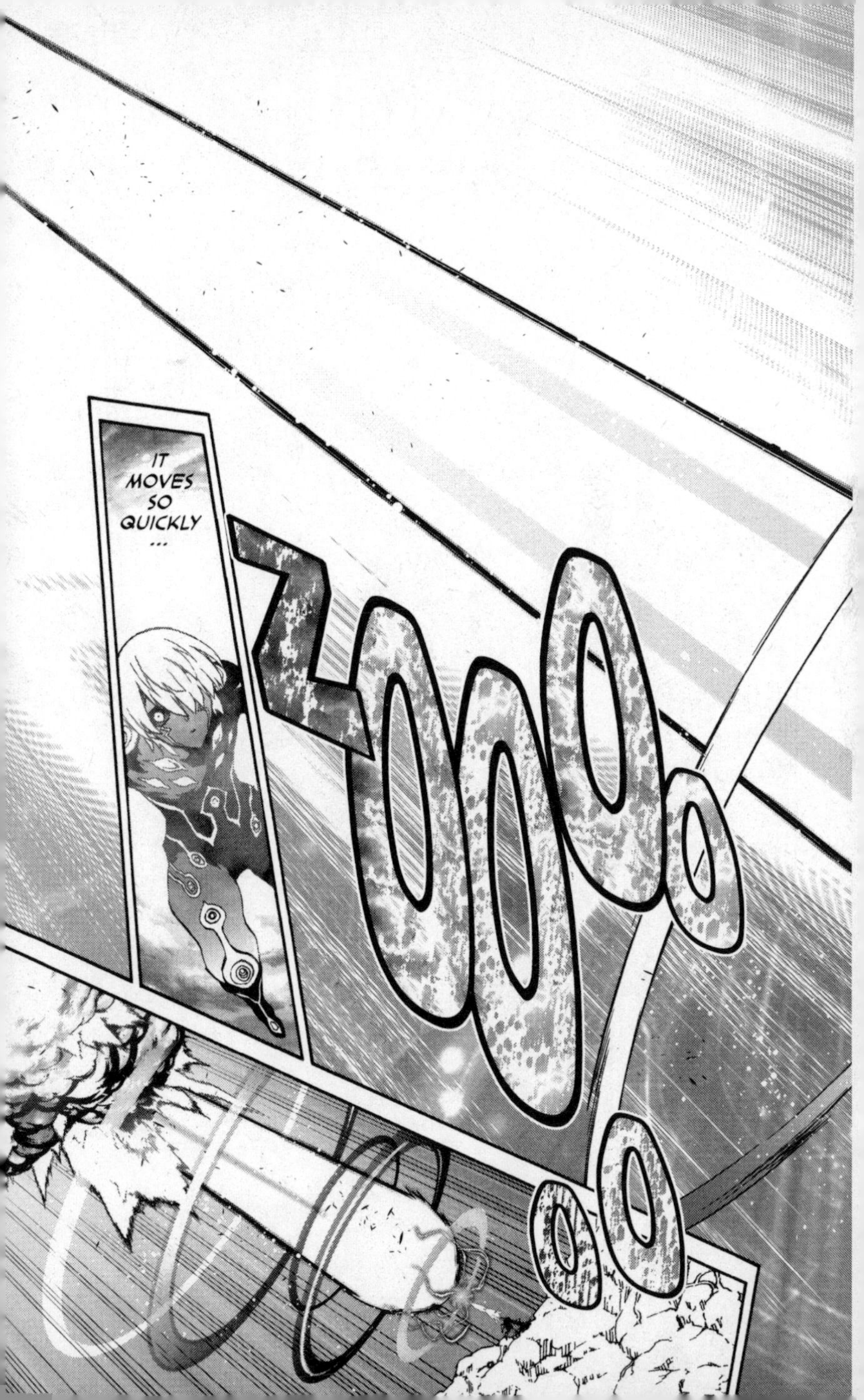
IT MOVES SO QUICKLY ...
ZOOOOOOO

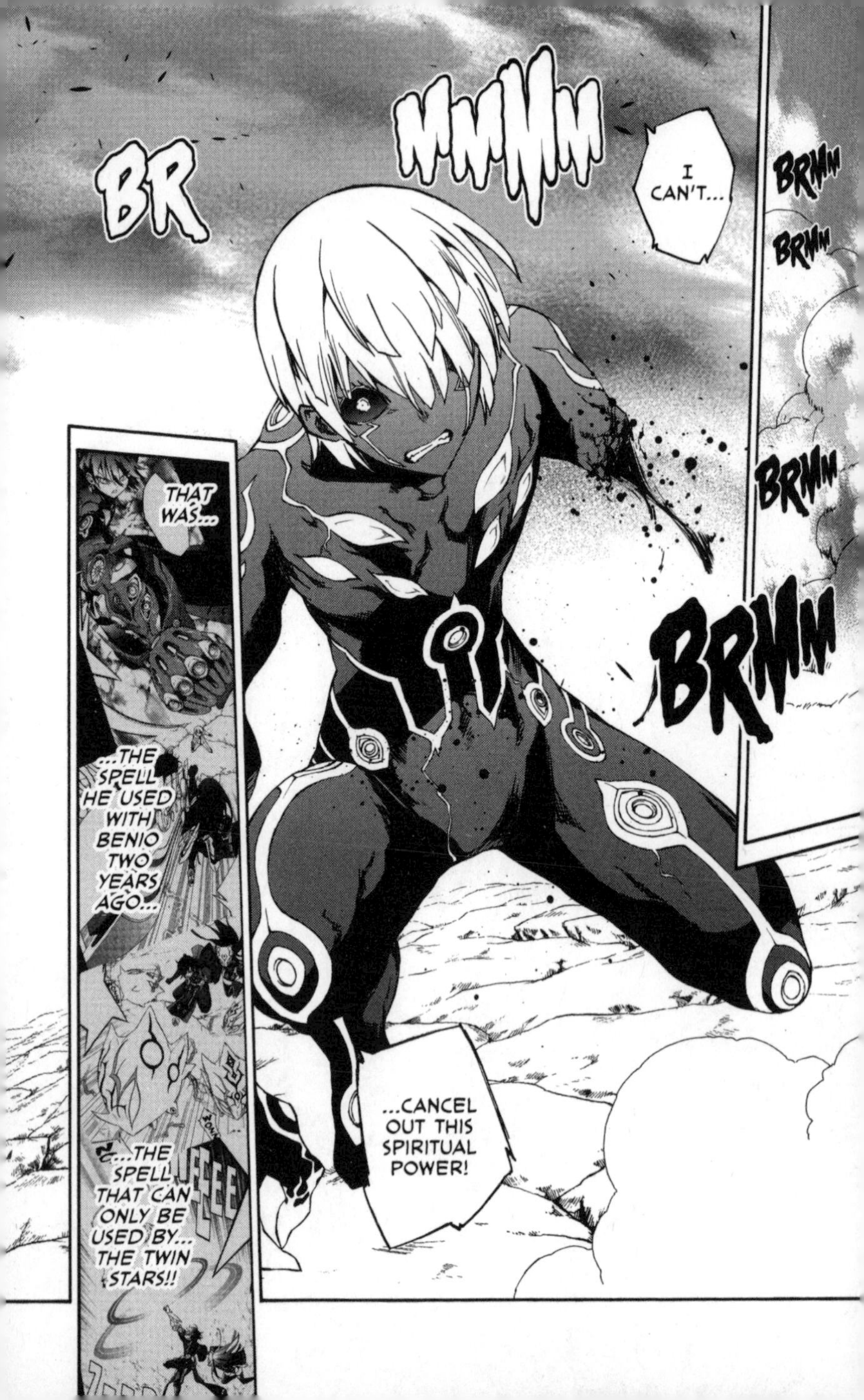
BRMM
BRMM
BRMM
BRMM
BR
MMMMM
I CAN'T...
...CANCEL OUT THIS SPIRITUAL POWER!
THAT WAS...
...THE SPELL HE USED WITH BENIO TWO YEARS AGO...
...THE SPELL THAT CAN ONLY BE USED BY... THE TWIN STARS!!

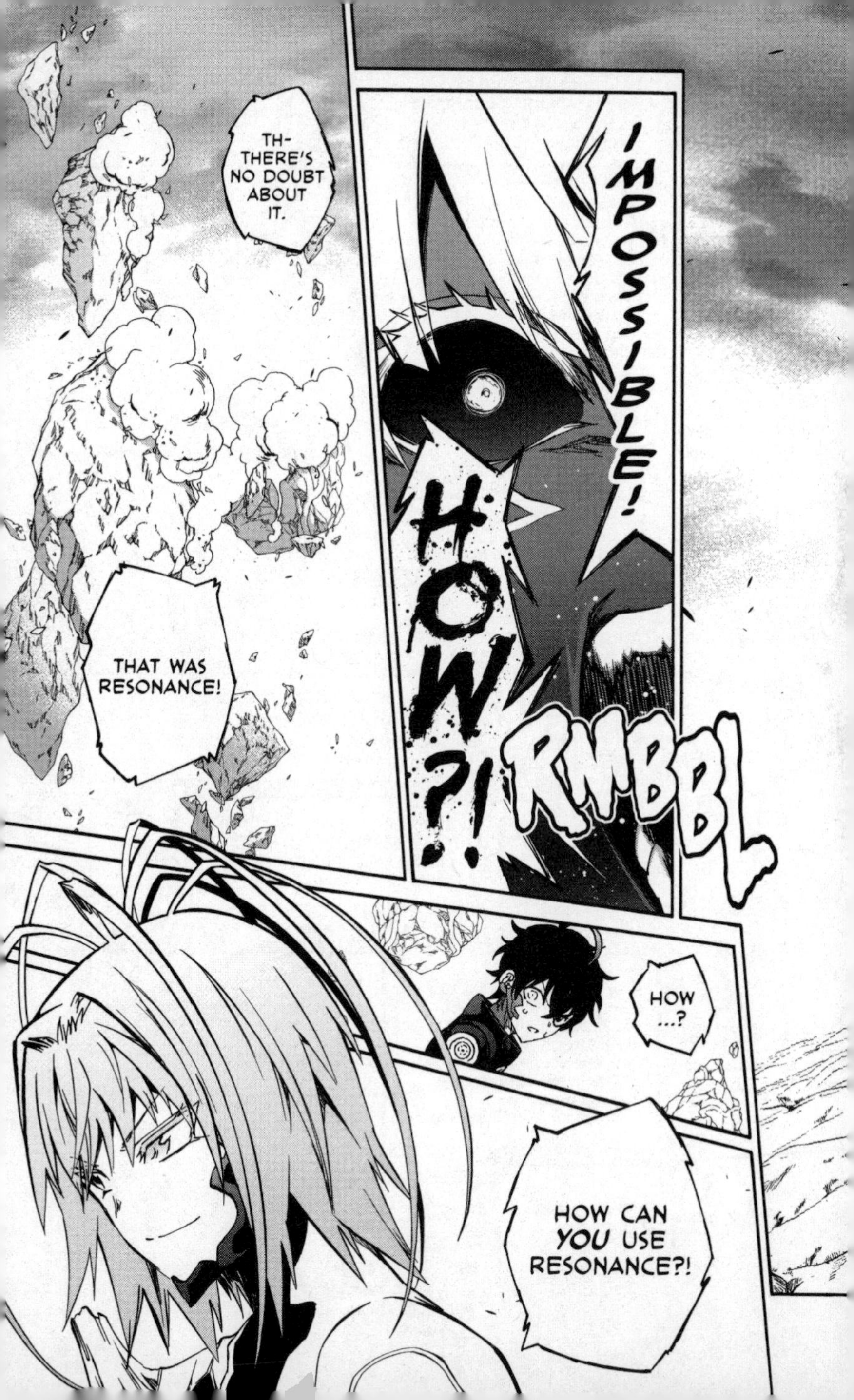
IMPOSSIBLE!
HOW?!
RMBBL
TH- THERE'S NO DOUBT ABOUT IT.
THAT WAS RESONANCE!
HOW ...?
HOW CAN YOU USE RESONANCE?!

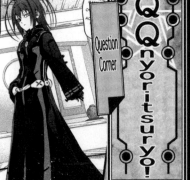

QQ nyoritsuryo!

Question Corner

AND SOME DELAYED IT LONG ENOUGH TO PROTECT THE REST OF US AND PAVE A WAY FORWARD!

Q Why does the hem of Tenma's hunting gear drag on the ground?
(From Sayo Watanabe)

A You know how you buy school uniforms slightly too big at the beginning of the year because you expect to grow into them? It's like that. Tenma assumed his hunting gear would fit perfectly by now...

Q What kind of person is Tenma attracted to?
(From Tomomi Numabe)

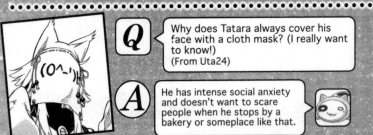

Tenma: "Huh? I'm into powerful exorcists and dumplings, and that's it."

Q Why does Tatara always cover his face with a cloth mask? (I really want to know!)
(From Uta24)

A He has intense social anxiety and doesn't want to scare people when he stops by a bakery or someplace like that.

Q How many stairs are there from the very bottom of the Platform of Courage to the Platform of the Starry Heavens at the top? I would probably get sore muscles midway up...
(From Black Tide Popcorn)

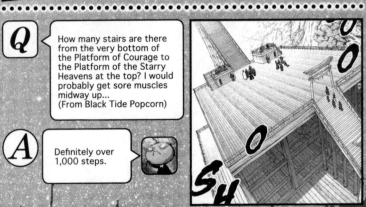

A Definitely over 1,000 steps.

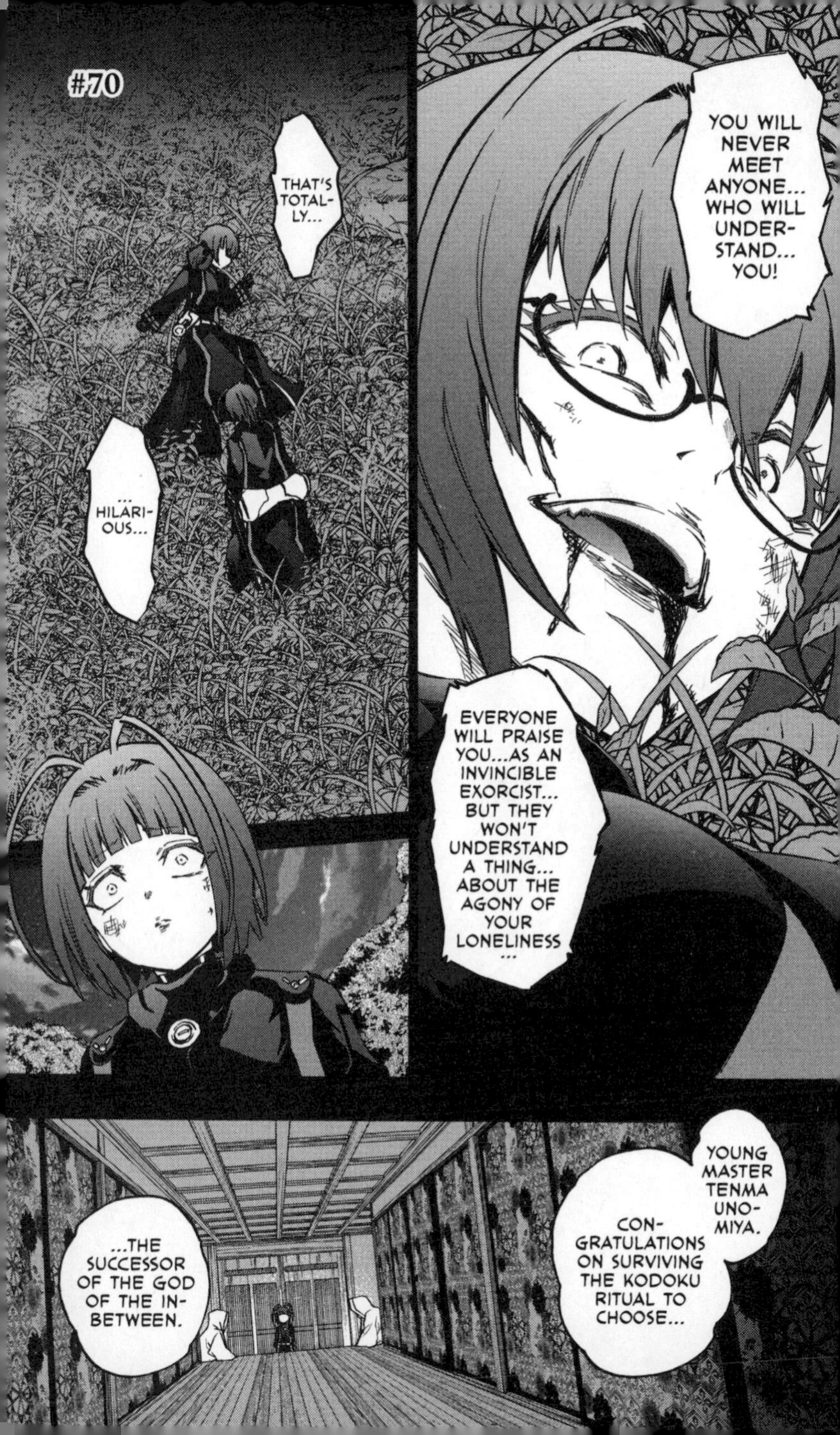
#70
YOU WILL NEVER MEET ANYONE... WHO WILL UNDERSTAND... YOU!
EVERYONE WILL PRAISE YOU...AS AN INVINCIBLE EXORCIST... BUT THEY WON'T UNDERSTAND A THING... ABOUT THE AGONY OF YOUR LONELINESS...
THAT'S TOTALLY...
...HILARIOUS...
YOUNG MASTER TENMA UNOMIYA.
CONGRATULATIONS ON SURVIVING THE KODOKU RITUAL TO CHOOSE...
...THE SUCCESSOR OF THE GOD OF THE IN-BETWEEN.

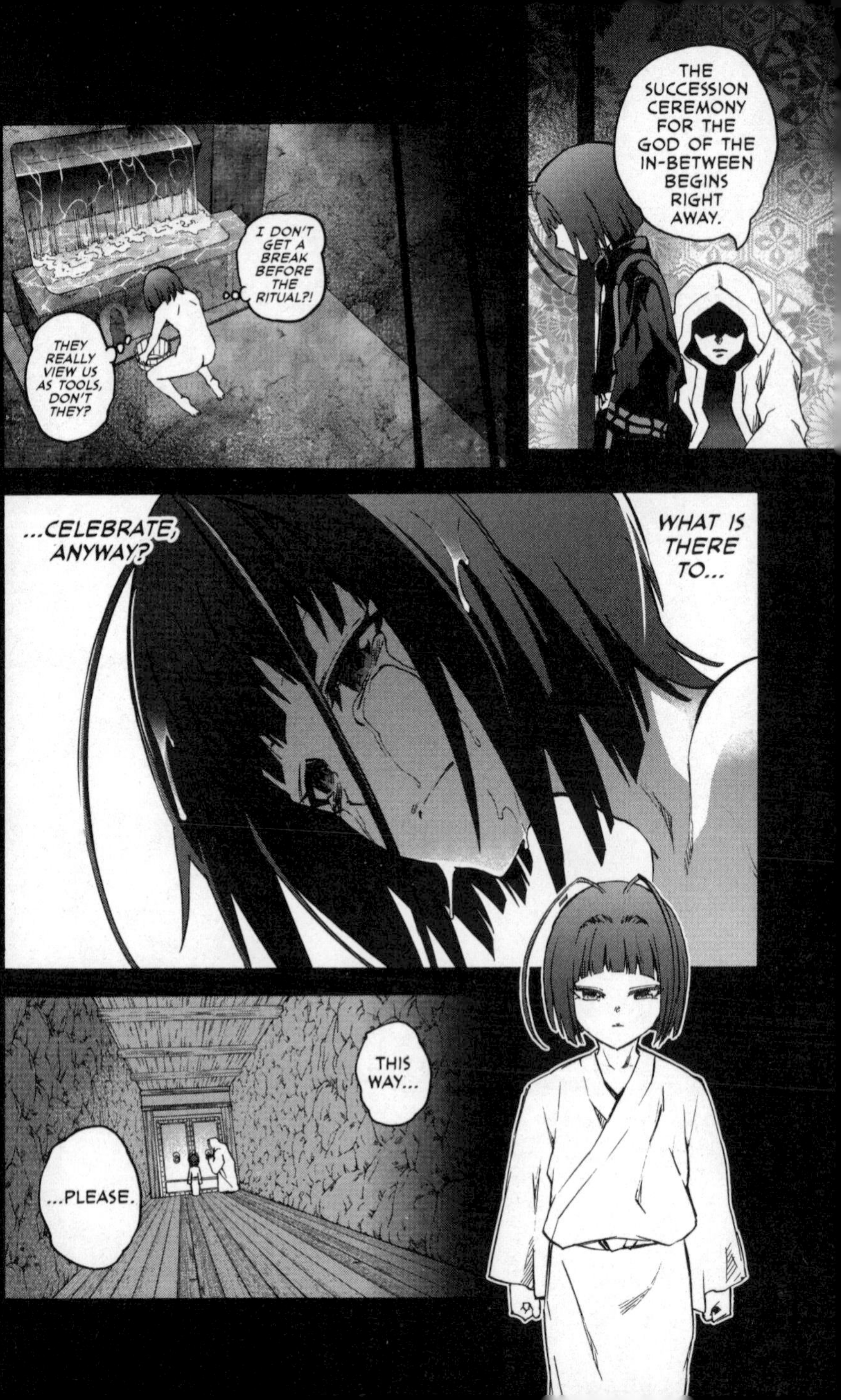
THE SUCCESSION CEREMONY FOR THE GOD OF THE IN-BETWEEN BEGINS RIGHT AWAY.
I DON'T GET A BREAK BEFORE THE RITUAL?!
THEY REALLY VIEW US AS TOOLS, DON'T THEY?
WHAT IS THERE TO...
...CELEBRATE, ANYWAY?
THIS WAY...
...PLEASE.

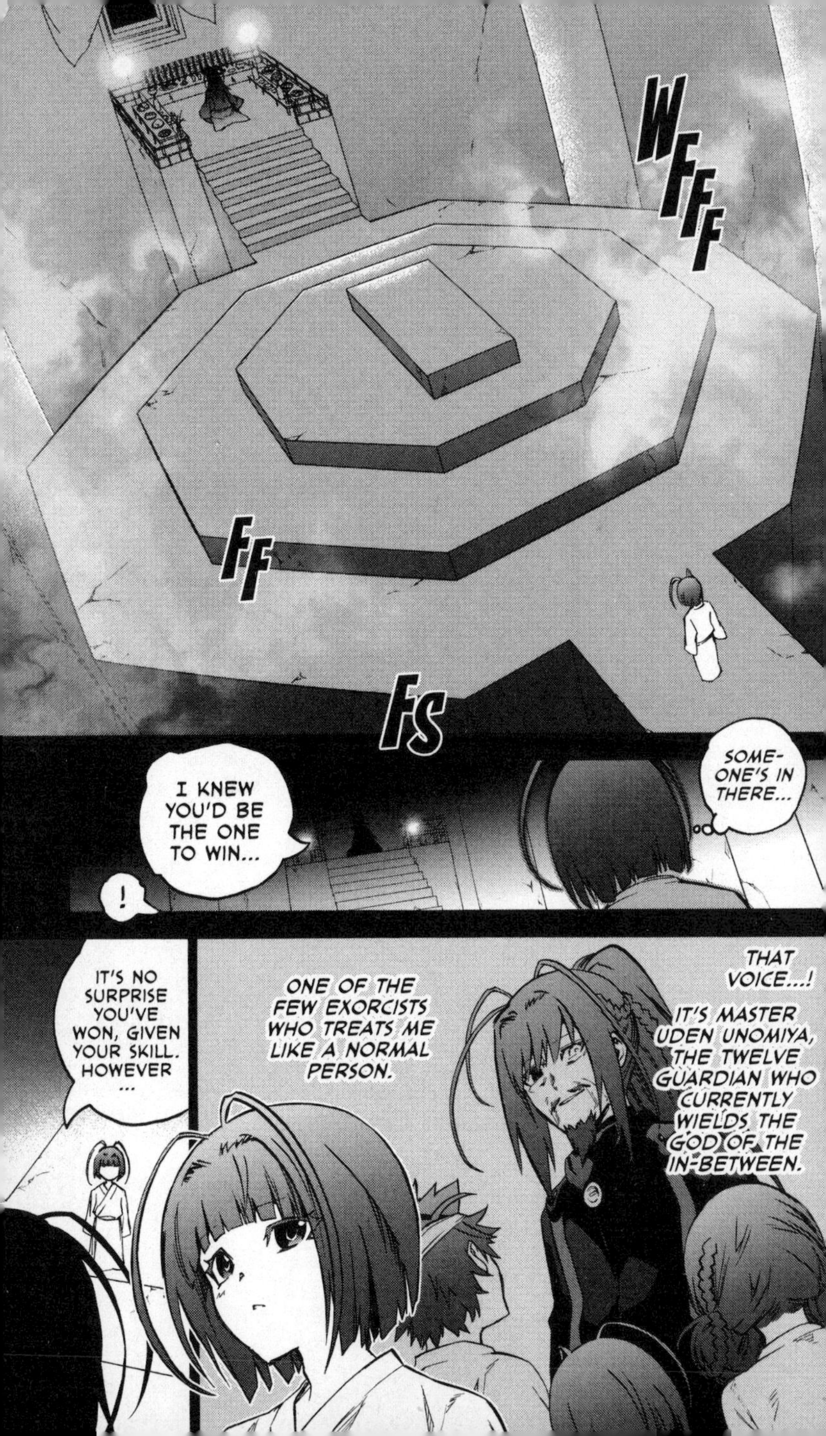
WFFFF
FF
FS
SOME-ONE'S IN THERE...
I KNEW YOU'D BE THE ONE TO WIN...
!
THAT VOICE...!
IT'S MASTER UDEN UNOMIYA, THE TWELVE GUARDIAN WHO CURRENTLY WIELDS THE GOD OF THE IN-BETWEEN.
ONE OF THE FEW EXORCISTS WHO TREATS ME LIKE A NORMAL PERSON.
IT'S NO SURPRISE YOU'VE WON, GIVEN YOUR SKILL. HOWEVER ...

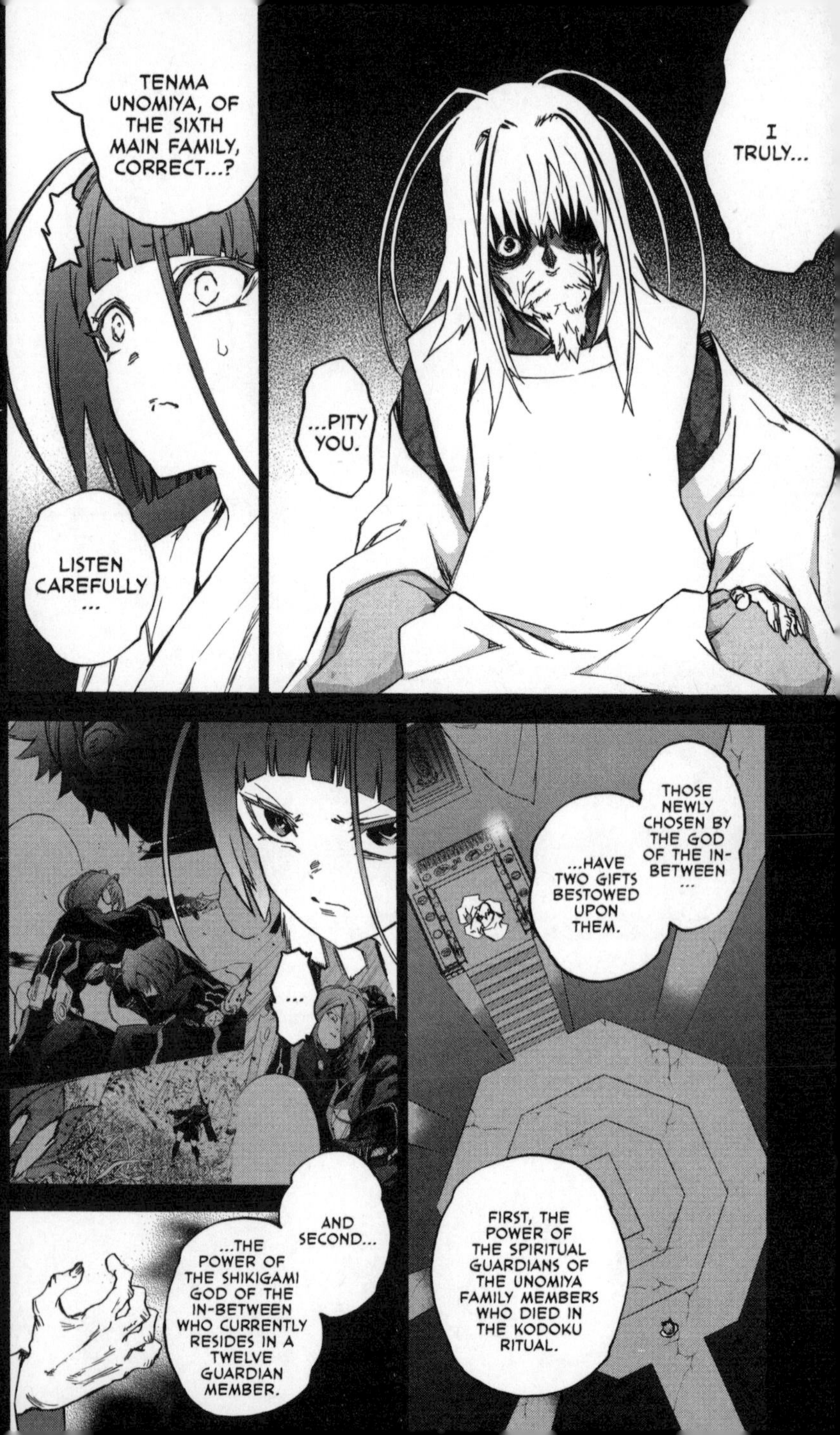
I TRULY...
...PITY YOU.
TENMA UNOMIYA, OF THE SIXTH MAIN FAMILY, CORRECT...?
LISTEN CAREFULLY ...
THOSE NEWLY CHOSEN BY THE GOD OF THE IN-BETWEEN ...
...HAVE TWO GIFTS BESTOWED UPON THEM.
FIRST, THE POWER OF THE SPIRITUAL GUARDIANS OF THE UNOMIYA FAMILY MEMBERS WHO DIED IN THE KODOKU RITUAL.
...
AND SECOND...
...THE POWER OF THE SHIKIGAMI GOD OF THE IN-BETWEEN WHO CURRENTLY RESIDES IN A TWELVE GUARDIAN MEMBER.

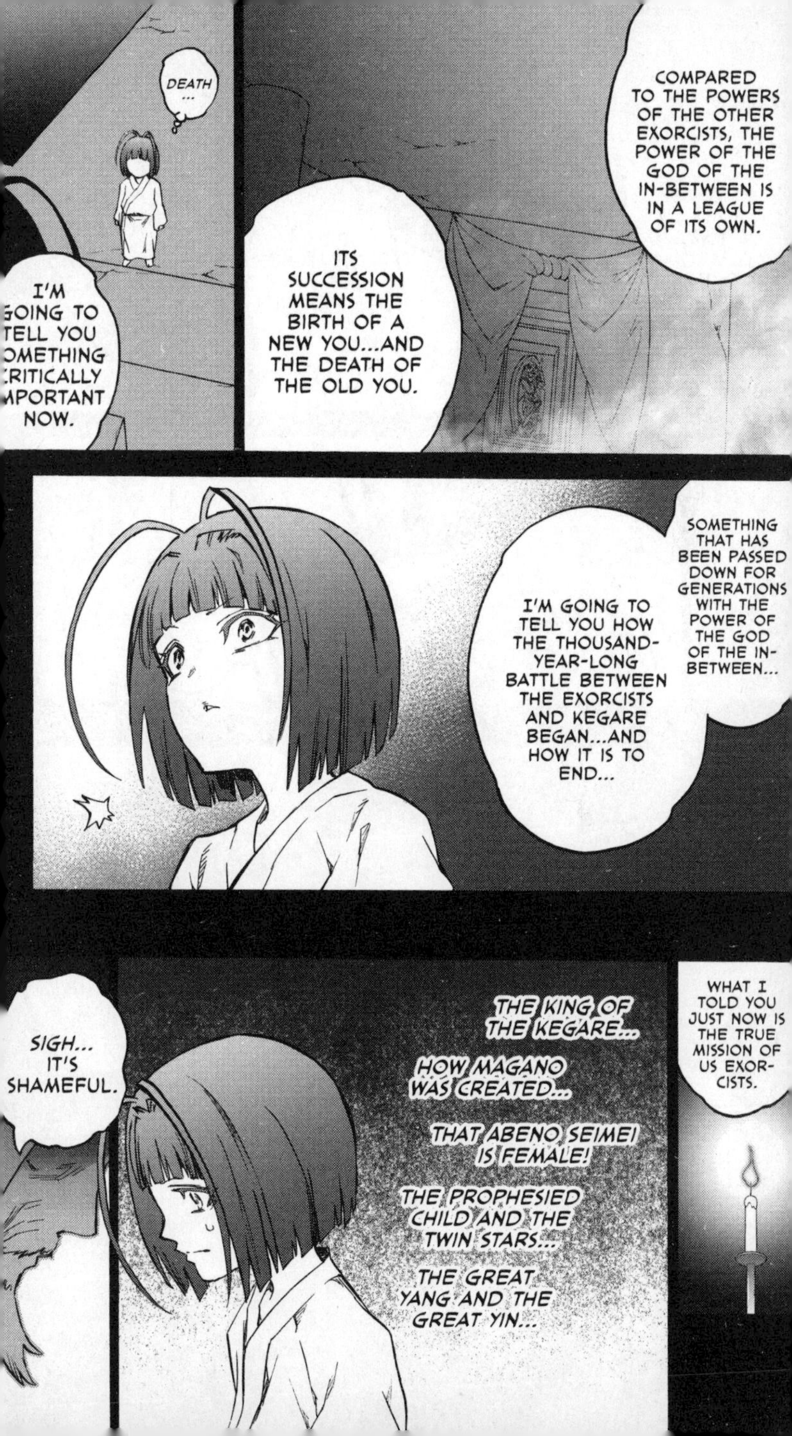
COMPARED TO THE POWERS OF THE OTHER EXORCISTS, THE POWER OF THE GOD OF THE IN-BETWEEN IS IN A LEAGUE OF ITS OWN.
ITS SUCCESSION MEANS THE BIRTH OF A NEW YOU...AND THE DEATH OF THE OLD YOU.
DEATH ...
I'M GOING TO TELL YOU OMETHING RITICALLY MPORTANT NOW.
SOMETHING THAT HAS BEEN PASSED DOWN FOR GENERATIONS WITH THE POWER OF THE GOD OF THE IN-BETWEEN...
I'M GOING TO TELL YOU HOW THE THOUSAND-YEAR-LONG BATTLE BETWEEN THE EXORCISTS AND KEGARE BEGAN...AND HOW IT IS TO END...
WHAT I TOLD YOU JUST NOW IS THE TRUE MISSION OF US EXORCISTS.
THE KING OF THE KEGARE...
HOW MAGANO WAS CREATED...
THAT ABENO SEIMEI IS FEMALE!
THE PROPHESIED CHILD AND THE TWIN STARS...
THE GREAT YANG AND THE GREAT YIN...
SIGH... IT'S SHAMEFUL.

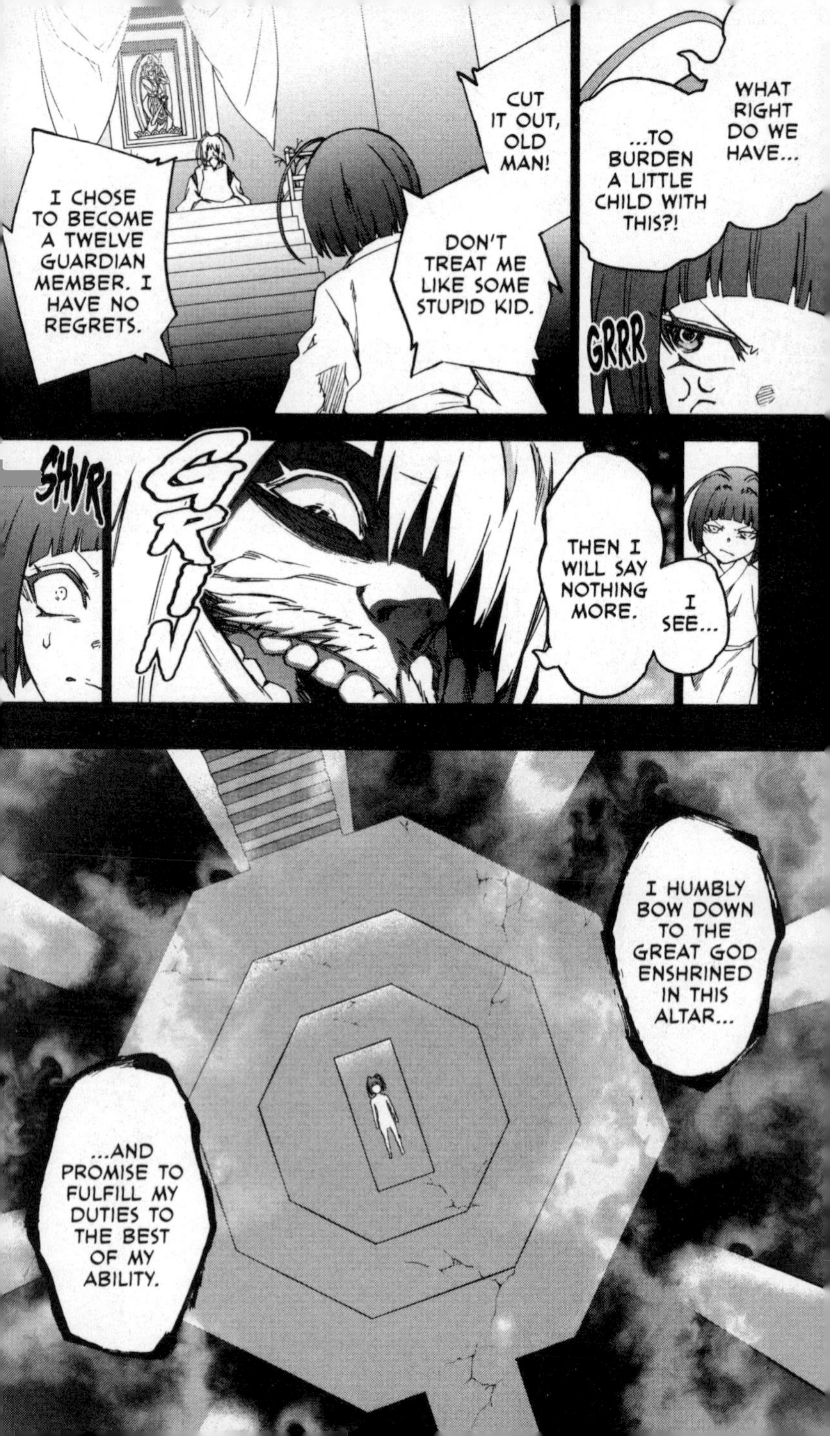
WHAT RIGHT DO WE HAVE...
...TO BURDEN A LITTLE CHILD WITH THIS?!
GRRR
CUT IT OUT, OLD MAN!
DON'T TREAT ME LIKE SOME STUPID KID.
I CHOSE TO BECOME A TWELVE GUARDIAN MEMBER. I HAVE NO REGRETS.
I SEE...
THEN I WILL SAY NOTHING MORE.
GRIN
SHVR
I HUMBLY BOW DOWN TO THE GREAT GOD ENSHRINED IN THIS ALTAR...
...AND PROMISE TO FULFILL MY DUTIES TO THE BEST OF MY ABILITY.

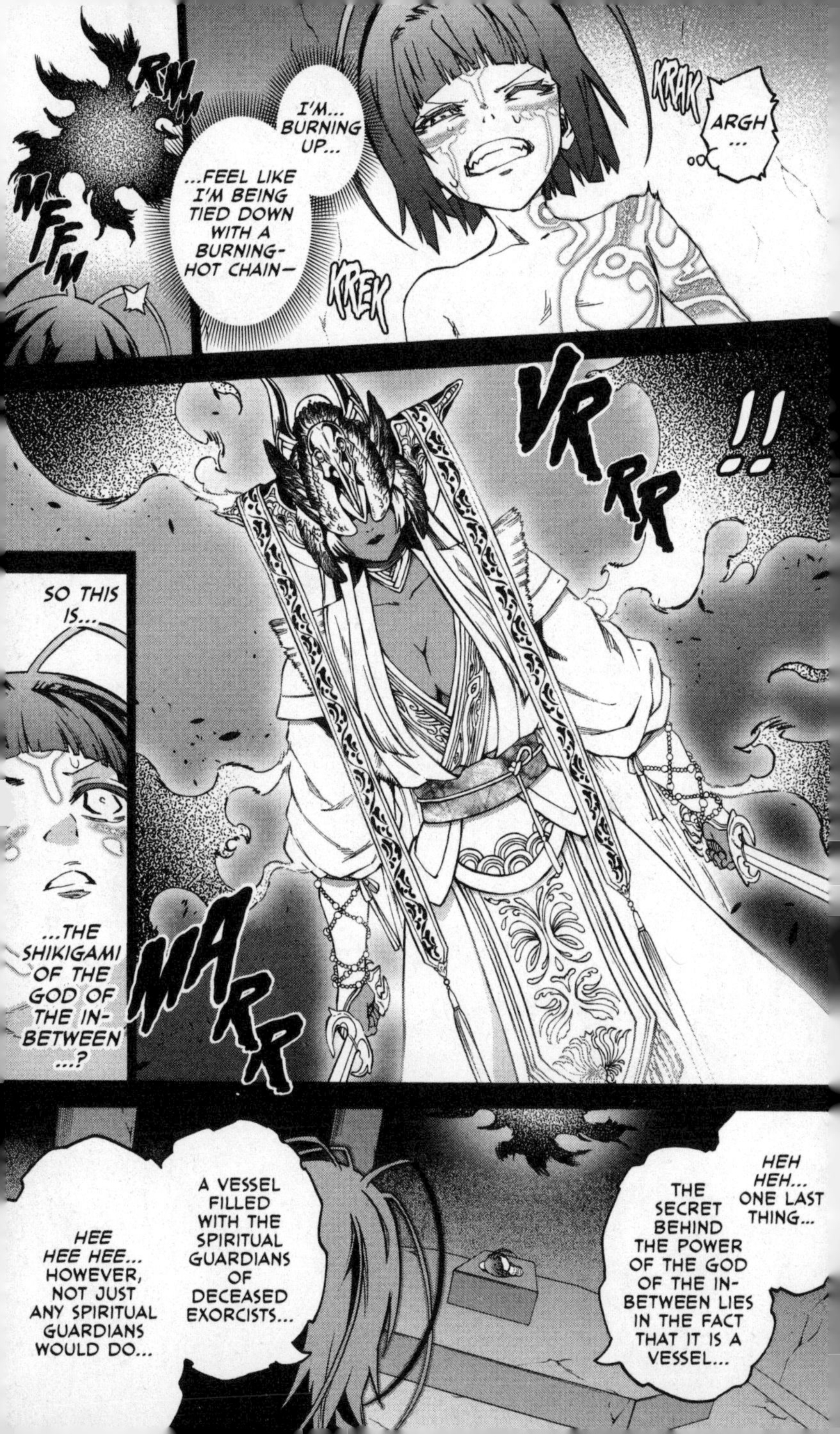
KRAK
ARGH...
I'M... BURNING UP...
...FEEL LIKE I'M BEING TIED DOWN WITH A BURNING-HOT CHAIN—
KREK
RMM
MFFM
VRRR!!
MARR
SO THIS IS...
...THE SHIKIGAMI OF THE GOD OF THE IN-BETWEEN...?
HEH HEH... ONE LAST THING...
THE SECRET BEHIND THE POWER OF THE GOD OF THE IN-BETWEEN LIES IN THE FACT THAT IT IS A VESSEL...
A VESSEL FILLED WITH THE SPIRITUAL GUARDIANS OF DECEASED EXORCISTS...
HEE HEE HEE... HOWEVER, NOT JUST ANY SPIRITUAL GUARDIANS WOULD DO...

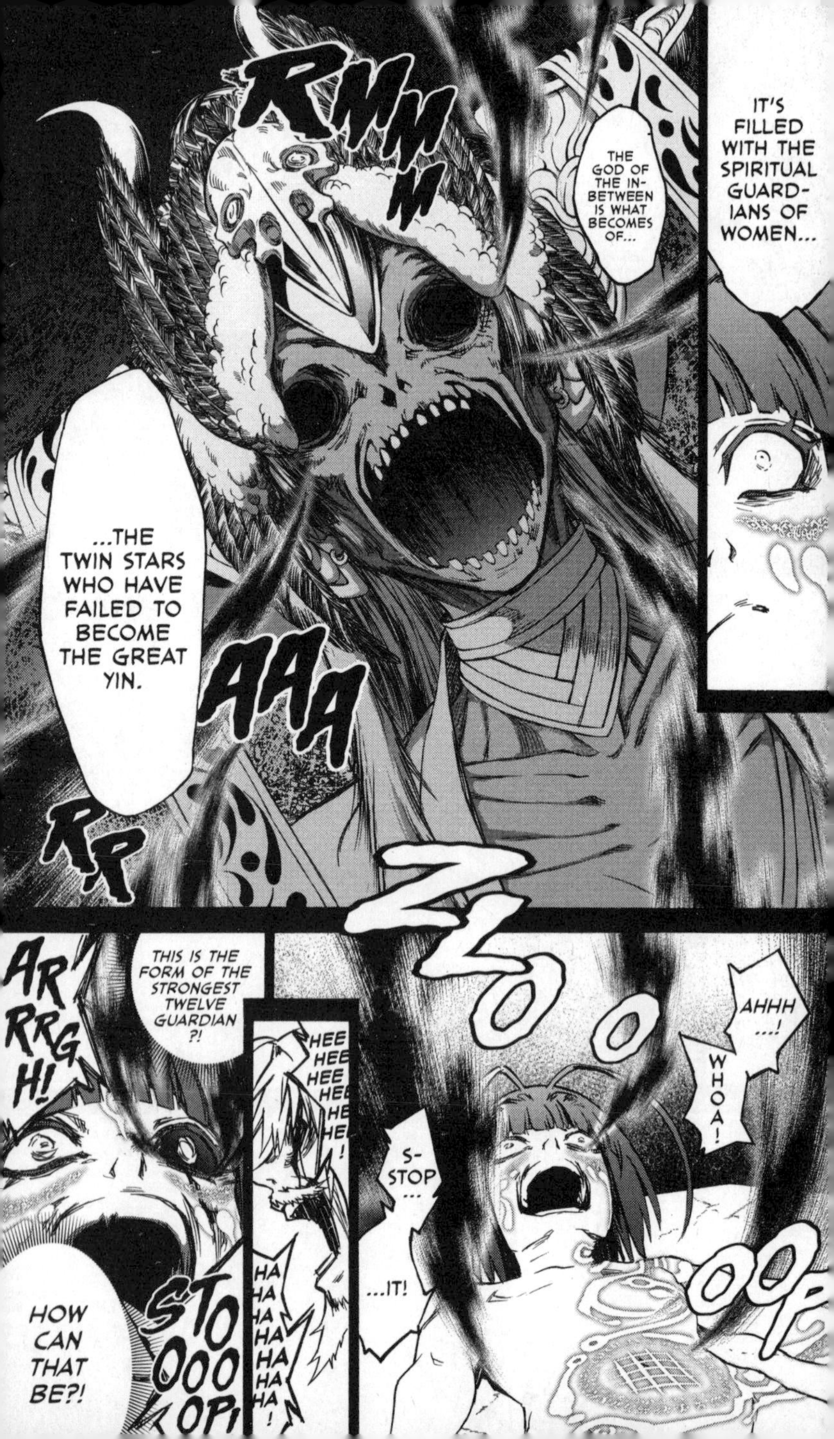

IT'S FILLED WITH THE SPIRITUAL GUARDIANS OF WOMEN...
RMMMM
THE GOD OF THE IN-BETWEEN IS WHAT BECOMES OF...
...THE TWIN STARS WHO HAVE FAILED TO BECOME THE GREAT YIN.
AAAA
RP
ZOOOO
AHHH ...!
WHOA!
S-STOP ...
...IT!
OOOF
HEE HEE HEE HEE HE HE!
HA HA HA HA HA HA HA HA!
THIS IS THE FORM OF THE STRONGEST TWELVE GUARDIAN ?!
ARRRGH!
HOW CAN THAT BE?!
STOOOOOP!

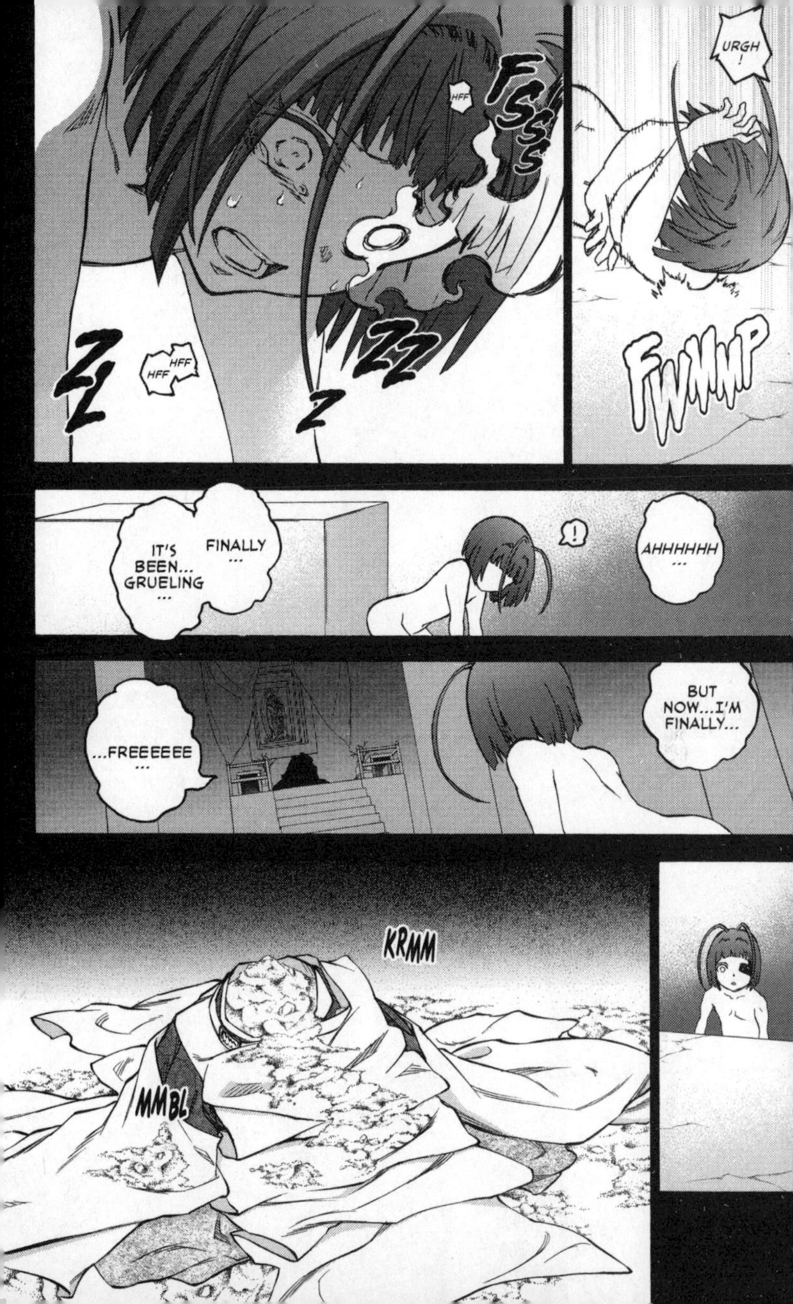
URGH!
FWMMP
HFF
FSSSS
ZZ
HFF HFF
Z
Z
AHHHHHH...
!
FINALLY...
IT'S BEEN... GRUELING...
BUT NOW...I'M FINALLY...
...FREEEEEE...
KRMM
MMBL

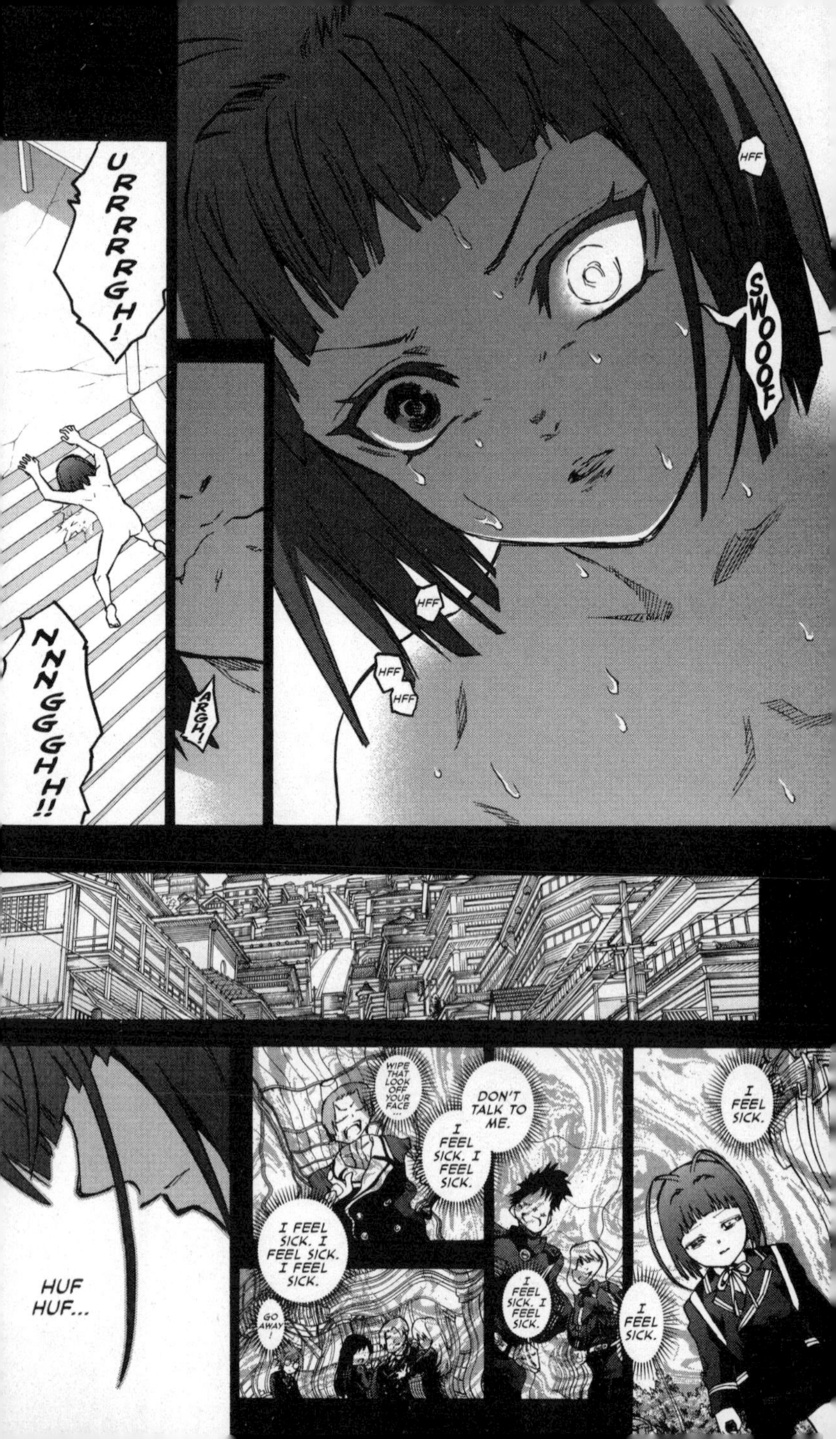
HFF
SWOOOF
HFF
HFF
HFF
ARGH!
URRRRGH!
NNNGGGH!!
I FEEL SICK.
I FEEL SICK.
I FEEL SICK. I FEEL SICK.
DON'T TALK TO ME.
WIPE THAT LOOK OFF YOUR FACE...
I FEEL SICK. I FEEL SICK.
I FEEL SICK. I FEEL SICK. I FEEL SICK.
GO AWAY!
HUF HUF...

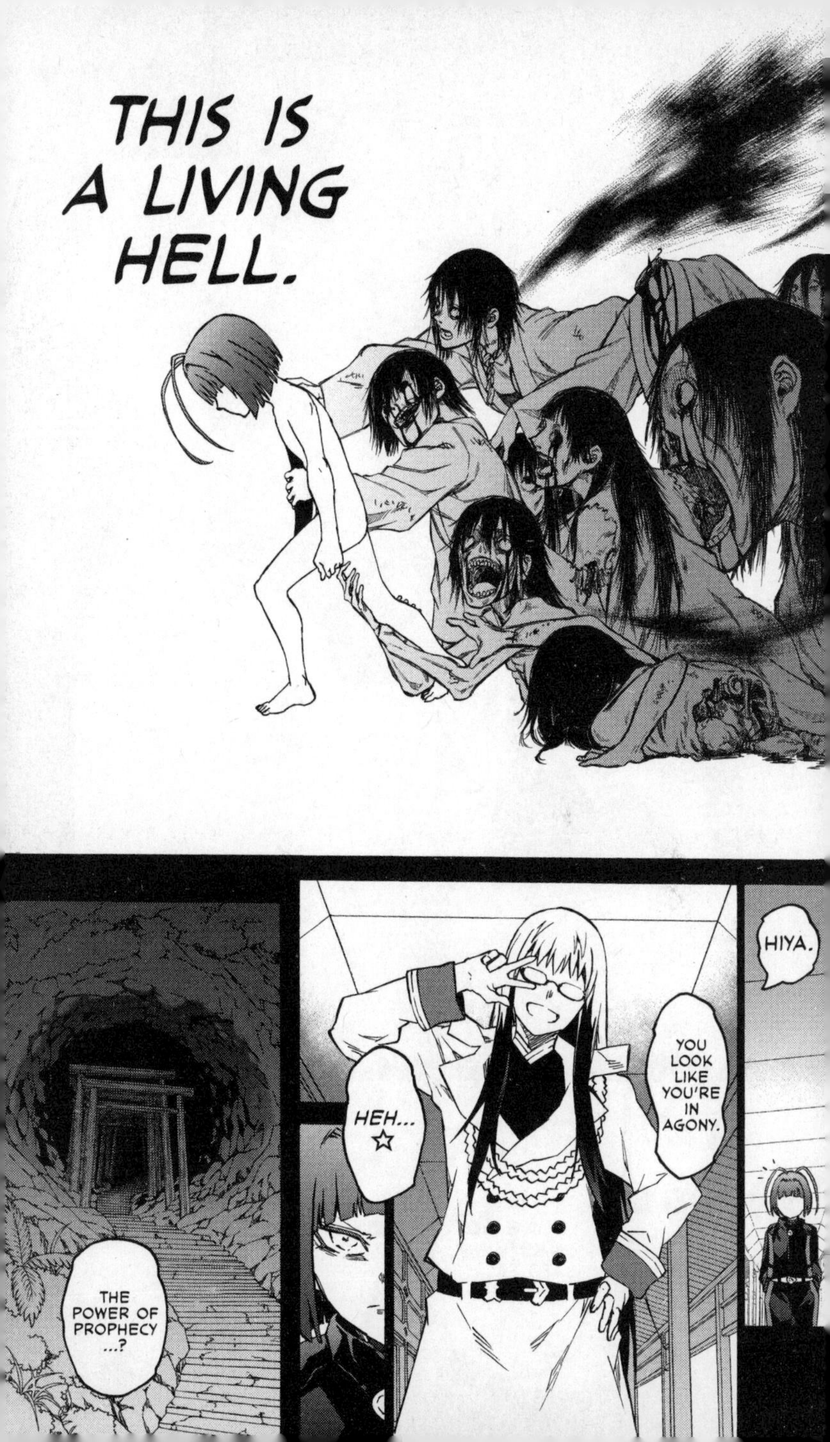
THIS IS A LIVING HELL.
HIYA.
YOU LOOK LIKE YOU'RE IN AGONY.
HEH... ☆
THE POWER OF PROPHECY ...?

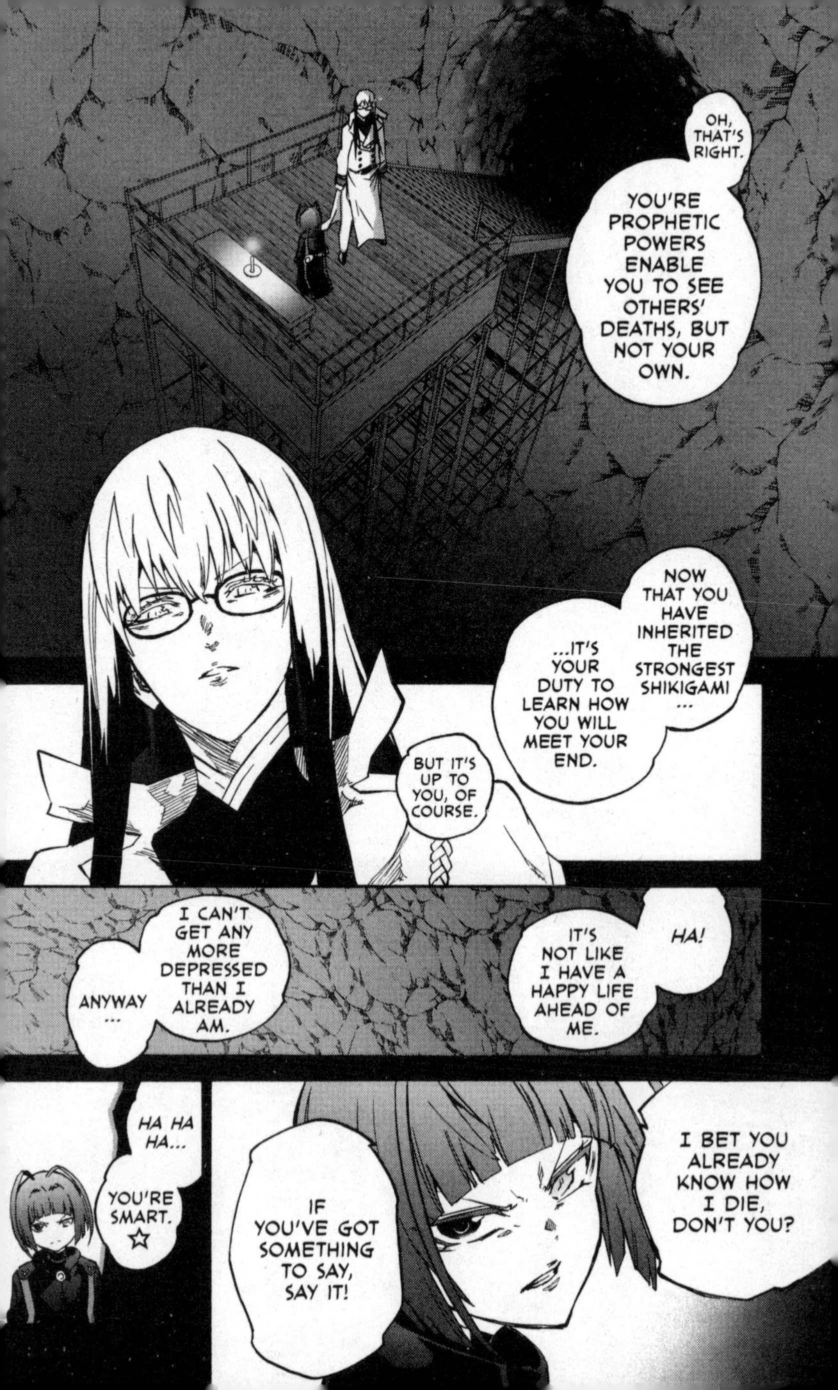
OH, THAT'S RIGHT.
YOU'RE PROPHETIC POWERS ENABLE YOU TO SEE OTHERS' DEATHS, BUT NOT YOUR OWN.
NOW THAT YOU HAVE INHERITED THE STRONGEST SHIKIGAMI ...
...IT'S YOUR DUTY TO LEARN HOW YOU WILL MEET YOUR END.
BUT IT'S UP TO YOU, OF COURSE.
HA!
IT'S NOT LIKE I HAVE A HAPPY LIFE AHEAD OF ME.
I CAN'T GET ANY MORE DEPRESSED THAN I ALREADY AM.
ANYWAY ...
I BET YOU ALREADY KNOW HOW I DIE, DON'T YOU?
IF YOU'VE GOT SOMETHING TO SAY, SAY IT!
HA HA HA...
YOU'RE SMART. ☆

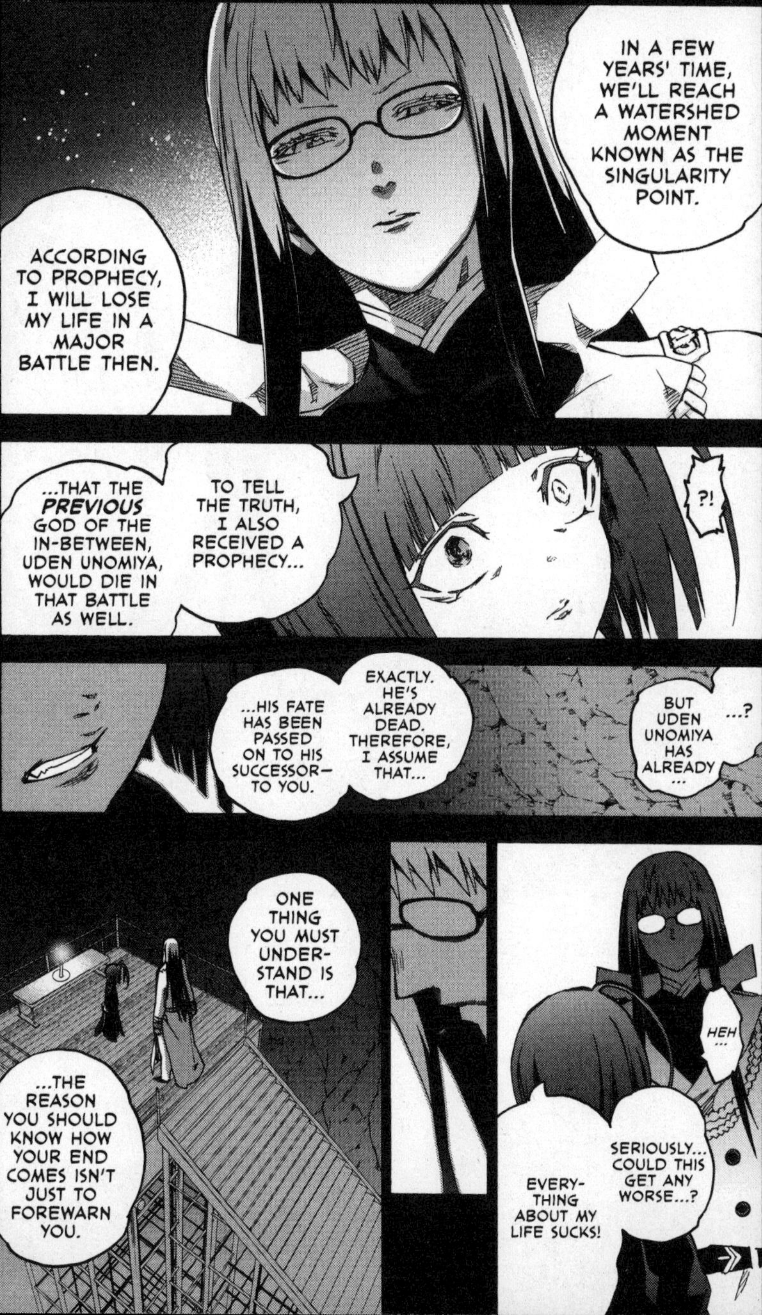
IN A FEW YEARS' TIME, WE'LL REACH A WATERSHED MOMENT KNOWN AS THE SINGULARITY POINT.
ACCORDING TO PROPHECY, I WILL LOSE MY LIFE IN A MAJOR BATTLE THEN.
?!
TO TELL THE TRUTH, I ALSO RECEIVED A PROPHECY...
...THAT THE *PREVIOUS* GOD OF THE IN-BETWEEN, UDEN UNOMIYA, WOULD DIE IN THAT BATTLE AS WELL.
...?
BUT UDEN UNOMIYA HAS ALREADY ...
EXACTLY. HE'S ALREADY DEAD. THEREFORE, I ASSUME THAT...
...HIS FATE HAS BEEN PASSED ON TO HIS SUCCESSOR— TO YOU.
HEH ...
SERIOUSLY... COULD THIS GET ANY WORSE...?
EVERY-THING ABOUT MY LIFE SUCKS!
ONE THING YOU MUST UNDER-STAND IS THAT...
...THE REASON YOU SHOULD KNOW HOW YOUR END COMES ISN'T JUST TO FOREWARN YOU.

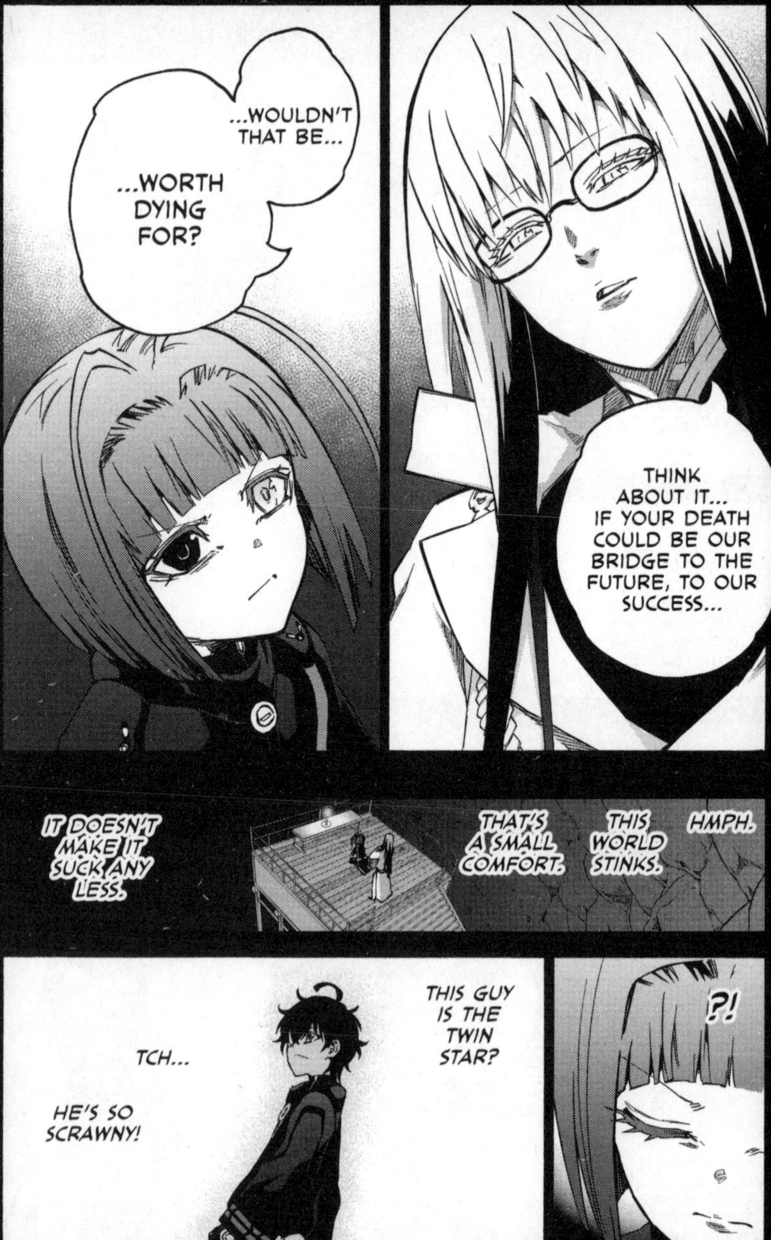
THINK ABOUT IT... IF YOUR DEATH COULD BE OUR BRIDGE TO THE FUTURE, TO OUR SUCCESS...
...WOULDN'T THAT BE...
...WORTH DYING FOR?
HMPH.
THIS WORLD STINKS.
THAT'S A SMALL COMFORT.
IT DOESN'T MAKE IT SUCK ANY LESS.
?!
THIS GUY IS THE TWIN STAR?
TCH...
HE'S SO SCRAWNY!

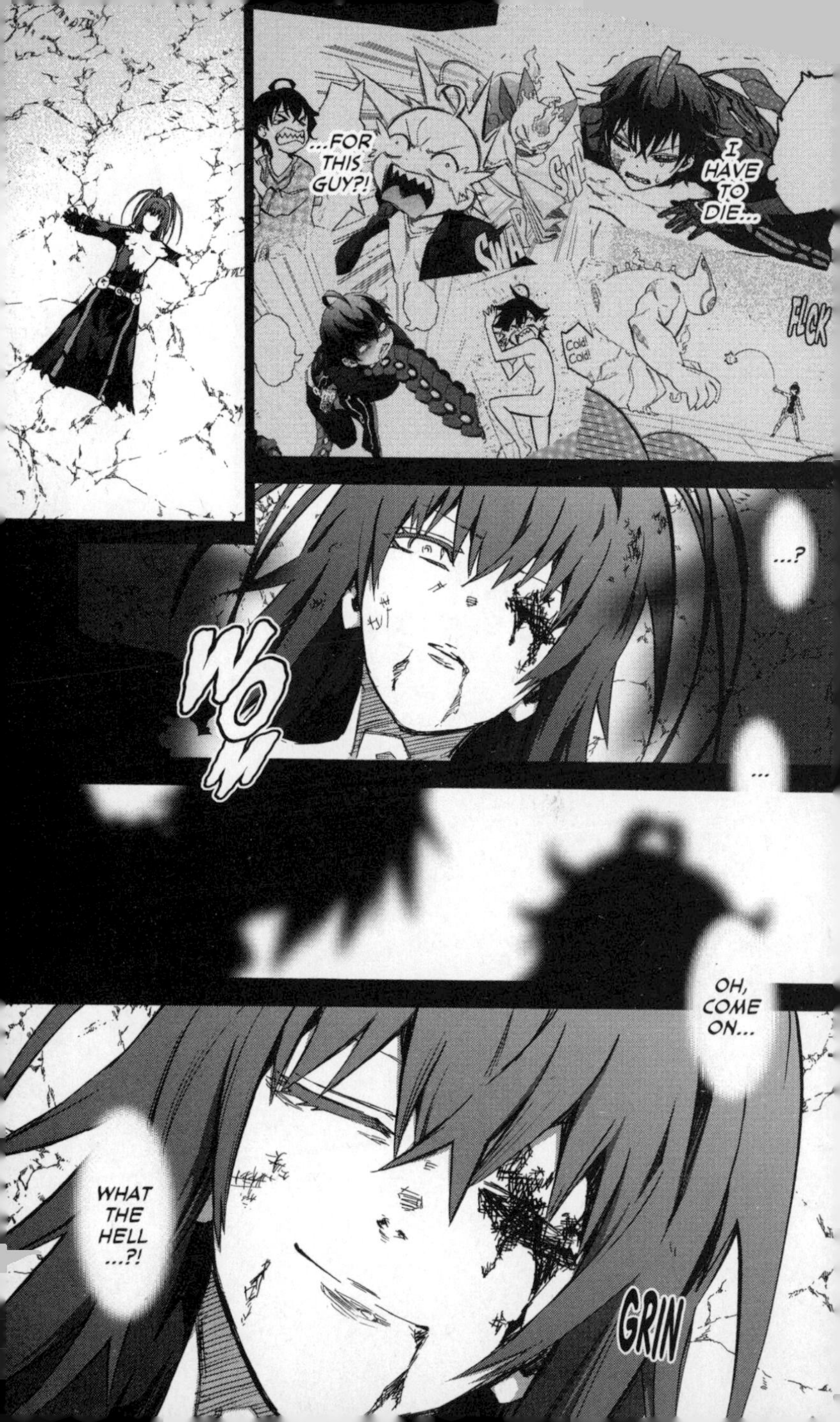
I HAVE TO DIE...
...FOR THIS GUY?!
Cold! Cold!
FLICK
...?
WOW
...
OH, COME ON...
GRIN
WHAT THE HELL ...?!

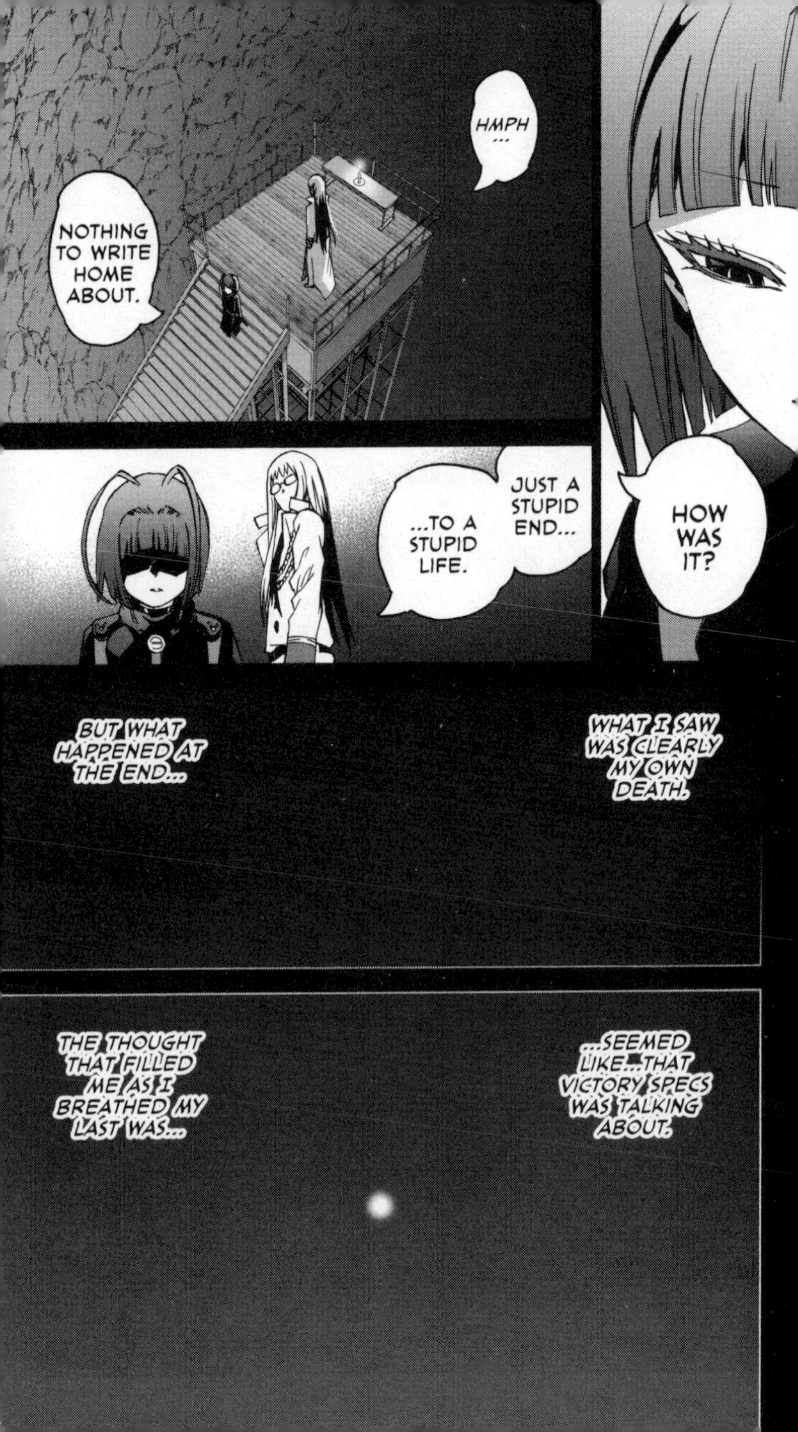
HOW WAS IT?
HMPH ...
NOTHING TO WRITE HOME ABOUT.
JUST A STUPID END...
...TO A STUPID LIFE.
WHAT I SAW WAS CLEARLY MY OWN DEATH.
BUT WHAT HAPPENED AT THE END...
...SEEMED LIKE...THAT VICTORY SPECS WAS TALKING ABOUT.
THE THOUGHT THAT FILLED ME AS I BREATHED MY LAST WAS...

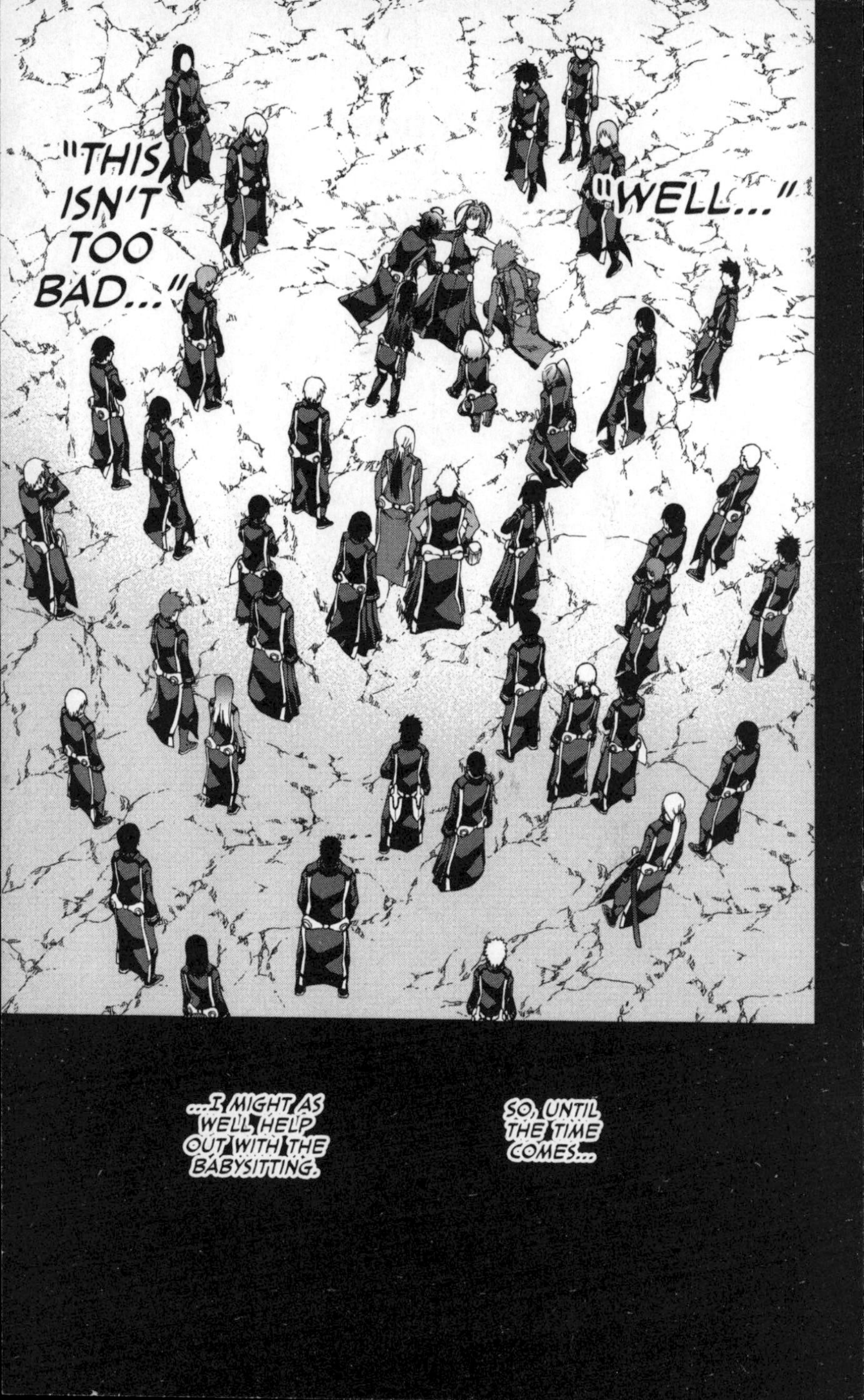
"WELL..."
"THIS ISN'T TOO BAD..."
SO, UNTIL THE TIME COMES...
...I MIGHT AS WELL HELP OUT WITH THE BABYSITTING.

#70 Tenma

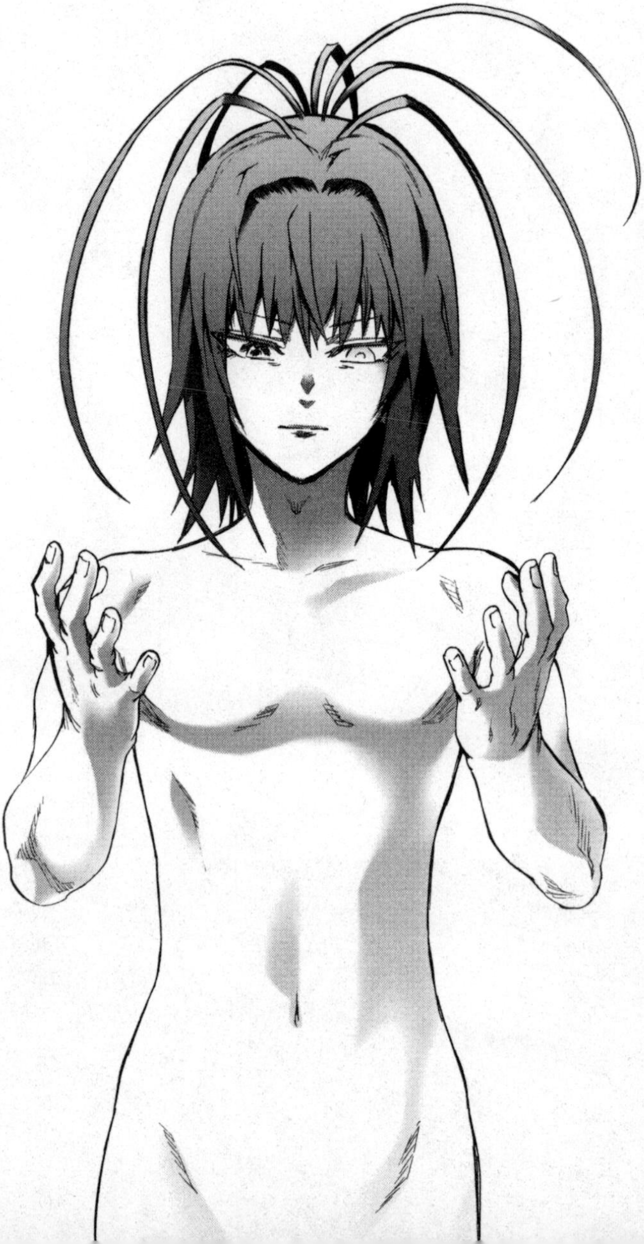

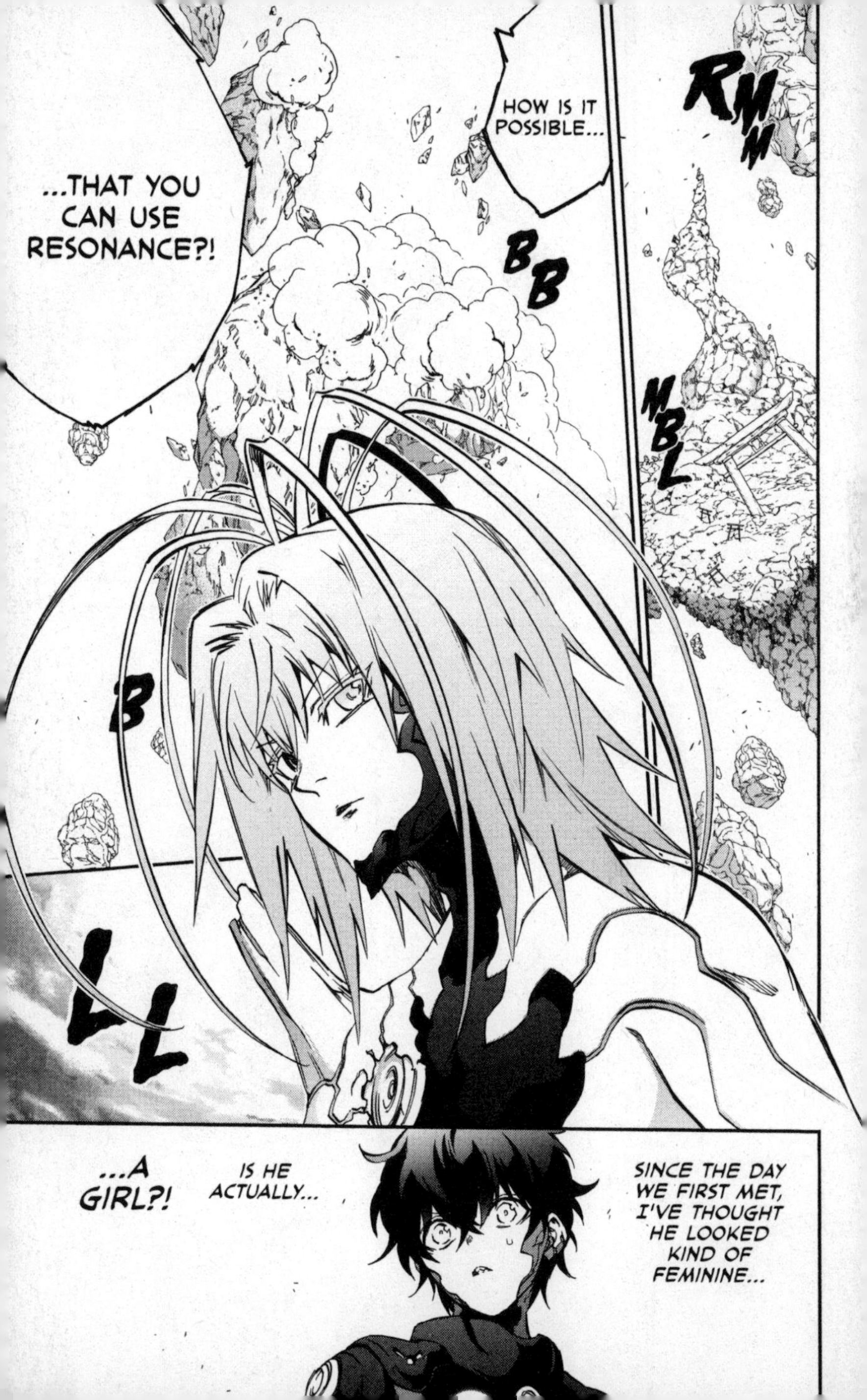

RMM
MBL
HOW IS IT POSSIBLE...
...THAT YOU CAN USE RESONANCE?!
BB
B
LL
SINCE THE DAY WE FIRST MET, I'VE THOUGHT HE LOOKED KIND OF FEMININE...
IS HE ACTUALLY...
...A GIRL?!

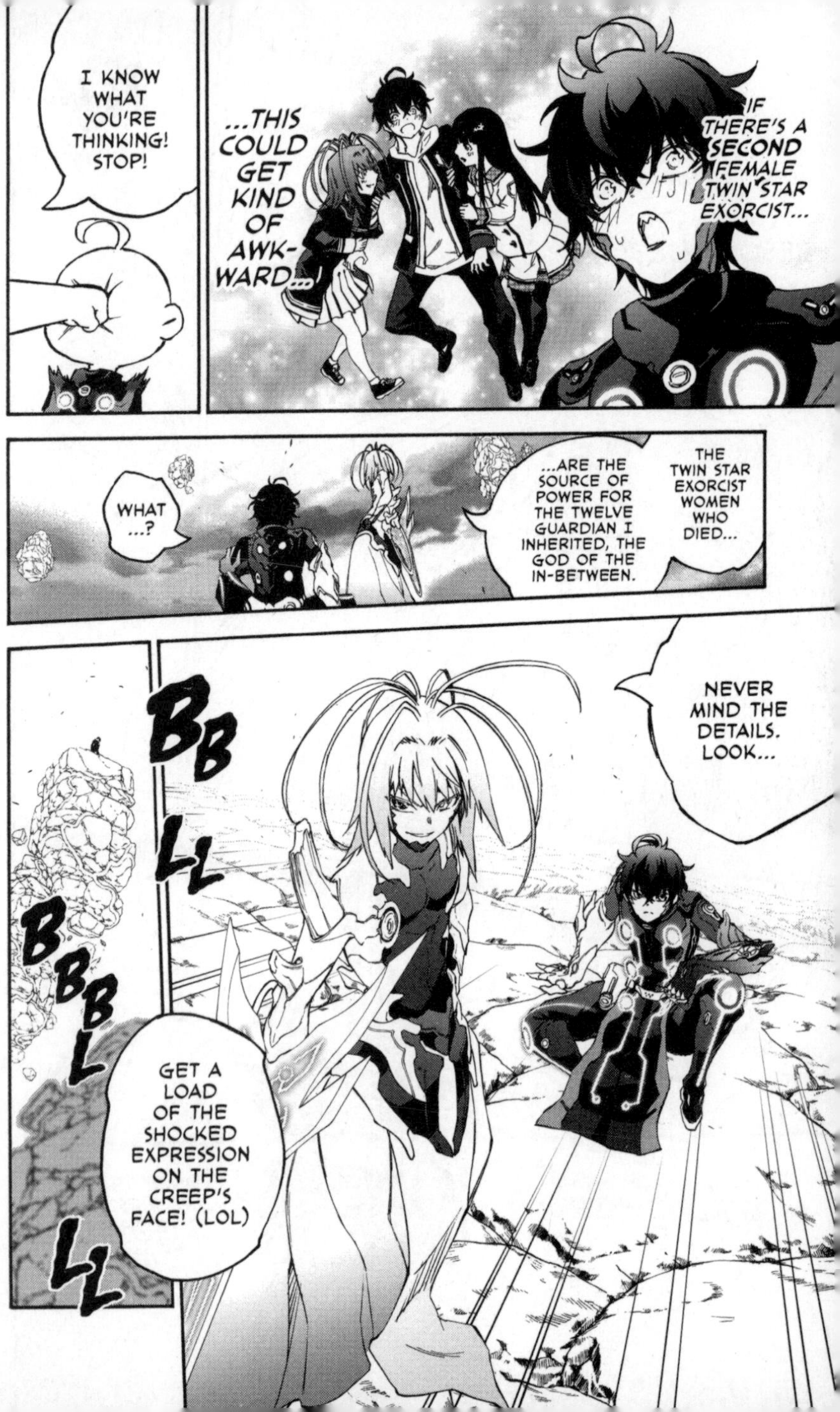
IF THERE'S A SECOND FEMALE TWIN STAR EXORCIST...
...THIS COULD GET KIND OF AWK-WARD...
I KNOW WHAT YOU'RE THINKING! STOP!
THE TWIN STAR EXORCIST WOMEN WHO DIED...
...ARE THE SOURCE OF POWER FOR THE TWELVE GUARDIAN I INHERITED, THE GOD OF THE IN-BETWEEN.
WHAT ...?
NEVER MIND THE DETAILS. LOOK...
BBLL
BBBLLL
GET A LOAD OF THE SHOCKED EXPRESSION ON THE CREEP'S FACE! (LOL)

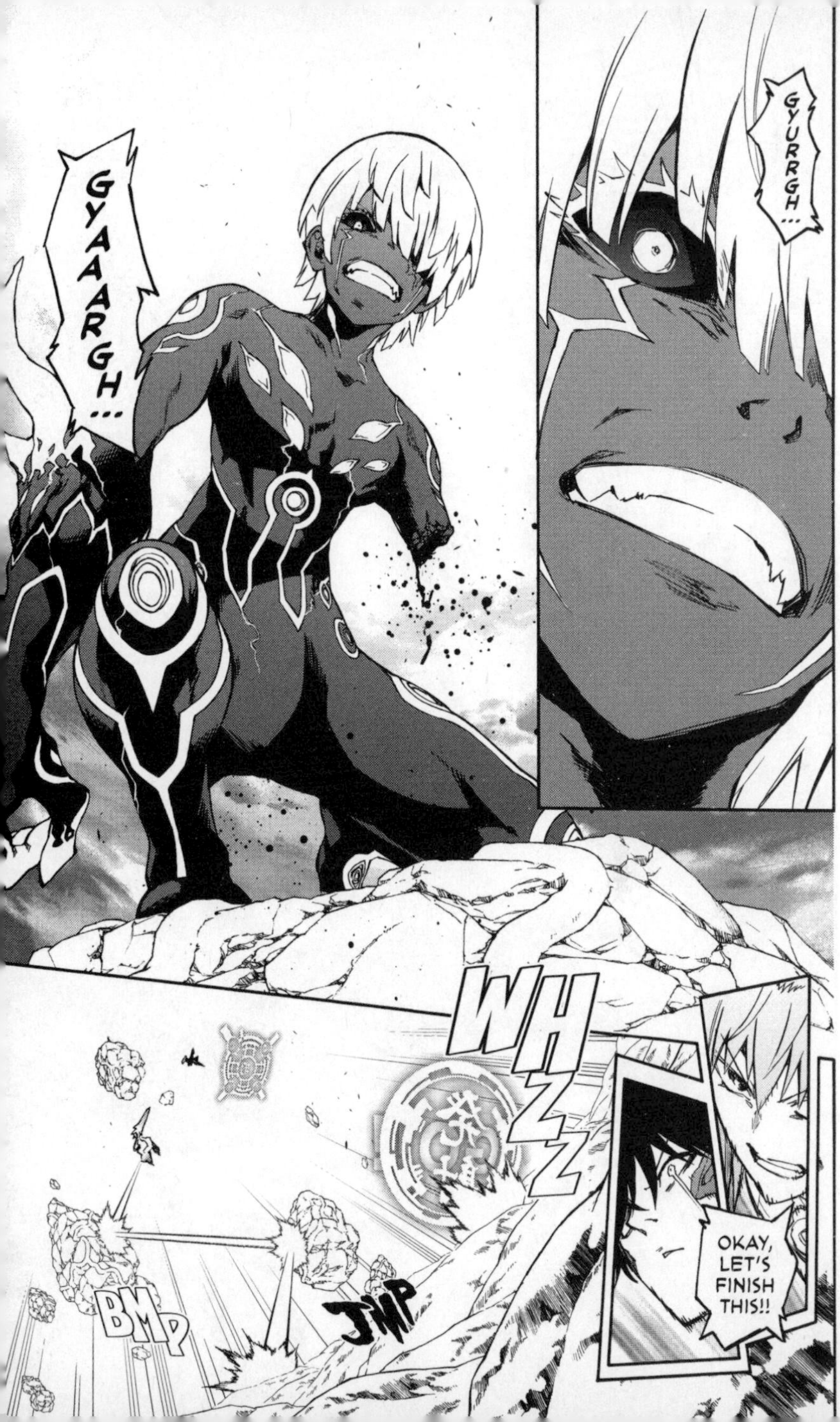
GYURRGH...
GYAAARGH...
WHZZ
OKAY, LET'S FINISH THIS!!
JMP
BMP

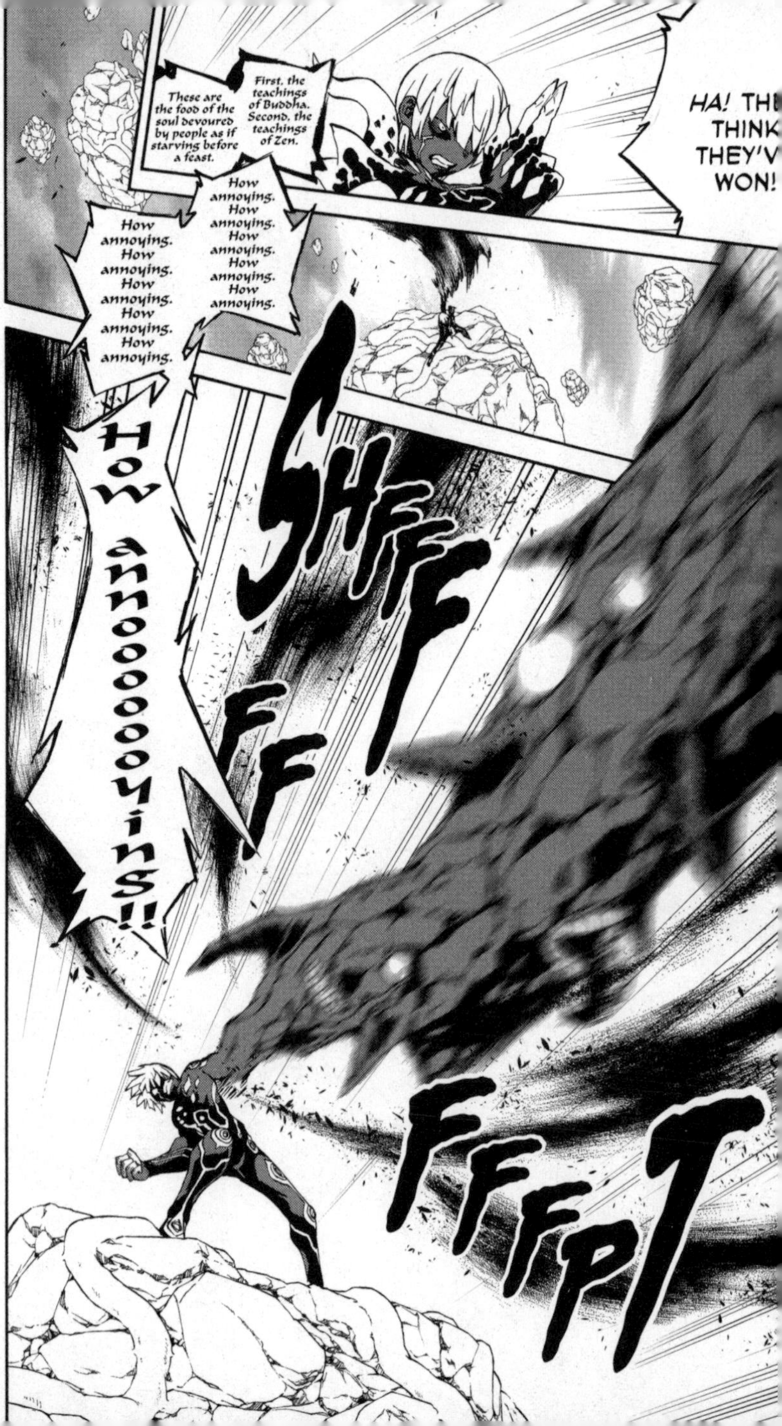

HA! TH THINK THEY'V WON!
First, the teachings of Buddha. Second, the teachings of Zen.
These are the food of the soul devoured by people as if starving before a feast.
How annoying. How annoying. How annoying. How annoying. How annoying.
How annoying. How annoying. How annoying. How annoying. How annoying.
How annooooooying!!
SHFFFF
FFFFPT

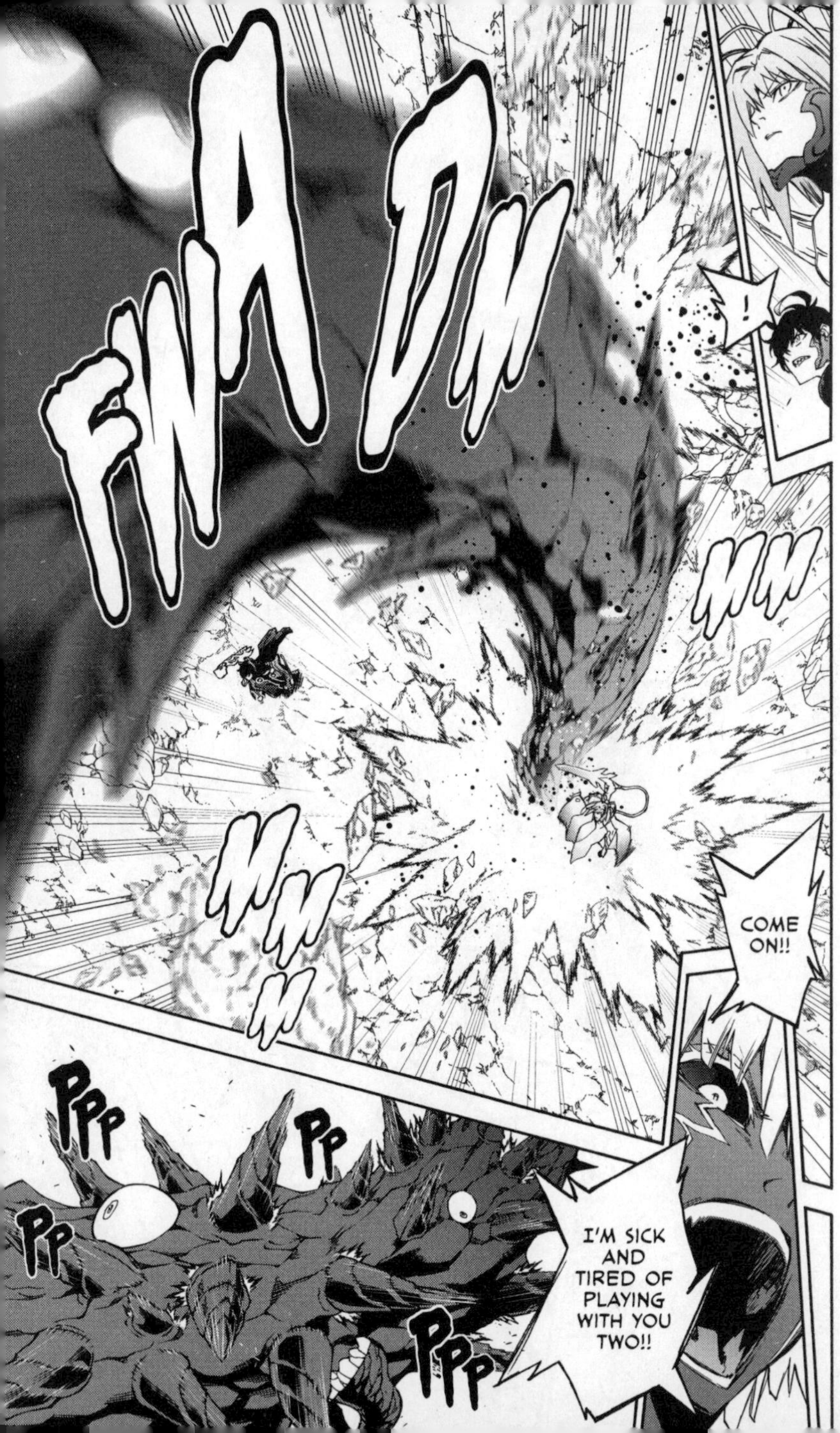
!
COME ON!!
I'M SICK AND TIRED OF PLAYING WITH YOU TWO!!

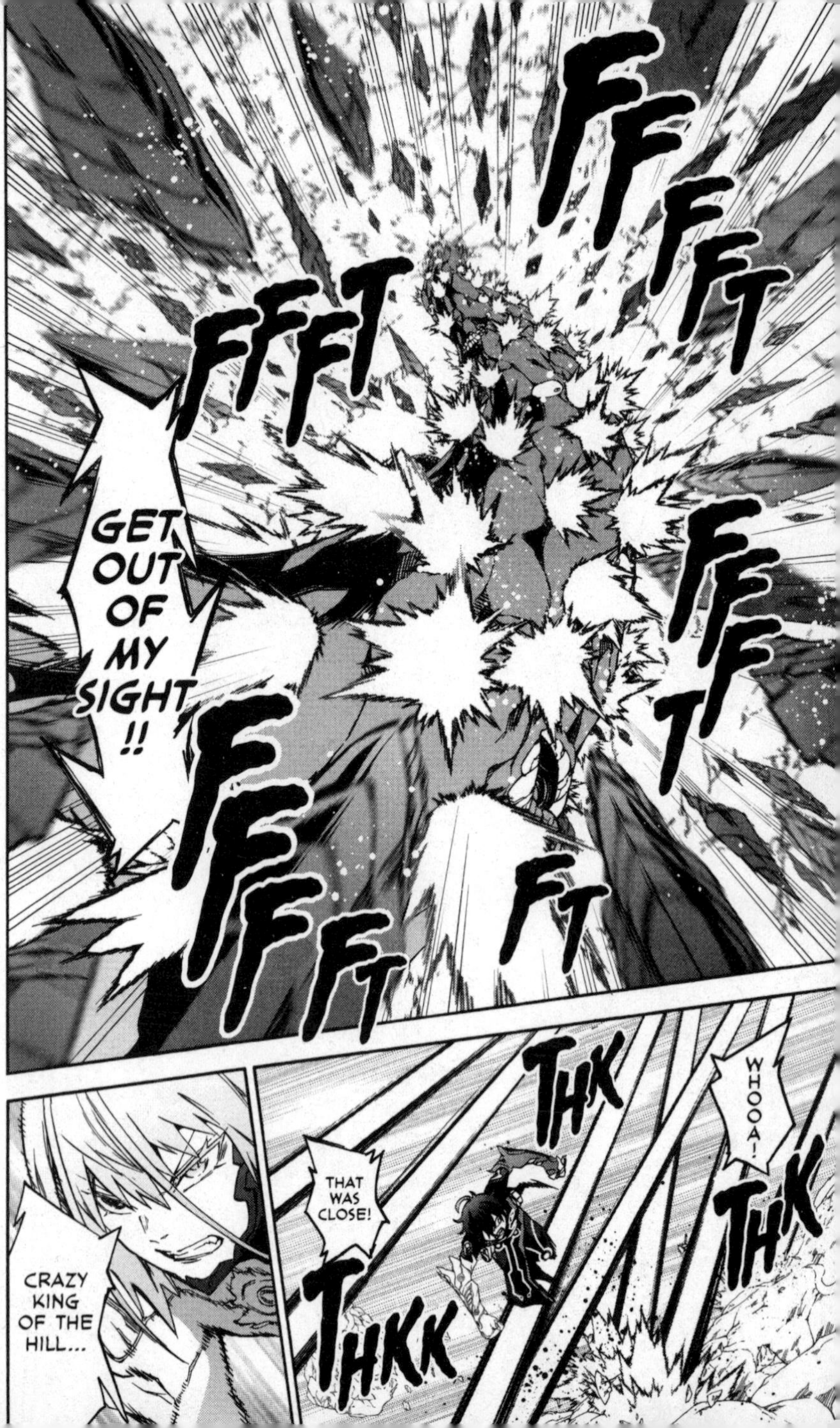
FFFFT
FFFT
GET OUT OF MY SIGHT!!
FFFT
FT
FFFFT
THK
WHOOA!
THAT WAS CLOSE!
THK
THKK
CRAZY KING OF THE HILL...

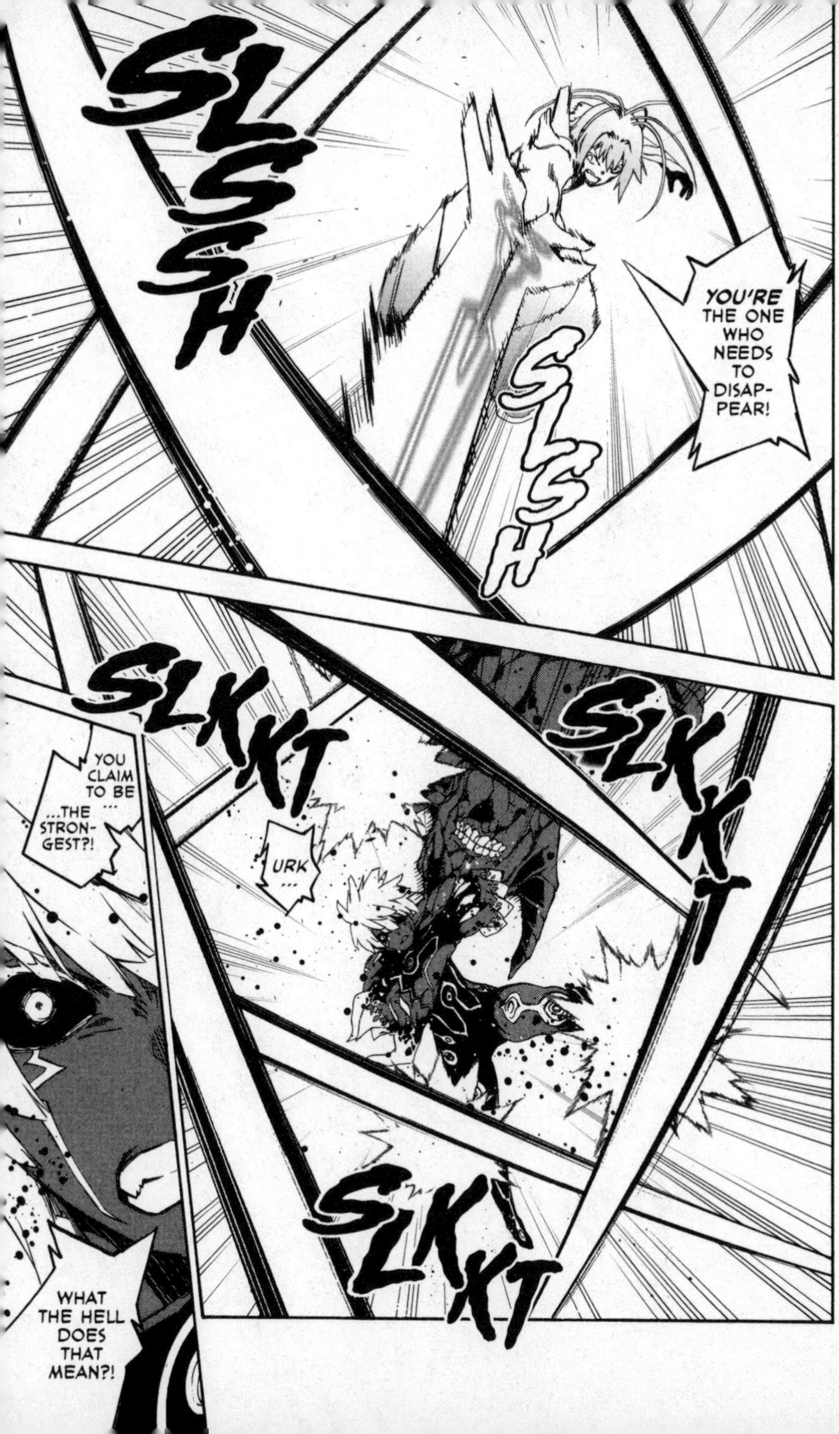
YOU'RE THE ONE WHO NEEDS TO DISAP-PEAR!
SLSSH
SLSSH
SLKKT
SLKKT
URK...
SLKKT
YOU CLAIM TO BE... ...THE STRONG-GEST?!
WHAT THE HELL DOES THAT MEAN?!

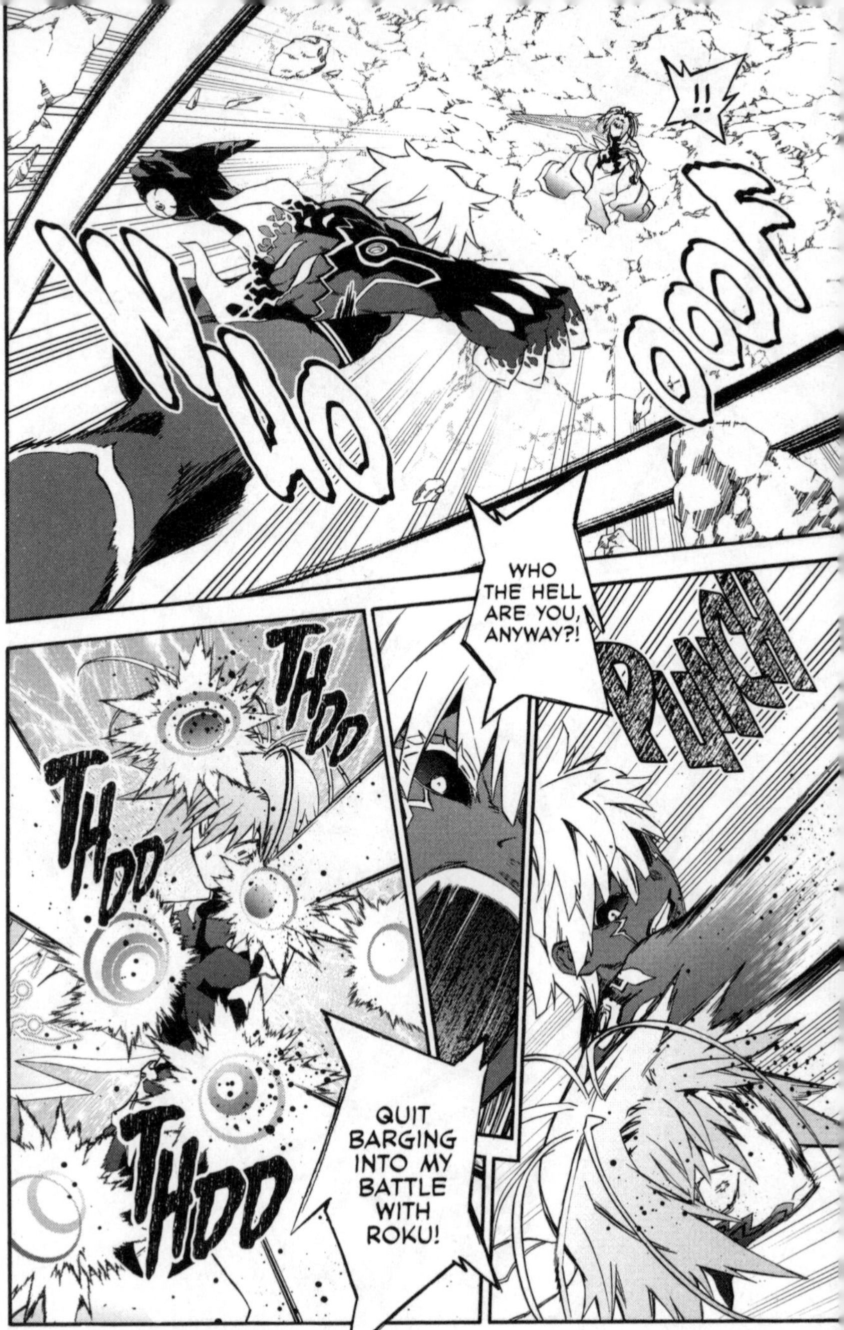
!!
WHOOOOF
WHO THE HELL ARE YOU, ANYWAY?!
PUNCH
THDD
THDD
THDD
QUIT BARGING INTO MY BATTLE WITH ROKU!

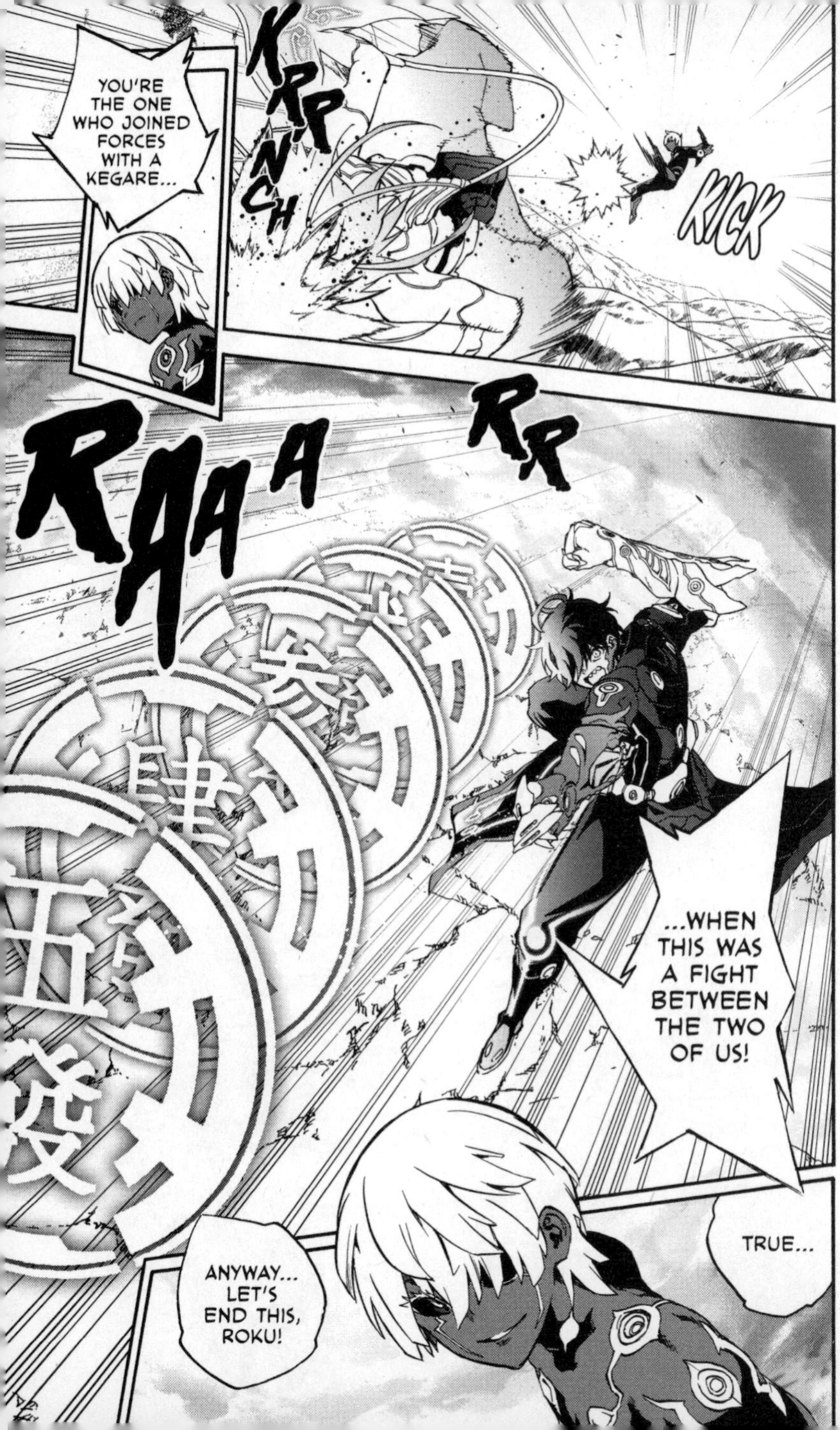
KRRNCH
KICK
YOU'RE THE ONE WHO JOINED FORCES WITH A KEGARE...
RAAAARR
...WHEN THIS WAS A FIGHT BETWEEN THE TWO OF US!
TRUE...
ANYWAY... LET'S END THIS, ROKU!

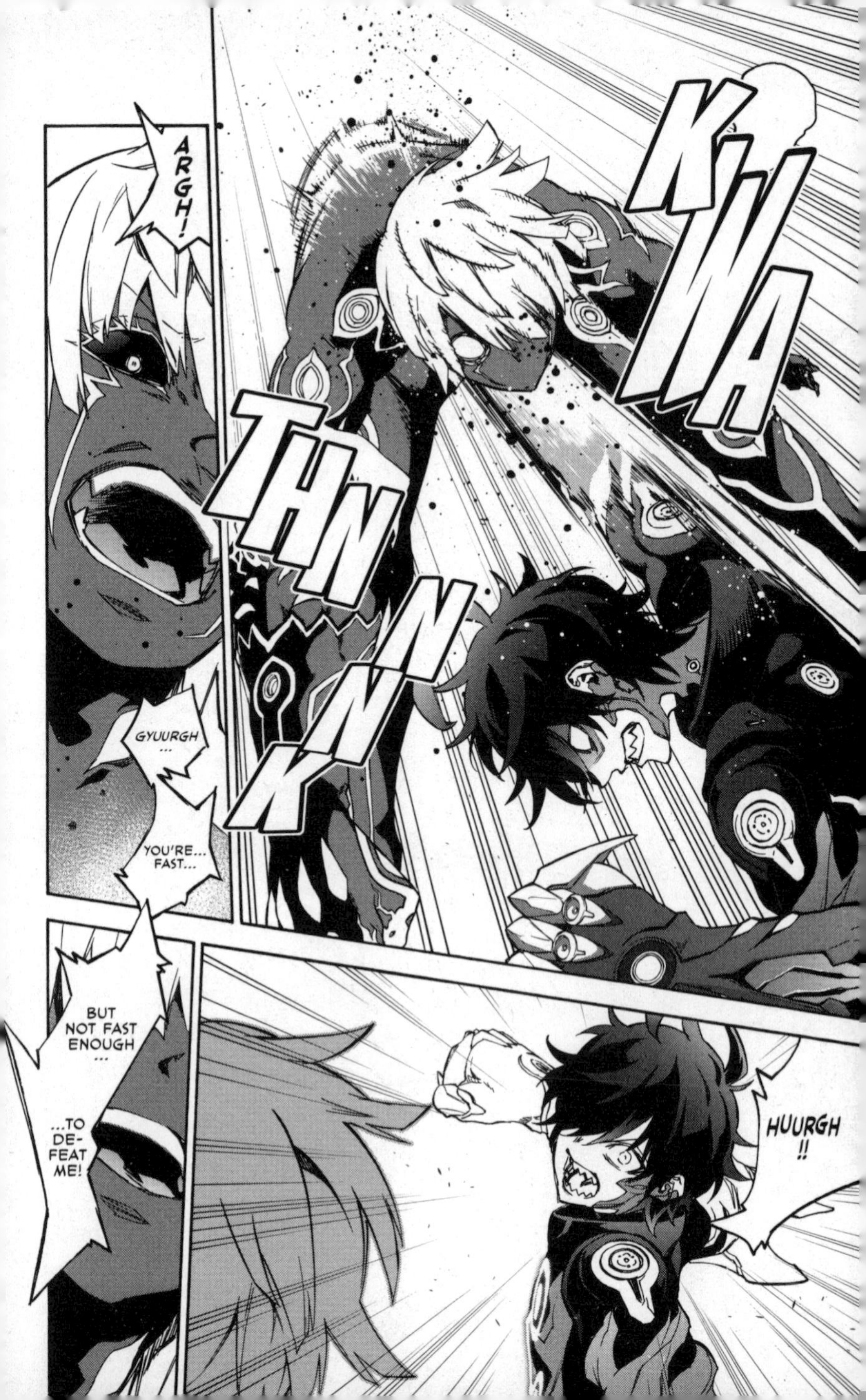
KWA
THNNNK
ARGH!
GYUURGH...
YOU'RE... FAST...
HUURGH!!
BUT NOT FAST ENOUGH...
...TO DE-FEAT ME!

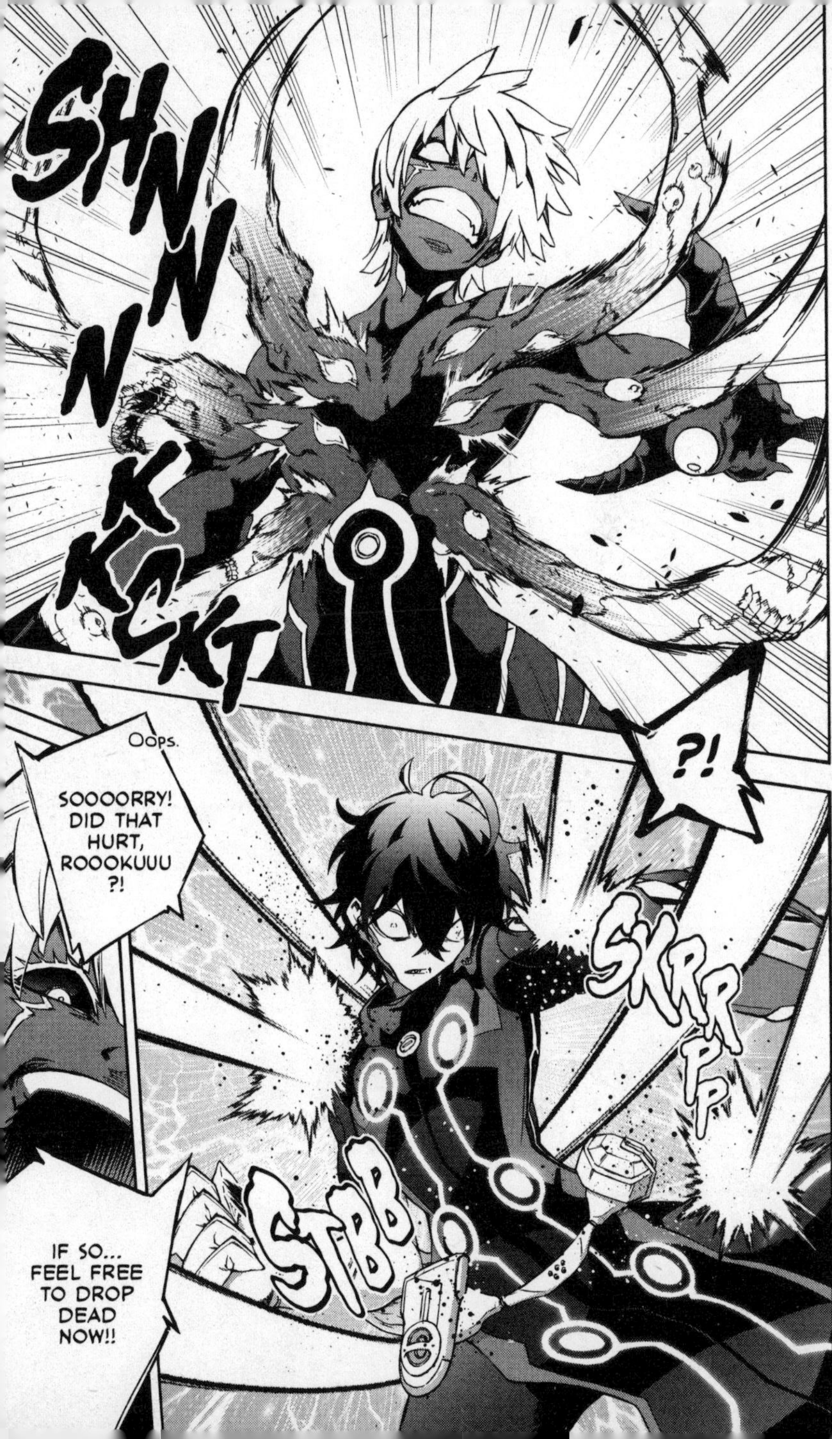
SHNNNKKKCKT
?!
Oops.
SOOOORRY! DID THAT HURT, ROOOKUUU ?!
SKRRPP
STBB
IF SO... FEEL FREE TO DROP DEAD NOW!!

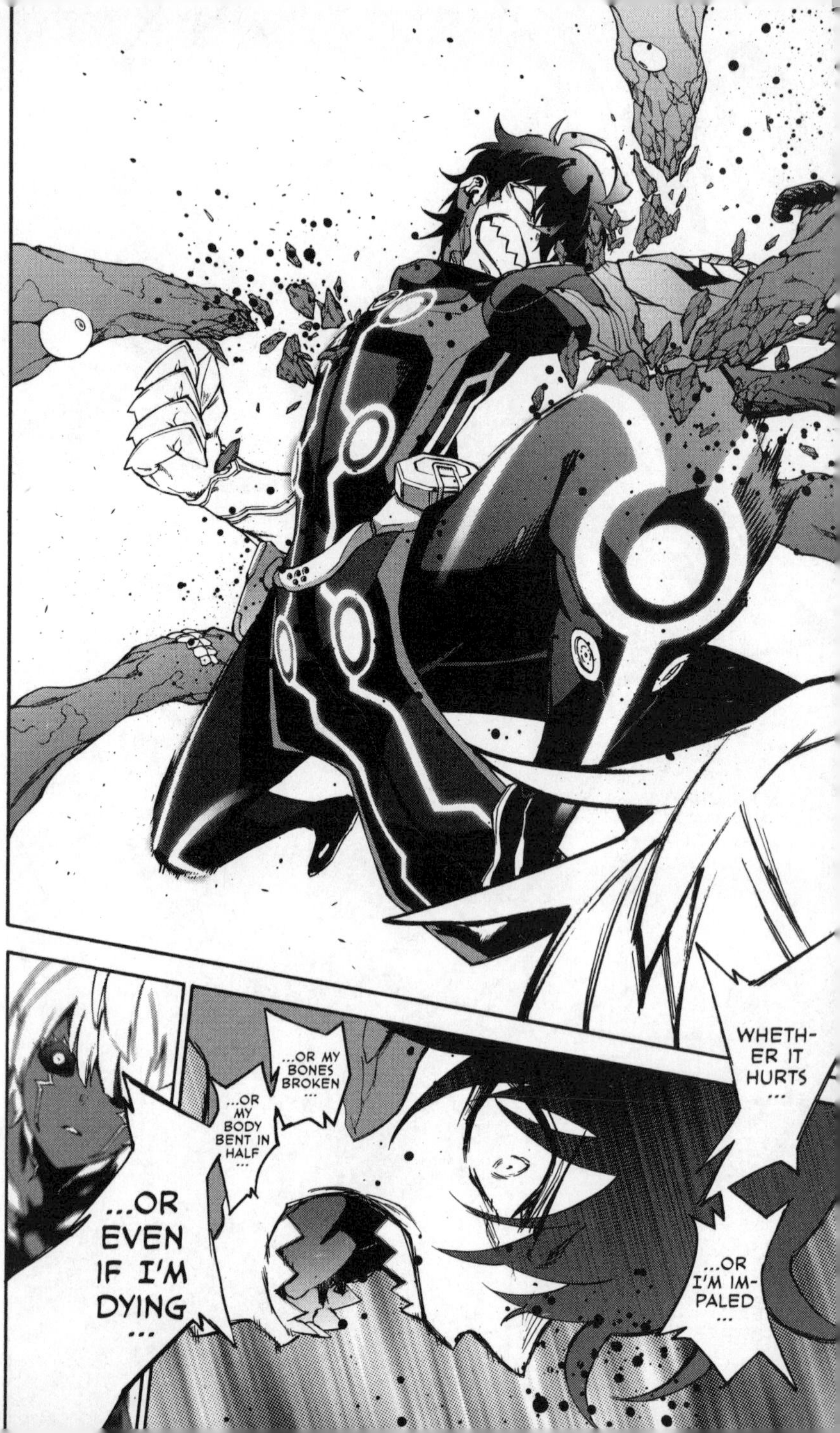
WHETHER IT HURTS...
...OR I'M IMPALED...
...OR MY BONES BROKEN...
...OR MY BODY BENT IN HALF...
...OR EVEN IF I'M DYING...

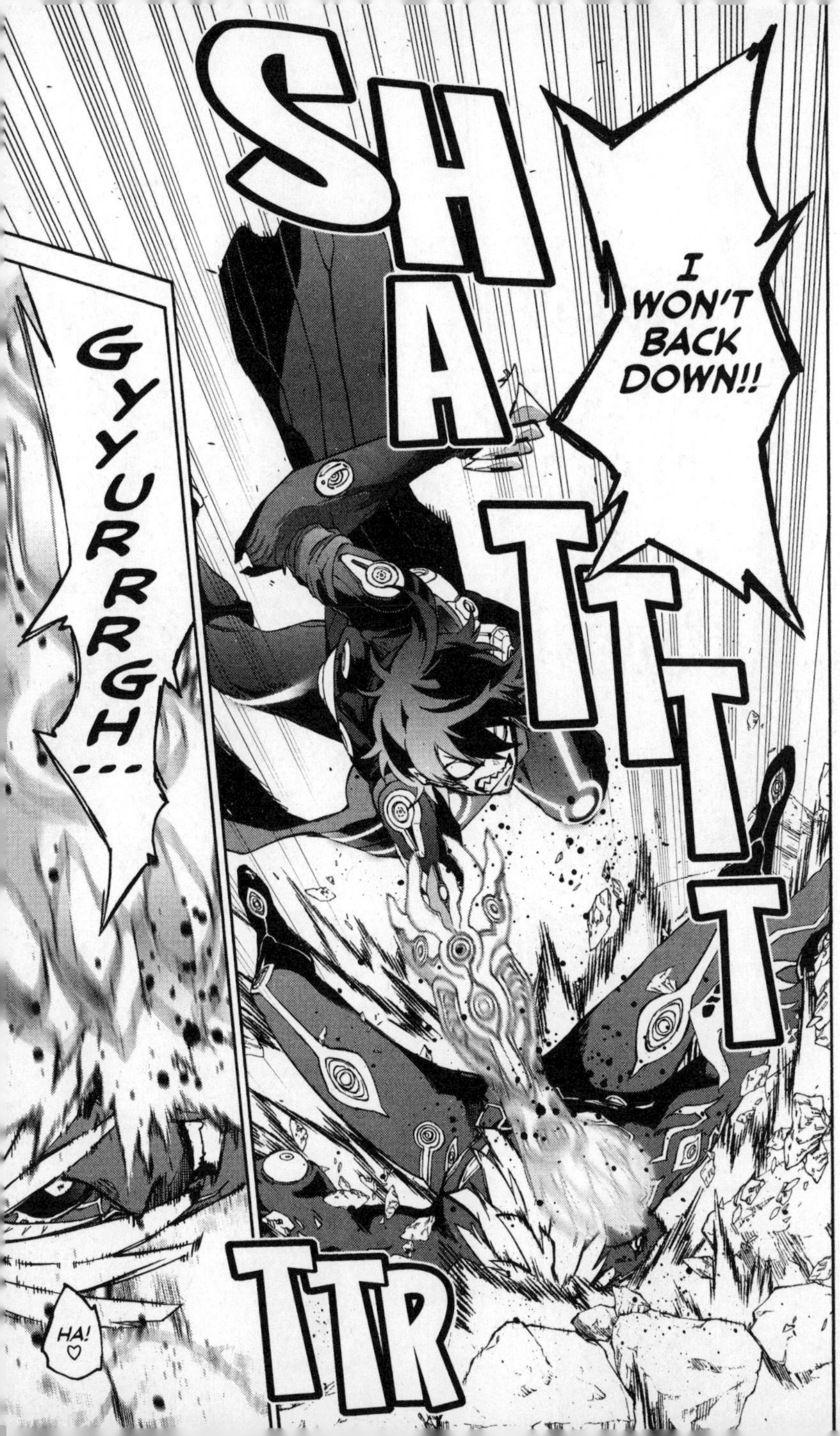
I WON'T BACK DOWN!!
SHATTTTTTR
GYYURRRGH...
HA! ♡

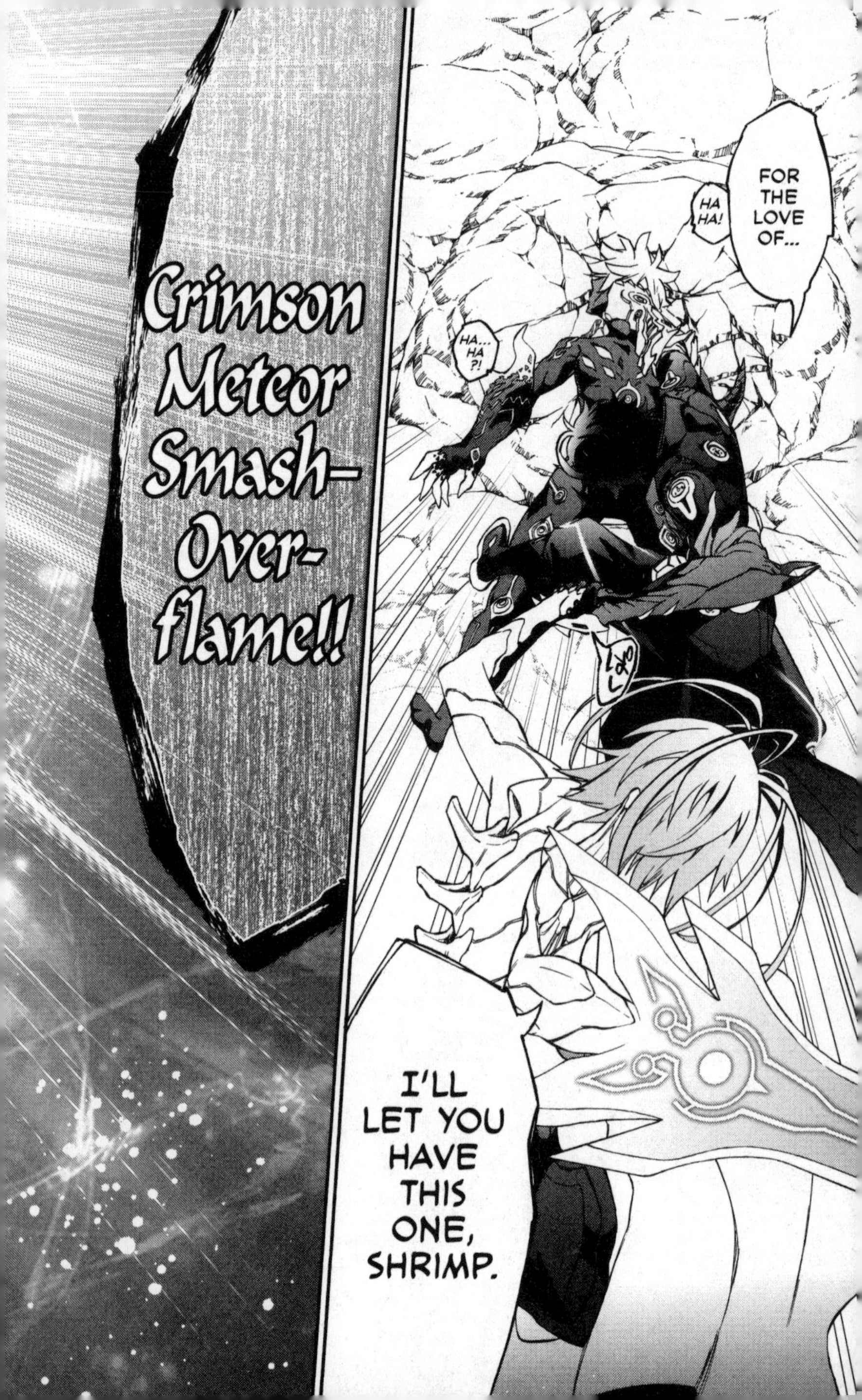
FOR THE LOVE OF...
HA HA!
HA... HA ?!
I'LL LET YOU HAVE THIS ONE, SHRIMP.
Crimson Meteor Smash-Over-flame!!

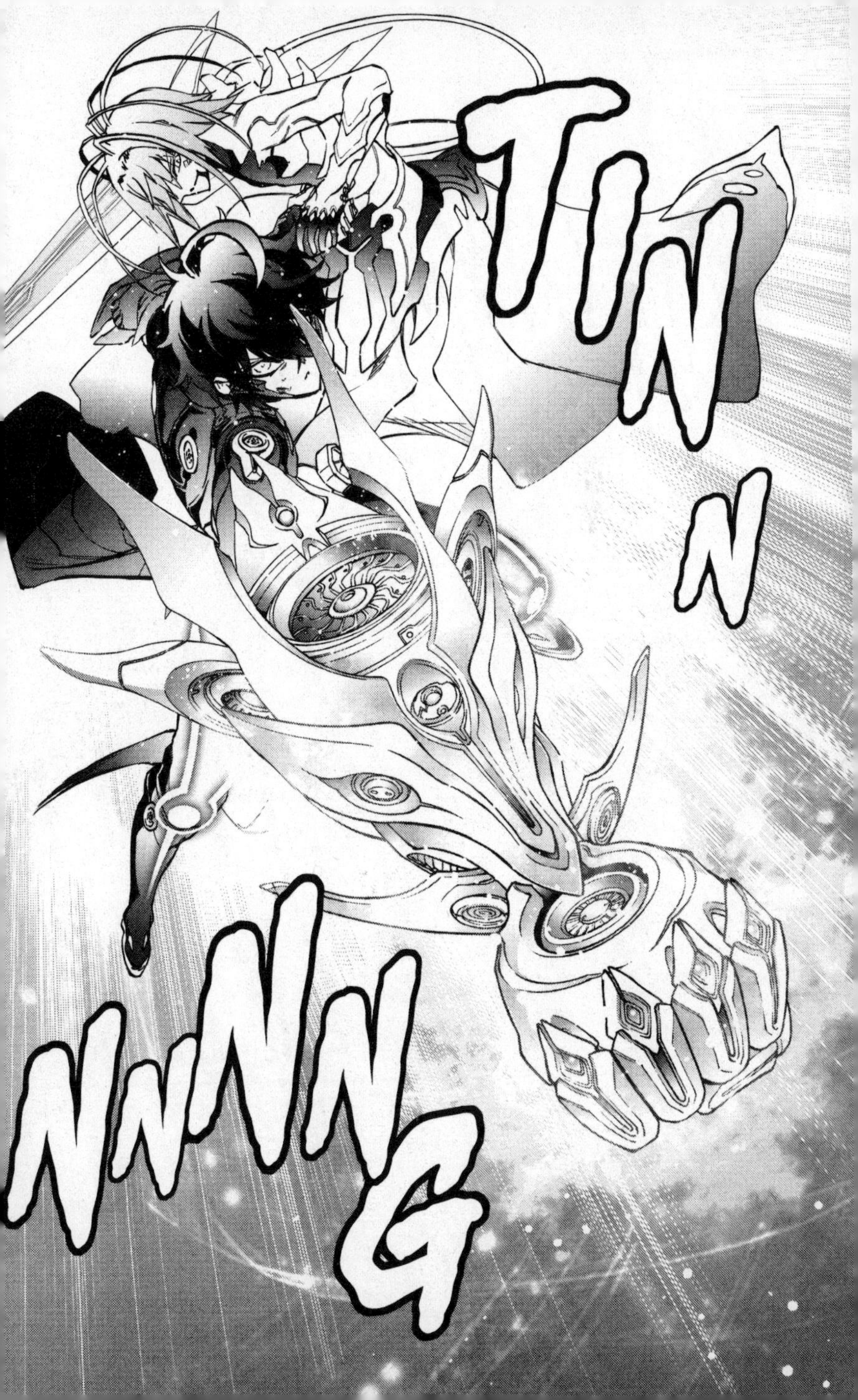
TINN
NNNNG

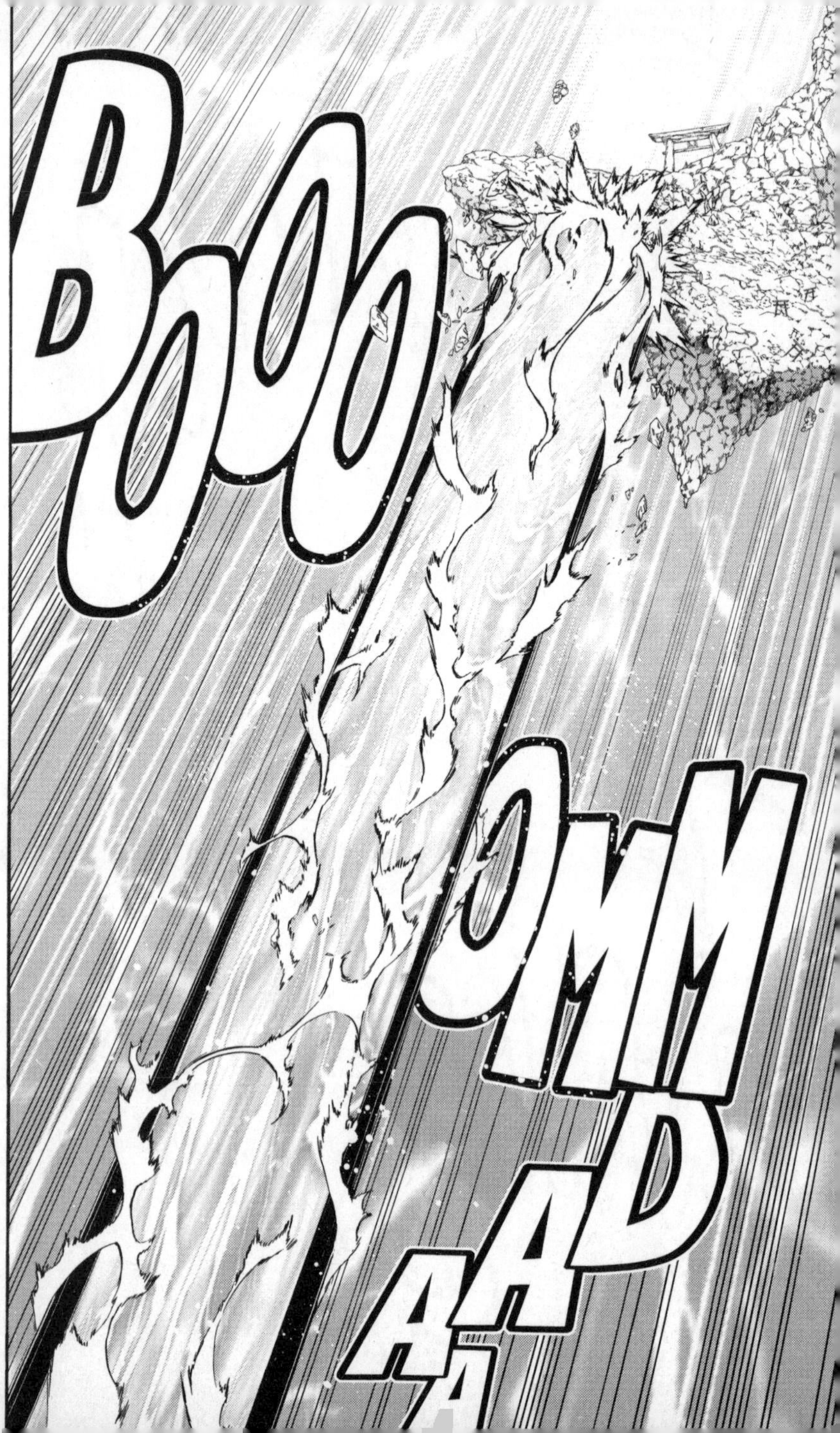
BOOOOMM
AAAD

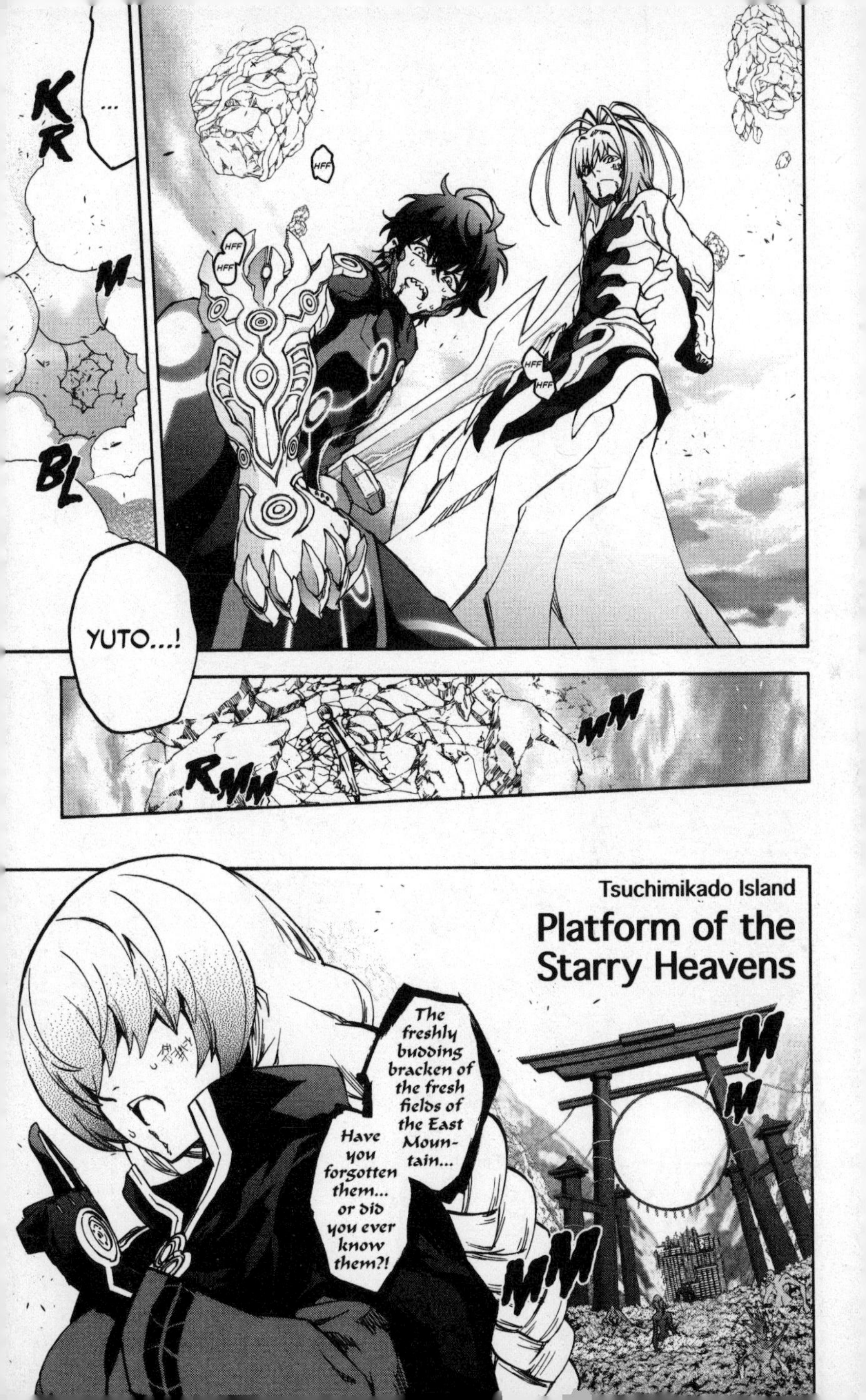
HFF
HFF
HFF
HFF
HFF
...
KR
M
BL
YUTO...!
MM
RMM
Tsuchimikado Island
Platform of the Starry Heavens
The freshly budding bracken of the fresh fields of the East Mountain...
Have you forgotten them... or did you ever know them?!
MM
M
MM

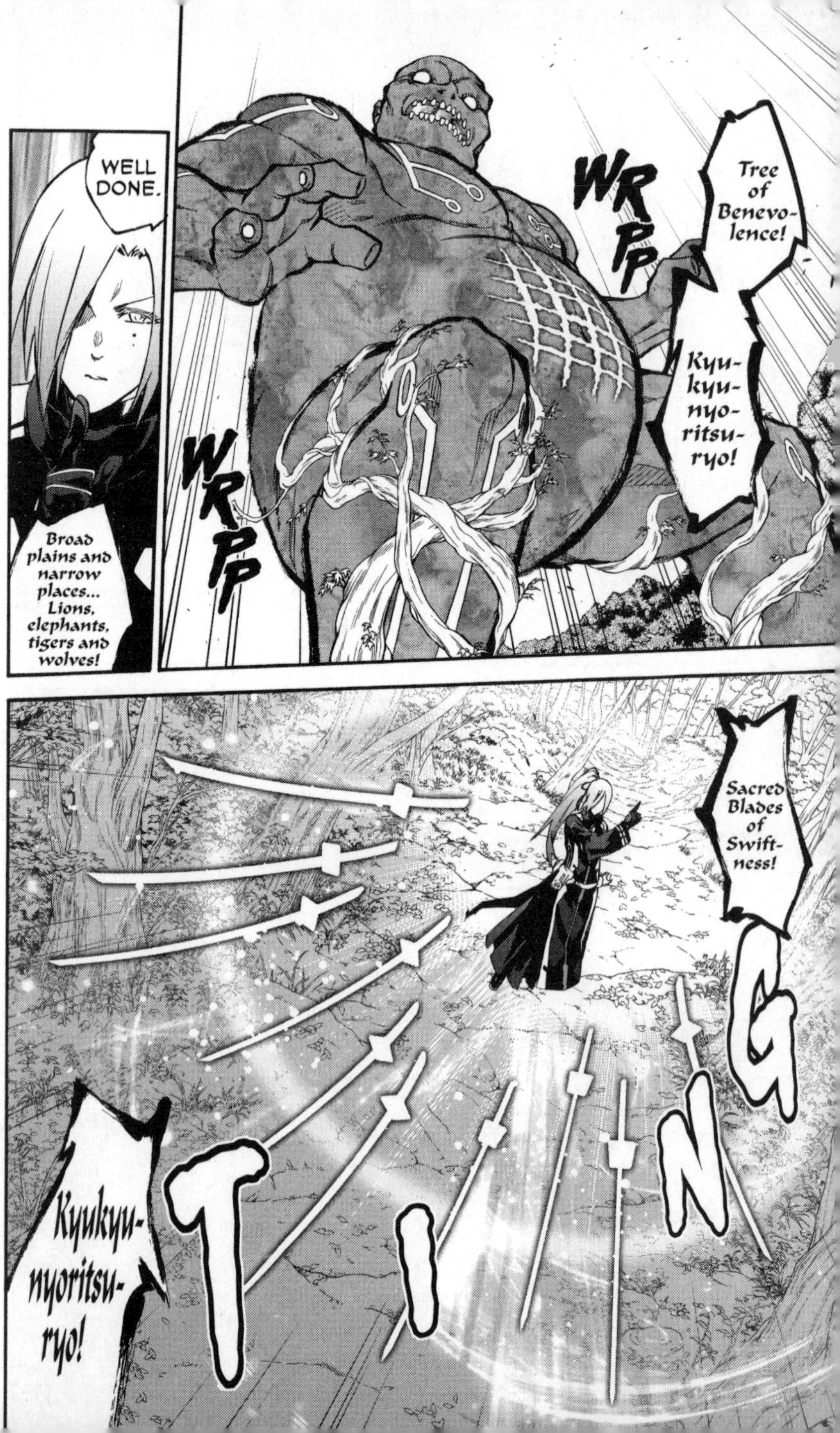
Tree of Benevolence!
Kyukyunyoritsuryo!
WRPP
WRPP
WELL DONE.
Broad plains and narrow places... Lions, elephants, tigers and wolves!
Sacred Blades of Swiftness!
TIING
Kyukyunyoritsuryo!

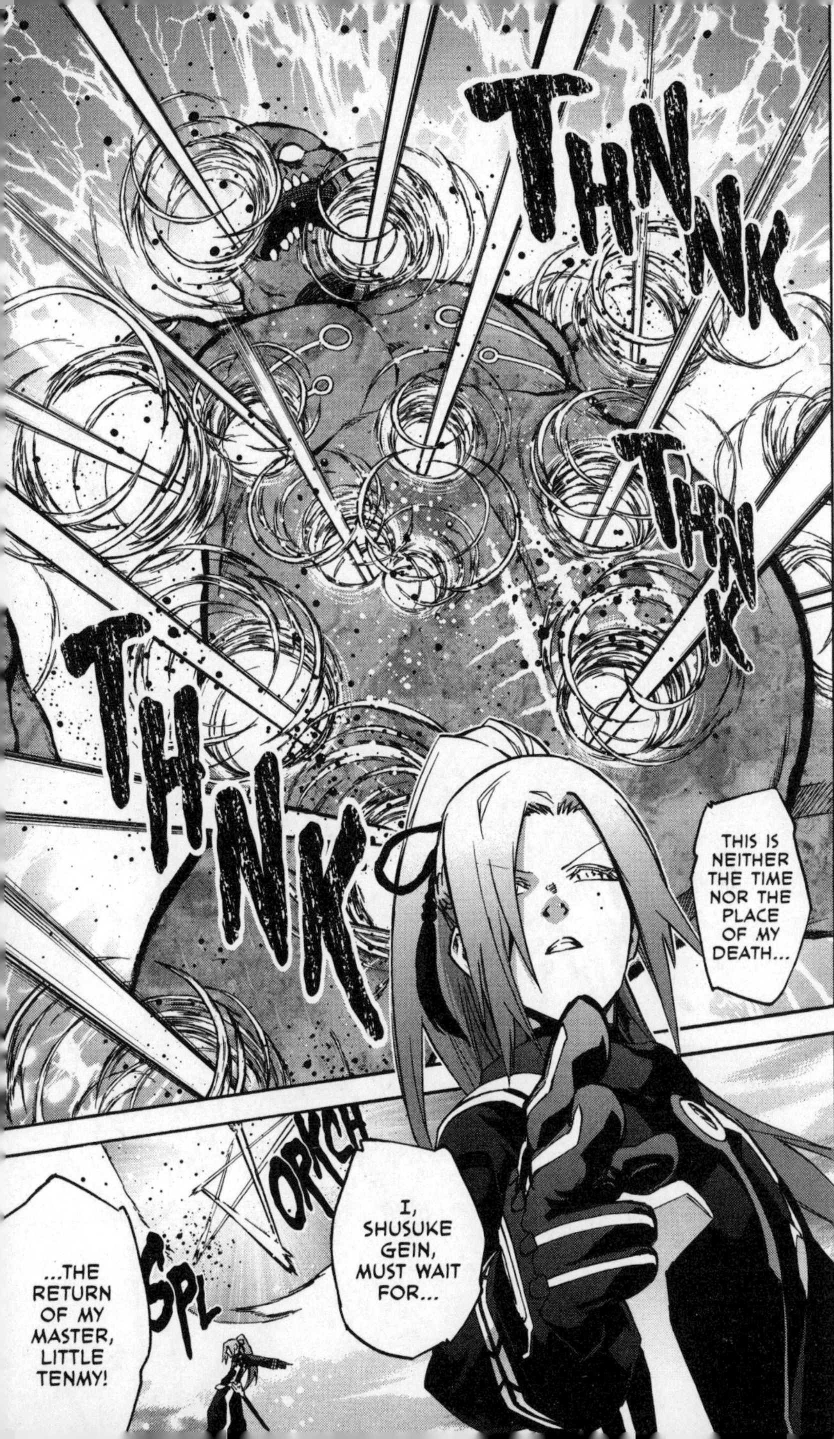
THNNK
THNK
THNNK
THIS IS NEITHER THE TIME NOR THE PLACE OF MY DEATH...
I, SHUSUKE GEIN, MUST WAIT FOR...
ORKCH
SPL
...THE RETURN OF MY MASTER, LITTLE TENMY!

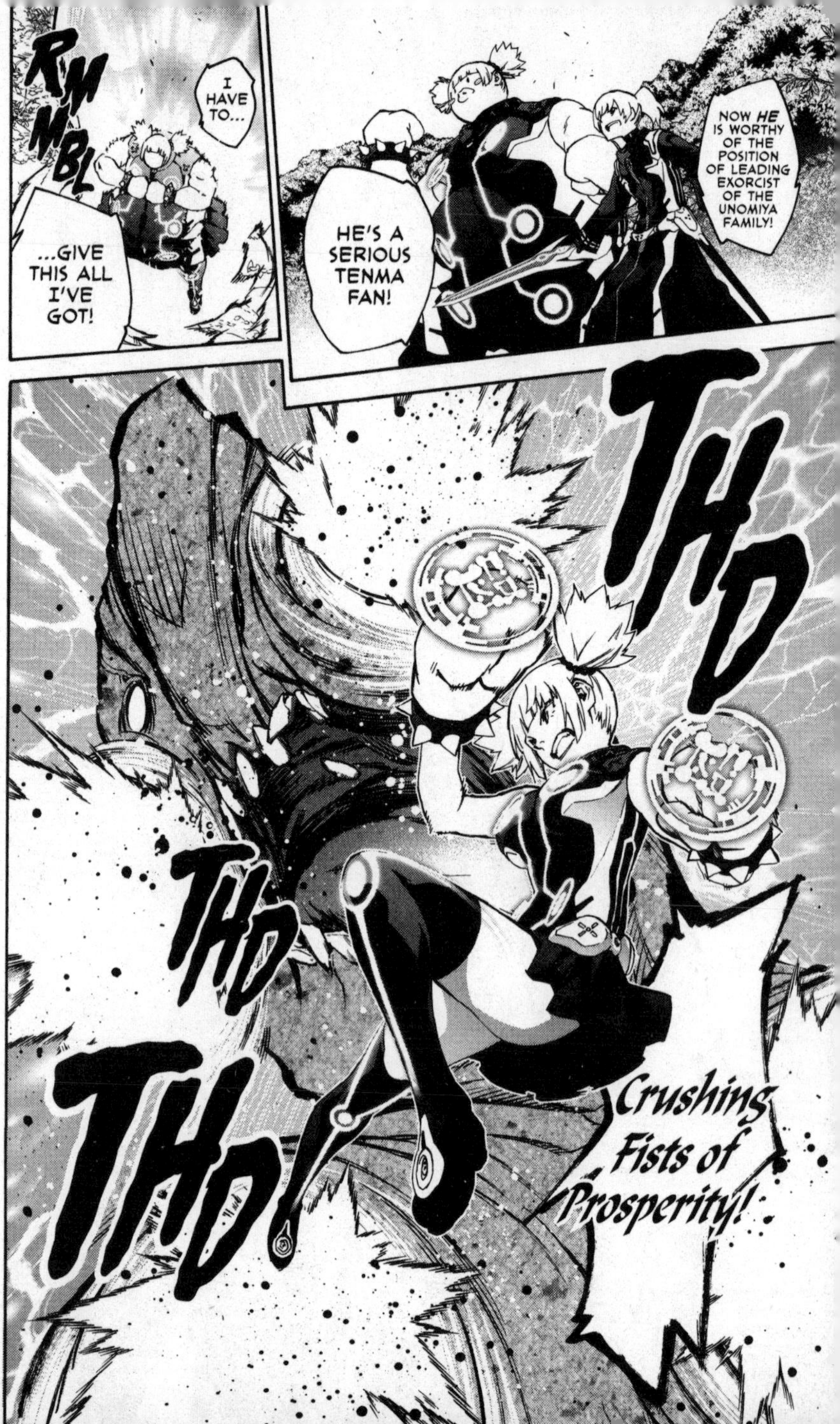
NOW HE IS WORTHY OF THE POSITION OF LEADING EXORCIST OF THE UNOMIYA FAMILY!
HE'S A SERIOUS TENMA FAN!
RMMBL
I HAVE TO...
...GIVE THIS ALL I'VE GOT!
THD
Crushing Fists of Prosperity!
THD
THD

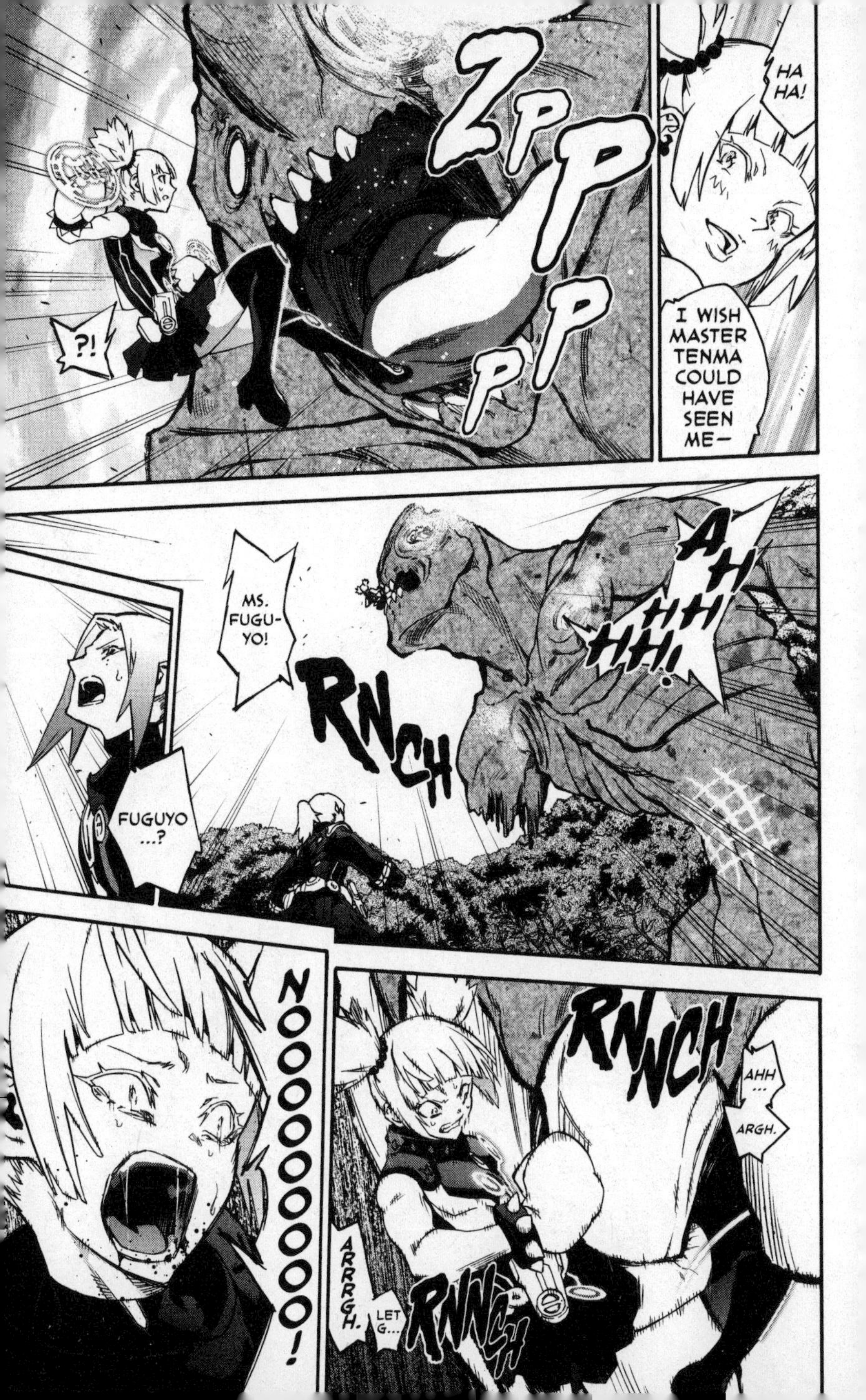
HA HA!
I WISH MASTER TENMA COULD HAVE SEEN ME—
ZPPPPP
?!
AHHHHHHH!
MS. FUGUYO!
RNCH
FUGUYO ...?
RNNCH
AHH ... ARGH.
ARRRGH.
LET G...
RNNCH
NOOOOOOOOOOO!

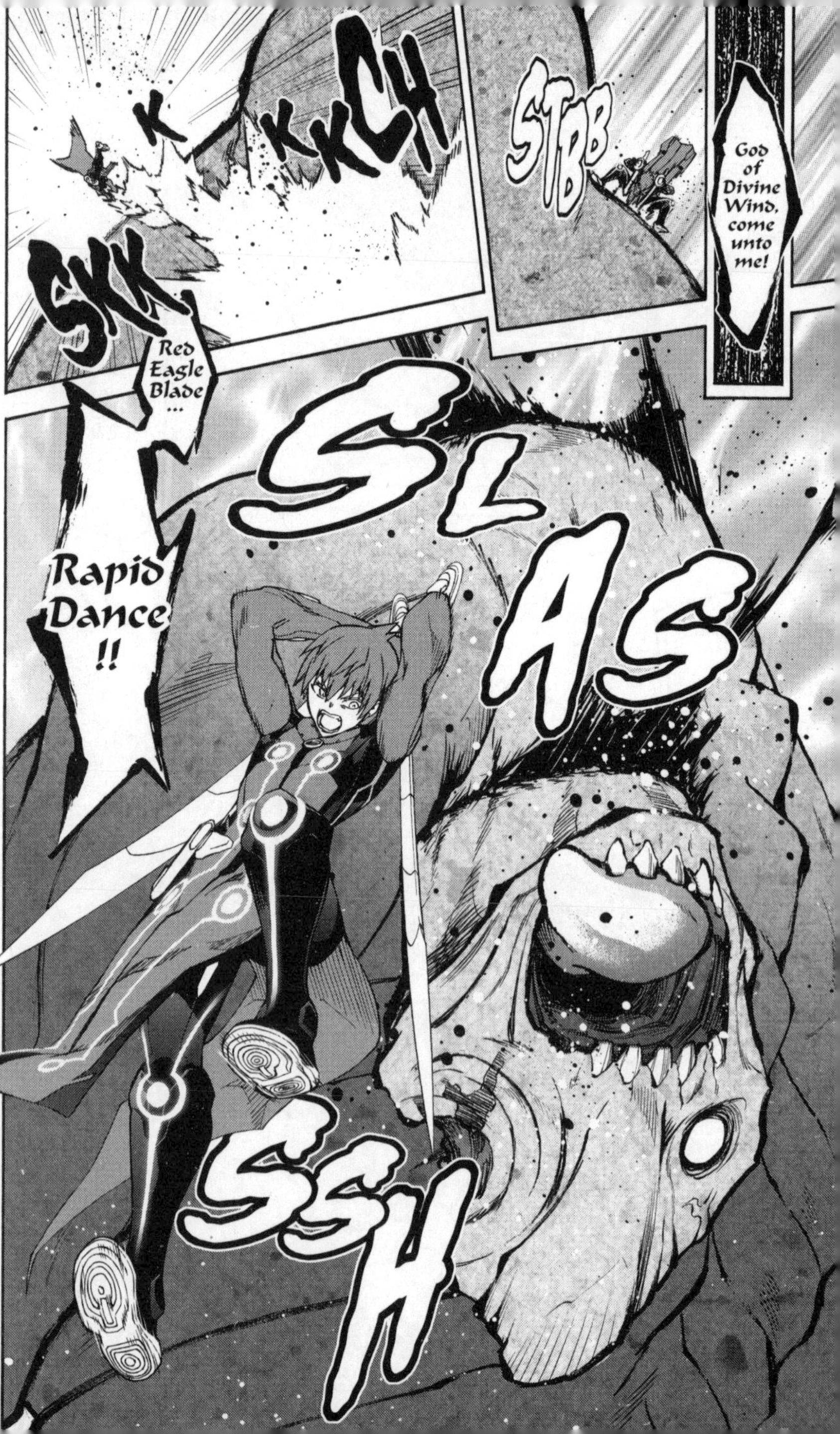
God of Divine Wind, come unto me!
STBB
K
KKCH
SKK
Red Eagle Blade...
SLAS
Rapid Dance!!
SSH

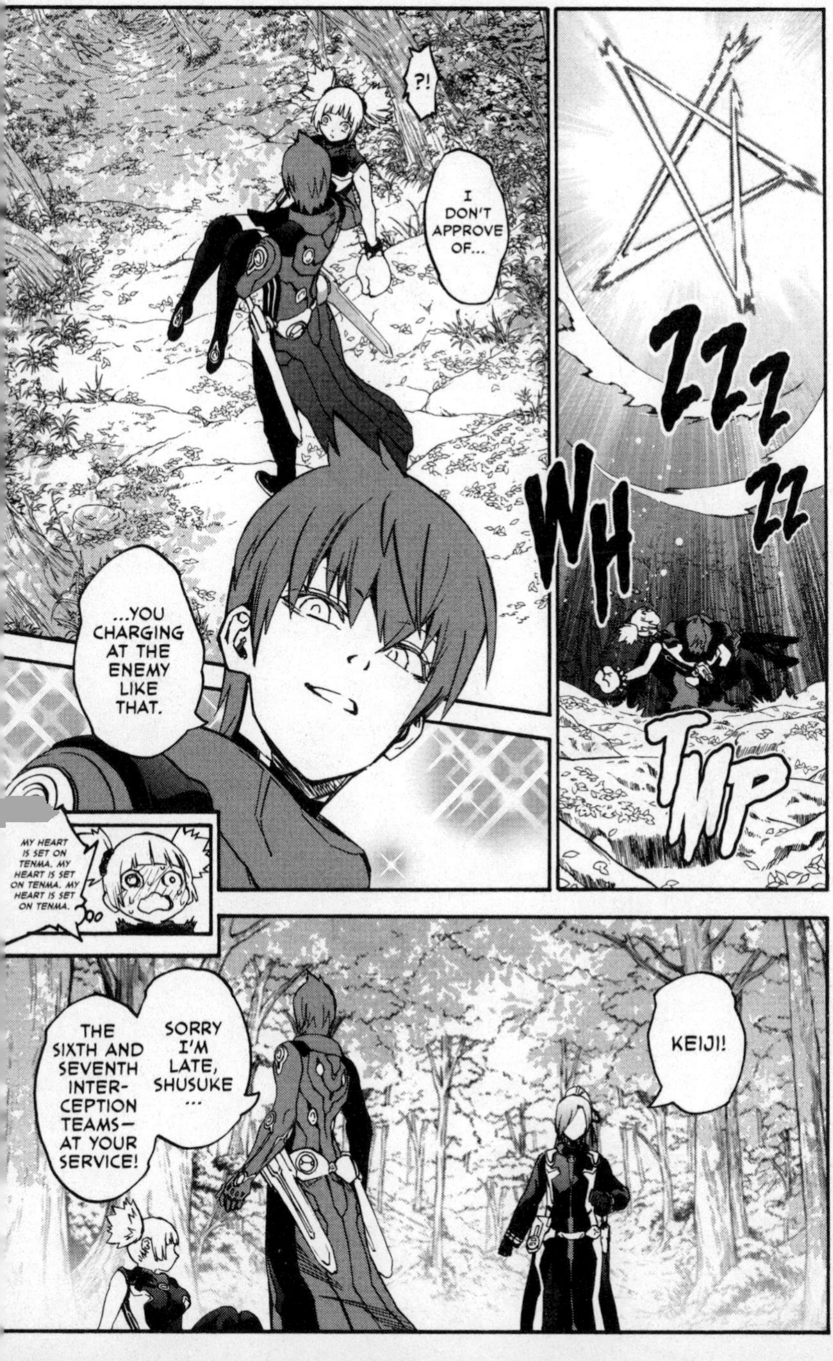
WHZZZZZ
TMP
?!
I DON'T APPROVE OF...
...YOU CHARGING AT THE ENEMY LIKE THAT.
MY HEART IS SET ON TENMA. MY HEART IS SET ON TENMA. MY HEART IS SET ON TENMA.
KEIJI!
SORRY I'M LATE, SHUSUKE...
THE SIXTH AND SEVENTH INTERCEPTION TEAMS—AT YOUR SERVICE!

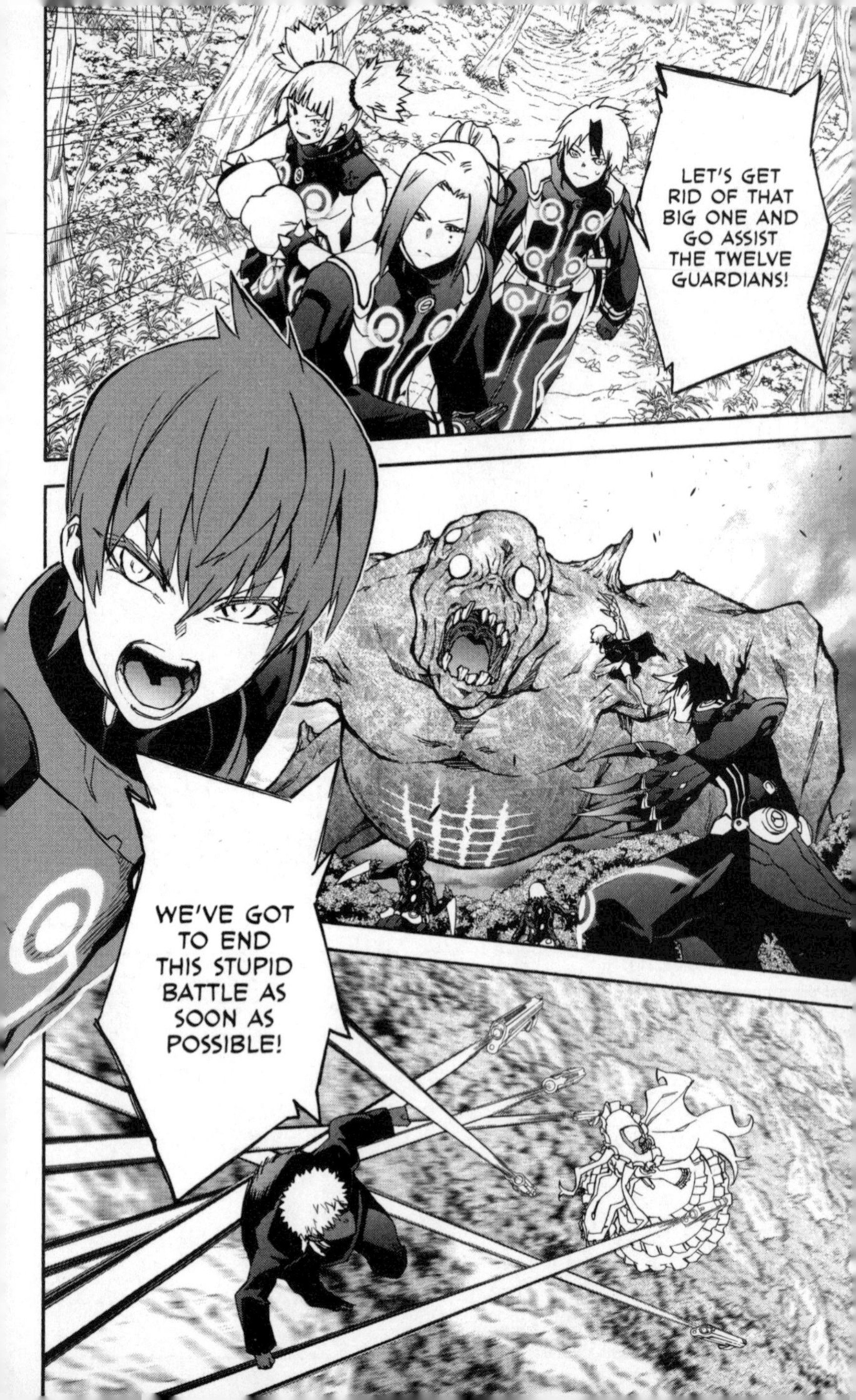
LET'S GET RID OF THAT BIG ONE AND GO ASSIST THE TWELVE GUARDIANS!
WE'VE GOT TO END THIS STUPID BATTLE AS SOON AS POSSIBLE!

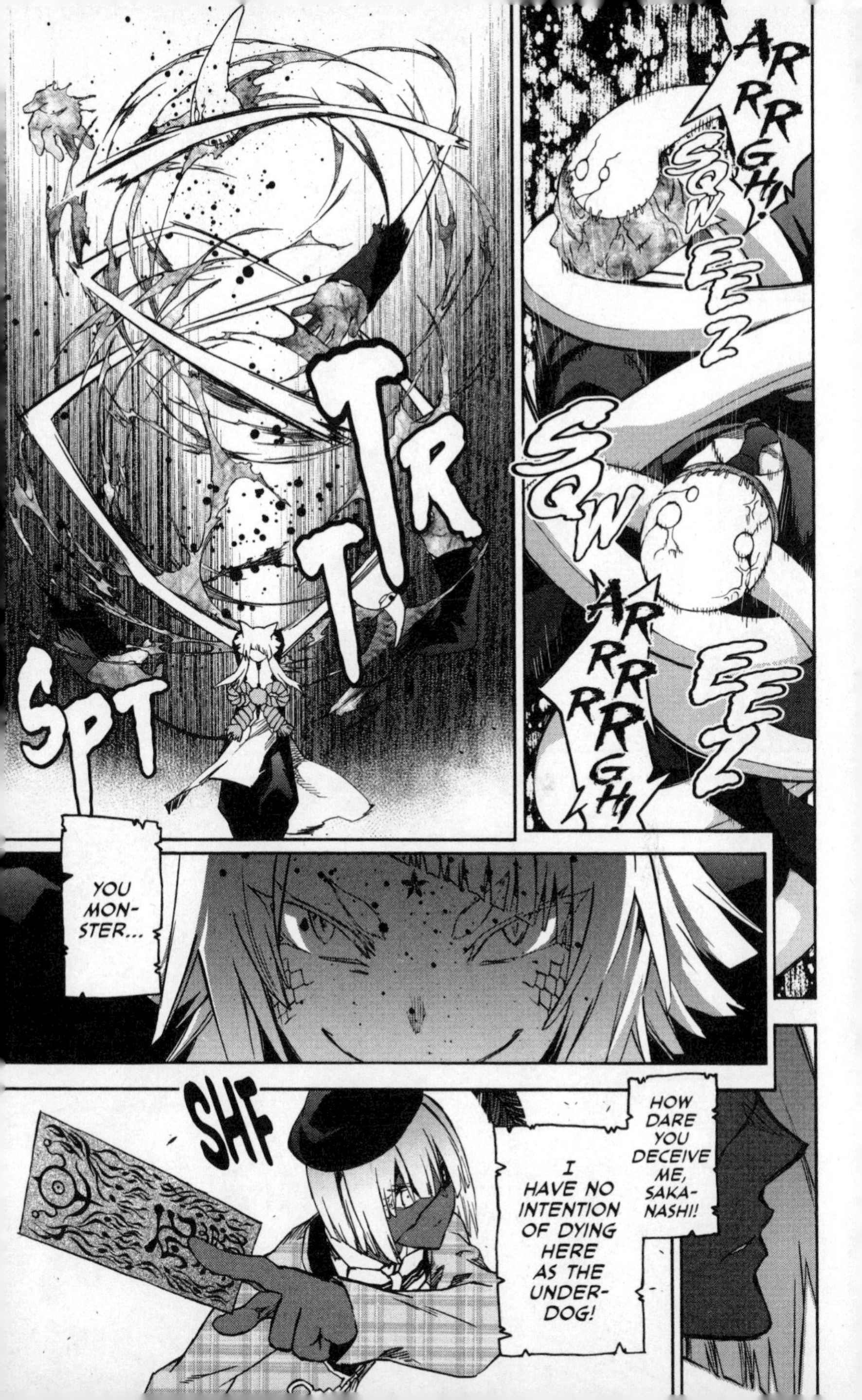
ARRRGH!
SQWEEZ
SQWEEZ
ARRRRRRGH!
TRT
SPT
YOU MONSTER...
HOW DARE YOU DECEIVE ME, SAKANASHI!
I HAVE NO INTENTION OF DYING HERE AS THE UNDERDOG!
SHF

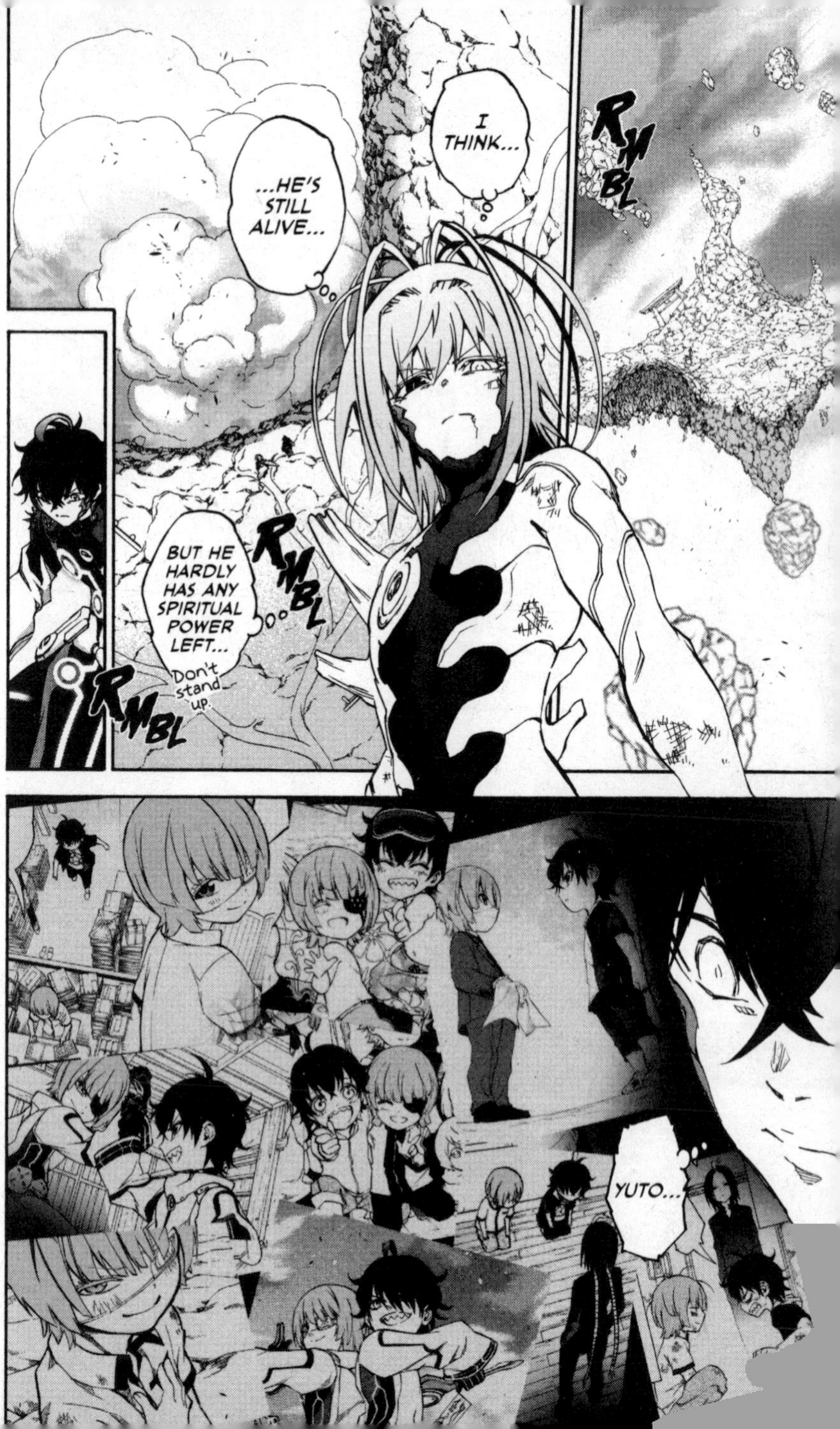
RMBL
I THINK...
...HE'S STILL ALIVE...
RMBL
BUT HE HARDLY HAS ANY SPIRITUAL POWER LEFT...
Don't stand up.
RMBL
YUTO...

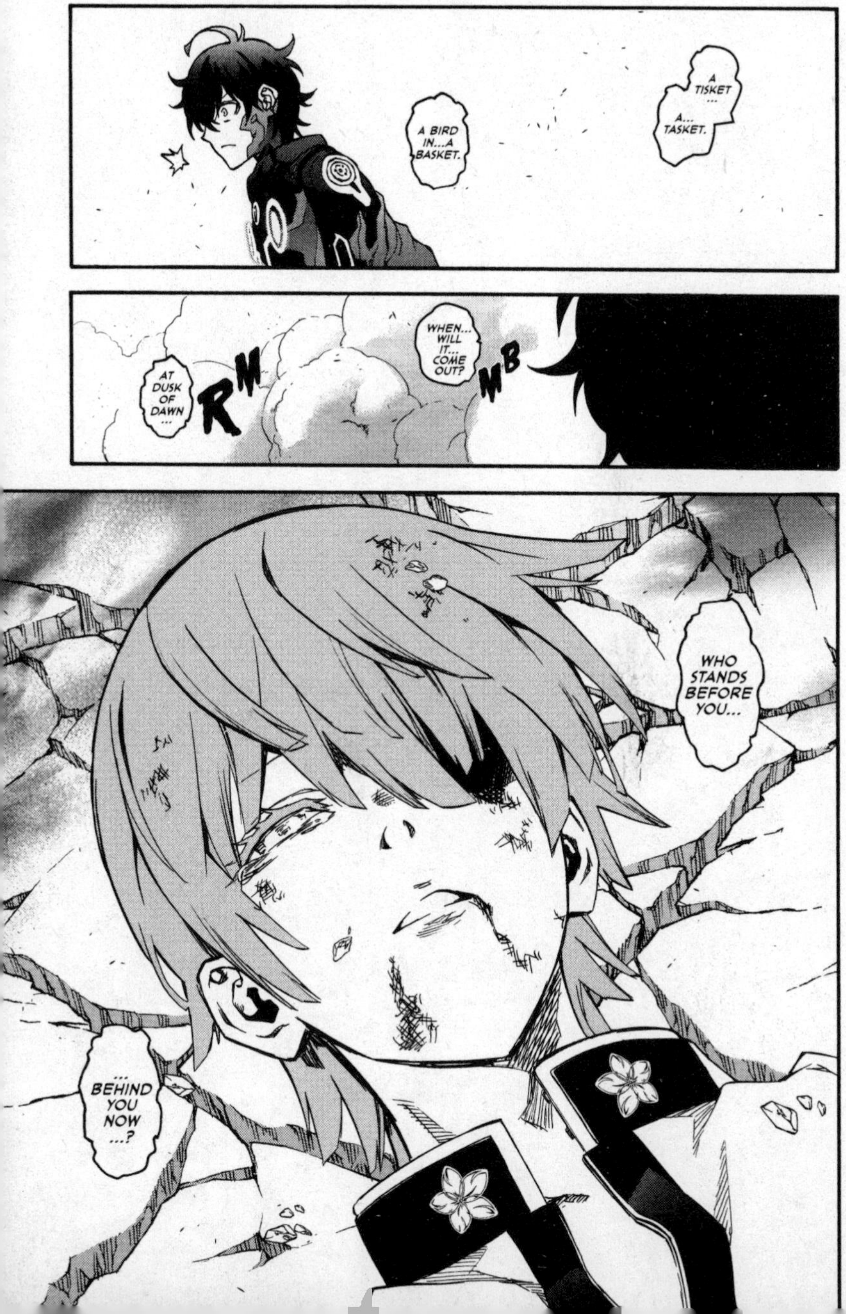
A TISKET... A... TASKET.
A BIRD IN...A BASKET.
WHEN... WILL IT... COME OUT?
RMMB
AT DUSK OF DAWN...
WHO STANDS BEFORE YOU...
...BEHIND YOU NOW...?

Twin Star Exorcists

O N M Y O J I

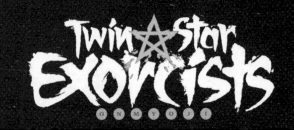

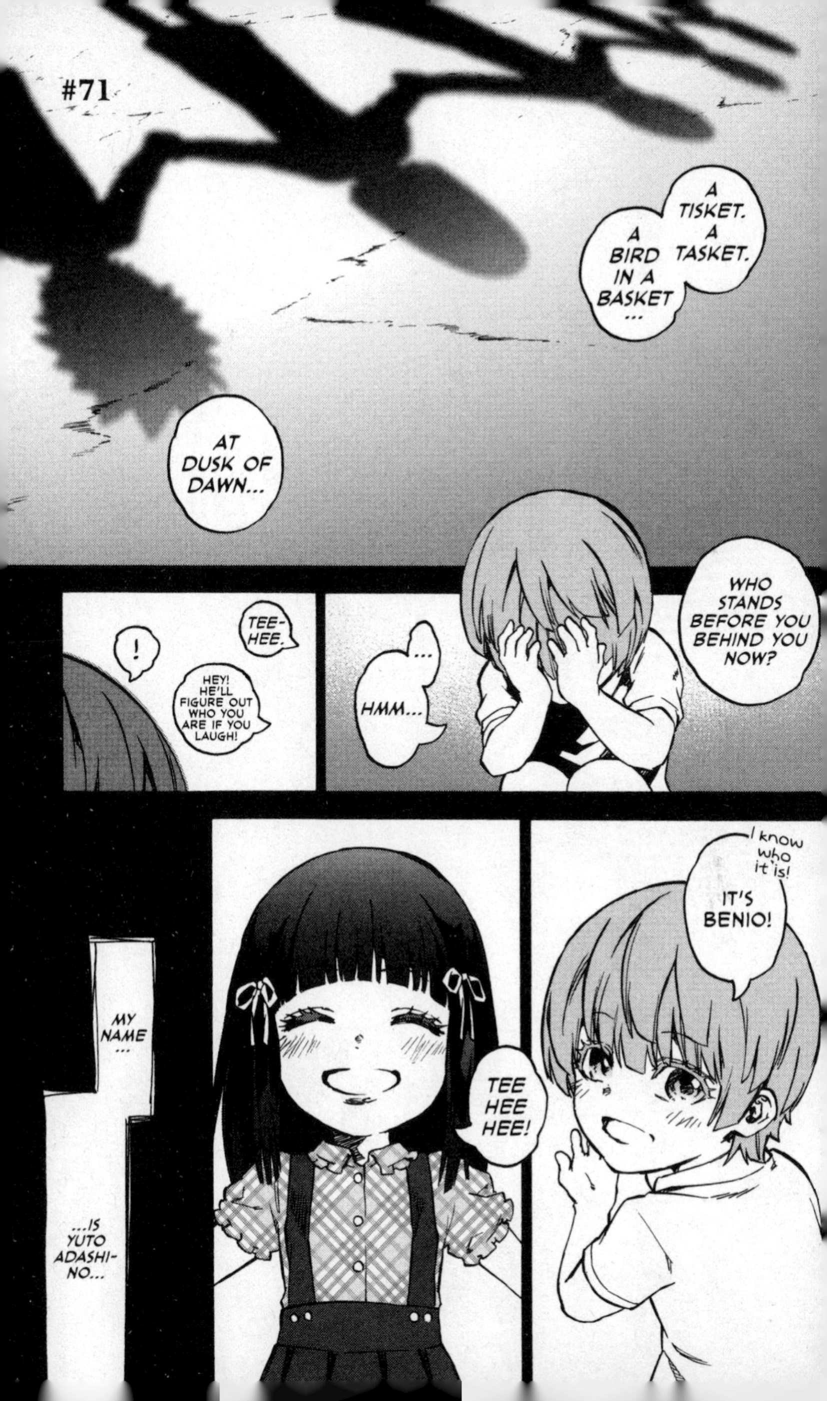
#71
A TISKET. A TASKET.
A BIRD IN A BASKET...
AT DUSK OF DAWN...
WHO STANDS BEFORE YOU BEHIND YOU NOW?
...
HMM...
TEE-HEE.
!
HEY! HE'LL FIGURE OUT WHO YOU ARE IF YOU LAUGH!
I know who it is!
IT'S BENIO!
TEE HEE HEE!
MY NAME...
...IS YUTO ADASHINO...

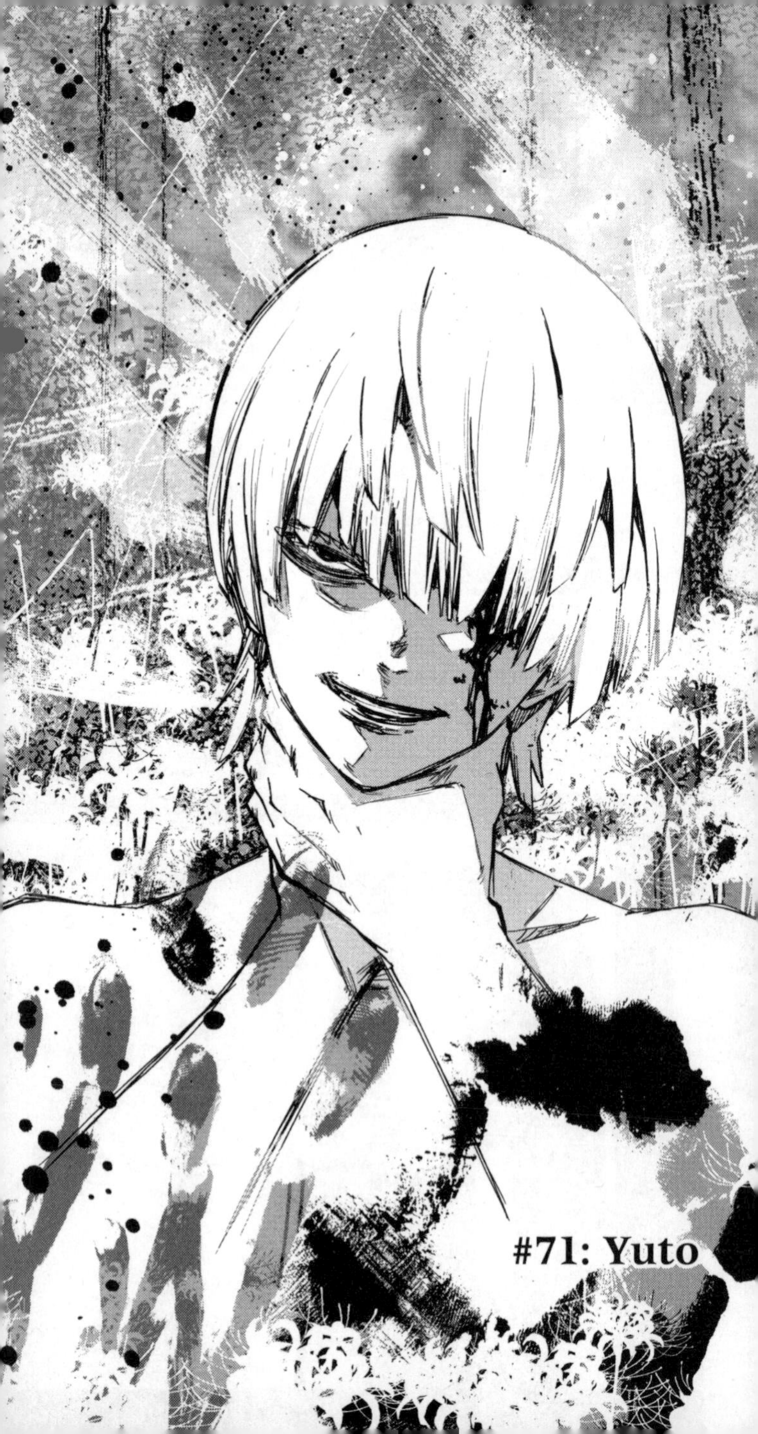
#71: Yuto

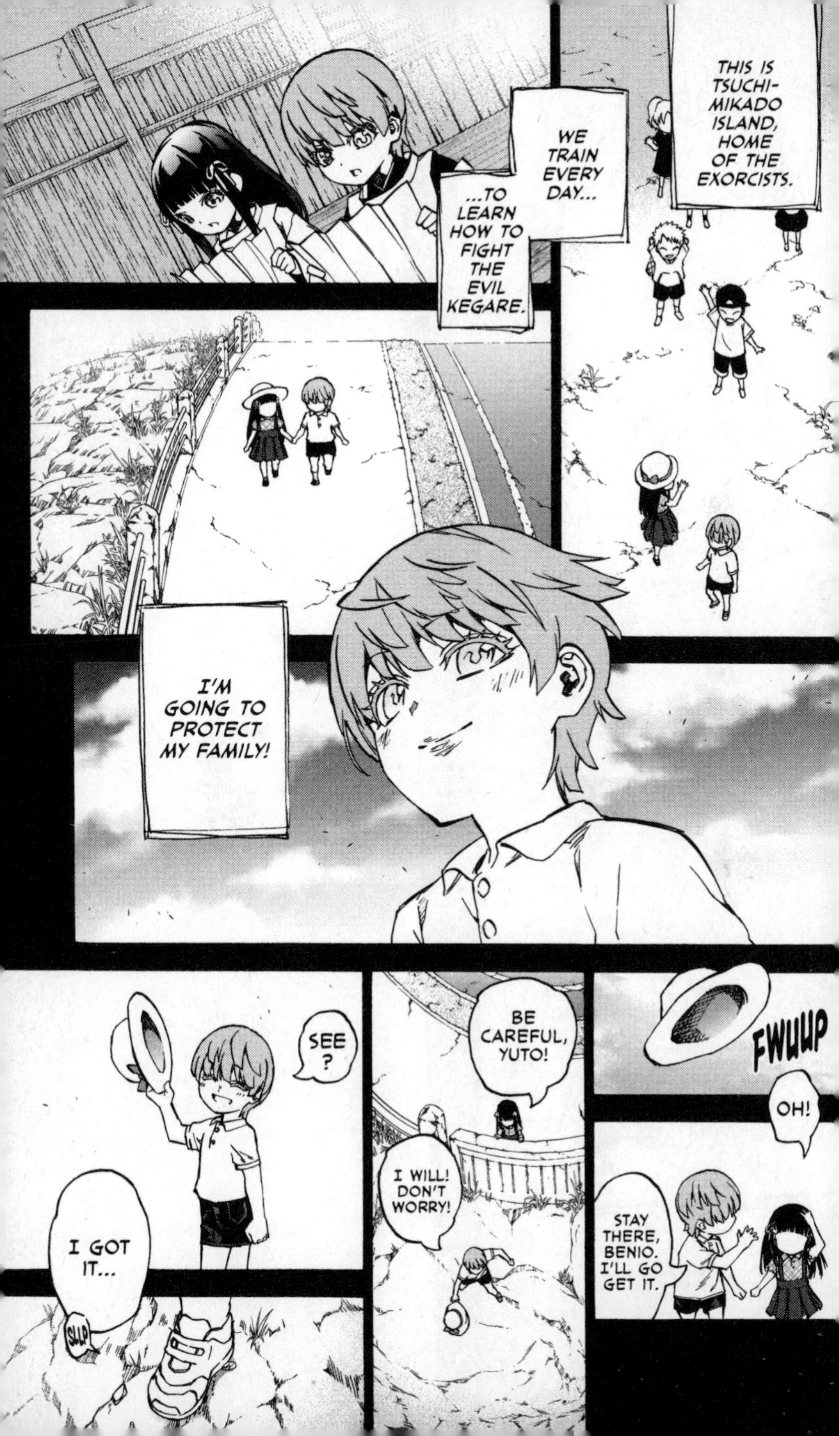
THIS IS TSUCHI-MIKADO ISLAND, HOME OF THE EXORCISTS.
WE TRAIN EVERY DAY...
...TO LEARN HOW TO FIGHT THE EVIL KEGARE.
I'M GOING TO PROTECT MY FAMILY!
FWUUP
OH!
STAY THERE, BENIO. I'LL GO GET IT.
BE CAREFUL, YUTO!
I WILL! DON'T WORRY!
SEE?
I GOT IT...
SLIP

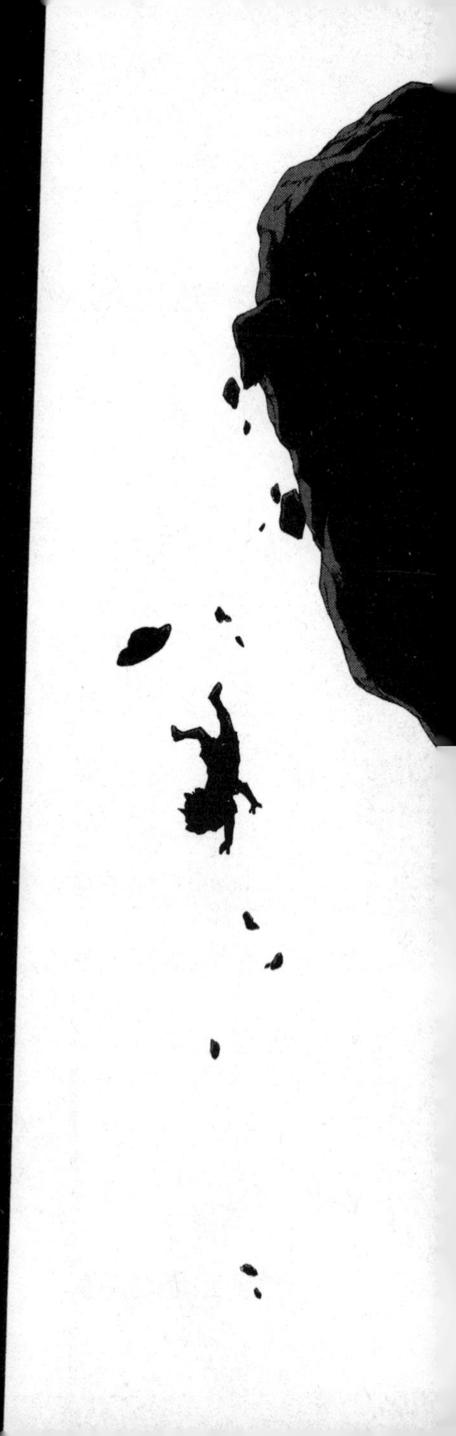

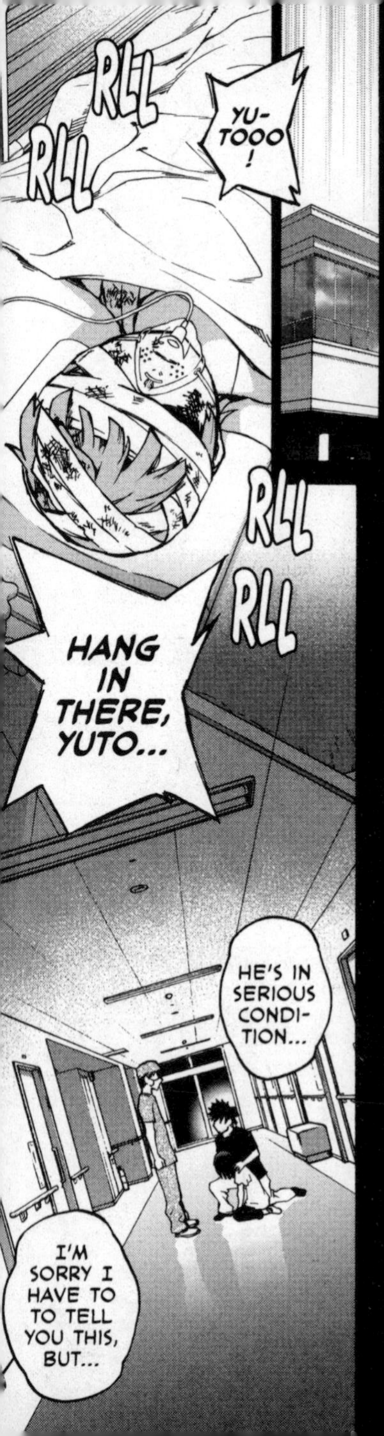
YU-TOOO!
RLL
RLL
RLL
RLL
HANG IN THERE, YUTO...
HE'S IN SERIOUS CONDITION...
I'M SORRY I HAVE TO TO TELL YOU THIS, BUT...

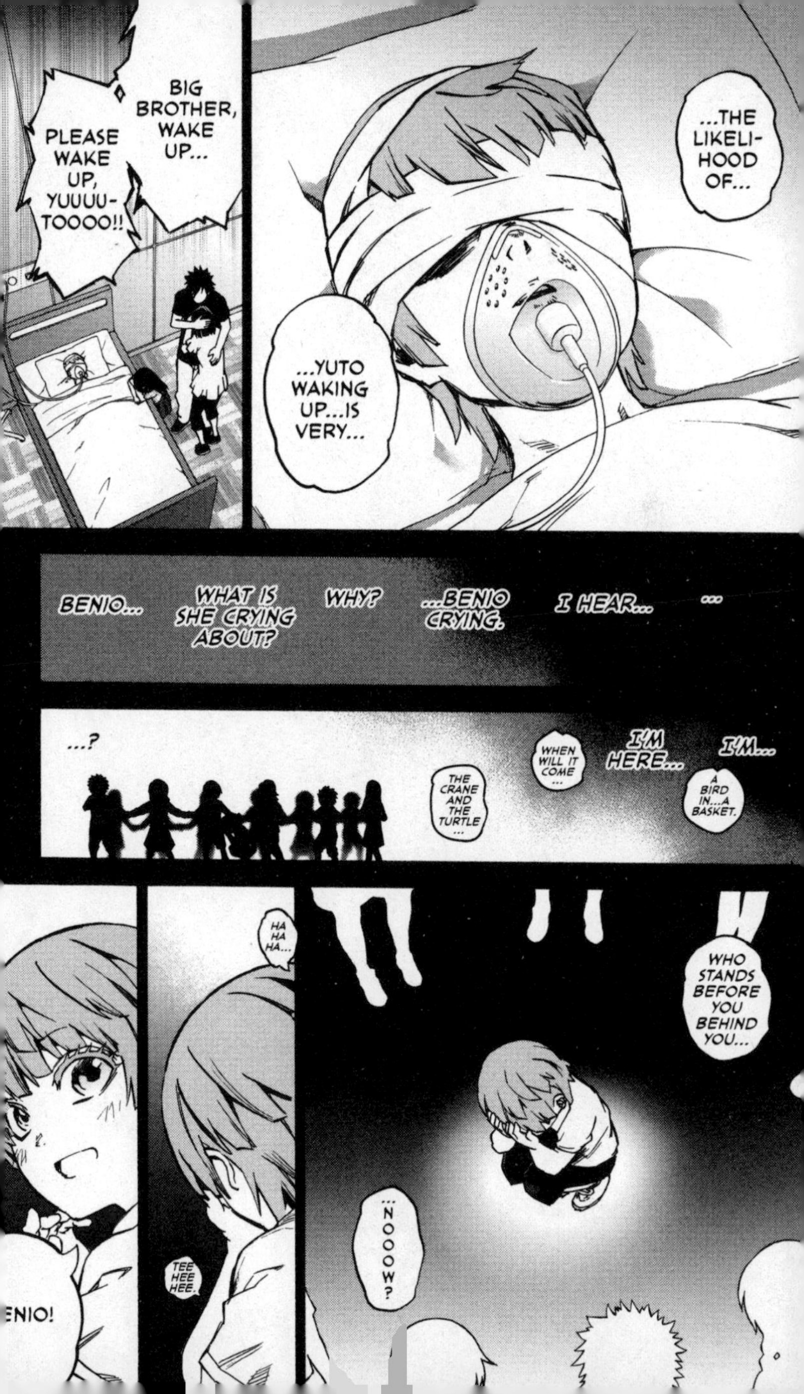
...THE LIKELI-HOOD OF...
...YUTO WAKING UP...IS VERY...
BIG BROTHER, WAKE UP...
PLEASE WAKE UP, YUUUU-TOOOO!!
...
I HEAR...
...BENIO CRYING.
WHY?
WHAT IS SHE CRYING ABOUT?
BENIO...
I'M...
A BIRD IN...A BASKET.
I'M HERE...
WHEN WILL IT COME...
THE CRANE AND THE TURTLE...
...?
WHO STANDS BEFORE YOU BEHIND YOU...
...NOOOW?
HA HA HA...
TEE HEE HEE.
ENIO!

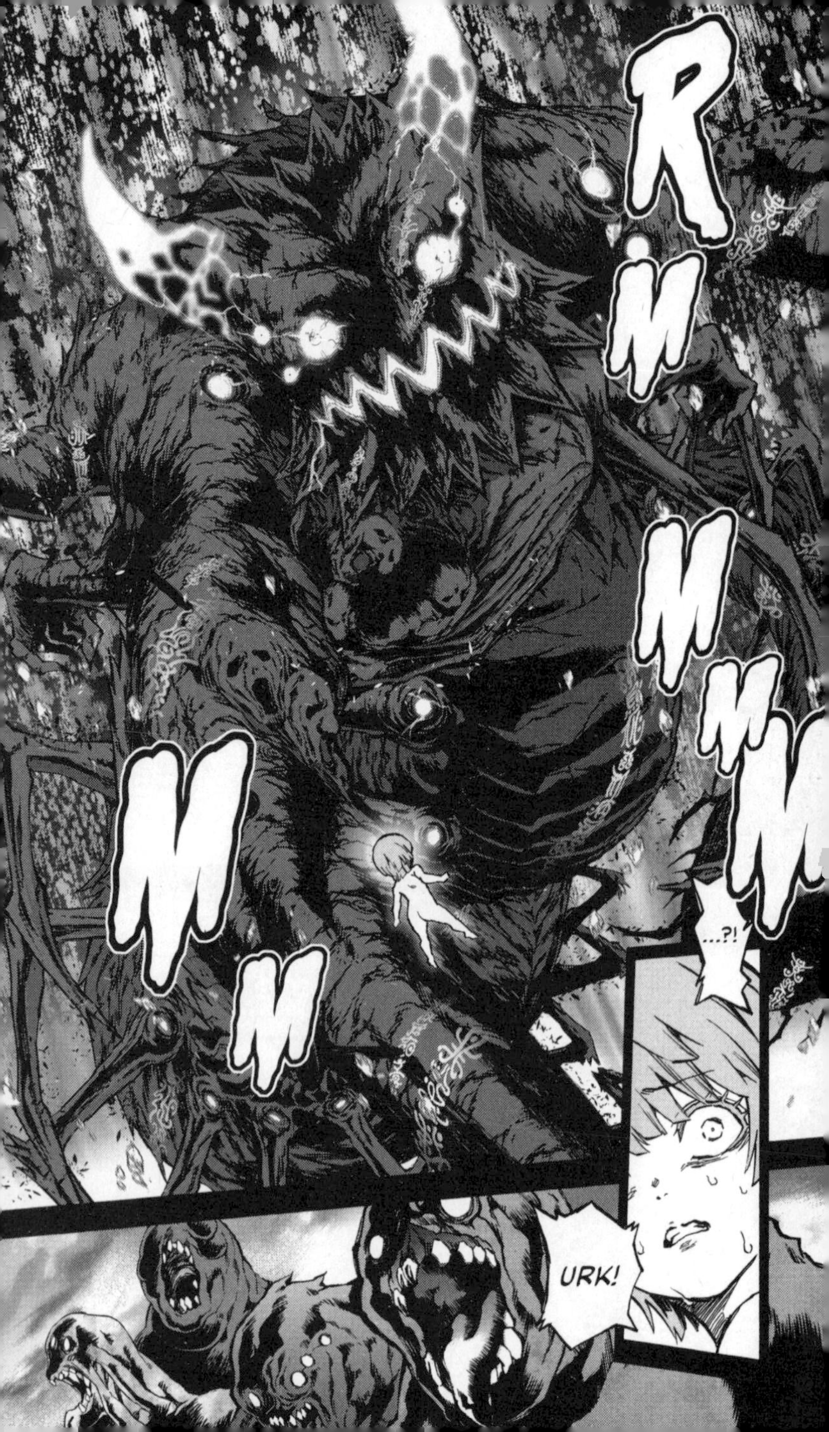
RMMMMMM
...?!
URK!

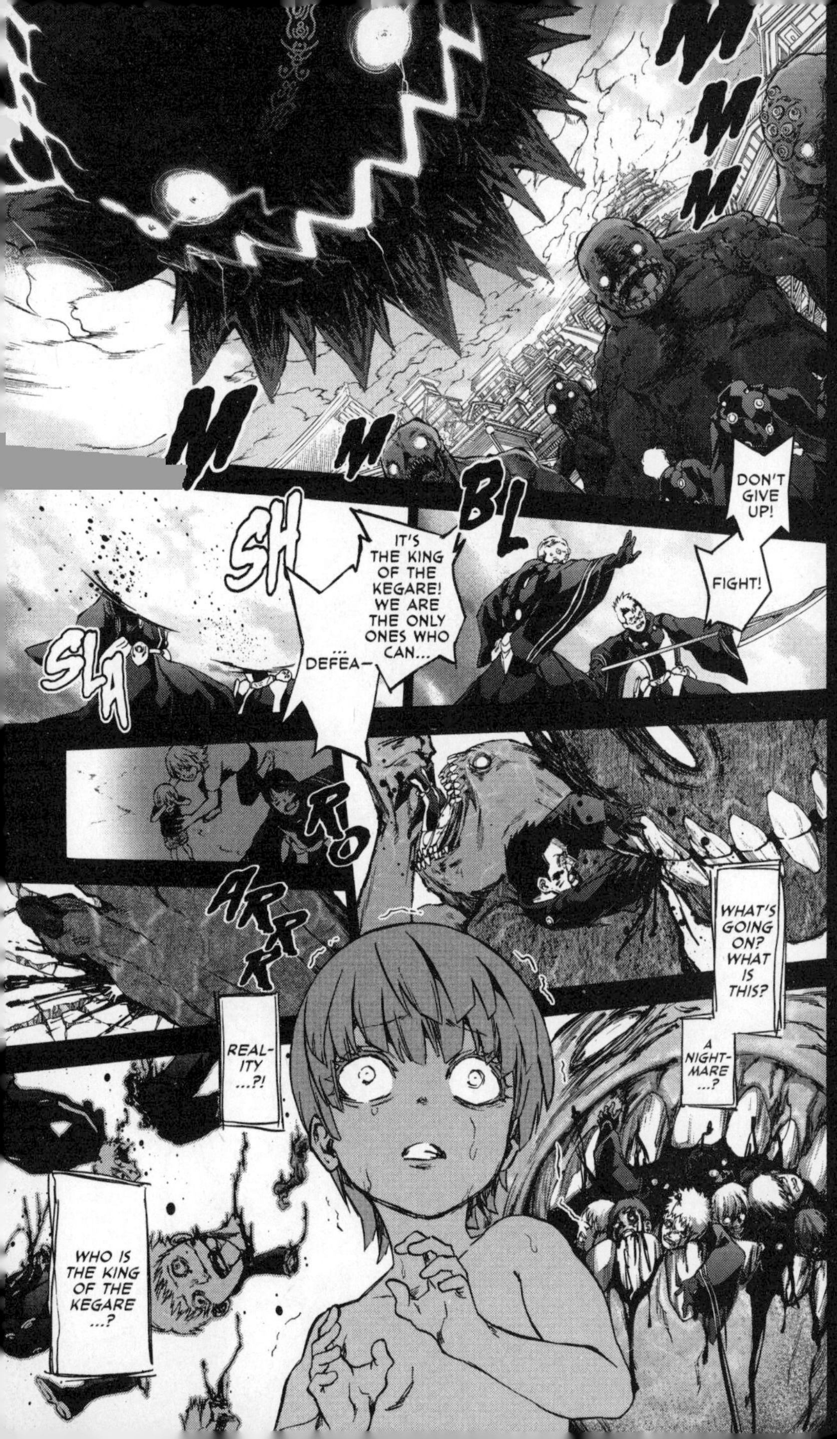
MMMM
MMBL
DON'T GIVE UP!
FIGHT!
IT'S THE KING OF THE KEGARE! WE ARE THE ONLY ONES WHO CAN...
... DEFEA—
SH
SLA
RO
ARRRR
WHAT'S GOING ON? WHAT IS THIS?
A NIGHT-MARE ...?
REAL-ITY ...?!
WHO IS THE KING OF THE KEGARE ...?

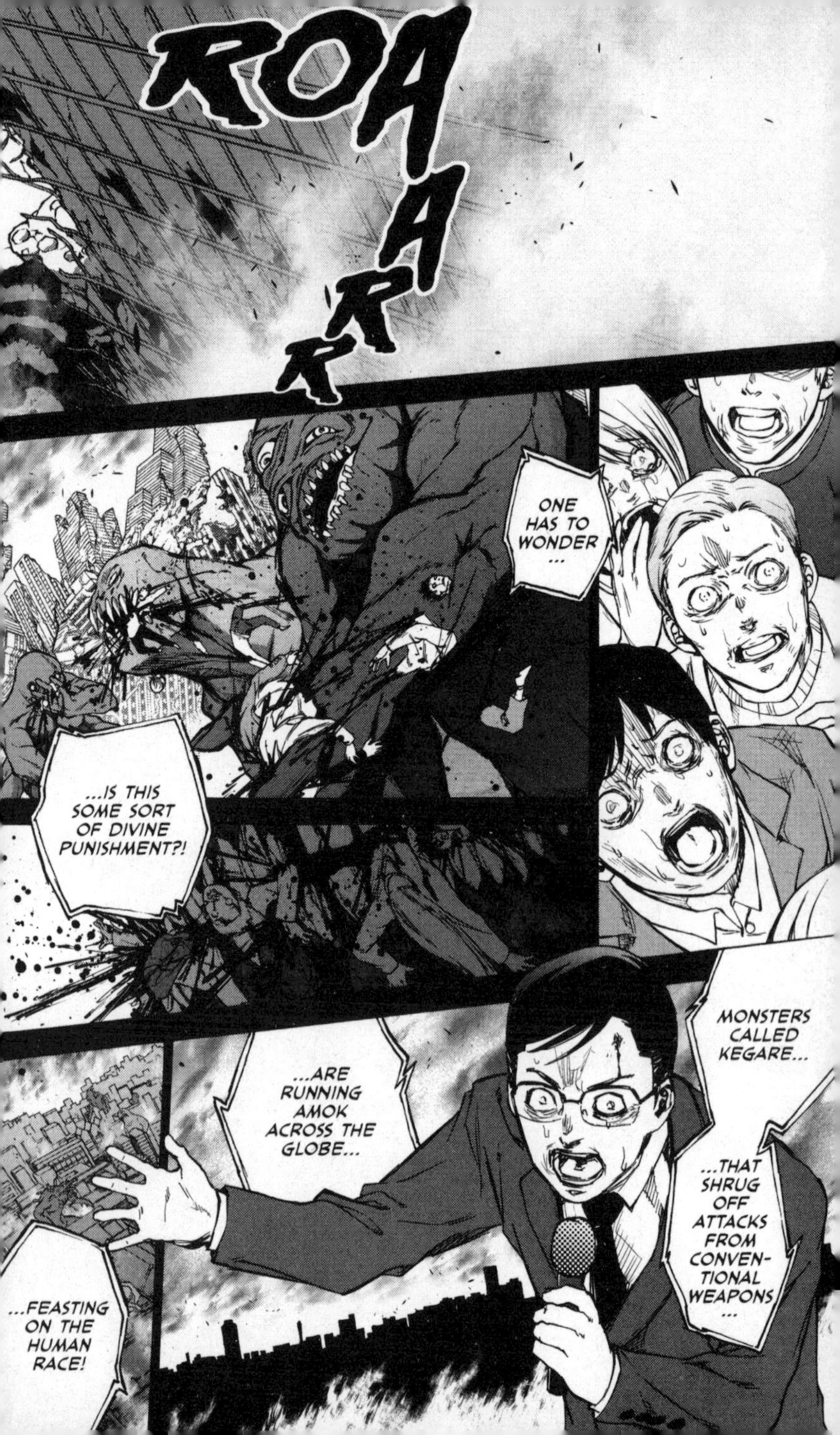
ROAARR
ONE HAS TO WONDER...
...IS THIS SOME SORT OF DIVINE PUNISHMENT?!
MONSTERS CALLED KEGARE...
...THAT SHRUG OFF ATTACKS FROM CONVENTIONAL WEAPONS...
...ARE RUNNING AMOK ACROSS THE GLOBE...
...FEASTING ON THE HUMAN RACE!

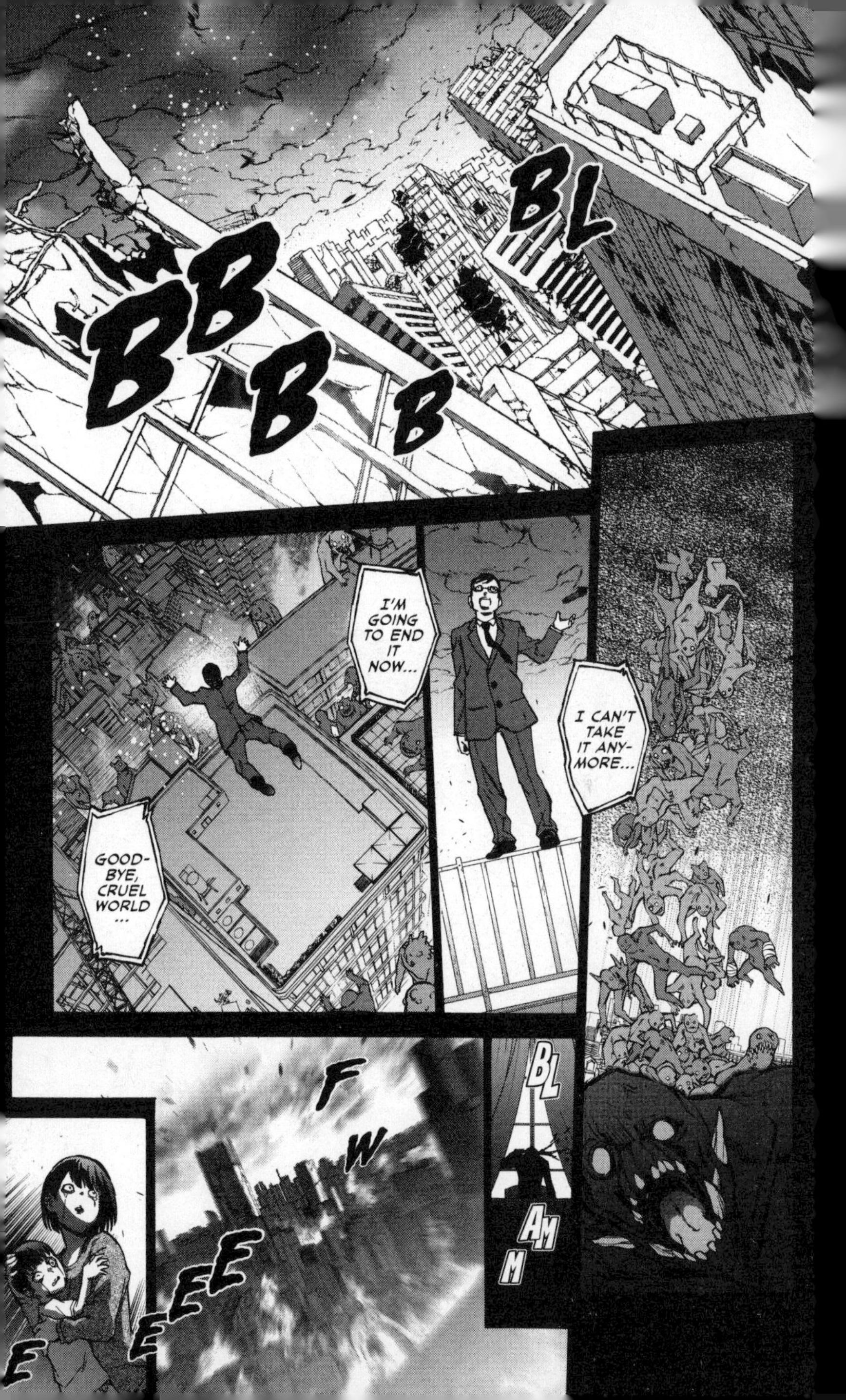
BL
BB
B
B
I CAN'T TAKE IT ANY-MORE...
I'M GOING TO END IT NOW...
GOOD-BYE, CRUEL WORLD ...
BLAMM
FW
EEEEE

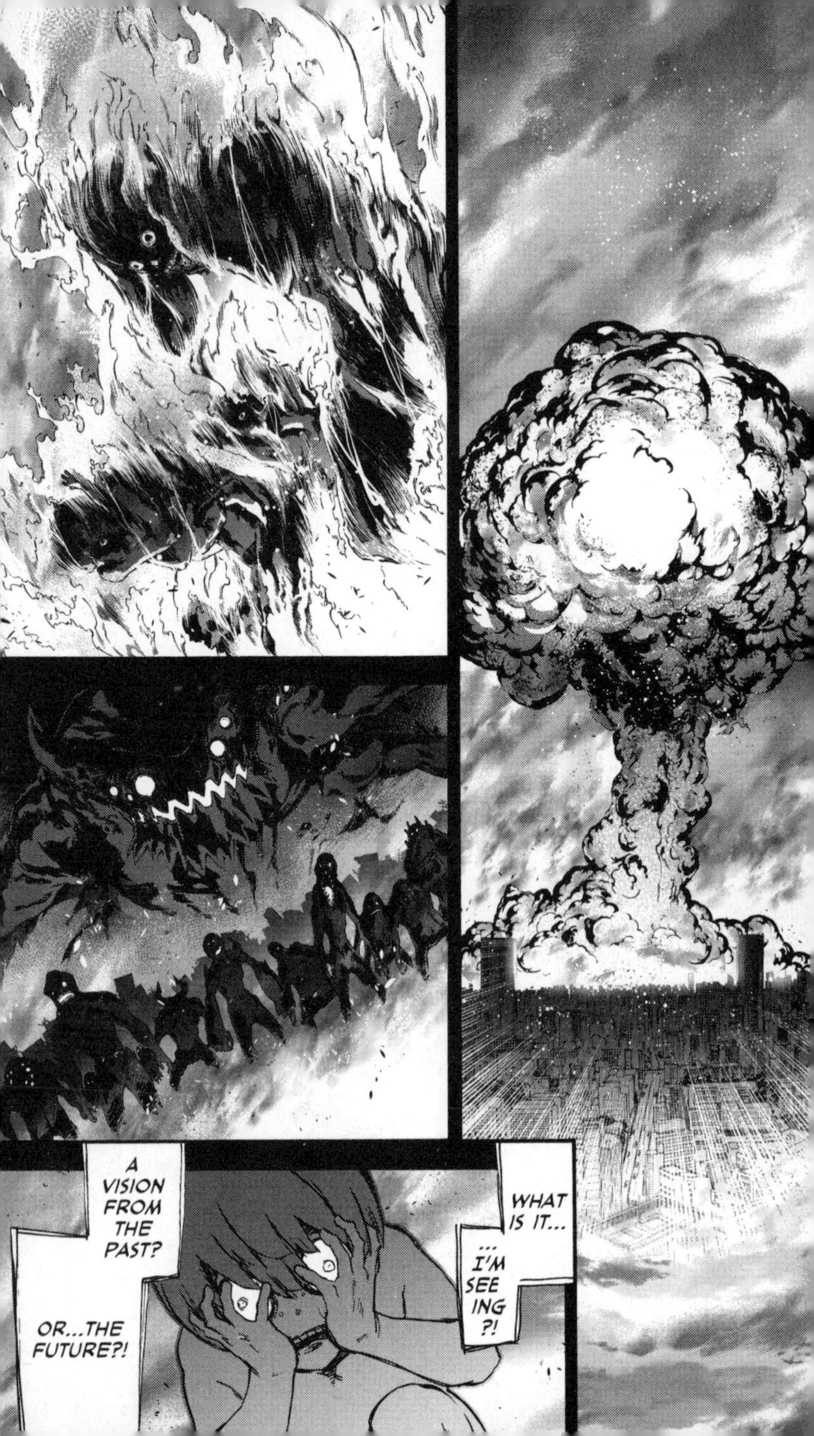
WHAT IS IT... ...I'M SEEING?!
A VISION FROM THE PAST?
OR...THE FUTURE?!

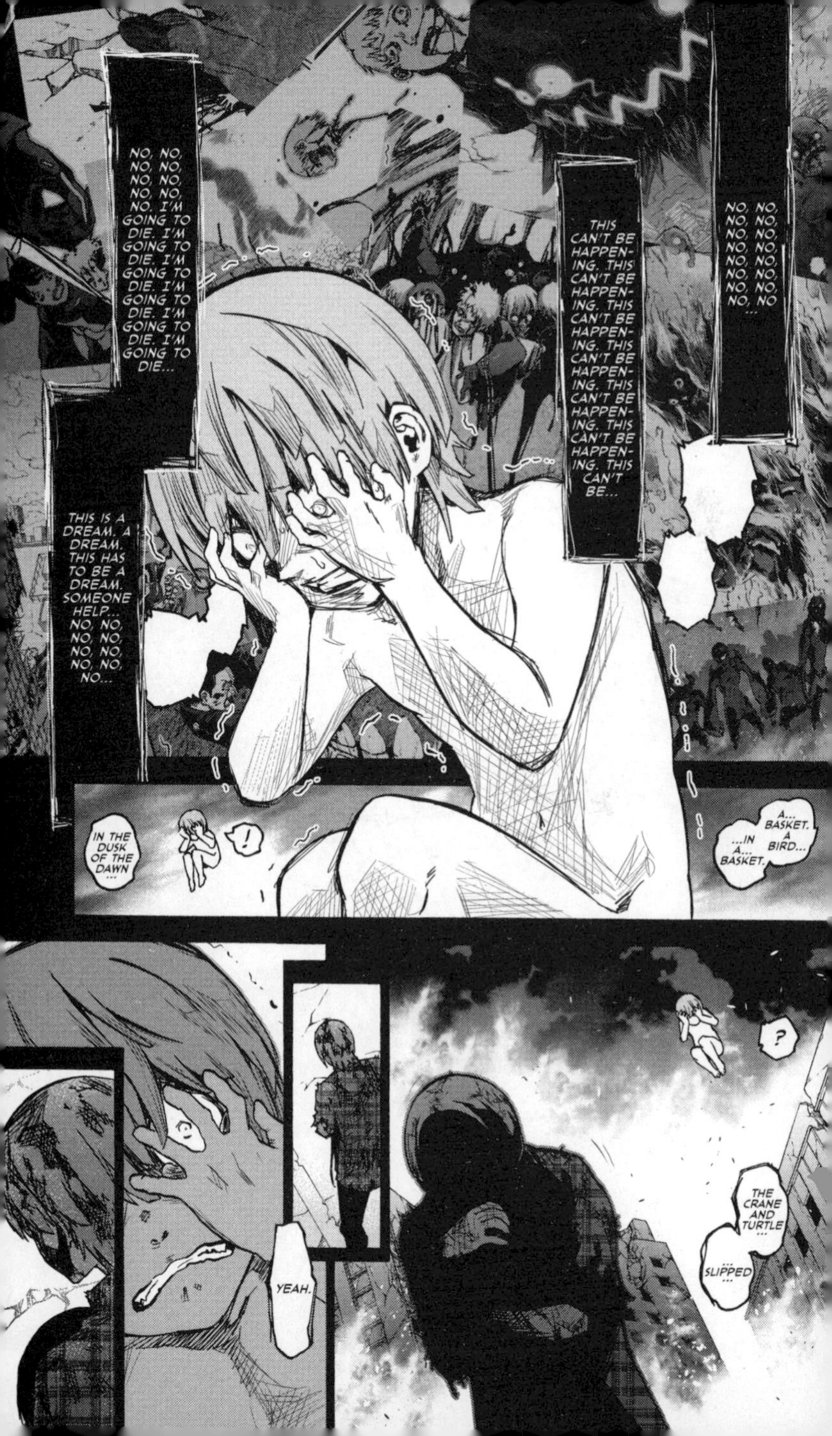
NO, NO, NO, NO, NO, NO, NO, NO, NO, NO, NO, NO, NO, NO, NO, NO...
THIS CAN'T BE HAPPEN-ING. THIS CAN'T BE HAPPEN-ING. THIS CAN'T BE HAPPEN-ING. THIS CAN'T BE HAPPEN-ING. THIS CAN'T BE HAPPEN-ING. THIS CAN'T BE HAPPEN-ING. THIS CAN'T BE...
NO, NO, NO, NO, NO, NO, NO. I'M GOING TO DIE. I'M GOING TO DIE. I'M GOING TO DIE. I'M GOING TO DIE. I'M GOING TO DIE. I'M GOING TO DIE...
THIS IS A DREAM. A DREAM. THIS HAS TO BE A DREAM. SOMEONE HELP... NO, NO, NO, NO, NO, NO, NO, NO, NO...
A... BASKET. A BIRD...
...IN A... BASKET.
!
IN THE DUSK OF THE DAWN...
?
THE CRANE AND TURTLE...
...SLIPPED...
YEAH.

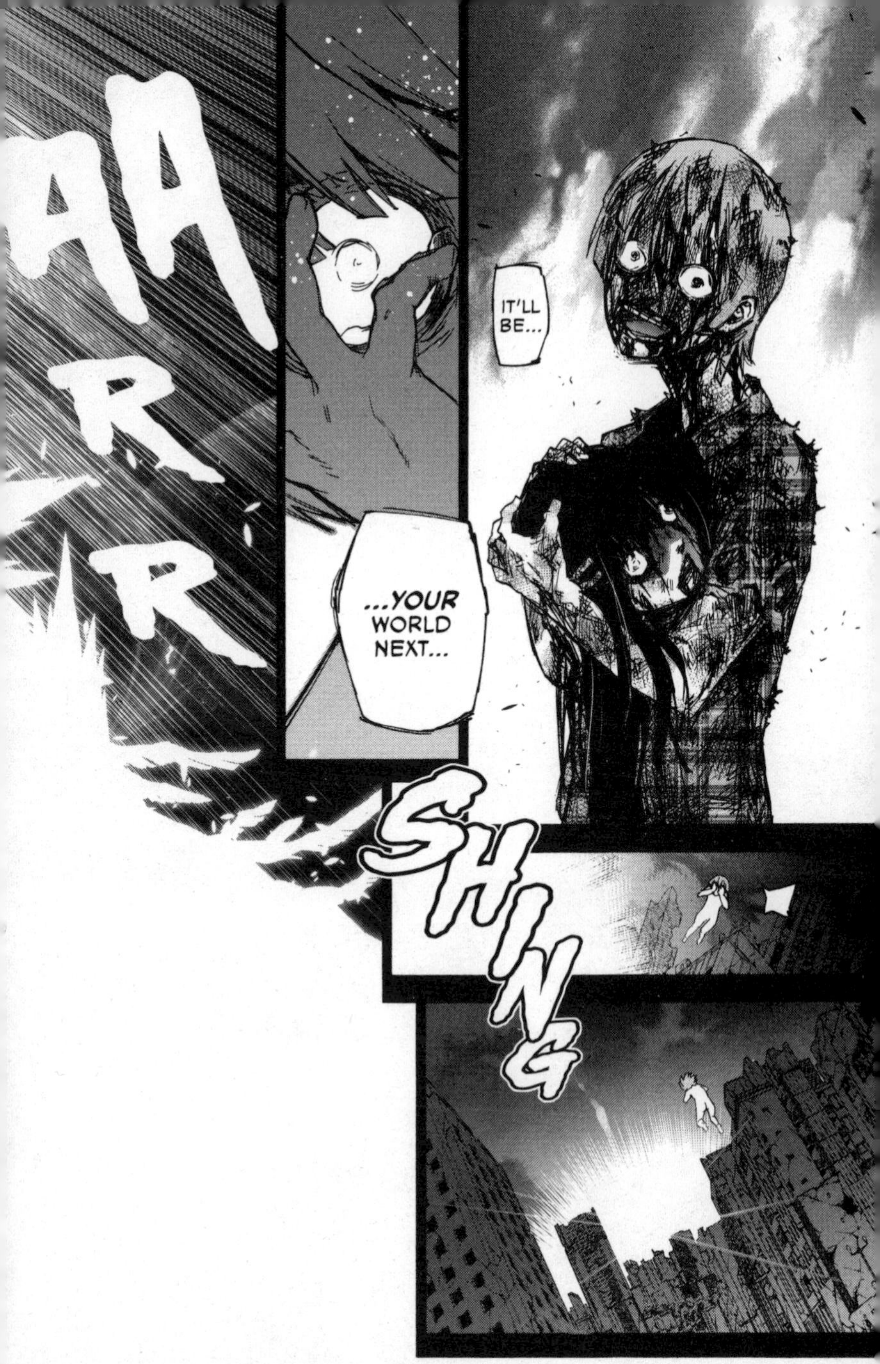
IT'LL BE...
...YOUR WORLD NEXT...
AARR
SHING

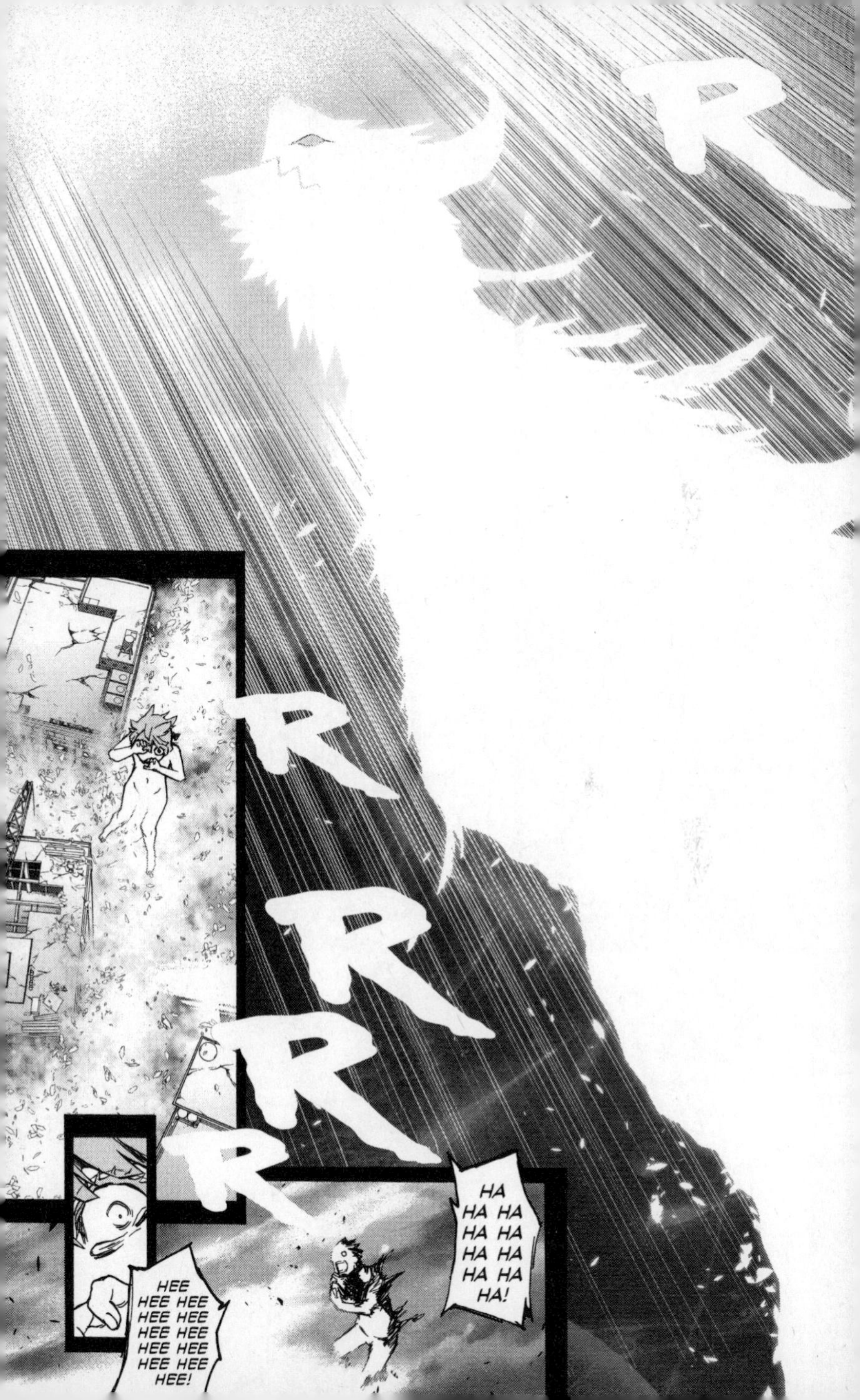
R
RRRRR
HA HA HA HA HA HA HA HA HA HA HA!
HEE HEE HEE HEE HEE HEE HEE HEE HEE HEE HEE HEE!

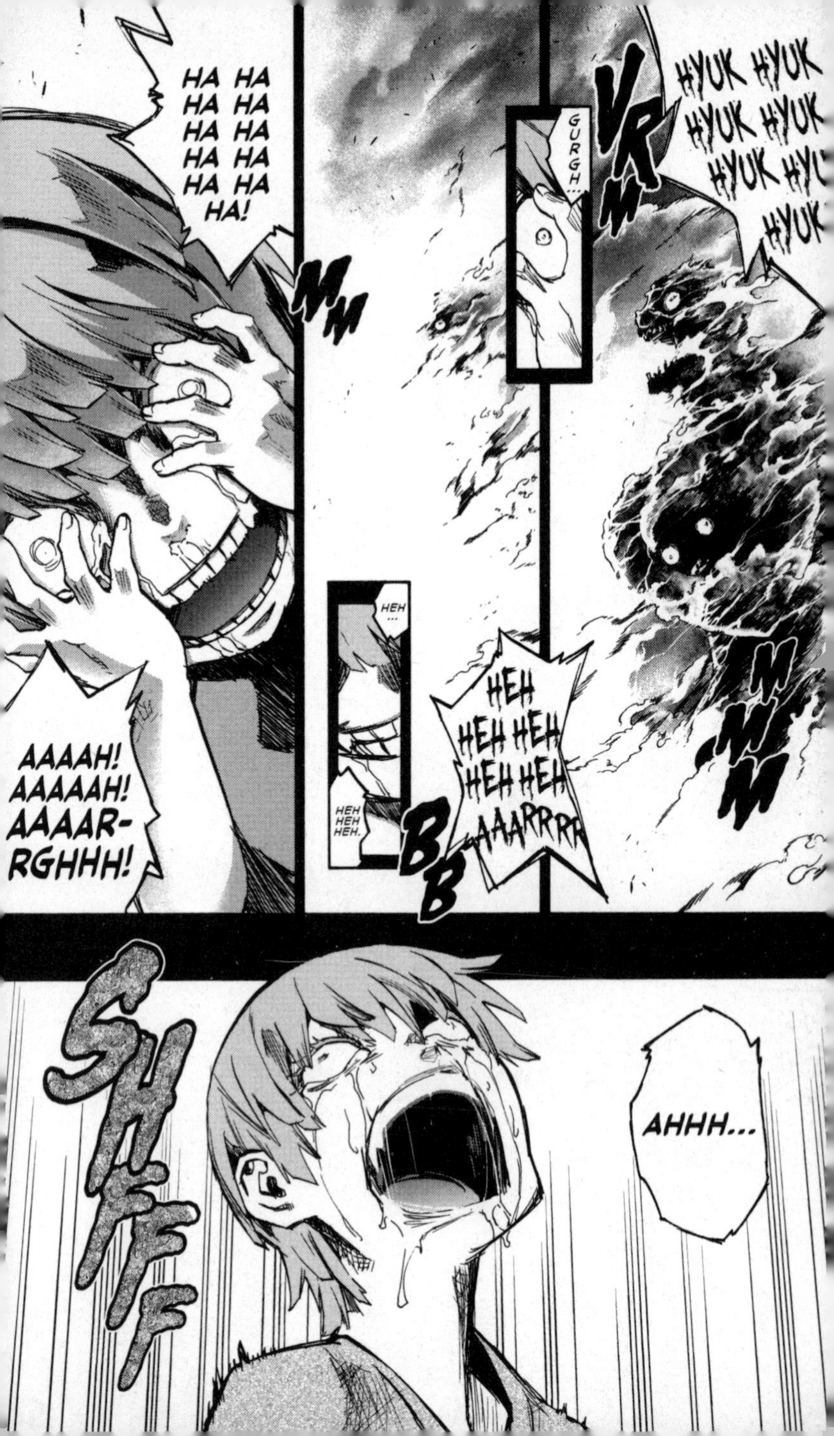

HYUK HYUK HYUK HYUK HYUK HYU HYUK
VRM
GURGH...
MMMM
HEH...
HEH HEH HEH HEH HEH AAARRRR
HEH HEH HEH.
BB
MM
HA HA HA HA HA HA HA HA HA HA HA!
AAAAH! AAAAAH! AAAAR-RGHHH!
AHHH...
SHFF

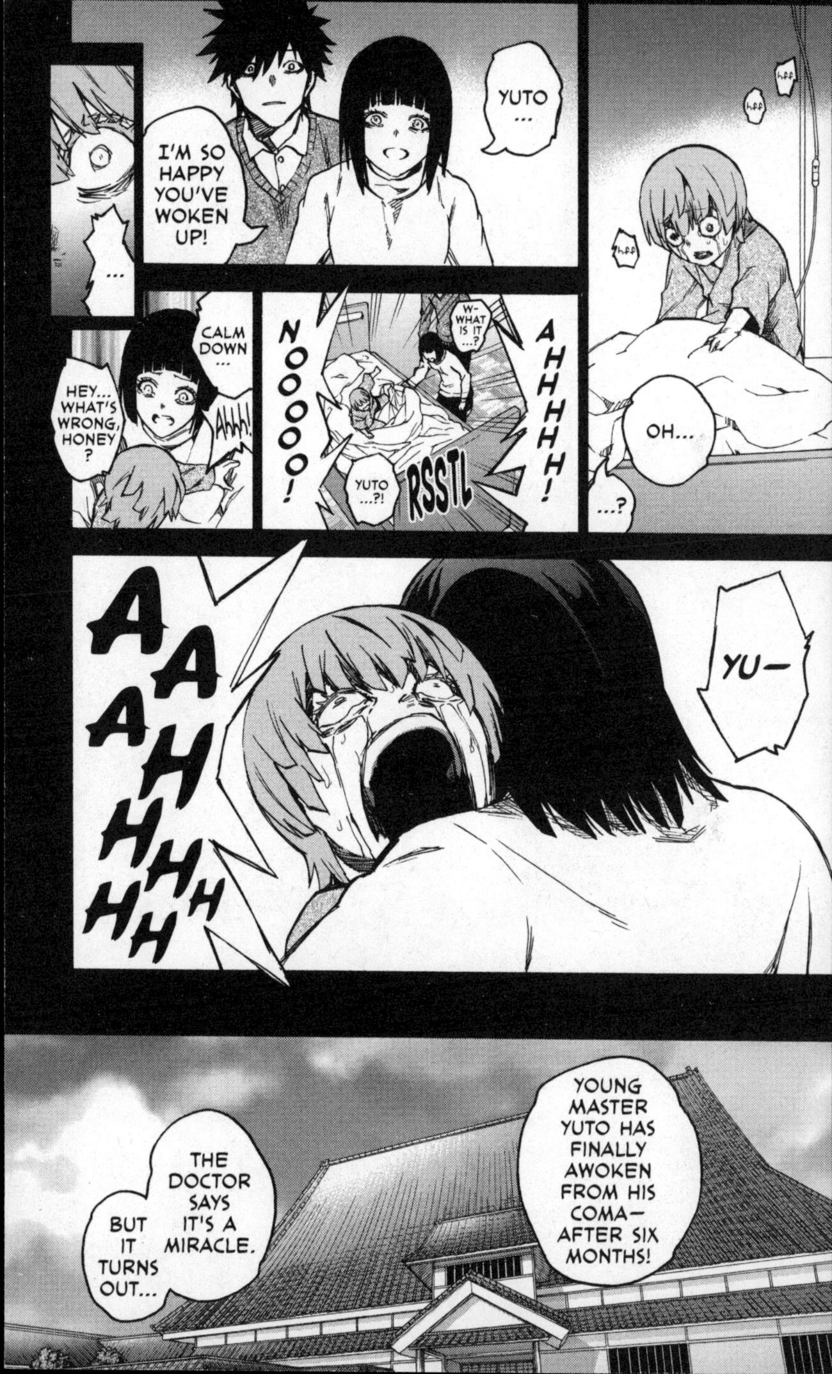
hff
hff
hff
OH...
...?
YUTO ...
I'M SO HAPPY YOU'VE WOKEN UP!
...
AHHHHHH!
W-WHAT IS IT ...?
NOOOOOO!
RSSTL
YUTO ...?!
CALM DOWN ...
HEY... WHAT'S WRONG, HONEY?
Ahhh!
YU—
AAAHHHHHHHH
YOUNG MASTER YUTO HAS FINALLY AWOKEN FROM HIS COMA—AFTER SIX MONTHS!
THE DOCTOR SAYS IT'S A MIRACLE.
BUT IT TURNS OUT...

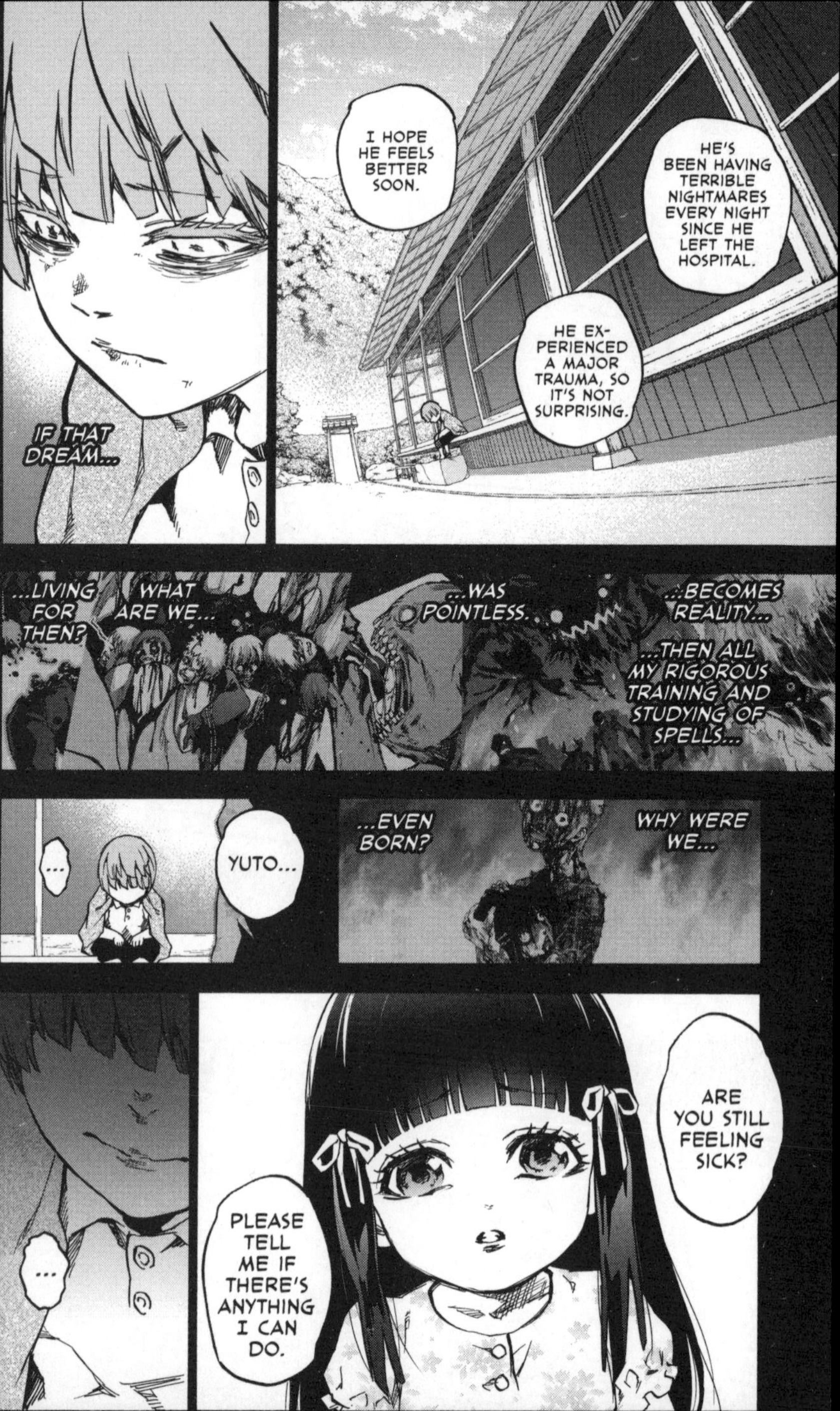
HE'S BEEN HAVING TERRIBLE NIGHTMARES EVERY NIGHT SINCE HE LEFT THE HOSPITAL.
HE EX-PERIENCED A MAJOR TRAUMA, SO IT'S NOT SURPRISING.
I HOPE HE FEELS BETTER SOON.
IF THAT DREAM...
...BECOMES REALITY...
...THEN ALL MY RIGOROUS TRAINING AND STUDYING OF SPELLS...
...WAS POINTLESS.
WHAT ARE WE...
...LIVING FOR THEN?
WHY WERE WE...
...EVEN BORN?
YUTO...
...
ARE YOU STILL FEELING SICK?
PLEASE TELL ME IF THERE'S ANYTHING I CAN DO.
...

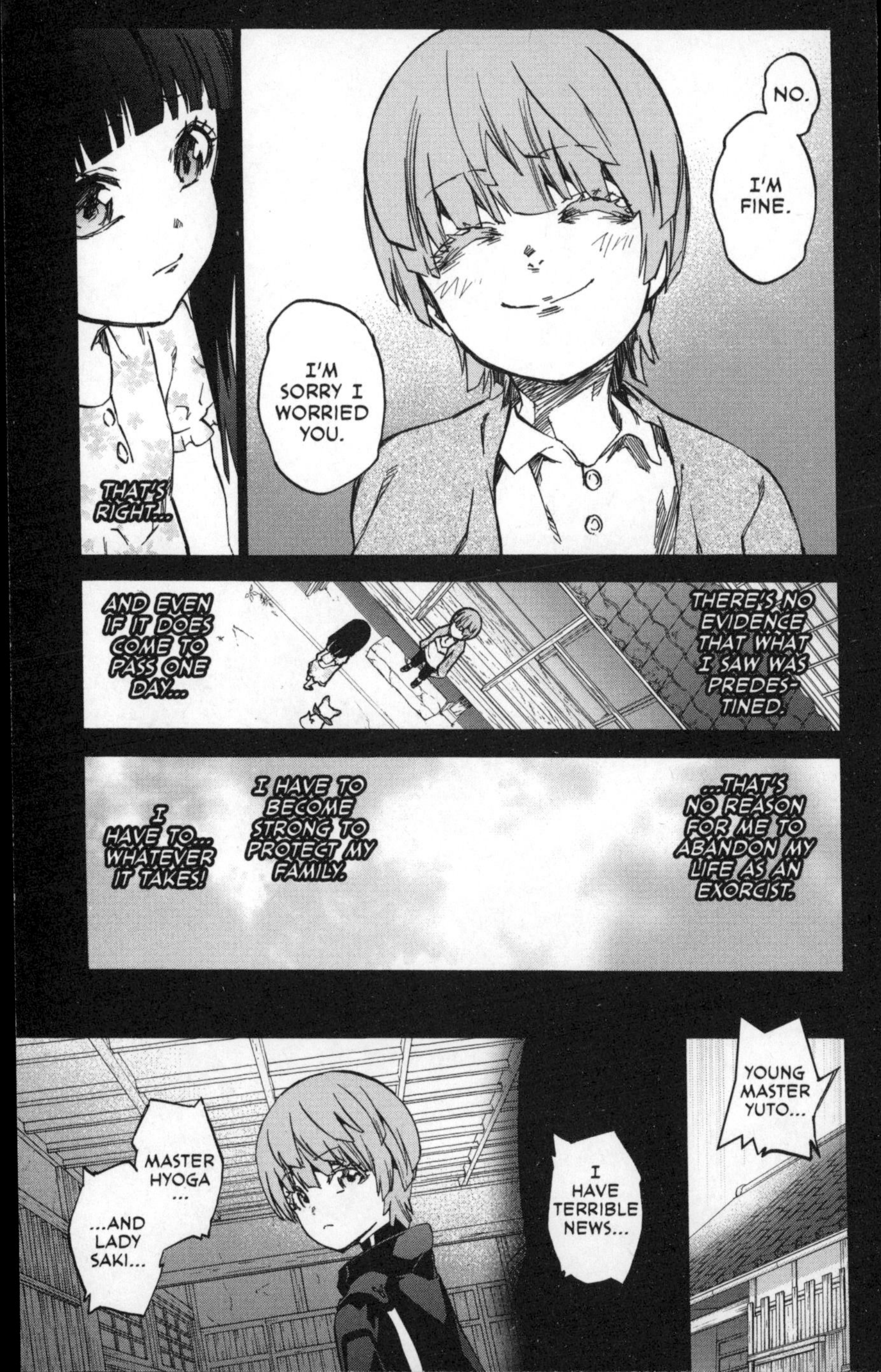
NO.
I'M FINE.
I'M SORRY I WORRIED YOU.
THAT'S RIGHT...
THERE'S NO EVIDENCE THAT WHAT I SAW WAS PREDES-TINED.
AND EVEN IF IT DOES COME TO PASS ONE DAY...
...THAT'S NO REASON FOR ME TO ABANDON MY LIFE AS AN EXORCIST.
I HAVE TO BECOME STRONG TO PROTECT MY FAMILY.
I HAVE TO... WHATEVER IT TAKES!
YOUNG MASTER YUTO...
I HAVE TERRIBLE NEWS...
MASTER HYOGA...
...AND LADY SAKI...

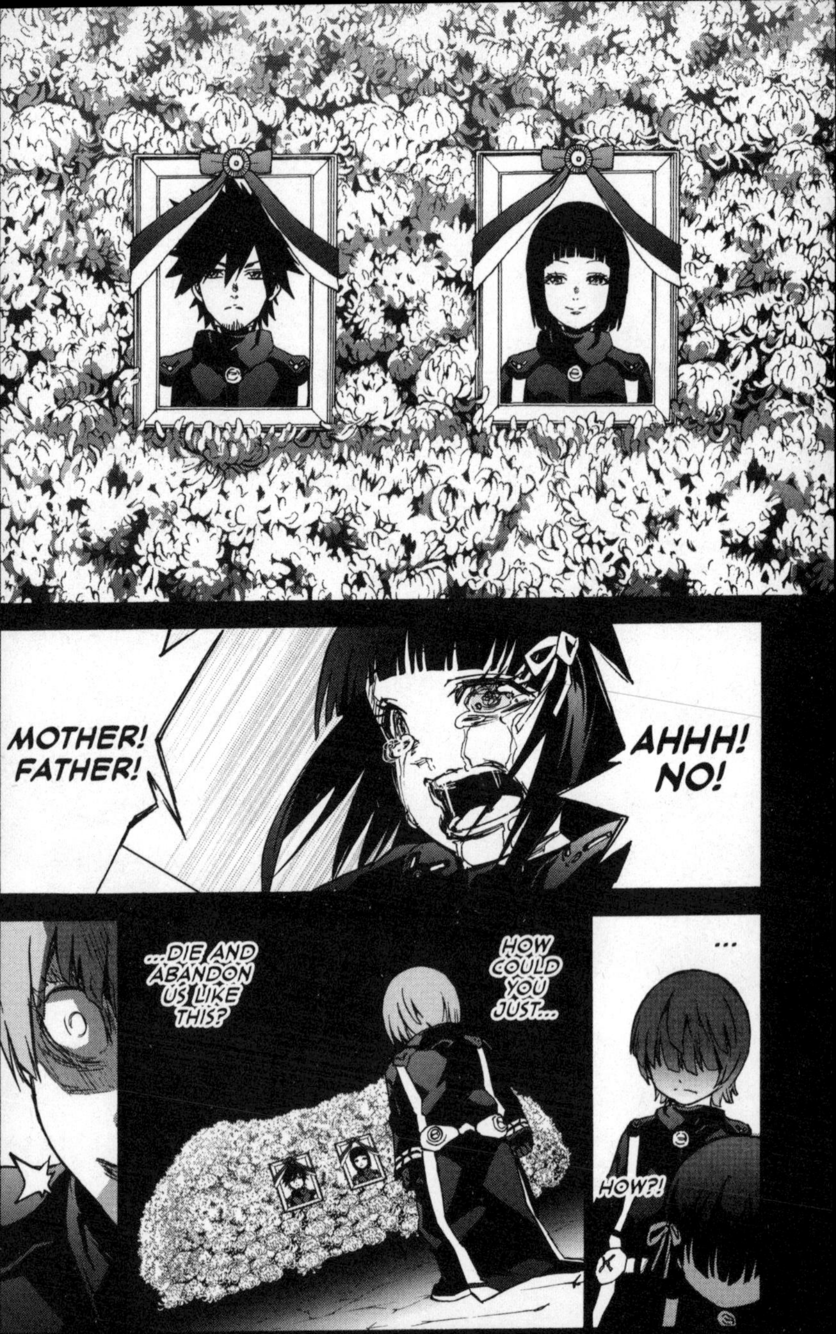
AHHH! NO!
MOTHER! FATHER!
...
HOW?!
HOW COULD YOU JUST...
...DIE AND ABANDON US LIKE THIS?

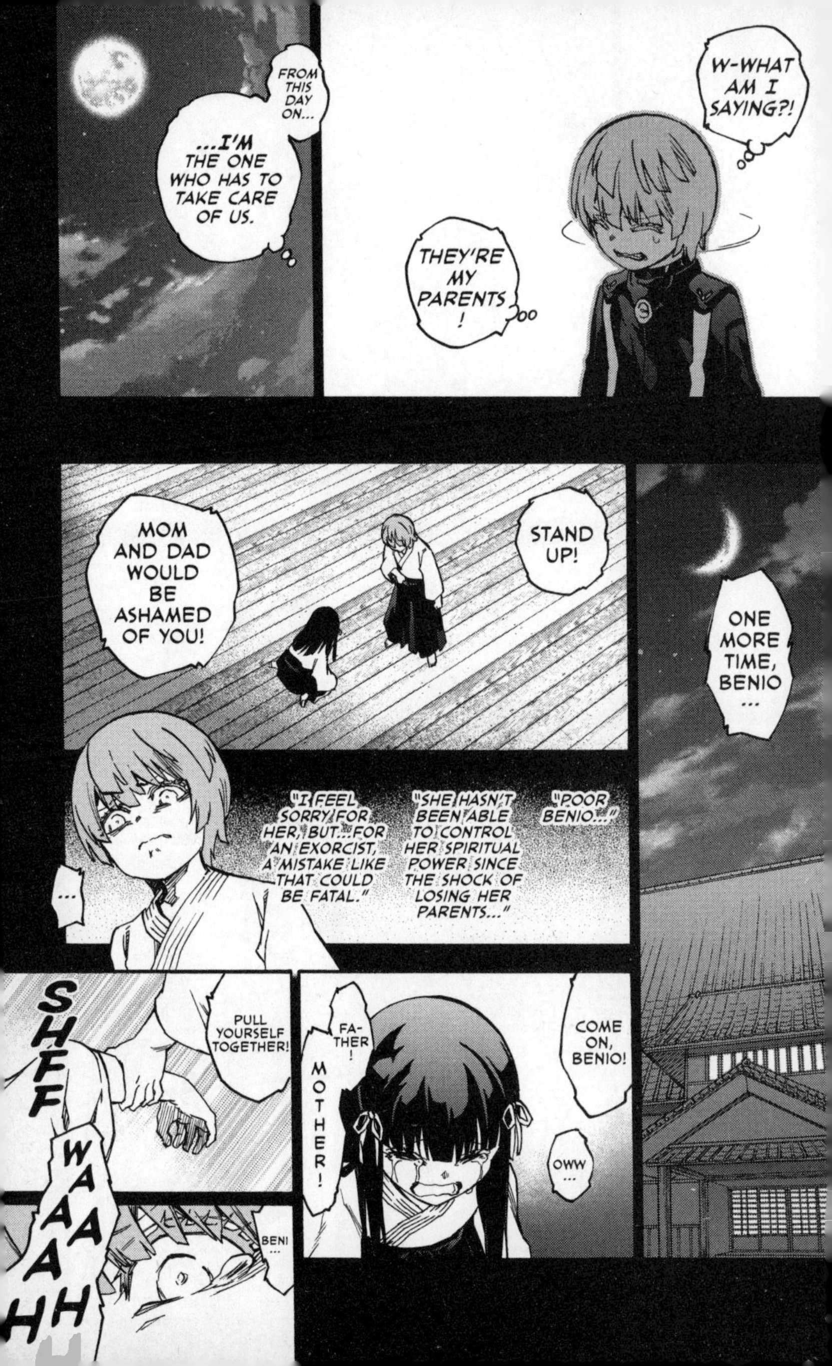
W-WHAT AM I SAYING?!
THEY'RE MY PARENTS!
FROM THIS DAY ON...
...I'M THE ONE WHO HAS TO TAKE CARE OF US.
ONE MORE TIME, BENIO...
STAND UP!
MOM AND DAD WOULD BE ASHAMED OF YOU!
"POOR BENIO..."
"SHE HASN'T BEEN ABLE TO CONTROL HER SPIRITUAL POWER SINCE THE SHOCK OF LOSING HER PARENTS..."
"I FEEL SORRY FOR HER, BUT...FOR AN EXORCIST, A MISTAKE LIKE THAT COULD BE FATAL."
...
COME ON, BENIO!
OWW...
FATHER!
MOTHER!
PULL YOURSELF TOGETHER!
SHFF
WAAAAHH
BENI...

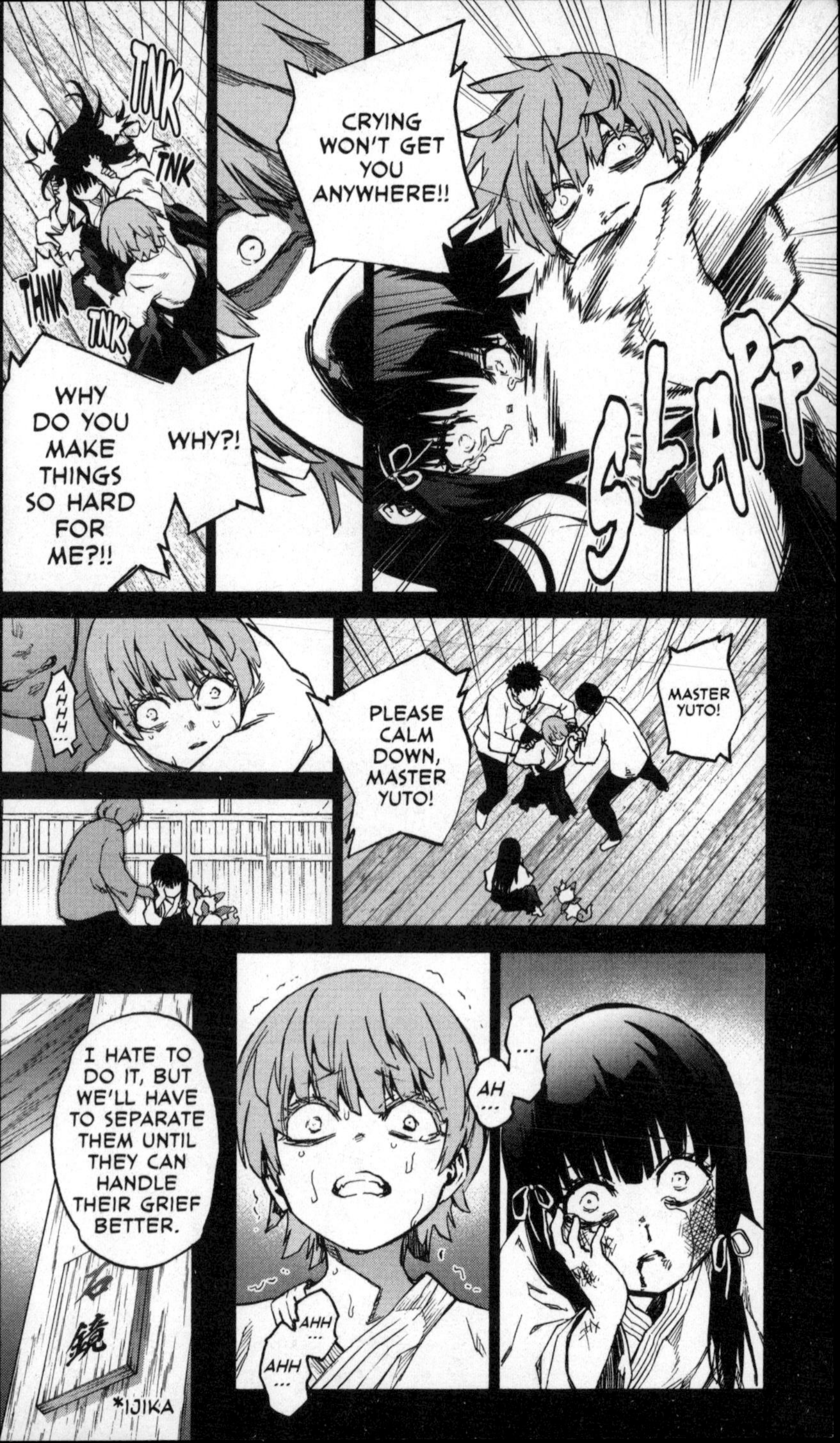
SLAPP
CRYING WON'T GET YOU ANYWHERE!!
TNK
TNK
THNK
TNK
WHY?!
WHY DO YOU MAKE THINGS SO HARD FOR ME?!!
MASTER YUTO!
PLEASE CALM DOWN, MASTER YUTO!
AHHH...
...
AH...
AHH...
AHH...
I HATE TO DO IT, BUT WE'LL HAVE TO SEPARATE THEM UNTIL THEY CAN HANDLE THEIR GRIEF BETTER.
石鏡
*IJIKA

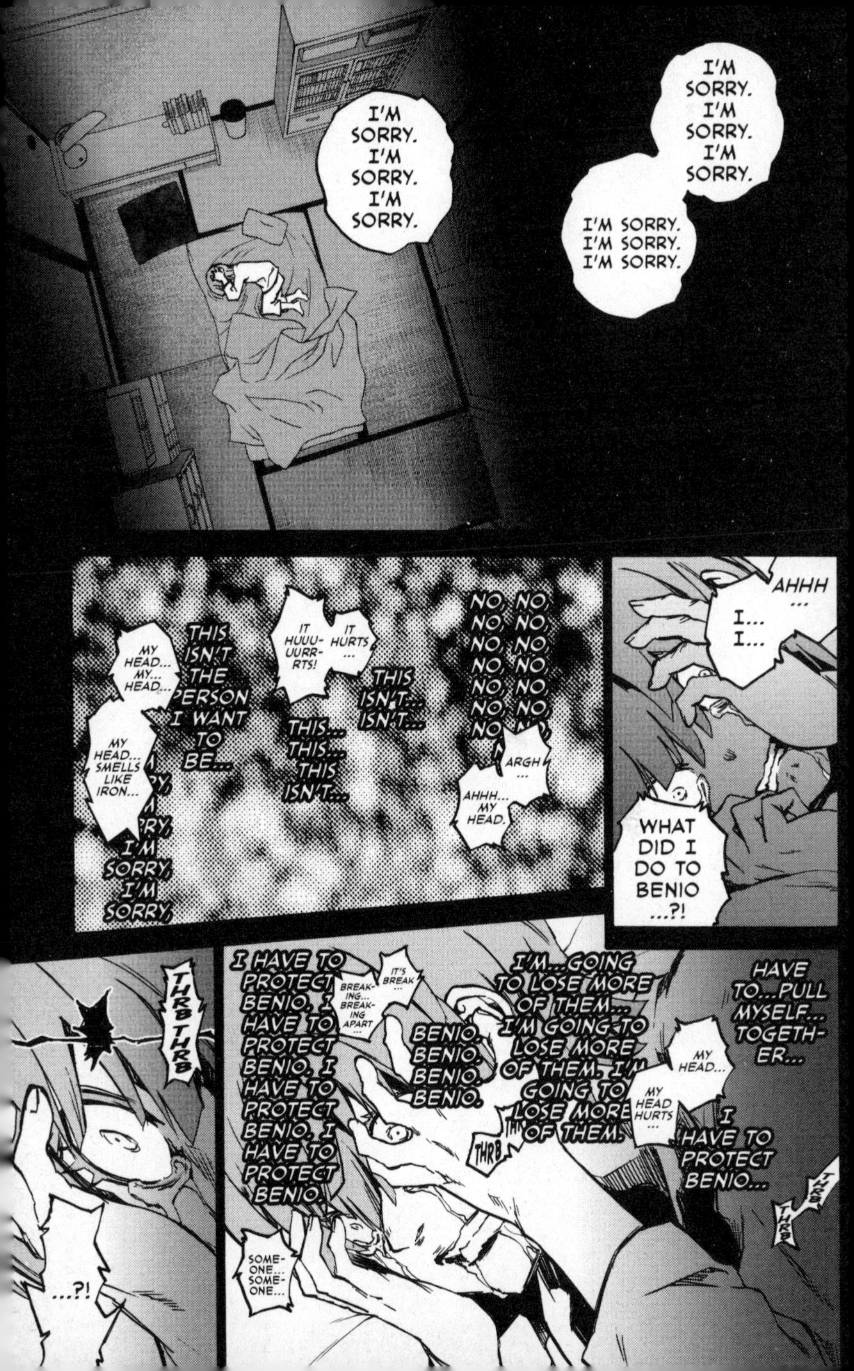
I'M SORRY. I'M SORRY. I'M SORRY.
I'M SORRY. I'M SORRY. I'M SORRY.
I'M SORRY. I'M SORRY. I'M SORRY.
AHHH... I... I...
WHAT DID I DO TO BENIO...?!
NO, NO, NO, NO, NO, NO, NO, NO, NO, NO, NO, NO, NO,
ARGH...
AHHH... MY HEAD.
IT HURTS...
IT HUUUUURRRTS!
THIS ISN'T... ISN'T...
THIS... THIS... THIS ISN'T...
THIS ISN'T THE PERSON I WANT TO BE...
MY HEAD... MY... HEAD...
MY HEAD... SMELLS LIKE IRON...
I'M SORRY, I'M SORRY,
HAVE TO... PULL MYSELF... TOGETHER...
MY HEAD...
MY HEAD HURTS...
I HAVE TO PROTECT BENIO...
THRB THRB
I'M... GOING TO LOSE MORE OF THEM... I'M GOING TO LOSE MORE OF THEM. I'M GOING TO LOSE MORE OF THEM.
THRB
BENIO. BENIO. BENIO. BENIO.
IT'S BREAK...
BREAKING... BREAKING APART...
I HAVE TO PROTECT BENIO. I HAVE TO PROTECT BENIO. I HAVE TO PROTECT BENIO. I HAVE TO PROTECT BENIO.
SOMEONE... SOMEONE...
THRB THRB
...?!

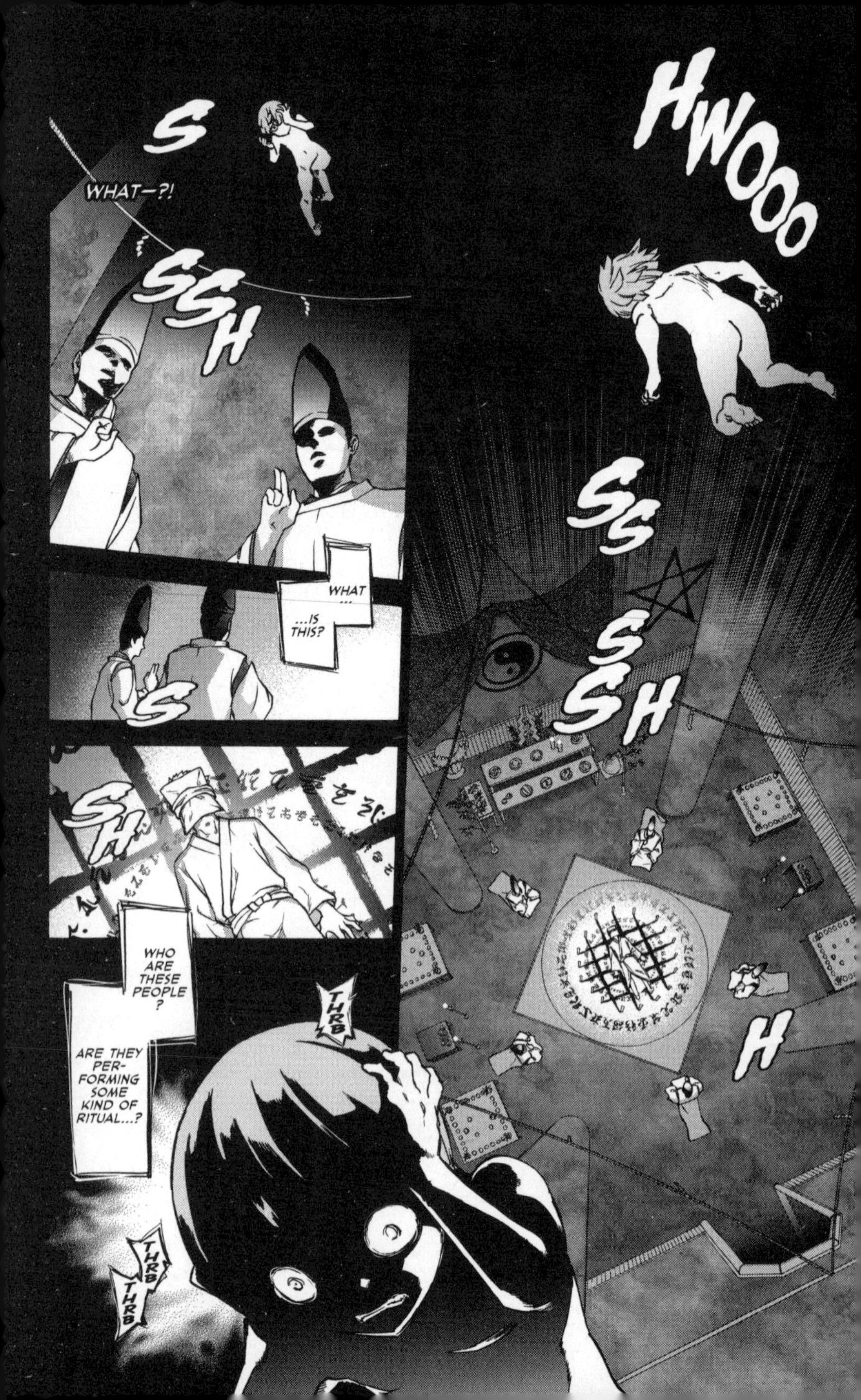
HWOOOO
SS
SSH
H
S
WHAT—?!
SSH
WHAT...
...IS THIS?
S
SH
WHO ARE THESE PEOPLE?
ARE THEY PER-FORMING SOME KIND OF RITUAL...?
THRB
THRB
THRB

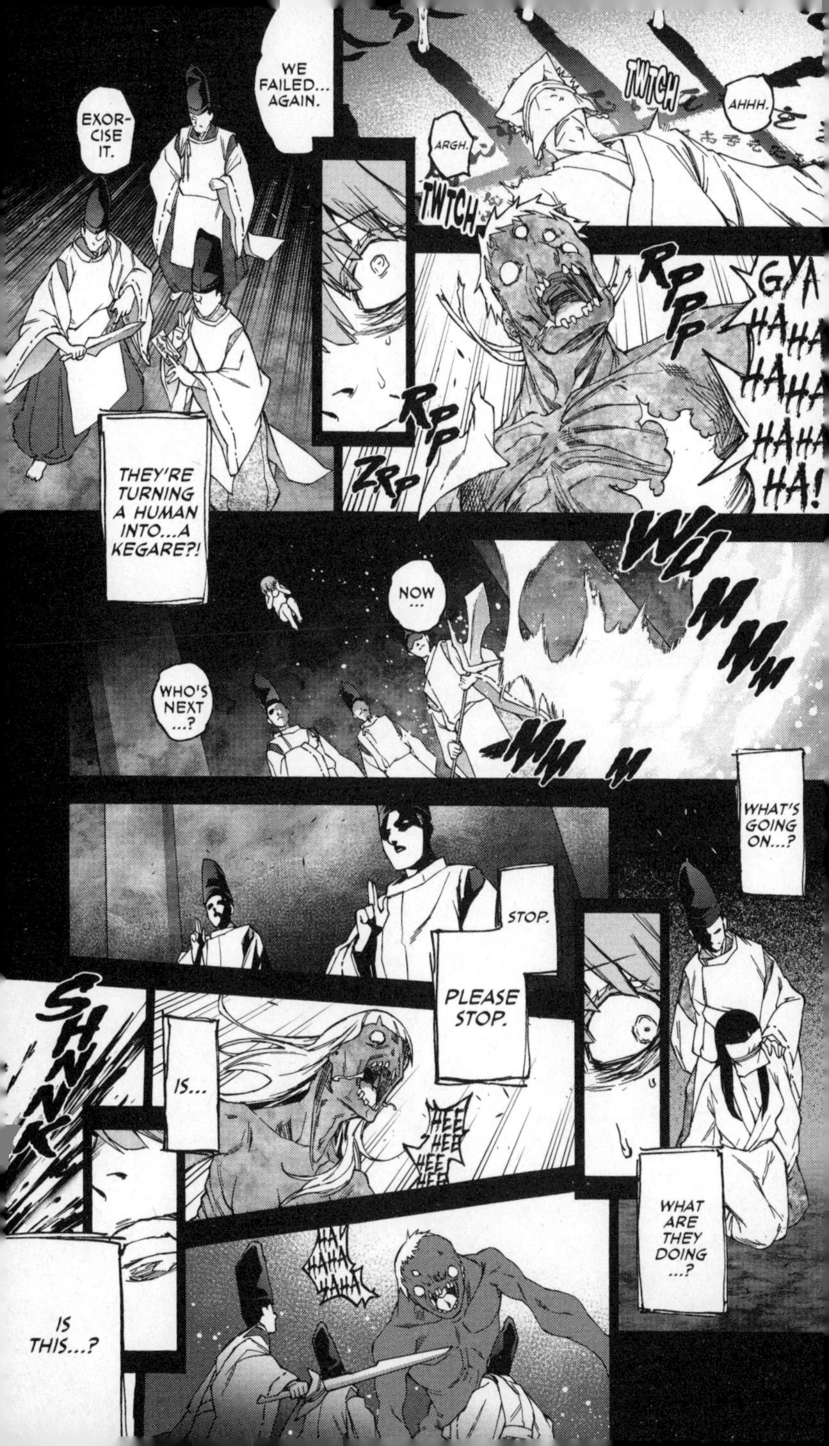
AHHH.
TWTCH
ARGH.
TWTCH
GYAHAHAHAHAHAHAHA!
RPPP
RPP
ZPP
WE FAILED... AGAIN.
EXORCISE IT.
THEY'RE TURNING A HUMAN INTO...A KEGARE?!
WUMMMMMMM
NOW...
WHO'S NEXT...?
WHAT'S GOING ON...?
STOP.
PLEASE STOP.
WHAT ARE THEY DOING...?
IS...
HEE HEE HEE HEE
SHNNK
HAHAHAHAHA
IS THIS...?

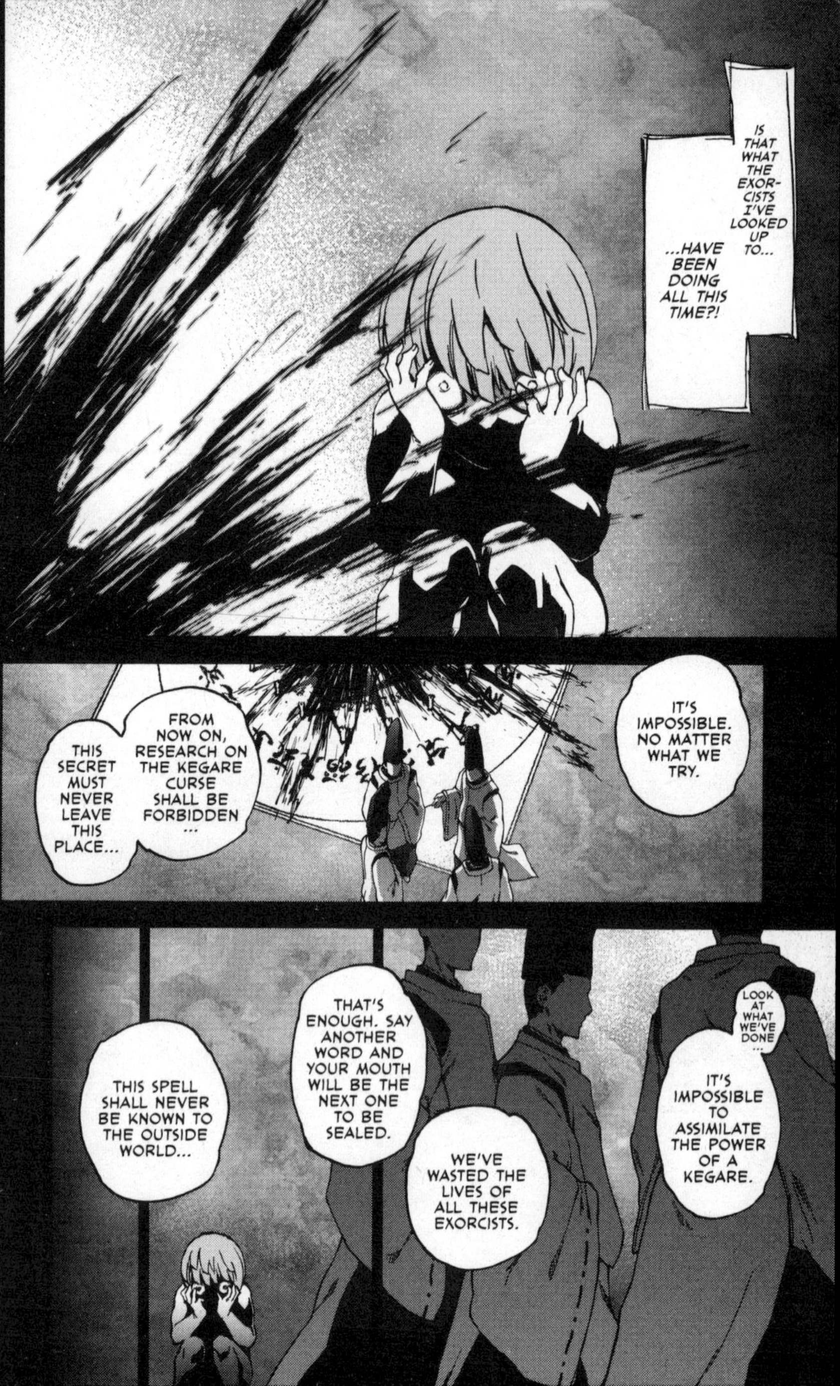
IS THAT WHAT THE EXORCISTS I'VE LOOKED UP TO...
...HAVE BEEN DOING ALL THIS TIME?!
IT'S IMPOSSIBLE. NO MATTER WHAT WE TRY.
FROM NOW ON, RESEARCH ON THE KEGARE CURSE SHALL BE FORBIDDEN...
THIS SECRET MUST NEVER LEAVE THIS PLACE...
LOOK AT WHAT WE'VE DONE...
IT'S IMPOSSIBLE TO ASSIMILATE THE POWER OF A KEGARE.
THAT'S ENOUGH. SAY ANOTHER WORD AND YOUR MOUTH WILL BE THE NEXT ONE TO BE SEALED.
WE'VE WASTED THE LIVES OF ALL THESE EXORCISTS.
THIS SPELL SHALL NEVER BE KNOWN TO THE OUTSIDE WORLD...

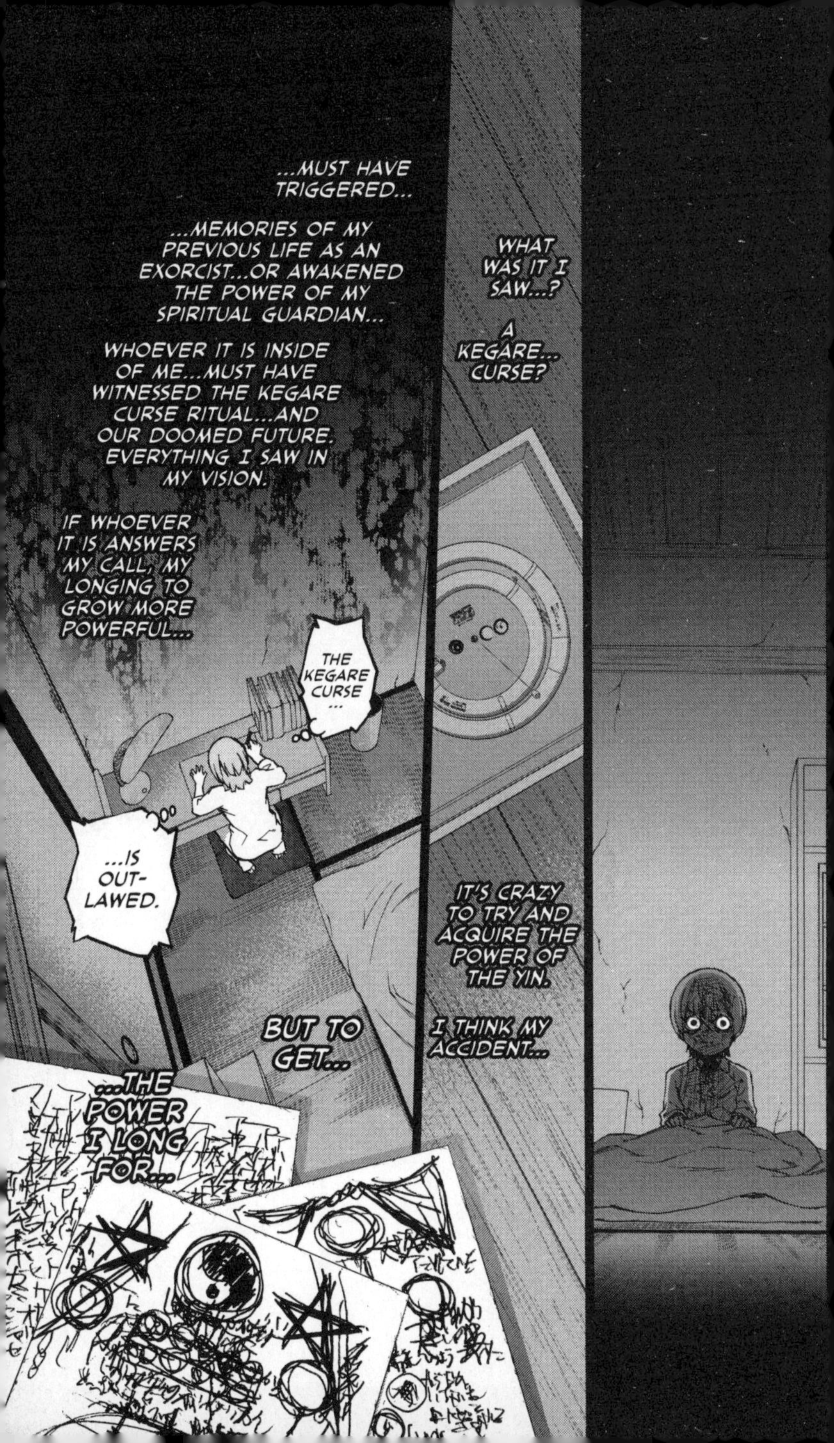
WHAT WAS IT I SAW...?
A KEGARE... CURSE?
IT'S CRAZY TO TRY AND ACQUIRE THE POWER OF THE YIN.
I THINK MY ACCIDENT...
...MUST HAVE TRIGGERED...
...MEMORIES OF MY PREVIOUS LIFE AS AN EXORCIST...OR AWAKENED THE POWER OF MY SPIRITUAL GUARDIAN...
WHOEVER IT IS INSIDE OF ME...MUST HAVE WITNESSED THE KEGARE CURSE RITUAL...AND OUR DOOMED FUTURE. EVERYTHING I SAW IN MY VISION.
IF WHOEVER IT IS ANSWERS MY CALL, MY LONGING TO GROW MORE POWERFUL...
THE KEGARE CURSE...
...IS OUT-LAWED.
BUT TO GET...
...THE POWER I LONG FOR...

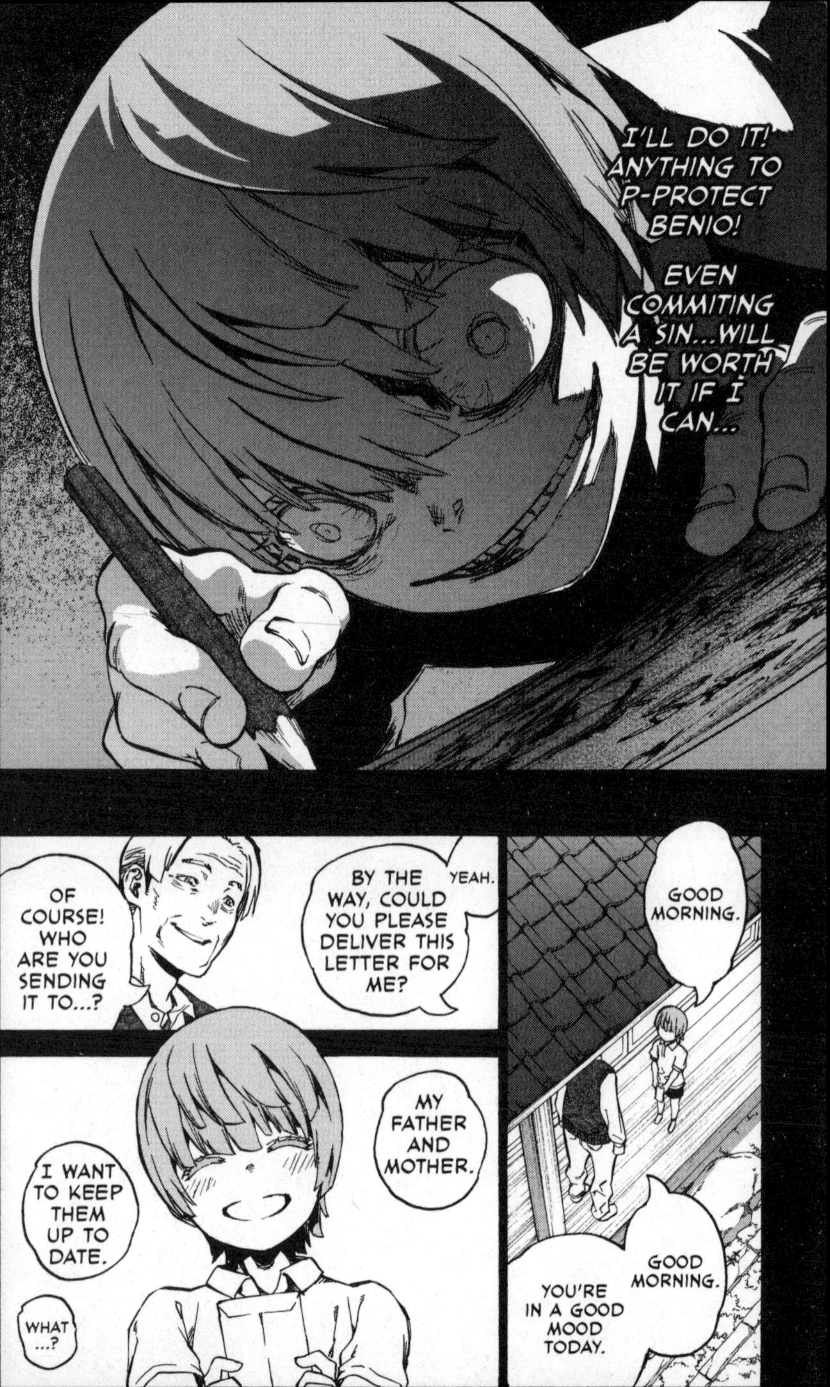

I'LL DO IT! ANYTHING TO P-PROTECT BENIO!
EVEN COMMITING A SIN...WILL BE WORTH IT IF I CAN...
GOOD MORNING.
GOOD MORNING.
YOU'RE IN A GOOD MOOD TODAY.
YEAH.
BY THE WAY, COULD YOU PLEASE DELIVER THIS LETTER FOR ME?
OF COURSE! WHO ARE YOU SENDING IT TO...?
MY FATHER AND MOTHER.
I WANT TO KEEP THEM UP TO DATE.
WHAT ...?

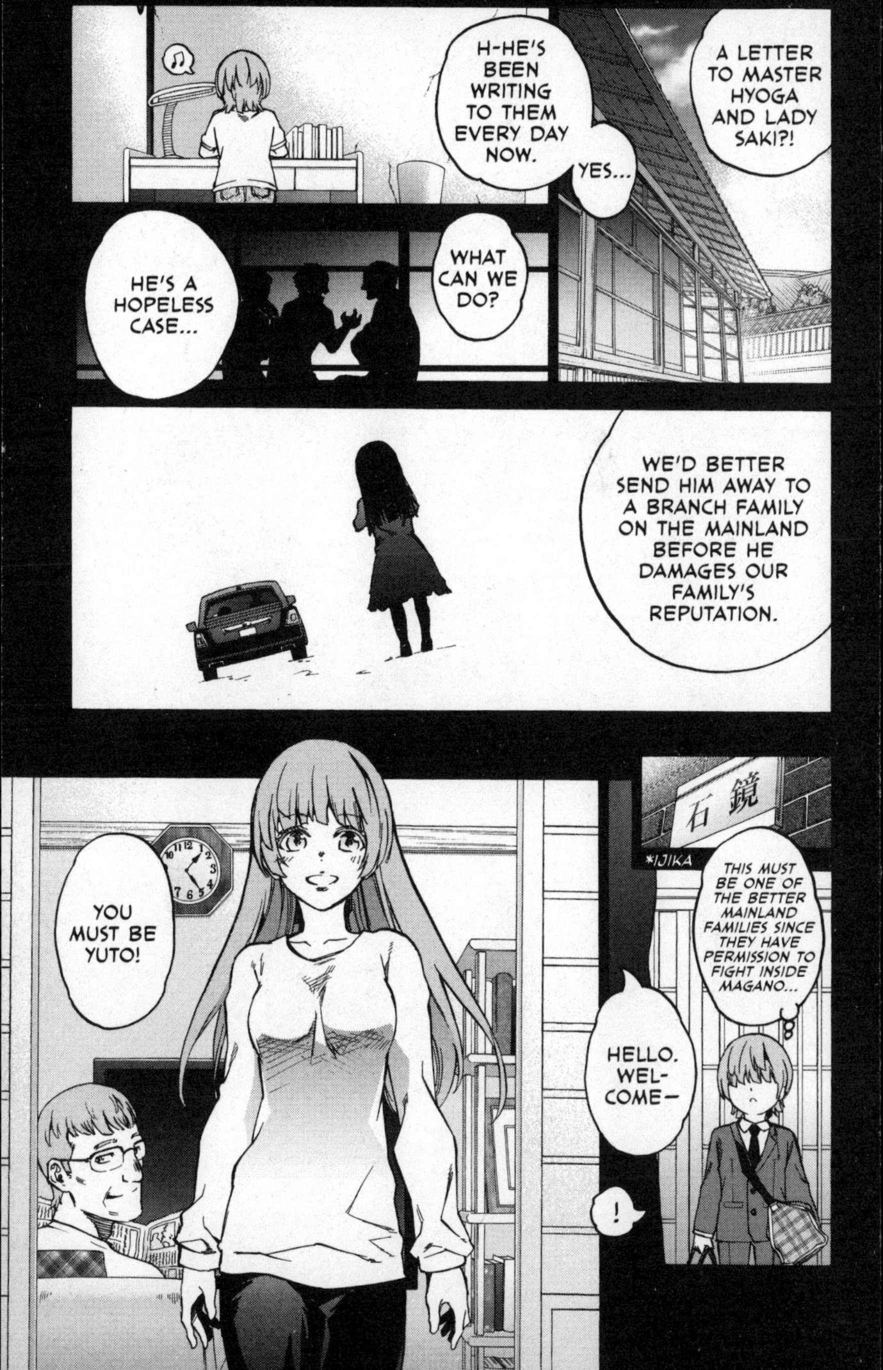
A LETTER TO MASTER HYOGA AND LADY SAKI?!
YES...
H-HE'S BEEN WRITING TO THEM EVERY DAY NOW.
♫
WHAT CAN WE DO?
HE'S A HOPELESS CASE...
WE'D BETTER SEND HIM AWAY TO A BRANCH FAMILY ON THE MAINLAND BEFORE HE DAMAGES OUR FAMILY'S REPUTATION.
石鏡
*IJIKA
THIS MUST BE ONE OF THE BETTER MAINLAND FAMILIES SINCE THEY HAVE PERMISSION TO FIGHT INSIDE MAGANO...
HELLO. WEL-COME—
!
YOU MUST BE YUTO!

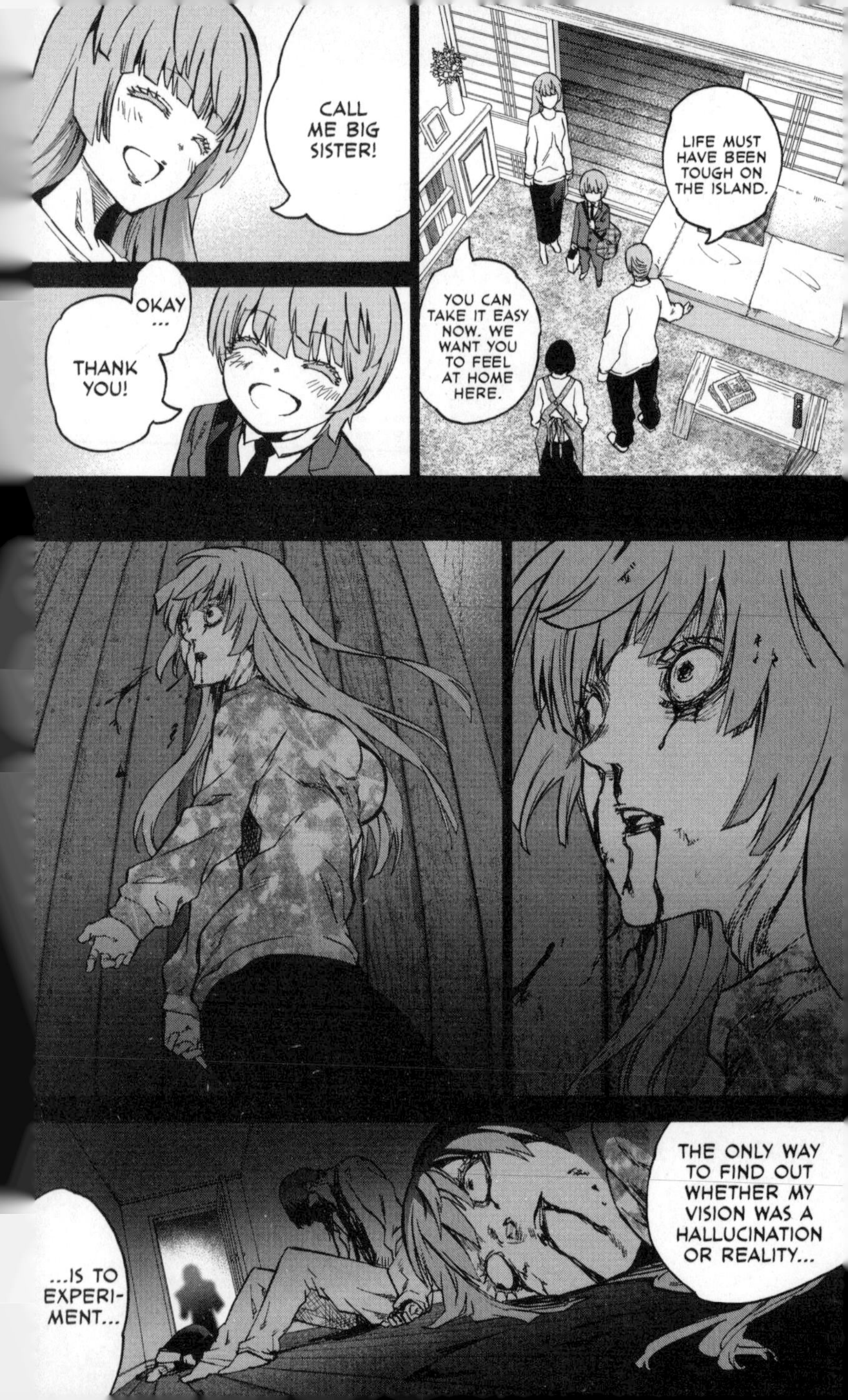
LIFE MUST HAVE BEEN TOUGH ON THE ISLAND.
YOU CAN TAKE IT EASY NOW. WE WANT YOU TO FEEL AT HOME HERE.
CALL ME BIG SISTER!
OKAY...
THANK YOU!
THE ONLY WAY TO FIND OUT WHETHER MY VISION WAS A HALLUCINATION OR REALITY...
...IS TO EXPERIMENT...

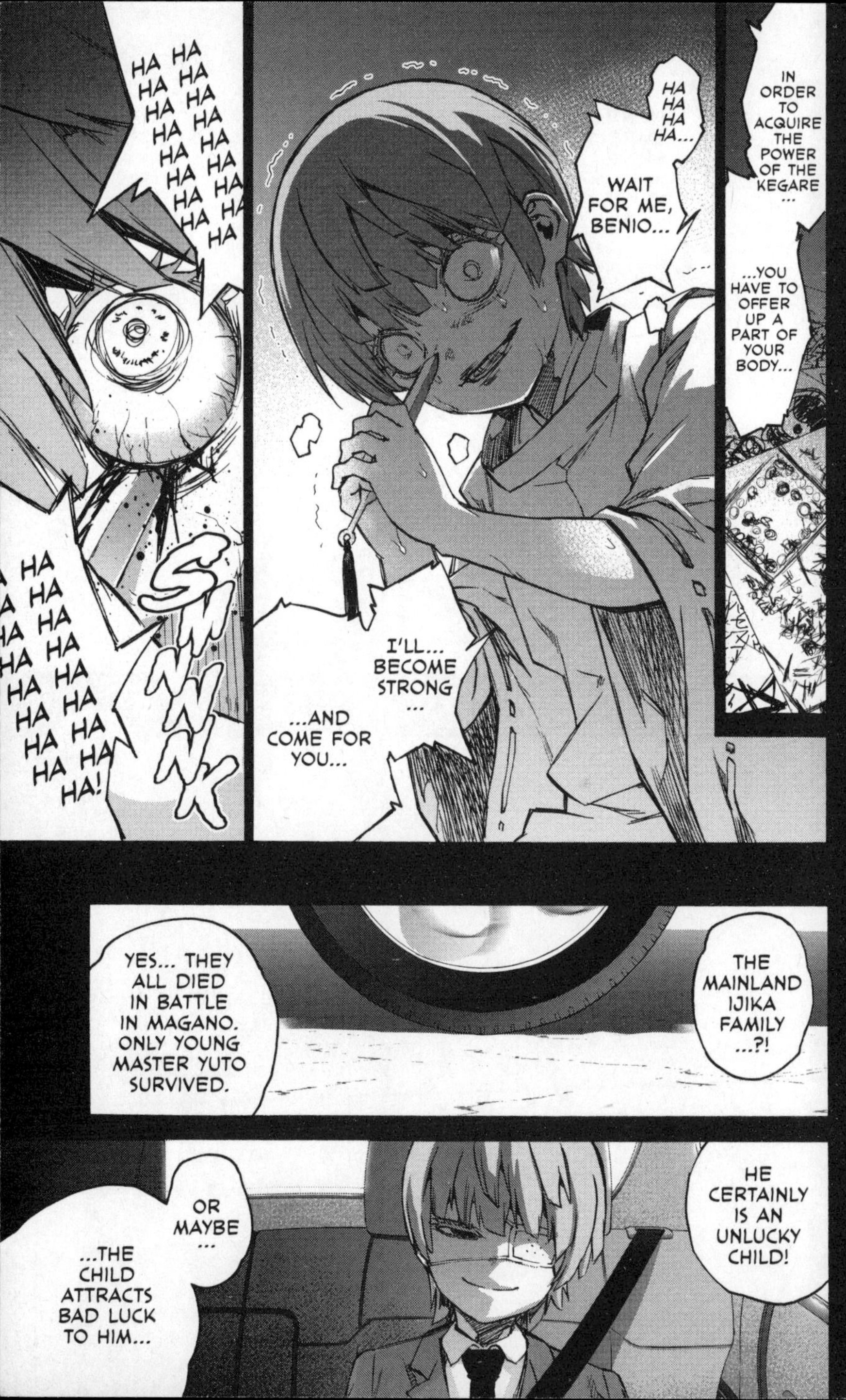

IN ORDER TO ACQUIRE THE POWER OF THE KEGARE...
...YOU HAVE TO OFFER UP A PART OF YOUR BODY...
HA HA HA HA...
WAIT FOR ME, BENIO...
I'LL... BECOME STRONG...
...AND COME FOR YOU...
HA HA HA HA HA HA HA HA HA HA HA HA HA HA HA HA HA
SHNNNK
HA HA HA HA HA HA HA HA HA HA HA HA HA HA HA HA HA!
THE MAINLAND IJIKA FAMILY...?!
YES... THEY ALL DIED IN BATTLE IN MAGANO. ONLY YOUNG MASTER YUTO SURVIVED.
HE CERTAINLY IS AN UNLUCKY CHILD!
OR MAYBE...
...THE CHILD ATTRACTS BAD LUCK TO HIM...

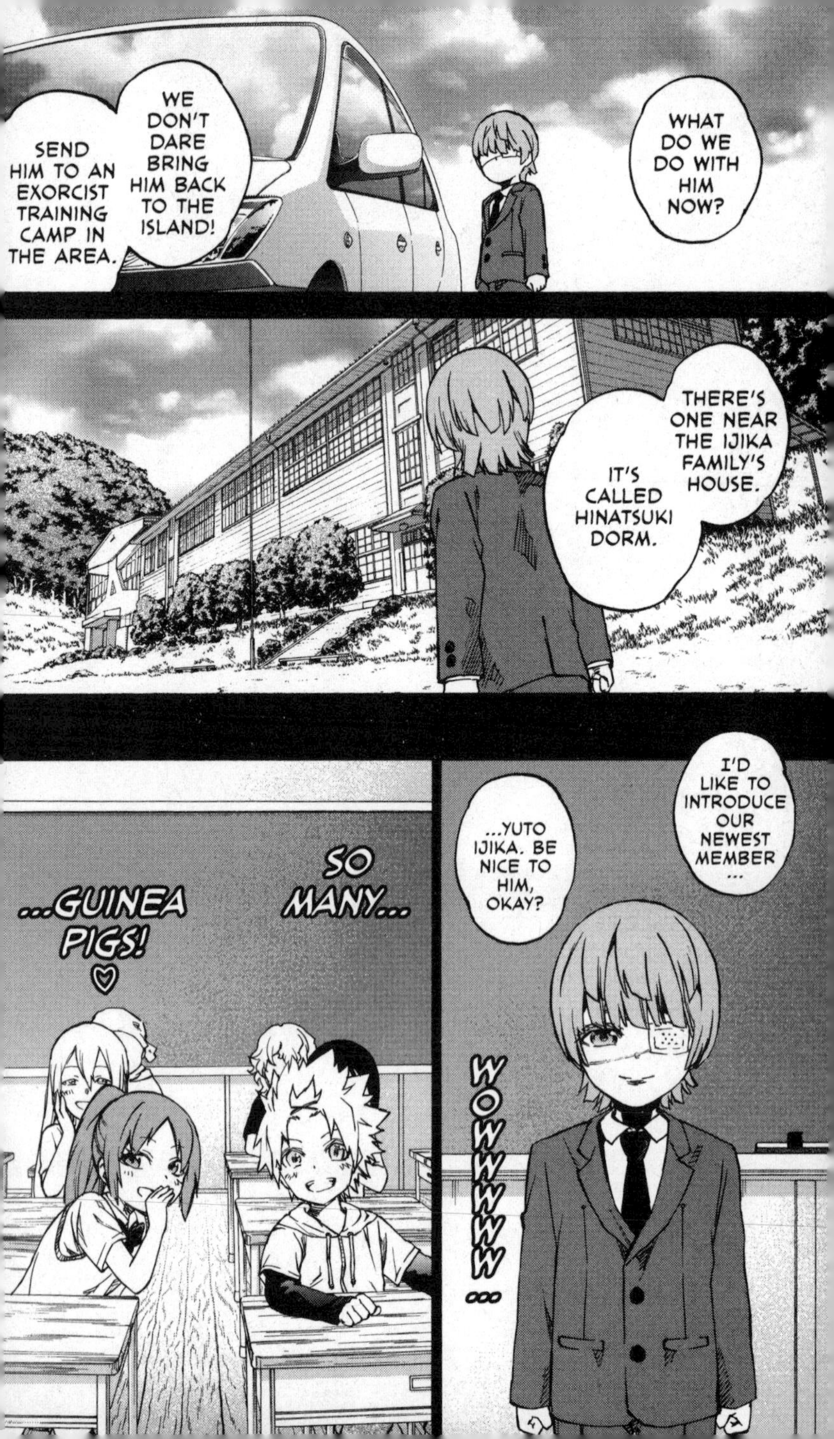
WHAT DO WE DO WITH HIM NOW?
WE DON'T DARE BRING HIM BACK TO THE ISLAND!
SEND HIM TO AN EXORCIST TRAINING CAMP IN THE AREA.
THERE'S ONE NEAR THE IJIKA FAMILY'S HOUSE.
IT'S CALLED HINATSUKI DORM.
I'D LIKE TO INTRODUCE OUR NEWEST MEMBER...
...YUTO IJIKA. BE NICE TO HIM, OKAY?
WOWWWWWW...
SO MANY...
...GUINEA PIGS! ♡

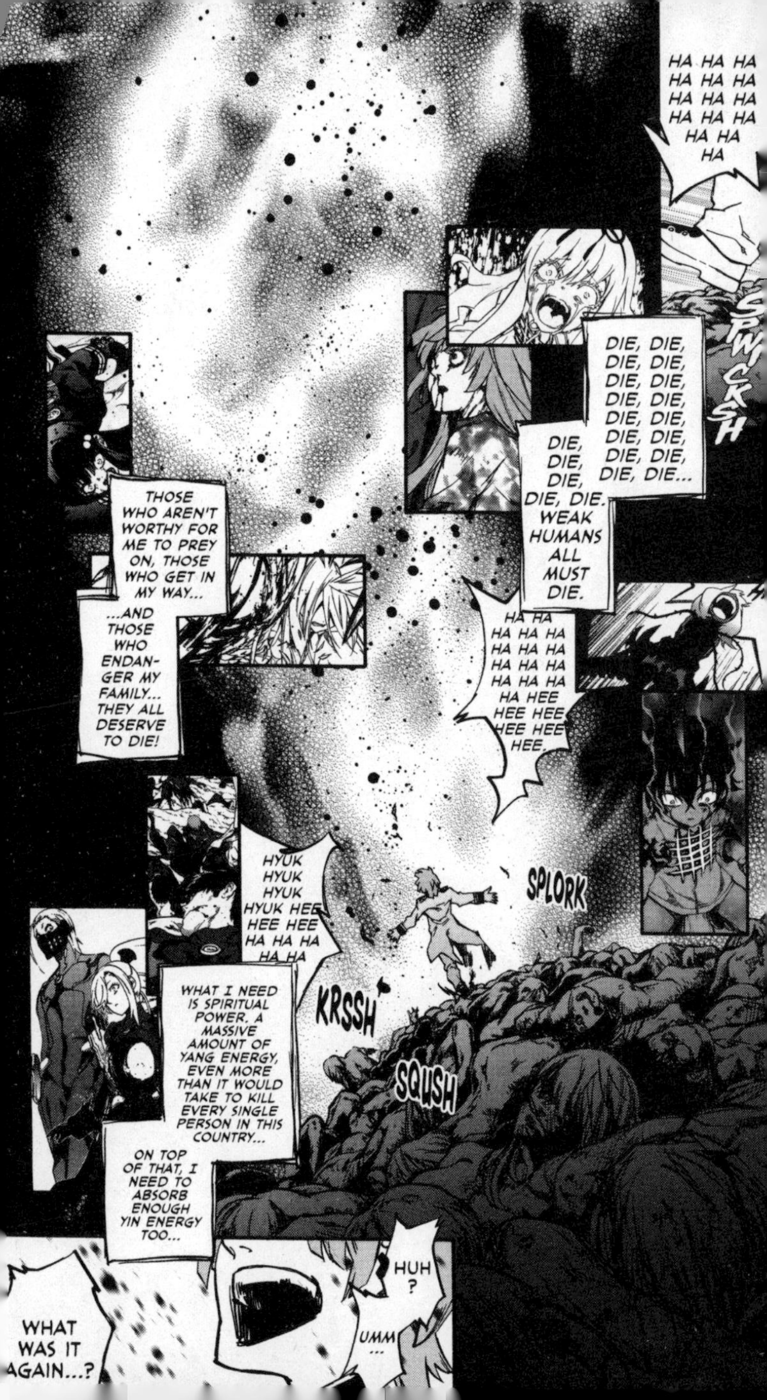

HA HA HA HA HA HA HA HA HA HA HA HA HA HA HA
SPWICKSH
DIE, DIE, DIE, DIE, DIE, DIE, DIE, DIE, DIE, DIE, DIE, DIE, DIE, DIE, DIE, DIE...
DIE, DIE, DIE, DIE, DIE. WEAK HUMANS ALL MUST DIE.
THOSE WHO AREN'T WORTHY FOR ME TO PREY ON, THOSE WHO GET IN MY WAY...
...AND THOSE WHO ENDANGER MY FAMILY... THEY ALL DESERVE TO DIE!
HA HA HA HA HA HA HA HA HA HA HA HA HA HA HA HA HEE HEE HEE HEE HEE HEE.
SPLORK
HYUK HYUK HYUK HYUK HEE HEE HEE HA HA HA HA HA
KRSSH
WHAT I NEED IS SPIRITUAL POWER. A MASSIVE AMOUNT OF YANG ENERGY, EVEN MORE THAN IT WOULD TAKE TO KILL EVERY SINGLE PERSON IN THIS COUNTRY...
SQUSH
ON TOP OF THAT, I NEED TO ABSORB ENOUGH YIN ENERGY TOO...
HUH?
UMM...
WHAT WAS IT AGAIN...?

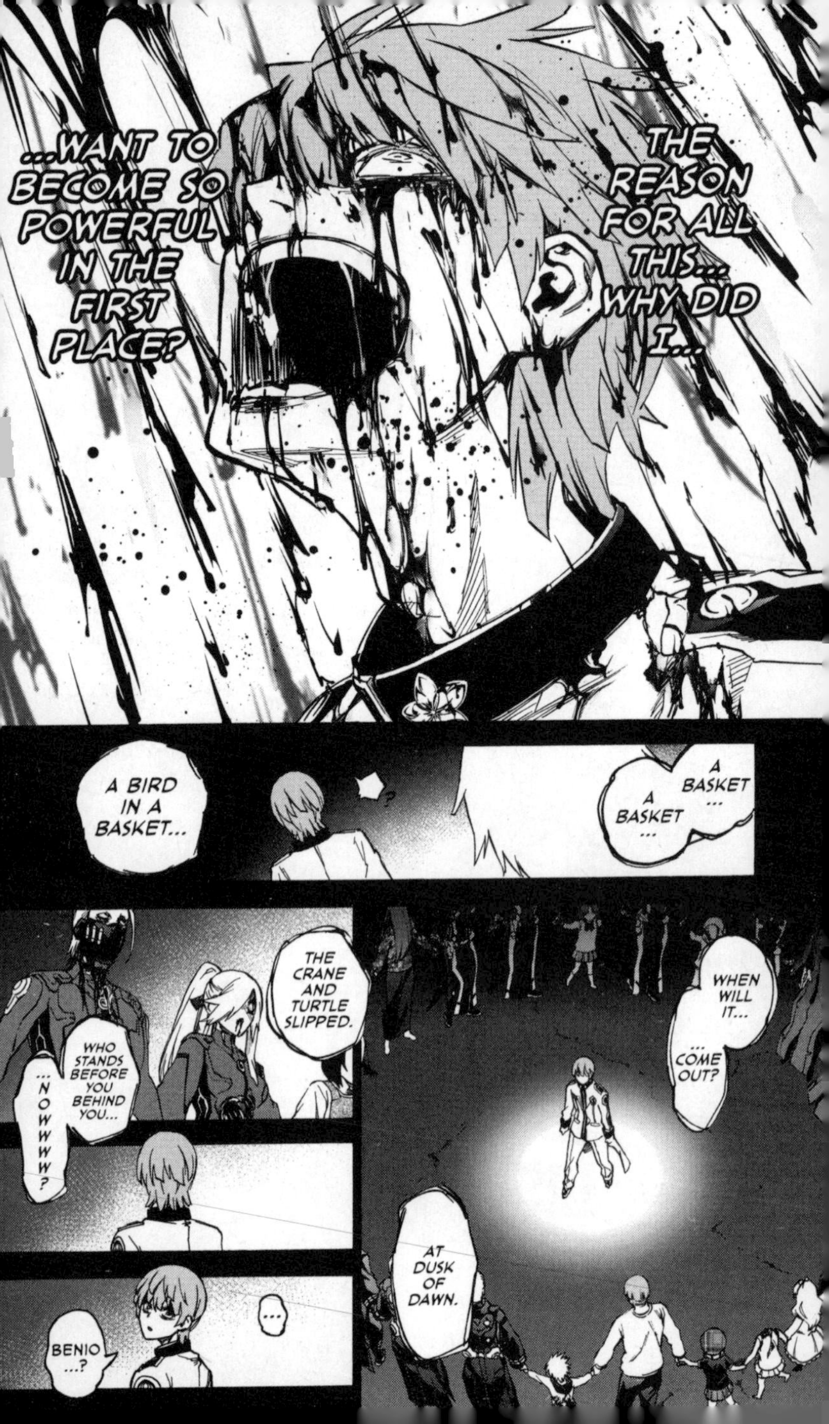
THE REASON FOR ALL THIS... WHY DID I...
...WANT TO BECOME SO POWERFUL IN THE FIRST PLACE?
A BASKET ...
A BASKET ...
A BIRD IN A BASKET...
WHEN WILL IT...
...COME OUT?
AT DUSK OF DAWN.
THE CRANE AND TURTLE SLIPPED.
WHO STANDS BEFORE YOU BEHIND YOU...
...NOWWWWW?
...
BENIO ...?

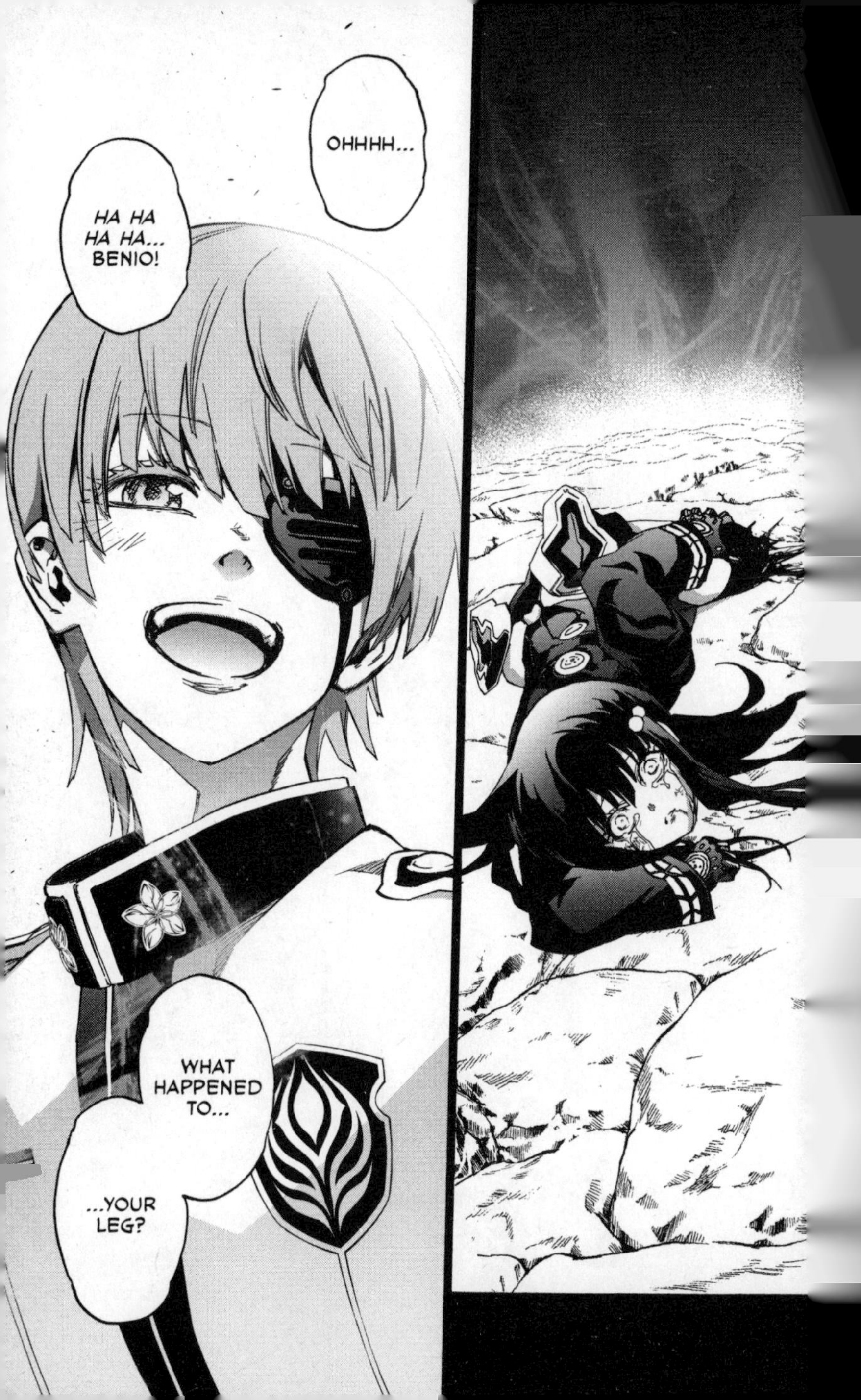
OHHHH...
HA HA HA HA... BENIO!
WHAT HAPPENED TO...
...YOUR LEG?

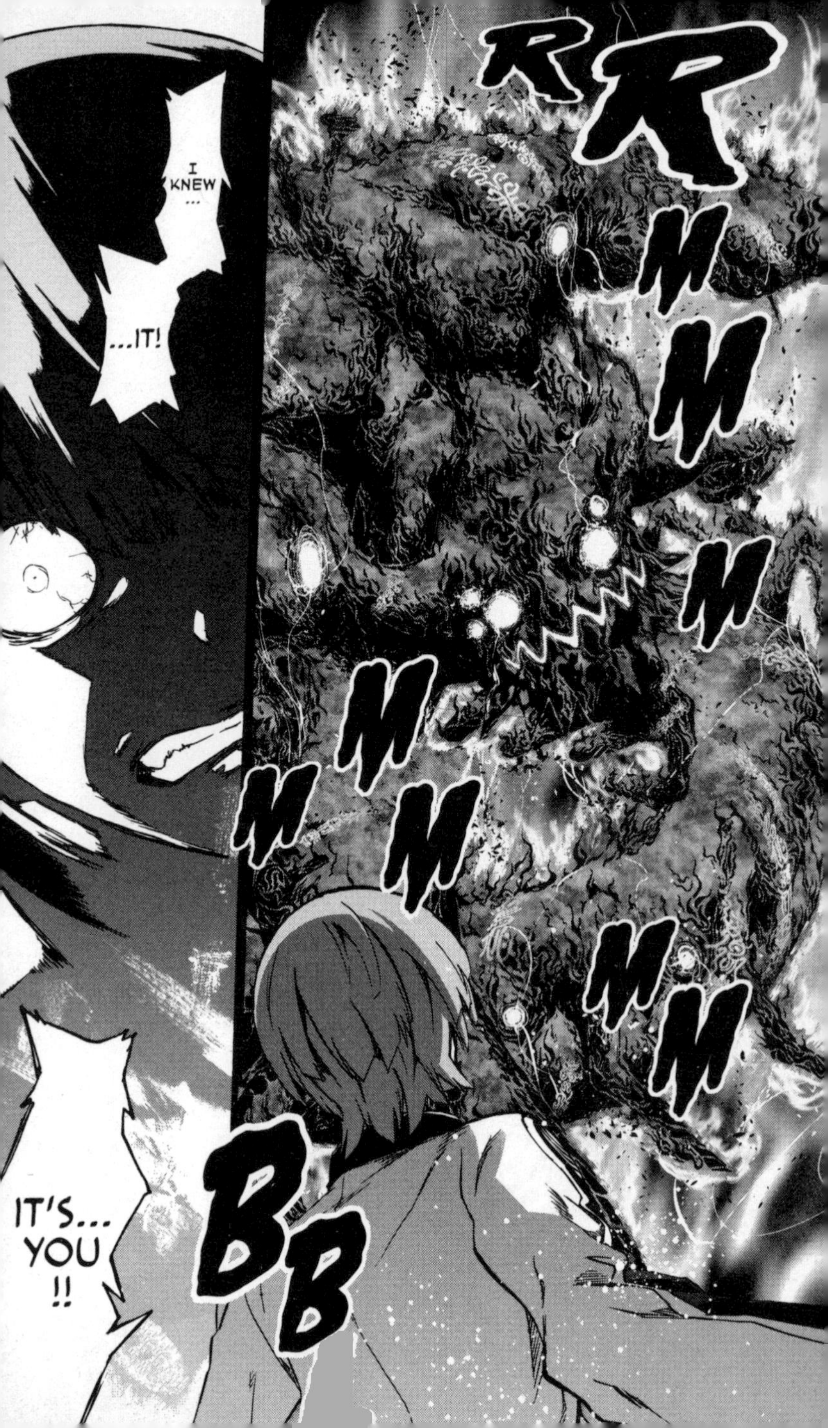
RRMMMMMMMM
BB
I KNEW...
...IT!
IT'S... YOU!!

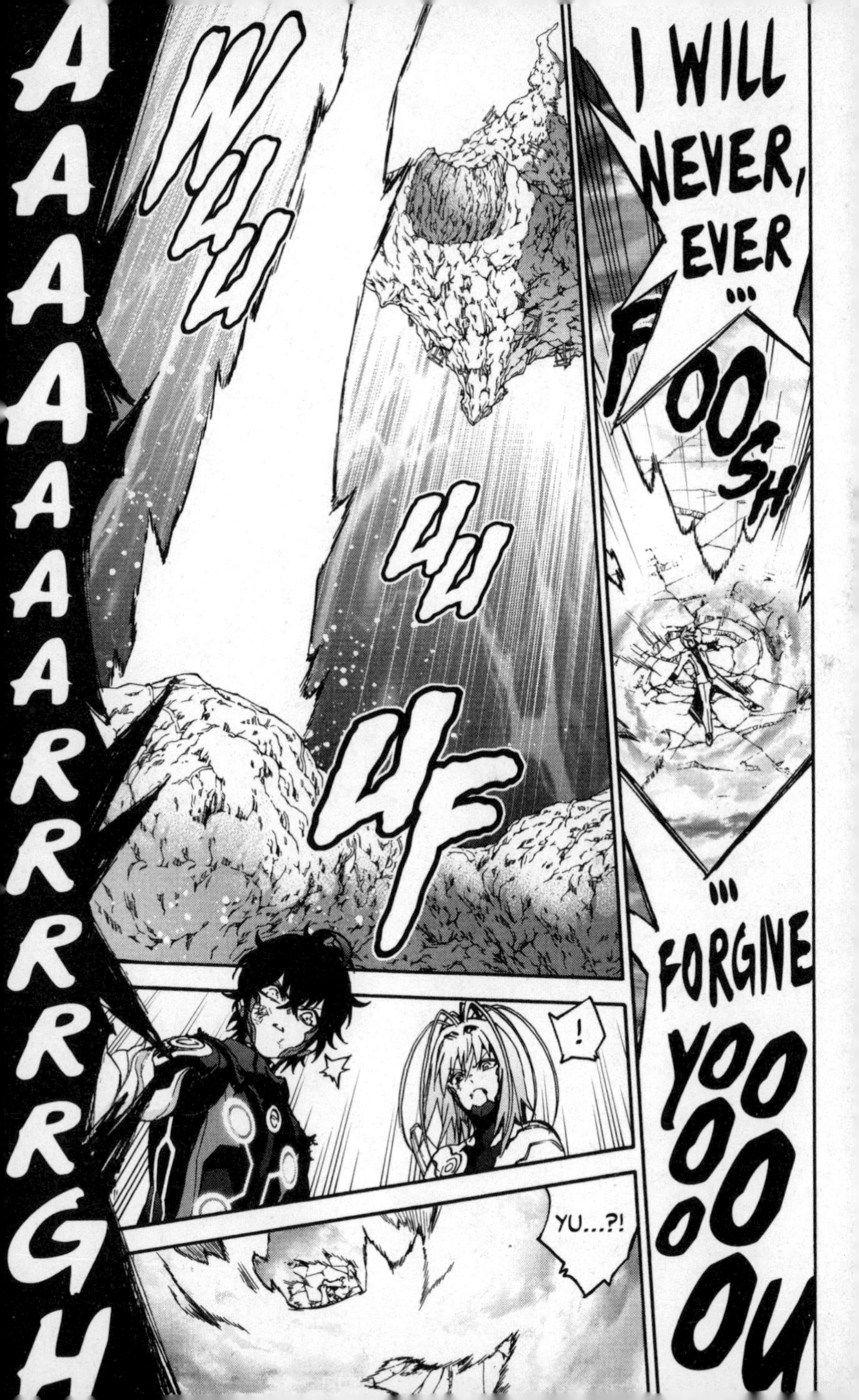
I WILL NEVER, EVER...
FOOSH
...FORGIVE YOOOOOOOU
WHUUUUUF
!
YU...?!
AAAAAAARRRRRRGH

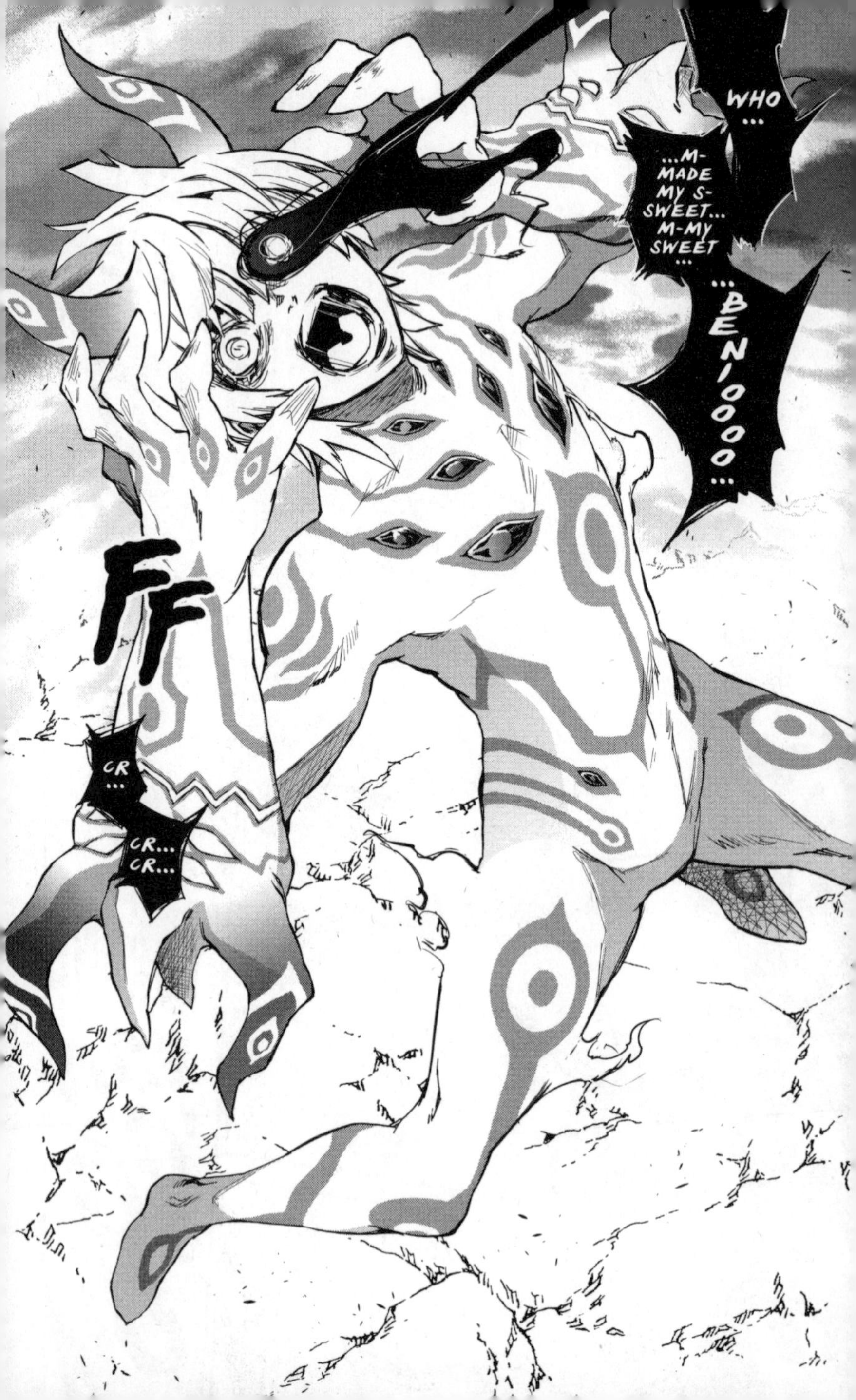
WHO...
...M-MADE MY S-SWEET... M-MY SWEET...
...BENIOOOO...
FF
CR...
CR... CR...

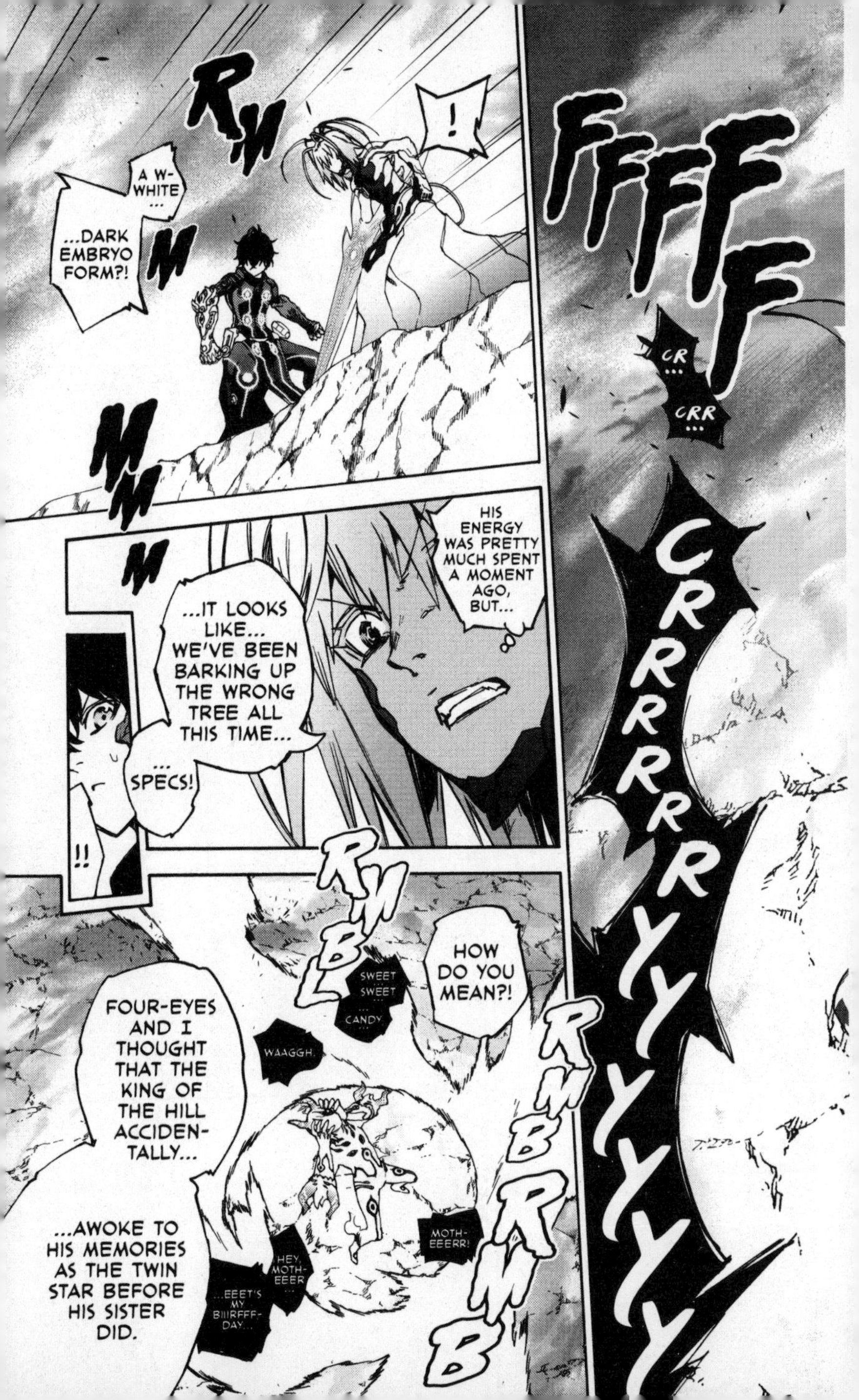
FFFFF
CR...
CRR...
CRRRRRRYYYYYY
RMMMMMM
!
A W-WHITE...
...DARK EMBRYO FORM?!
HIS ENERGY WAS PRETTY MUCH SPENT A MOMENT AGO, BUT...
...IT LOOKS LIKE... WE'VE BEEN BARKING UP THE WRONG TREE ALL THIS TIME...
...SPECS!
!!
RMBL
RMBRMB
HOW DO YOU MEAN?!
SWEET... SWEET... CANDY...
FOUR-EYES AND I THOUGHT THAT THE KING OF THE HILL ACCIDENTALLY...
WAAGGH.
MOTH-EEERR!
HEY, MOTH-EEER...
...EEET'S MY BIIIRFFF-DAY...
...AWOKE TO HIS MEMORIES AS THE TWIN STAR BEFORE HIS SISTER DID.

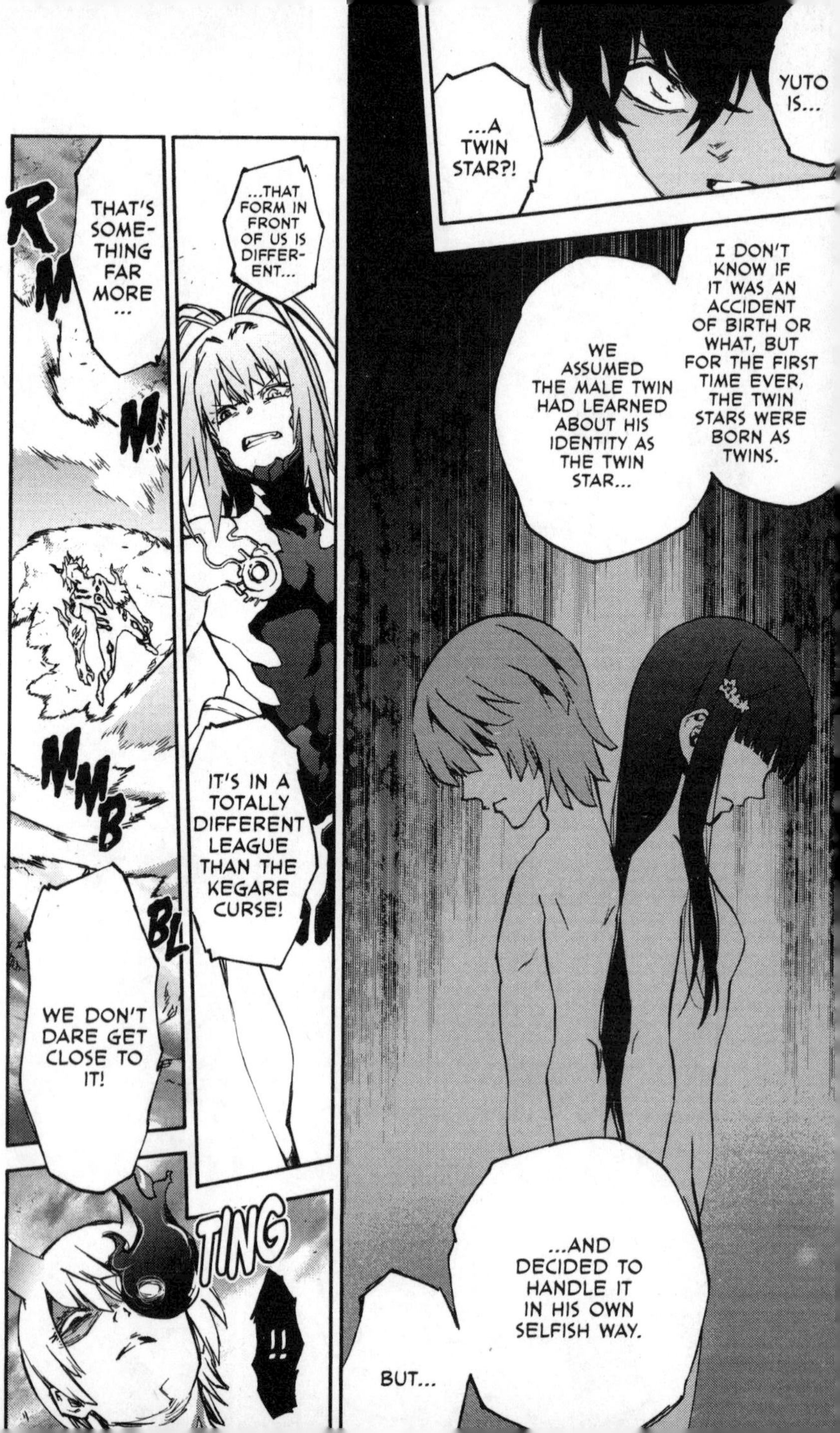

YUTO IS...
...A TWIN STAR?!
I DON'T KNOW IF IT WAS AN ACCIDENT OF BIRTH OR WHAT, BUT FOR THE FIRST TIME EVER, THE TWIN STARS WERE BORN AS TWINS.
WE ASSUMED THE MALE TWIN HAD LEARNED ABOUT HIS IDENTITY AS THE TWIN STAR...
...AND DECIDED TO HANDLE IT IN HIS OWN SELFISH WAY.
BUT...
...THAT FORM IN FRONT OF US IS DIFFERENT...
IT'S IN A TOTALLY DIFFERENT LEAGUE THAN THE KEGARE CURSE!
THAT'S SOMETHING FAR MORE...
RM
M
MMB
BL
WE DON'T DARE GET CLOSE TO IT!
TING
!!

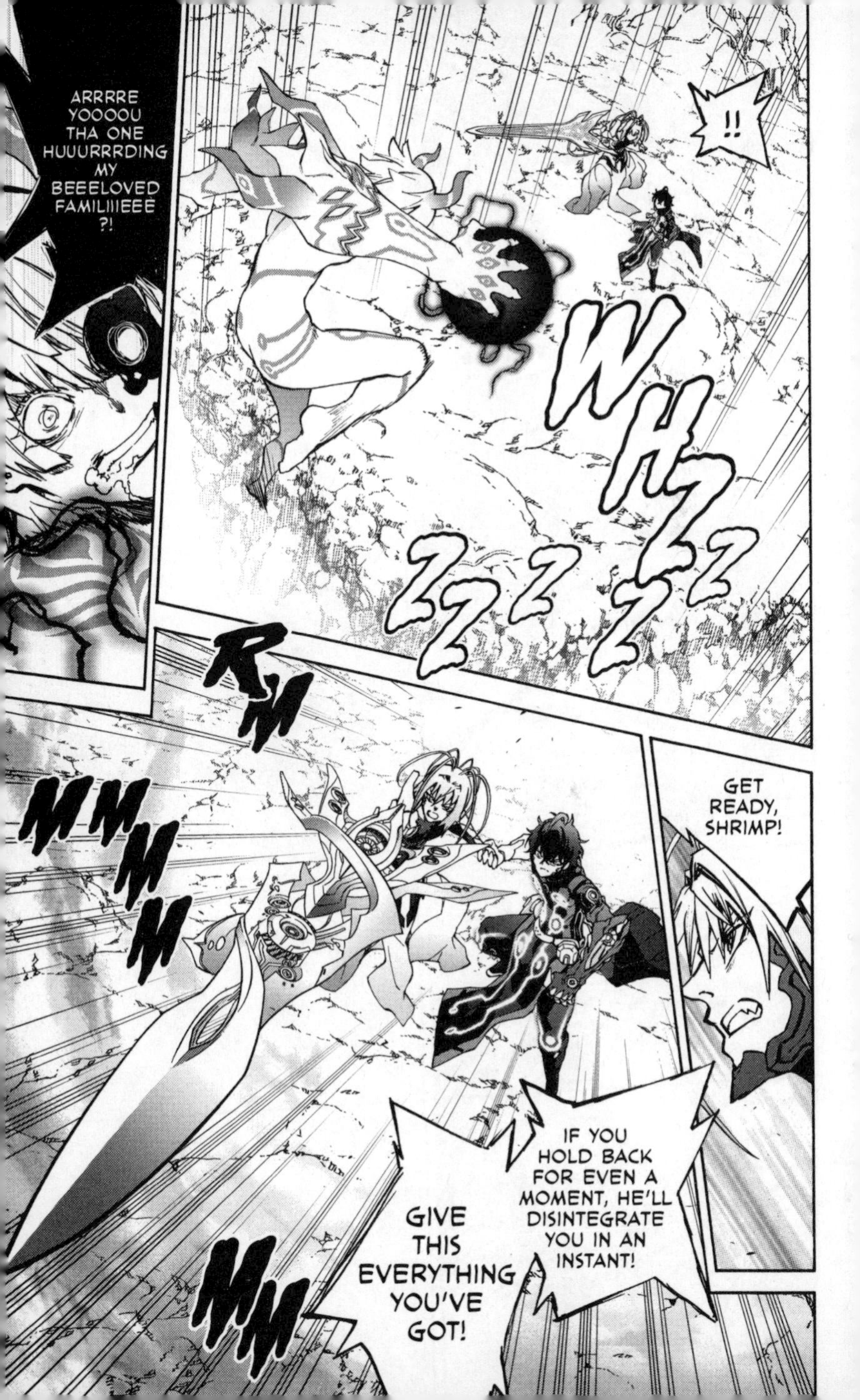
!!
WHZZZZZZZZ
ARRRRE YOOOOU THA ONE HUUURRRDING MY BEEELOVED FAMILIIIEEE ?!
GET READY, SHRIMP!
RMMMMMMM
IF YOU HOLD BACK FOR EVEN A MOMENT, HE'LL DISINTEGRATE YOU IN AN INSTANT!
GIVE THIS EVERYTHING YOU'VE GOT!

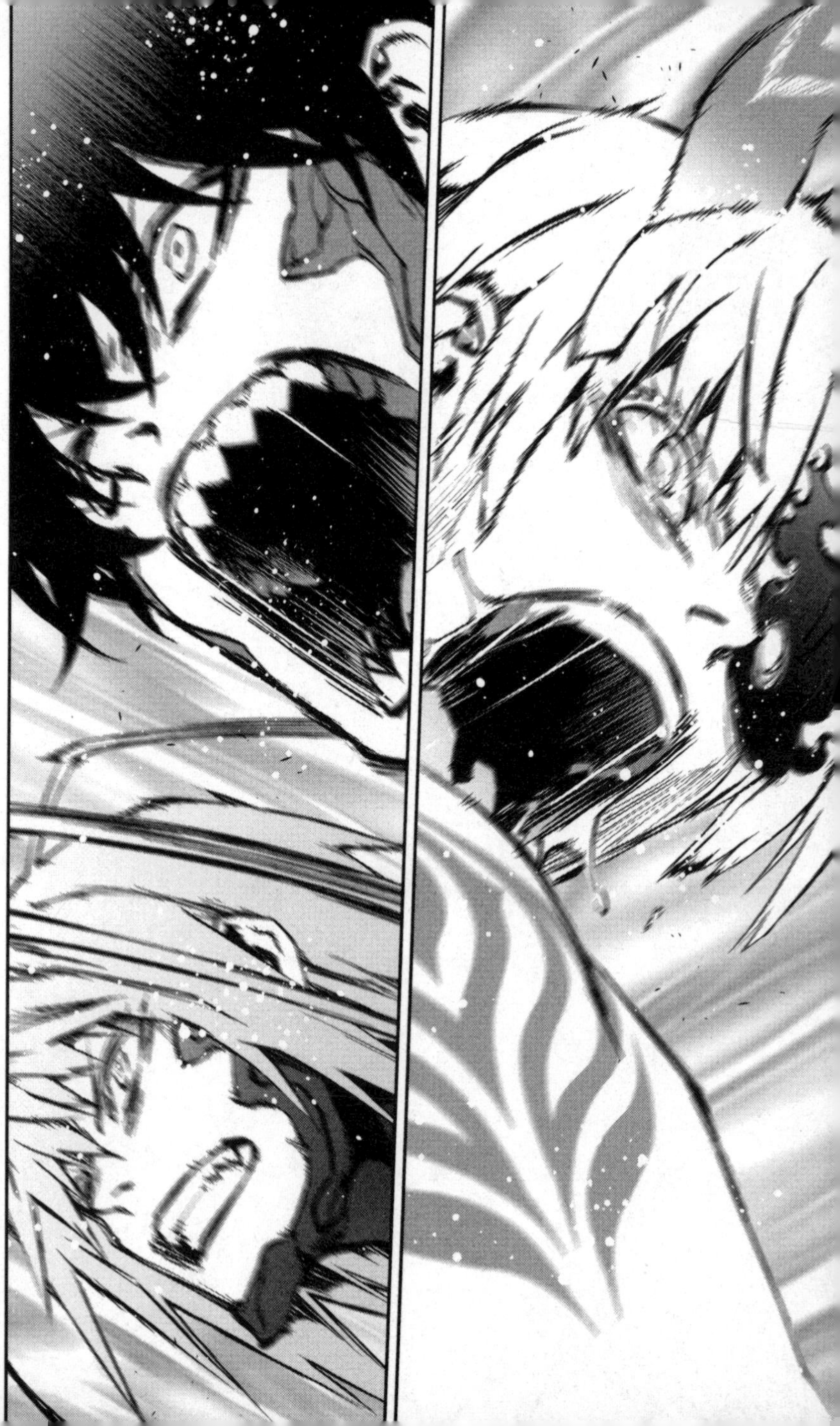

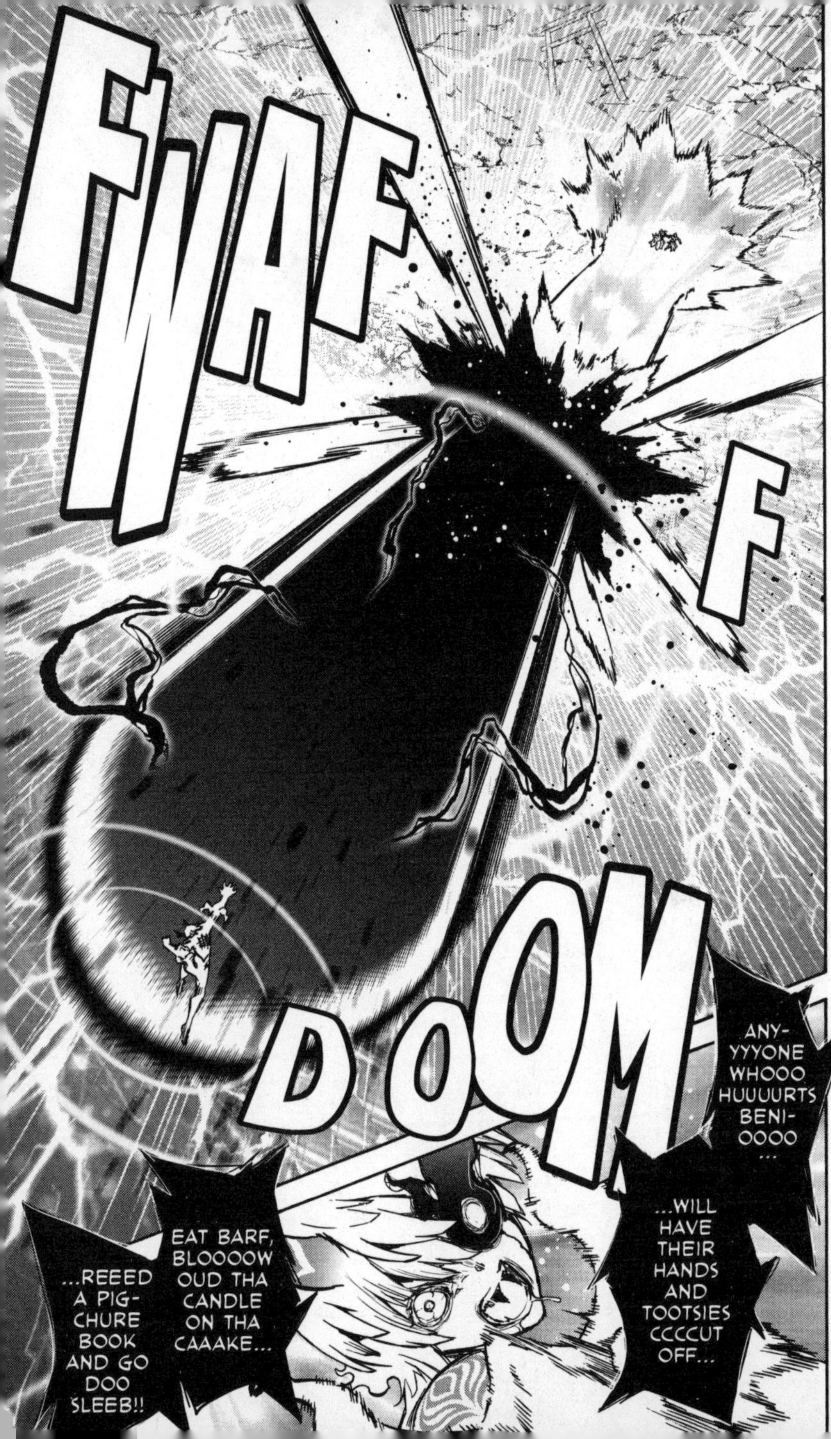
FWAF
F
DOOM
ANY-YYYONE WHOOO HUUUURTS BENI-OOOO...
...WILL HAVE THEIR HANDS AND TOOTSIES CCCCUT OFF...
EAT BARF, BLOOOOW OUD THA CANDLE ON THA CAAAKE...
...REEED A PIG-CHURE BOOK AND GO DOO SLEEB!!

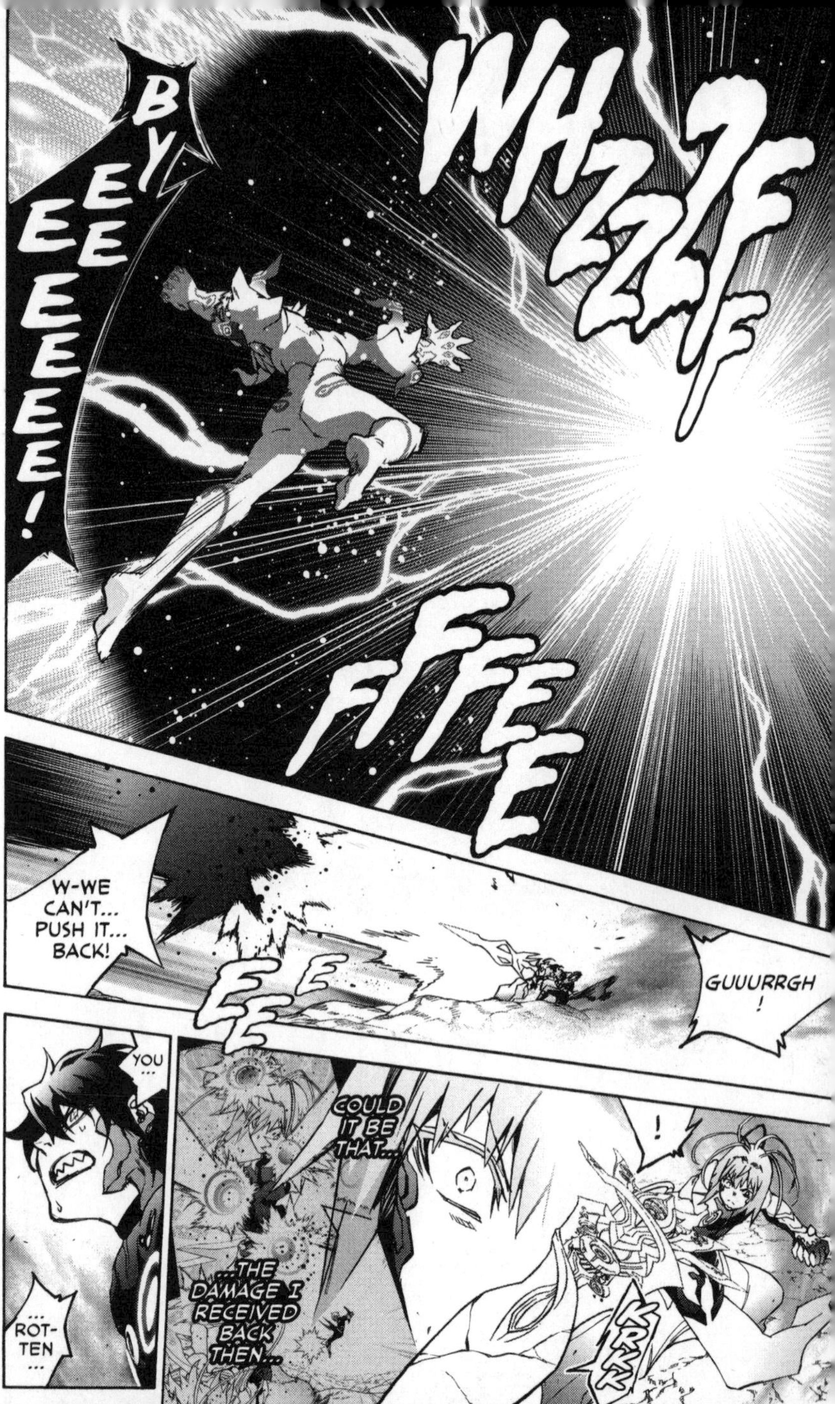
WHZZFFF
BYEEEEEEEEEE!
FFFEE
GUUURRGH!
W-WE CAN'T... PUSH IT... BACK!
EEE
!
COULD IT BE THAT...
...THE DAMAGE I RECEIVED BACK THEN...
KRKK
YOU...
...ROTTEN...

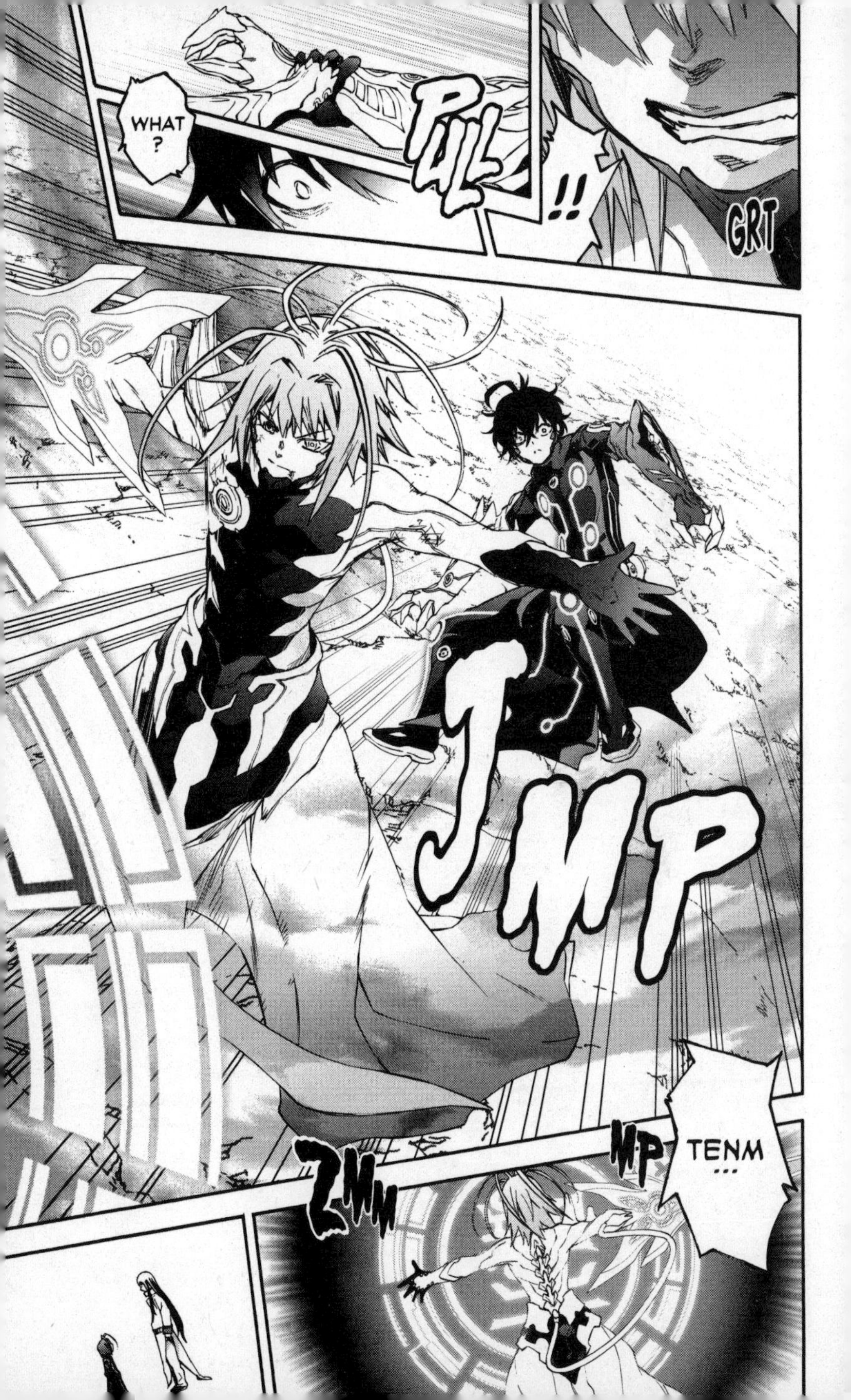
GRT
!!
PULL
WHAT ?
JMP
TENM ...
MP
ZMM

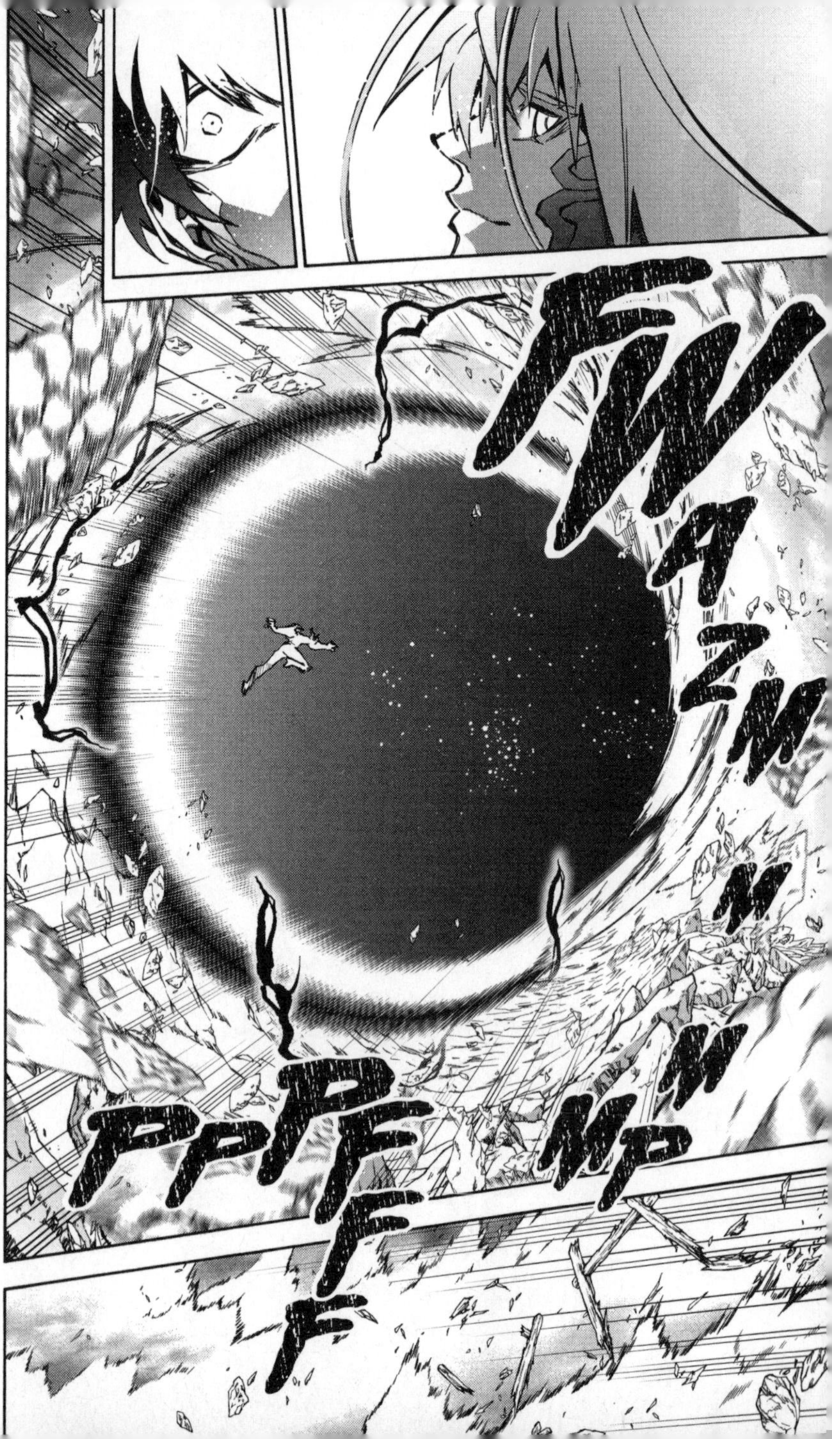
FWAZWWWWMP
PPPFF

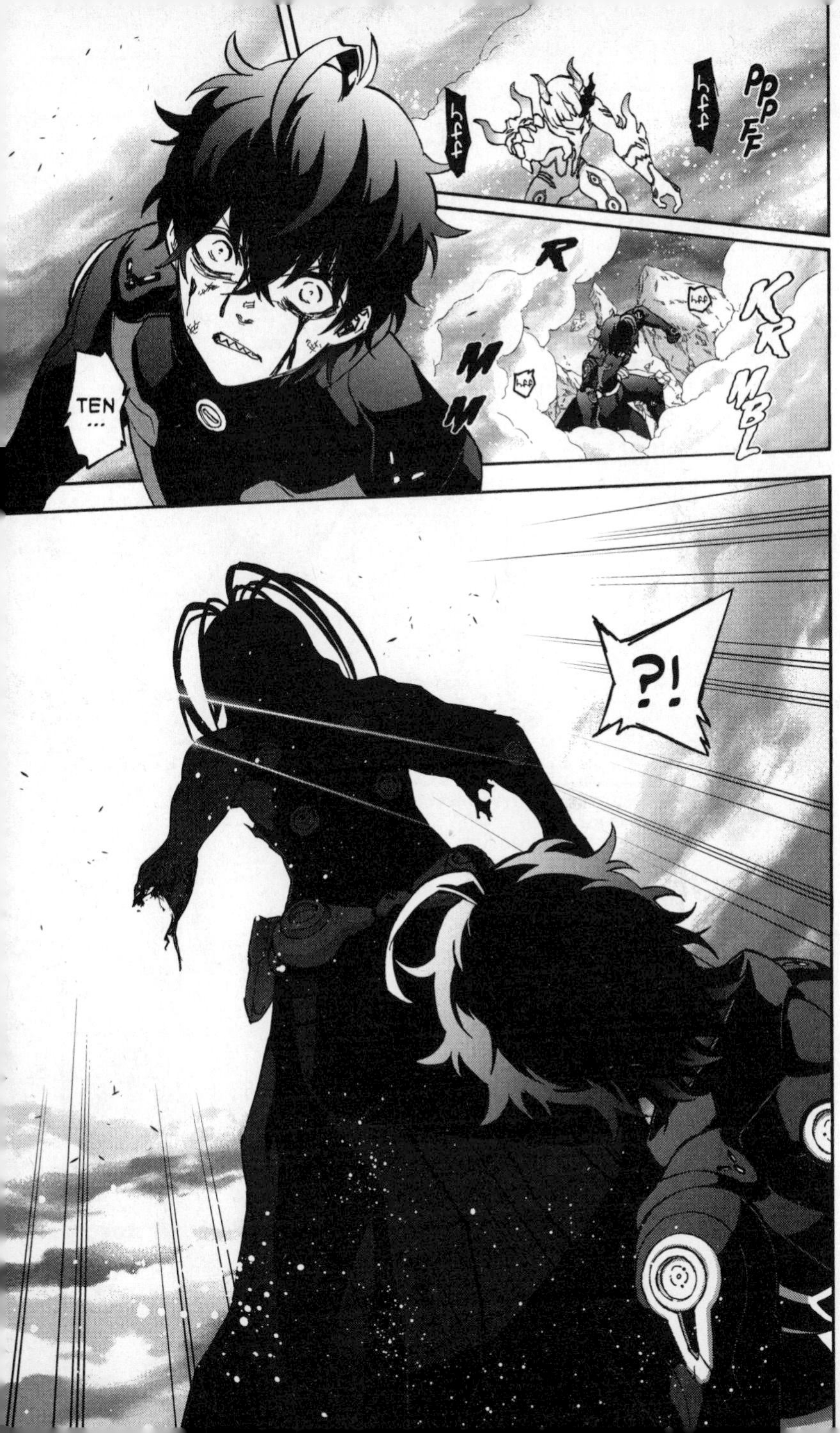
PPPFF
hfff
hfff
KRMBL
hff
RMM
hff
TEN...
?!

Q Q nyoritsuryo!

Question Corner

Q At my school, my friends are divided into Shimon fans and Tenma fans. I'm a Shimon fan. What about you, Sensei?
(From Eriko Okamoto)

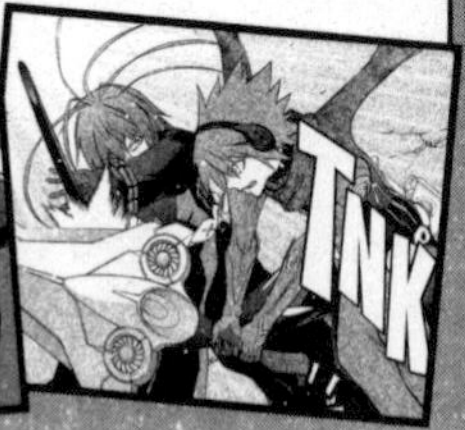
TNK

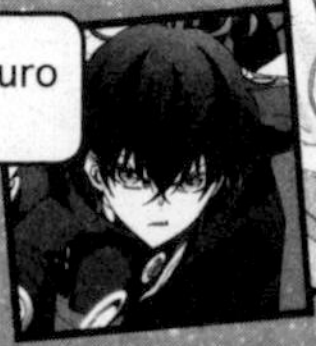

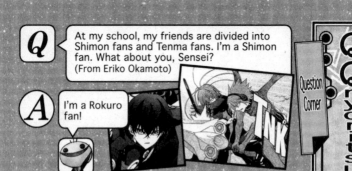

A I'm a Rokuro fan!

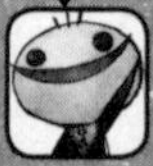

Q Please tell me who your top three favorite Twelve Guardian members are.
(From Yuito Murata)

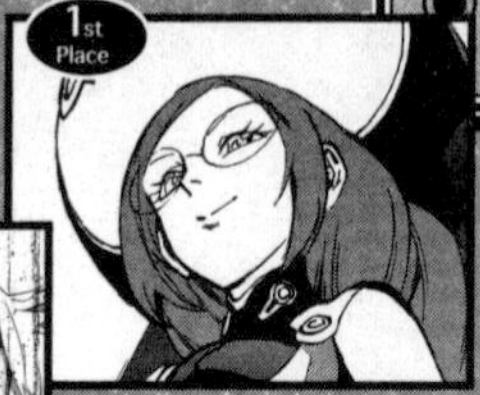
1st Place

A Probably...

1. Sakura Sada
2. Tatara
3. Kankuro Mitosaka

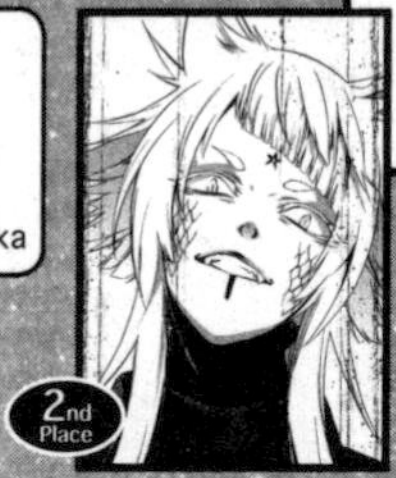
2nd Place

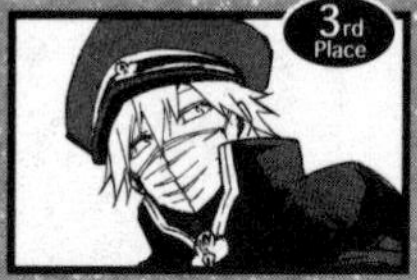
3rd Place

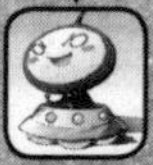

Q How does Cordelia feel about Shozan?
(From Love Twin Star Exorcists)

A Cordelia: "P-E-R-V-E-R-T."
➡(Apparently he always ogles her when she works out.)

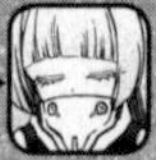

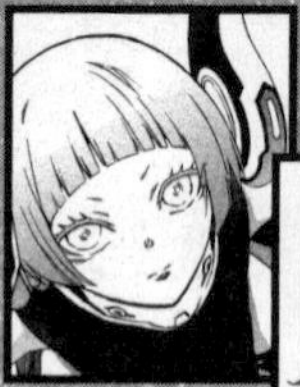

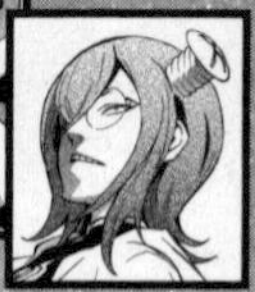

Request R Birthday requests! ♡

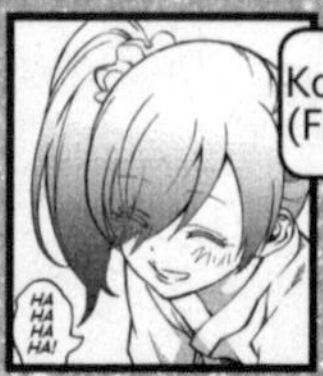
HA HA HA HA!

Kotoko: October 10
(From Milk Chocolate)

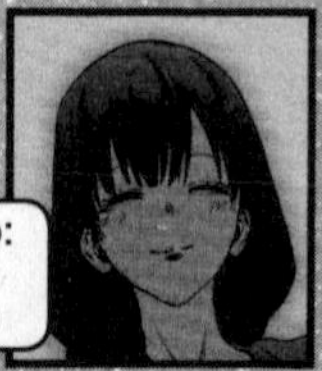

Mao Tsuchimikado: February 4
(From Uta No. 24)

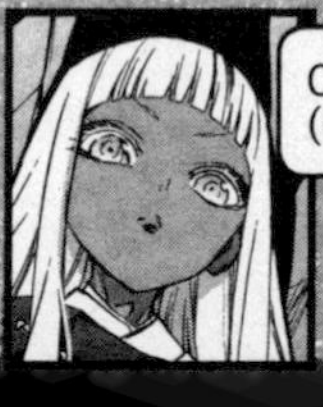

Chinu: March 10
(From Rokuron)

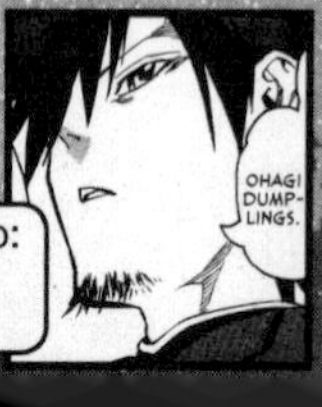
OHAGI DUMPLINGS.

Hyoga Adashino: September 15
(From Hyoga)

#72

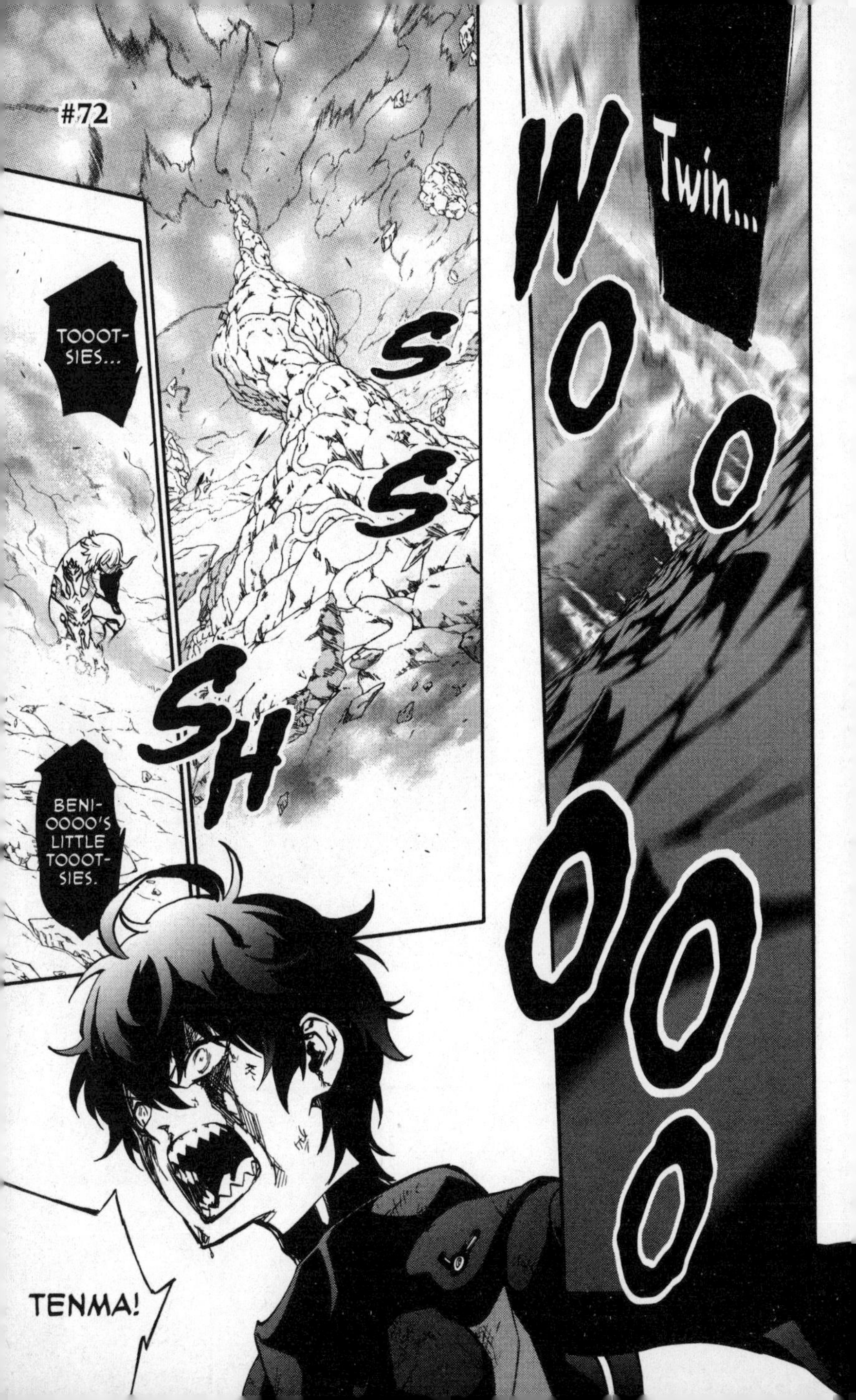
Twin...
WOOOOOOO
SSSH
TOOOT-SIES...
BENI-OOOO'S LITTLE TOOOT-SIES.
TENMA!

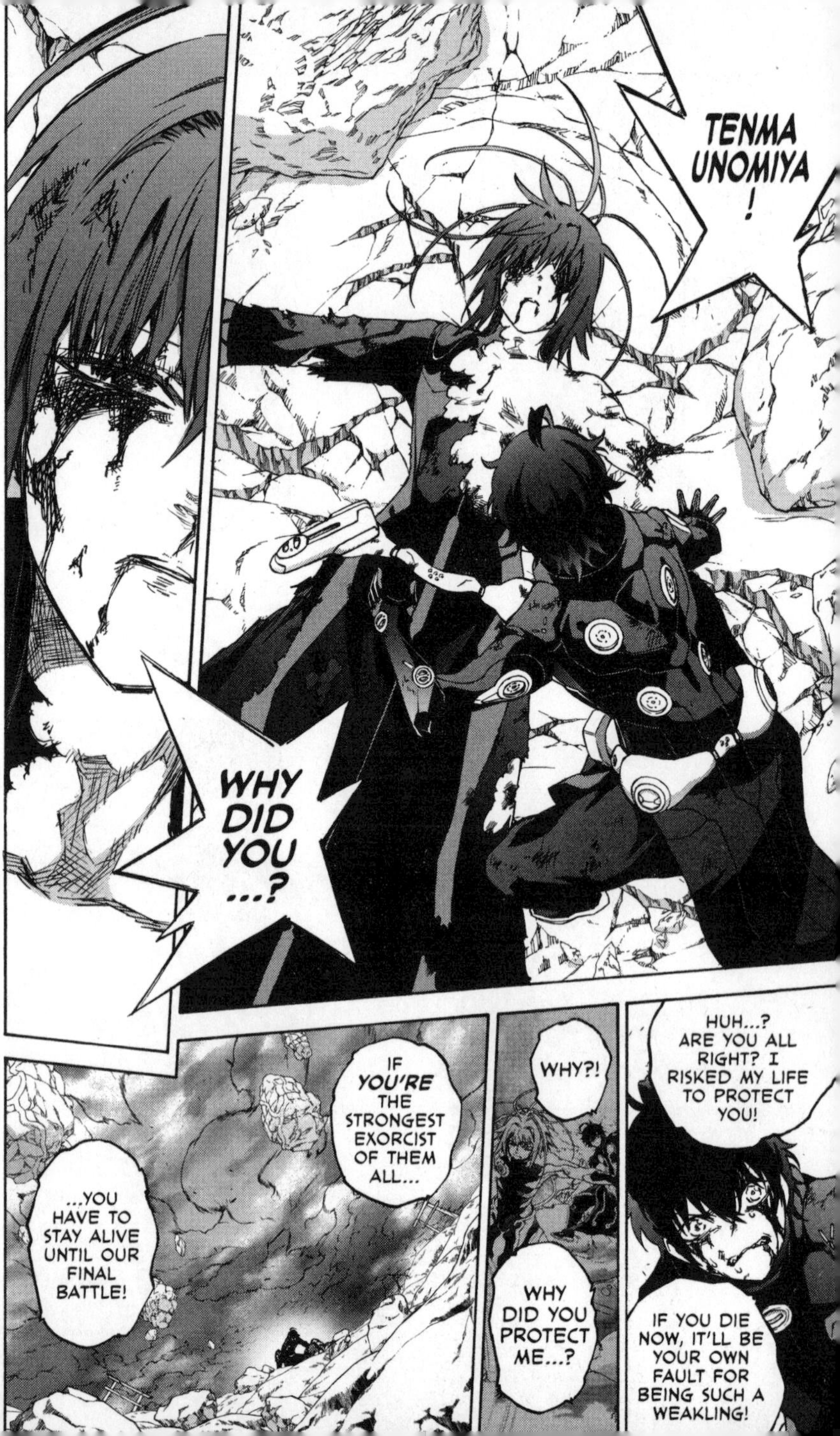
TENMA UNOMIYA!
WHY DID YOU ...?
HUH...? ARE YOU ALL RIGHT? I RISKED MY LIFE TO PROTECT YOU!
IF YOU DIE NOW, IT'LL BE YOUR OWN FAULT FOR BEING SUCH A WEAKLING!
WHY?!
WHY DID YOU PROTECT ME...?
IF YOU'RE THE STRONGEST EXORCIST OF THEM ALL...
...YOU HAVE TO STAY ALIVE UNTIL OUR FINAL BATTLE!

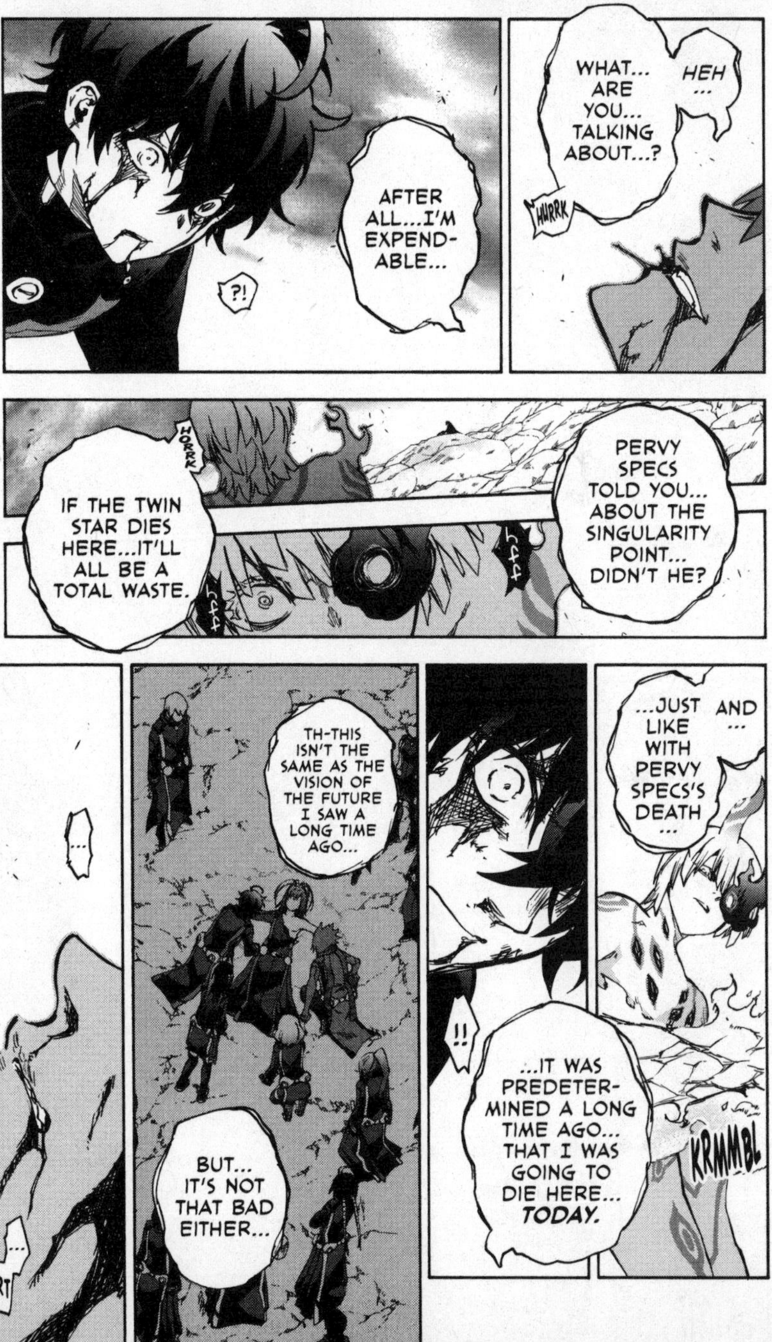
HEH ...
WHAT... ARE YOU... TALKING ABOUT...?
HURRK
AFTER ALL...I'M EXPENDABLE...
?!
PERVY SPECS TOLD YOU... ABOUT THE SINGULARITY POINT... DIDN'T HE?
HFF
HORRK
IF THE TWIN STAR DIES HERE...IT'LL ALL BE A TOTAL WASTE.
HFF
AND ...
...JUST LIKE WITH PERVY SPECS'S DEATH ...
!!
...IT WAS PREDETERMINED A LONG TIME AGO... THAT I WAS GOING TO DIE HERE... *TODAY.*
KRMMBL
TH-THIS ISN'T THE SAME AS THE VISION OF THE FUTURE I SAW A LONG TIME AGO...
BUT... IT'S NOT THAT BAD EITHER...
...
...
GRT

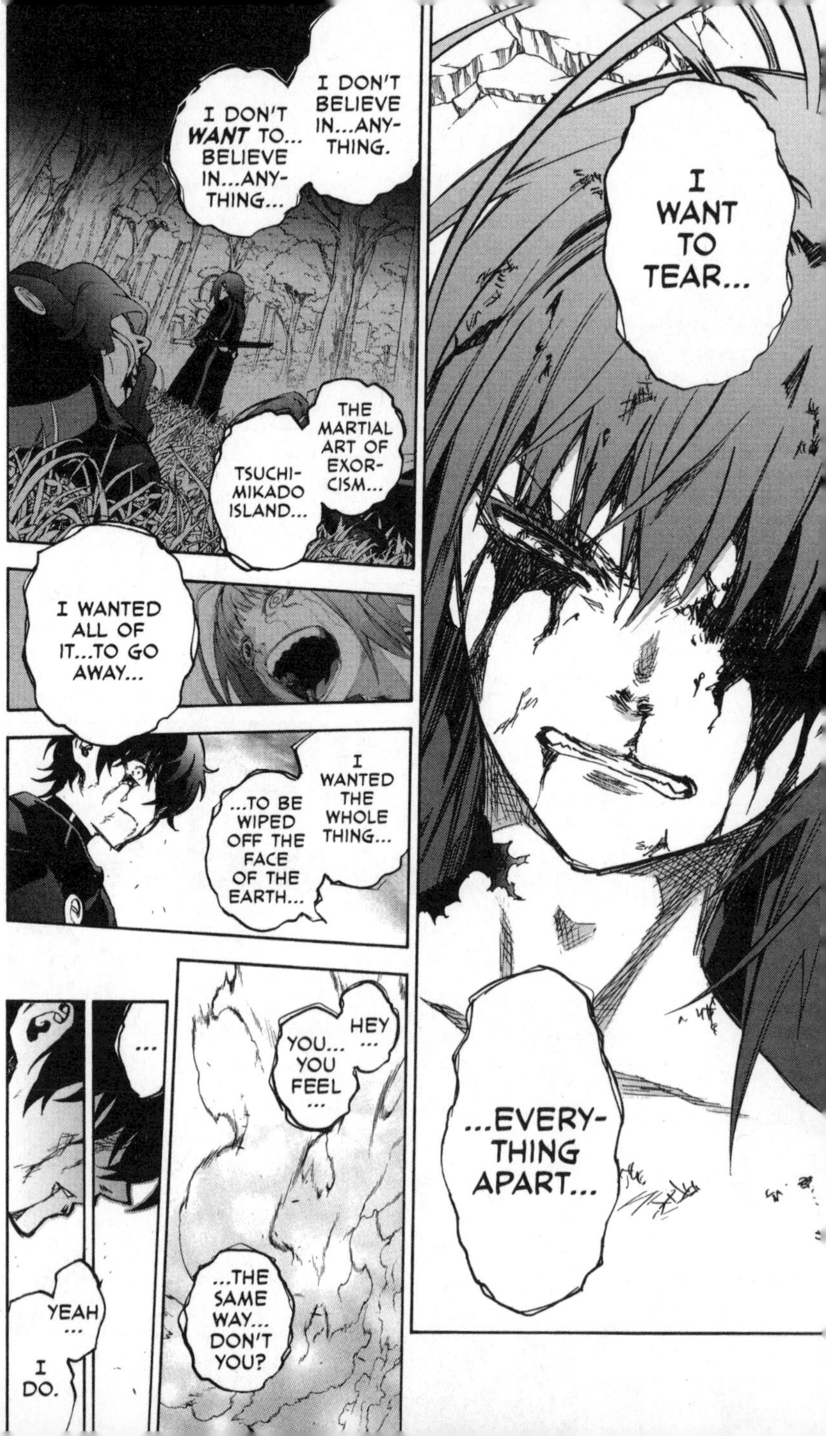
I WANT TO TEAR...
...EVERYTHING APART...
I DON'T BELIEVE IN...ANYTHING.
I DON'T *WANT* TO... BELIEVE IN...ANYTHING...
THE MARTIAL ART OF EXORCISM...
TSUCHIMIKADO ISLAND...
I WANTED ALL OF IT...TO GO AWAY...
I WANTED THE WHOLE THING...
...TO BE WIPED OFF THE FACE OF THE EARTH...
HEY...
YOU... YOU FEEL...
...THE SAME WAY... DON'T YOU?
...
YEAH...
I DO.

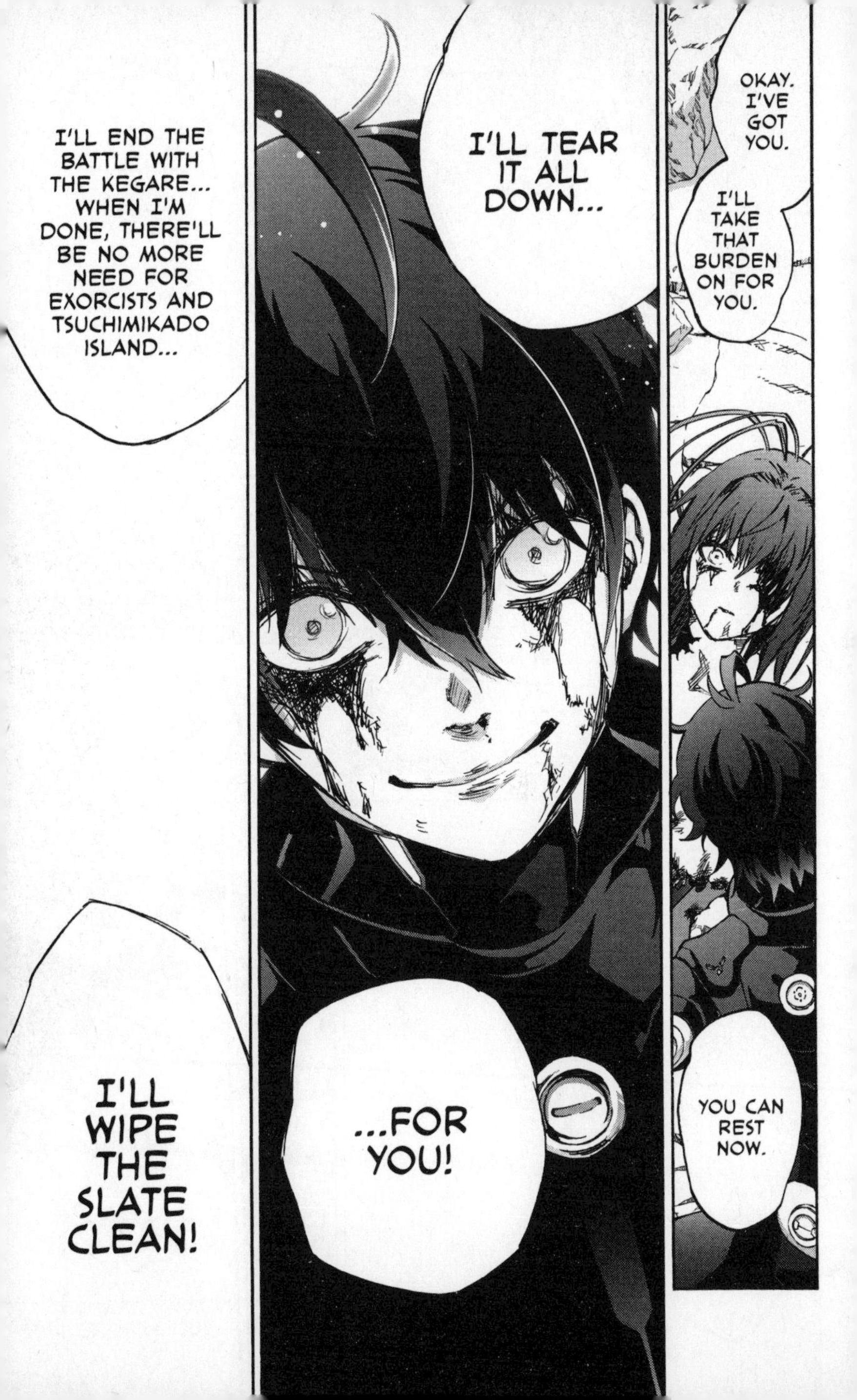
OKAY. I'VE GOT YOU.
I'LL TAKE THAT BURDEN ON FOR YOU.
YOU CAN REST NOW.
I'LL TEAR IT ALL DOWN...
...FOR YOU!
I'LL END THE BATTLE WITH THE KEGARE... WHEN I'M DONE, THERE'LL BE NO MORE NEED FOR EXORCISTS AND TSUCHIMIKADO ISLAND...
I'LL WIPE THE SLATE CLEAN!

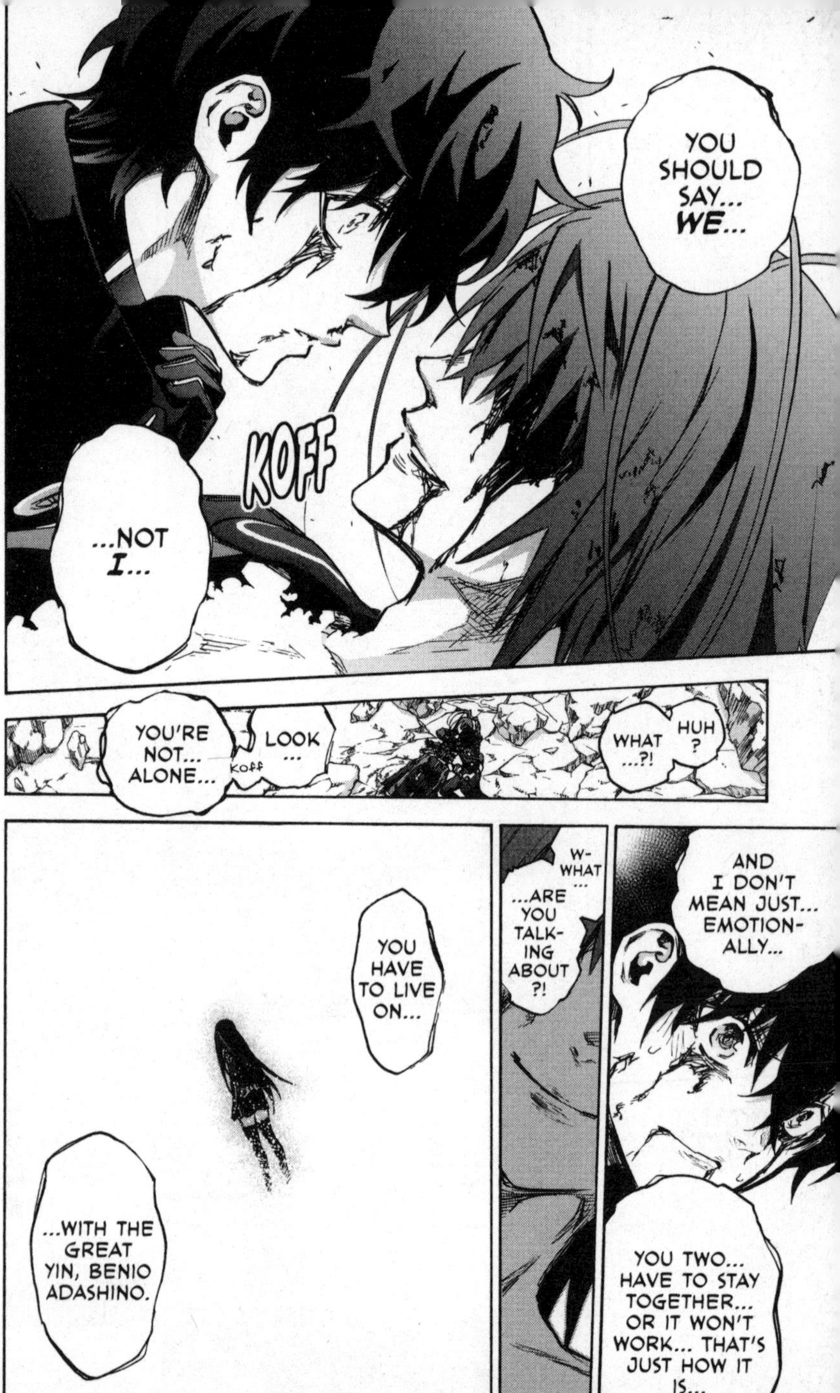
YOU SHOULD SAY... WE...
KOFF
...NOT I...
HUH?
WHAT...?!
LOOK...
Koff
YOU'RE NOT... ALONE...
AND I DON'T MEAN JUST... EMOTIONALLY...
YOU TWO... HAVE TO STAY TOGETHER... OR IT WON'T WORK... THAT'S JUST HOW IT IS...
W-WHAT...
...ARE YOU TALKING ABOUT?!
YOU HAVE TO LIVE ON...
...WITH THE GREAT YIN, BENIO ADASHINO.

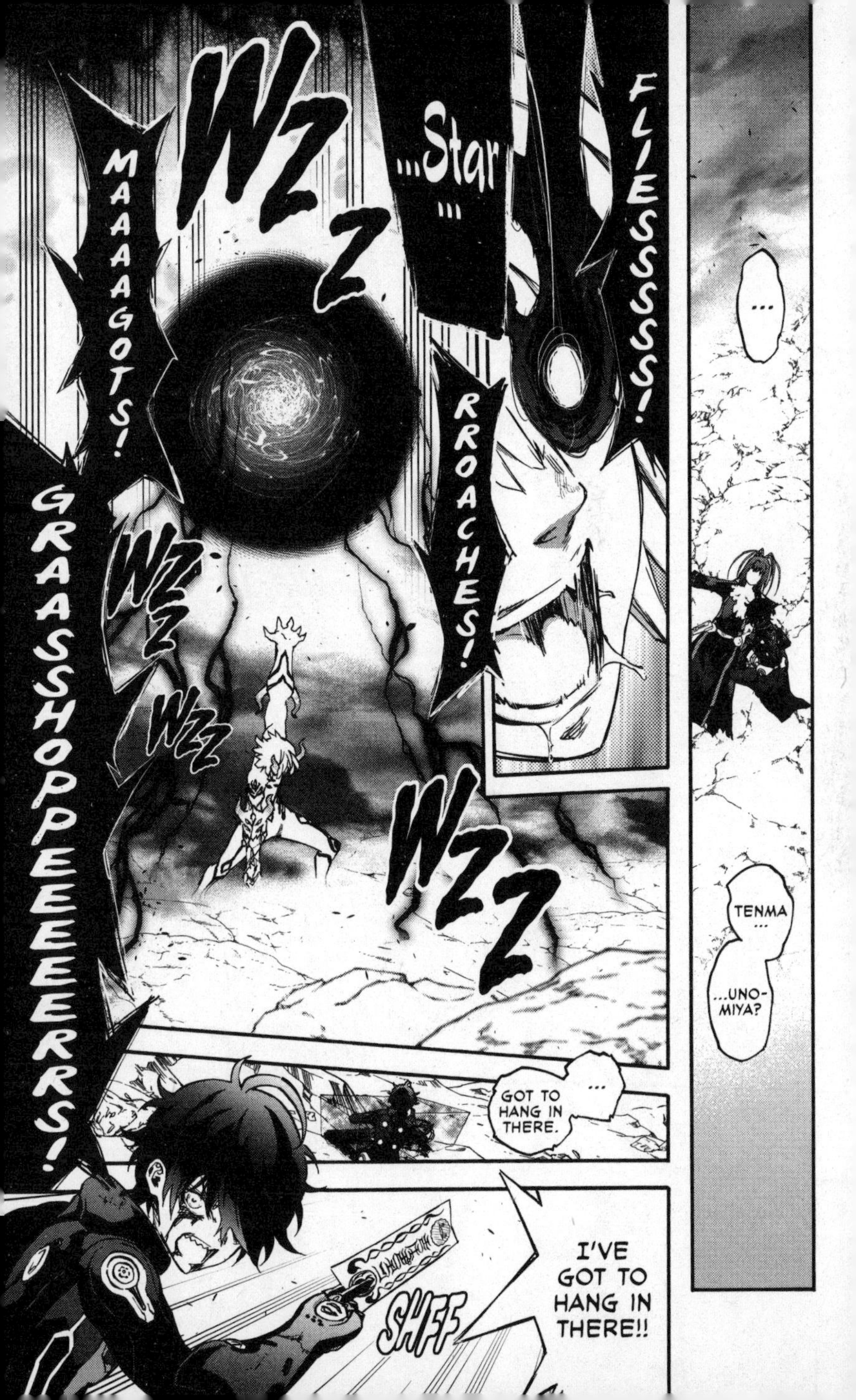
...
TENMA...
...UNO-MIYA?
FLIESSSSS!
...Star!!!
WZZ
MAAAAGOTS!
RROACHES!
GRAAASSHOPPEEEEERRS!
WZZ
WZZ
WZZ
... GOT TO HANG IN THERE.
I'VE GOT TO HANG IN THERE!!
SHFF

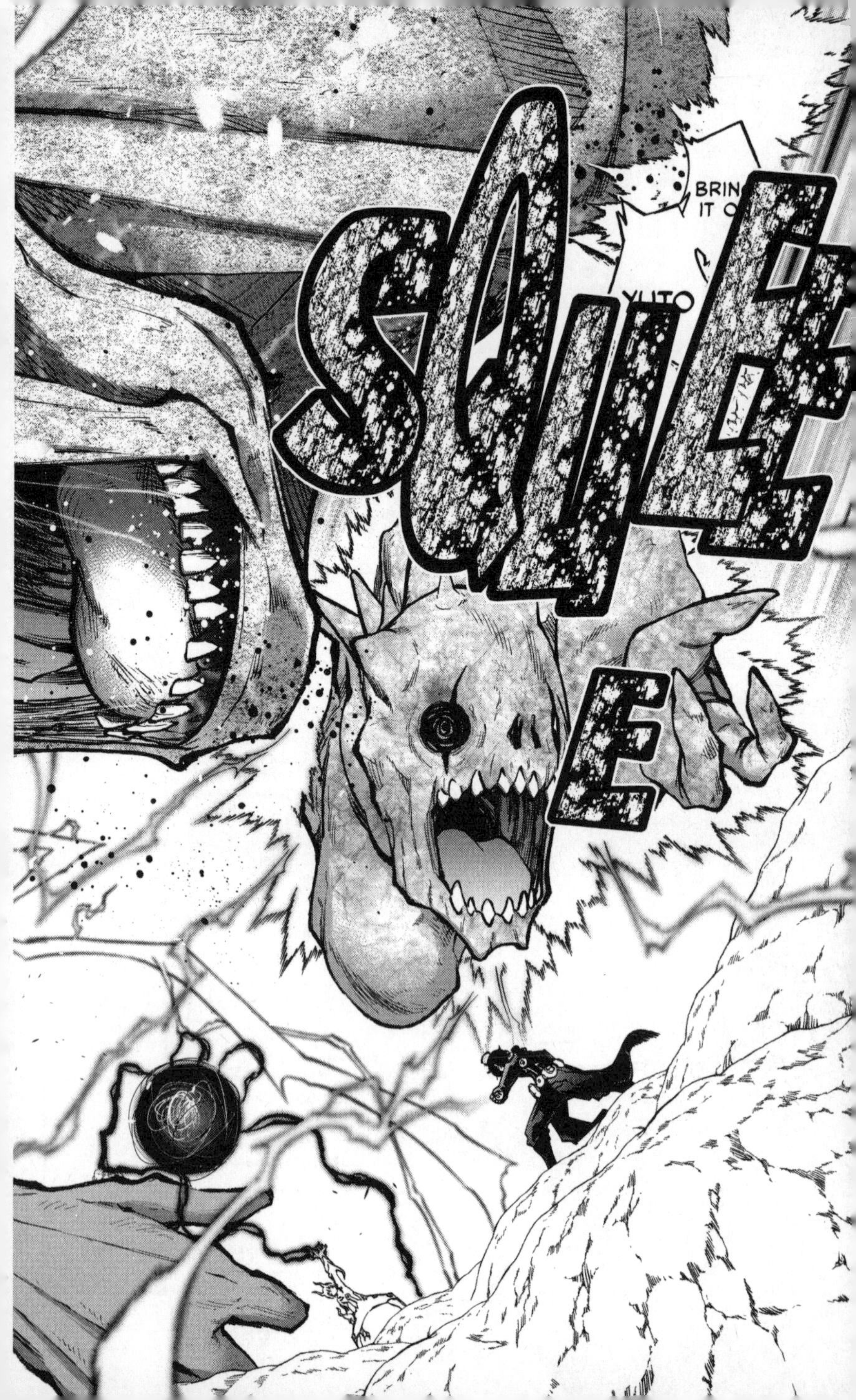
BRIN
IT O
YUITO

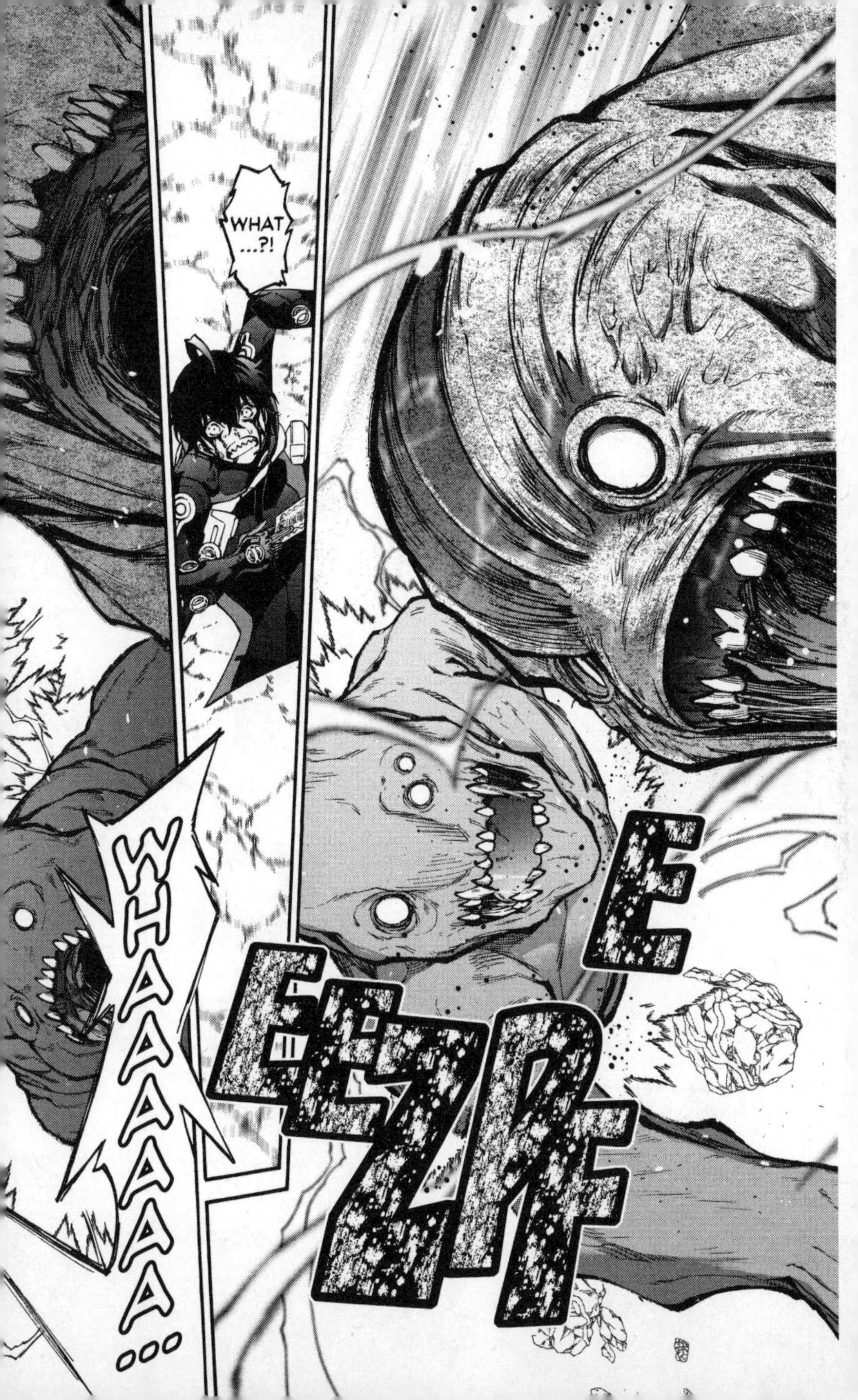
WHAT ...?!
WHAAAAAA...

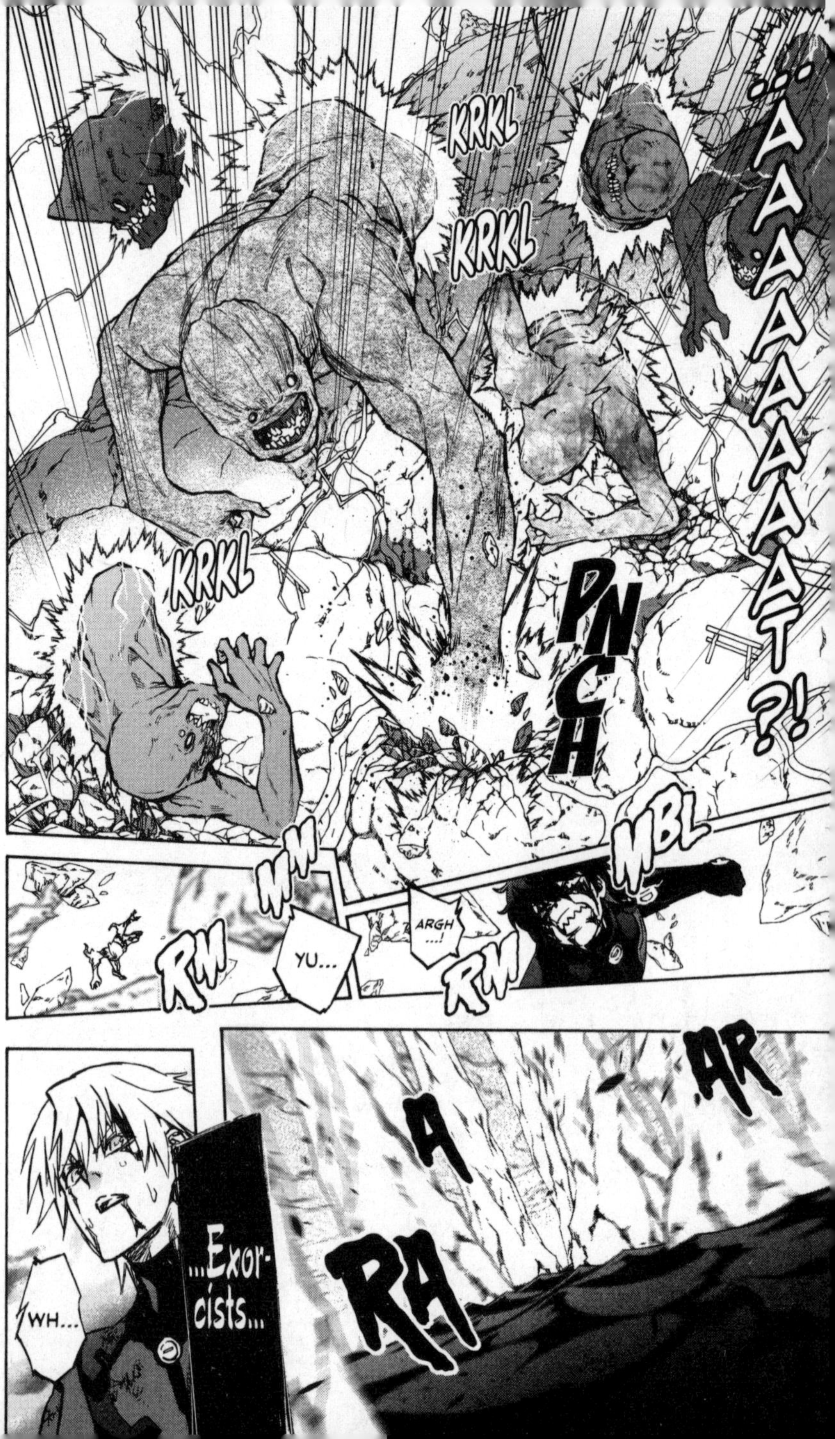
...AAAAAAAAAT?!
KRKL
KRKL
PNCH
KRKL
MBL
ARGH ...!
RM
MM
YU...
RM
AR
A
RA
...Exor-cists...
WH...

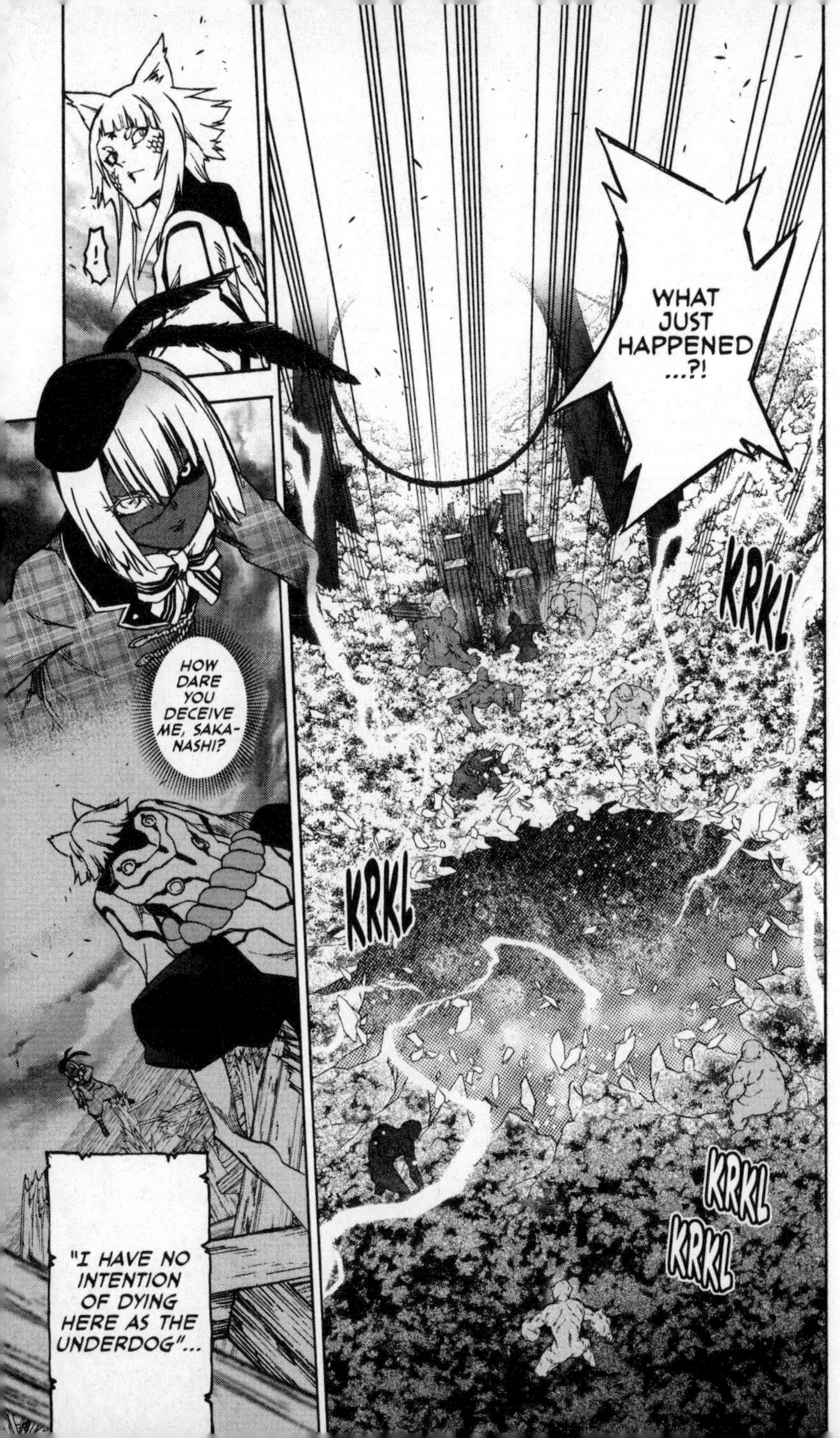
WHAT JUST HAPPENED ...?!
KRKL
KRKL
KRKL
KRKL
!
HOW DARE YOU DECEIVE ME, SAKA-NASHI?
"I HAVE NO INTENTION OF DYING HERE AS THE UNDERDOG"...

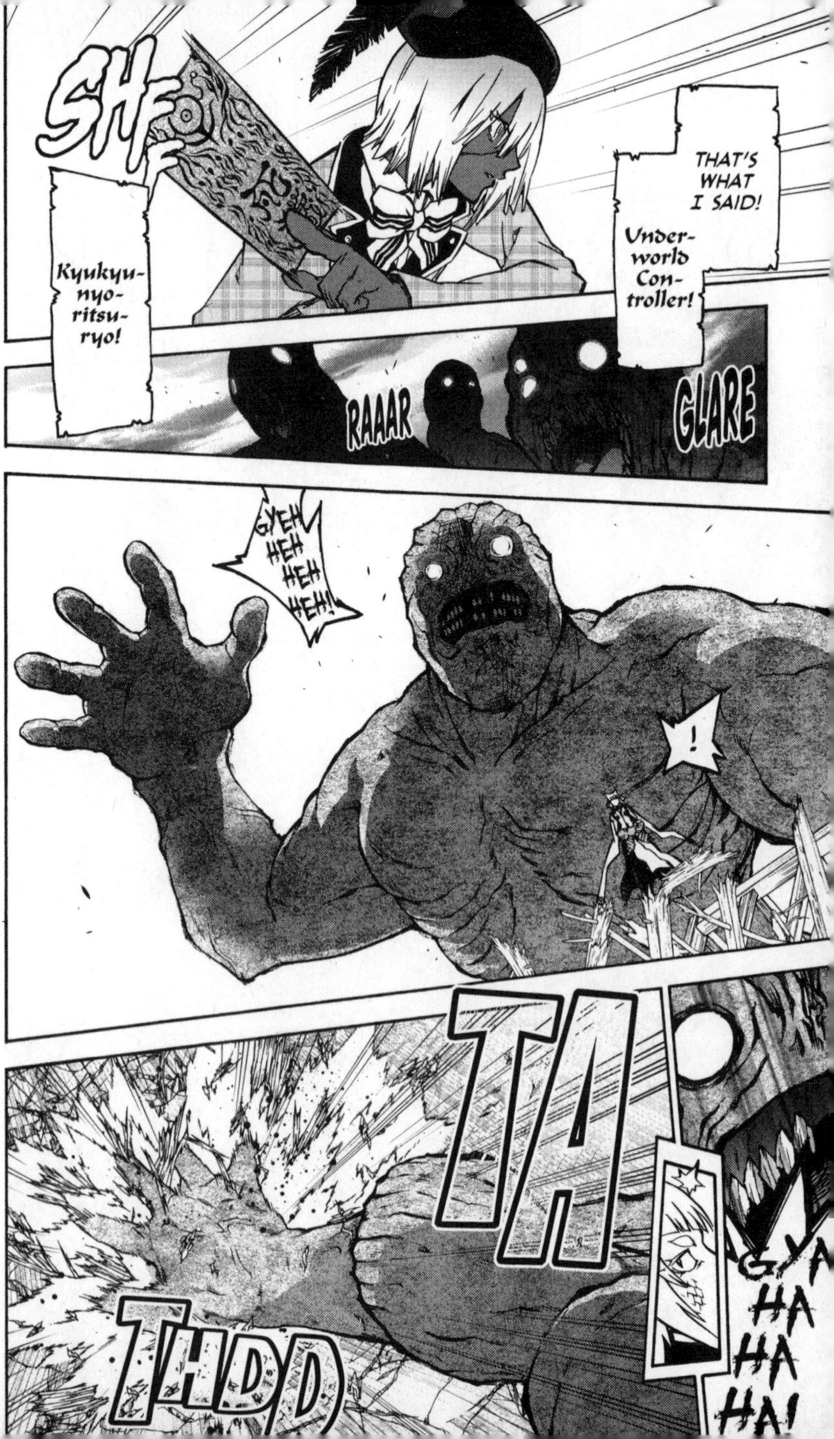
THAT'S WHAT I SAID!
Under-world Con-troller!
SH
Kyukyu-nyo-ritsu-ryo!
GLARE
RAAAR
GYEH HEH HEH HEH!
!
GYAHAHAHAHA!
TA
THDD

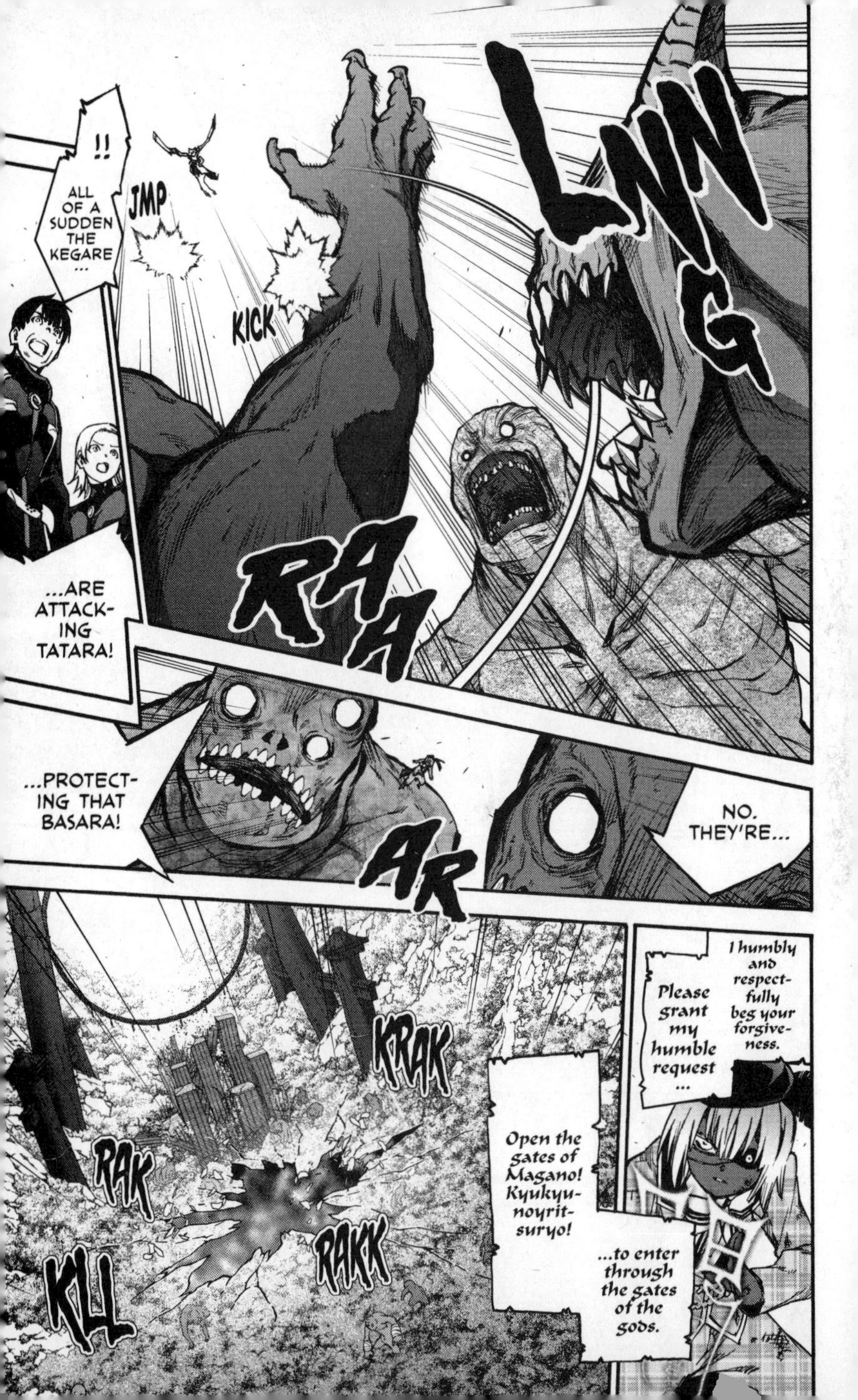

LNNG
KICK
JMP
!!
ALL OF A SUDDEN THE KEGARE...
RAAA
...ARE ATTACK-ING TATARA!
NO. THEY'RE...
AR
...PROTECT-ING THAT BASARA!
I humbly and respect-fully beg your forgive-ness.
Please grant my humble request...
Open the gates of Magano! Kyukyu-noyrit-suryo!
...to enter through the gates of the gods.
KRAK
RAK
RAKK
KLL

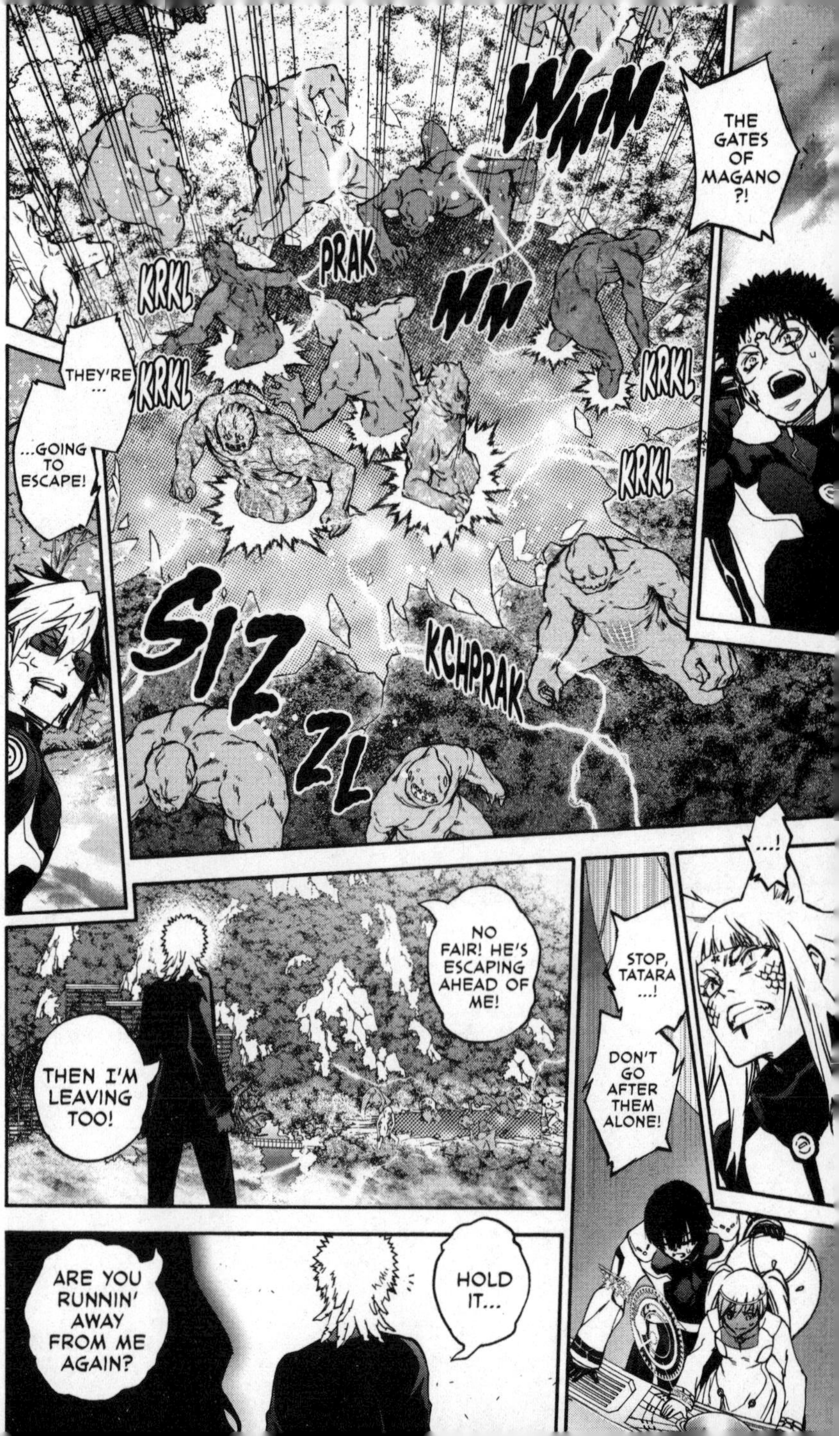
THE GATES OF MAGANO ?!
WMM
PRAK
KRKL
MM
KRKL
KRKL
KRKL
SIZZL
KCHPRAK
THEY'RE ...
...GOING TO ESCAPE!
...!
STOP, TATARA ...!
DON'T GO AFTER THEM ALONE!
NO FAIR! HE'S ESCAPING AHEAD OF ME!
THEN I'M LEAVING TOO!
HOLD IT...
ARE YOU RUNNIN' AWAY FROM ME AGAIN?

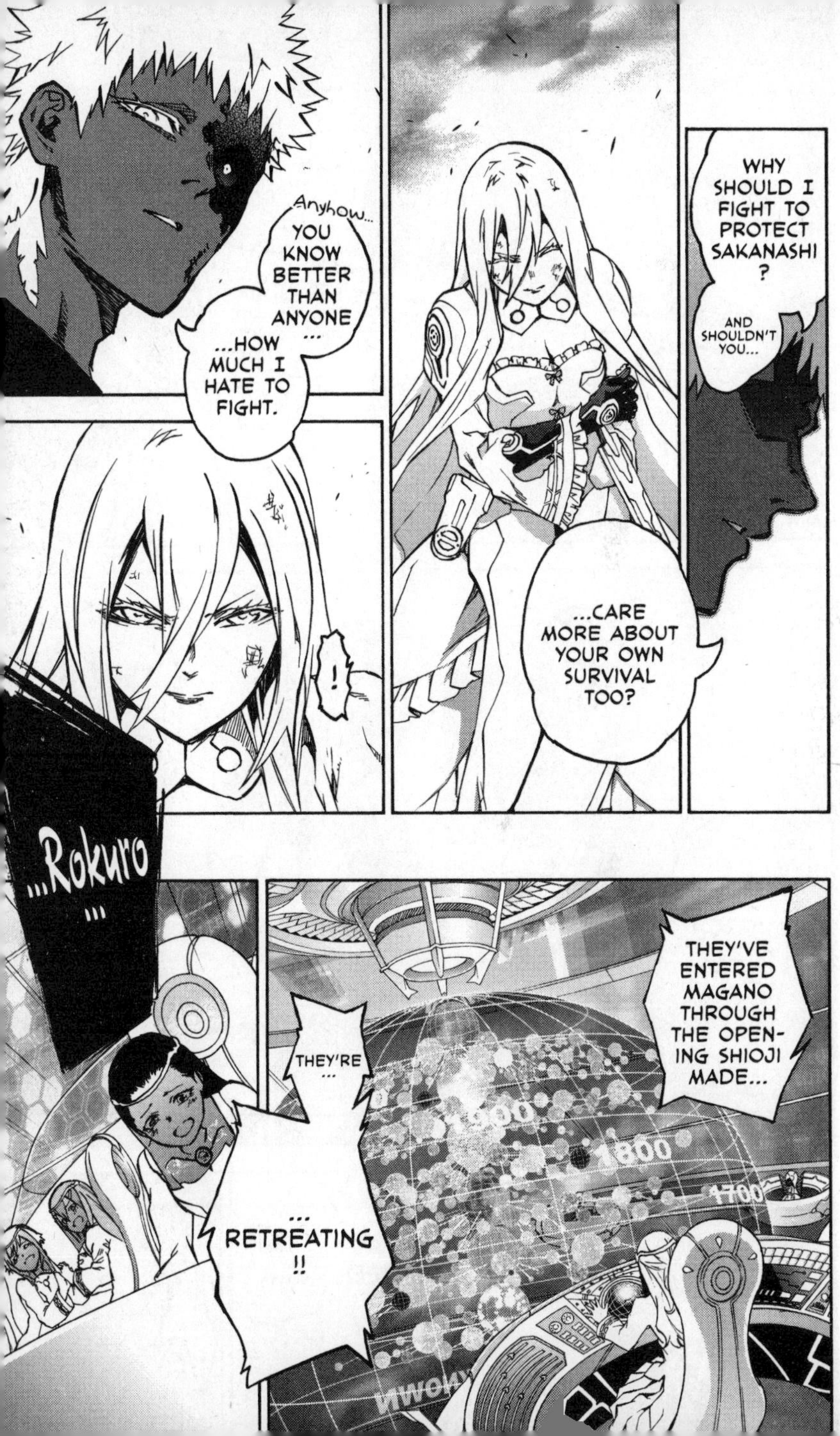
WHY SHOULD I FIGHT TO PROTECT SAKANASHI?
AND SHOULDN'T YOU...
...CARE MORE ABOUT YOUR OWN SURVIVAL TOO?
Anyhow... YOU KNOW BETTER THAN ANYONE...
...HOW MUCH I HATE TO FIGHT.
!
...Rokuro...
THEY'VE ENTERED MAGANO THROUGH THE OPENING SHIOJI MADE...
1900
1800
1700
THEY'RE...
...RETREATING!!

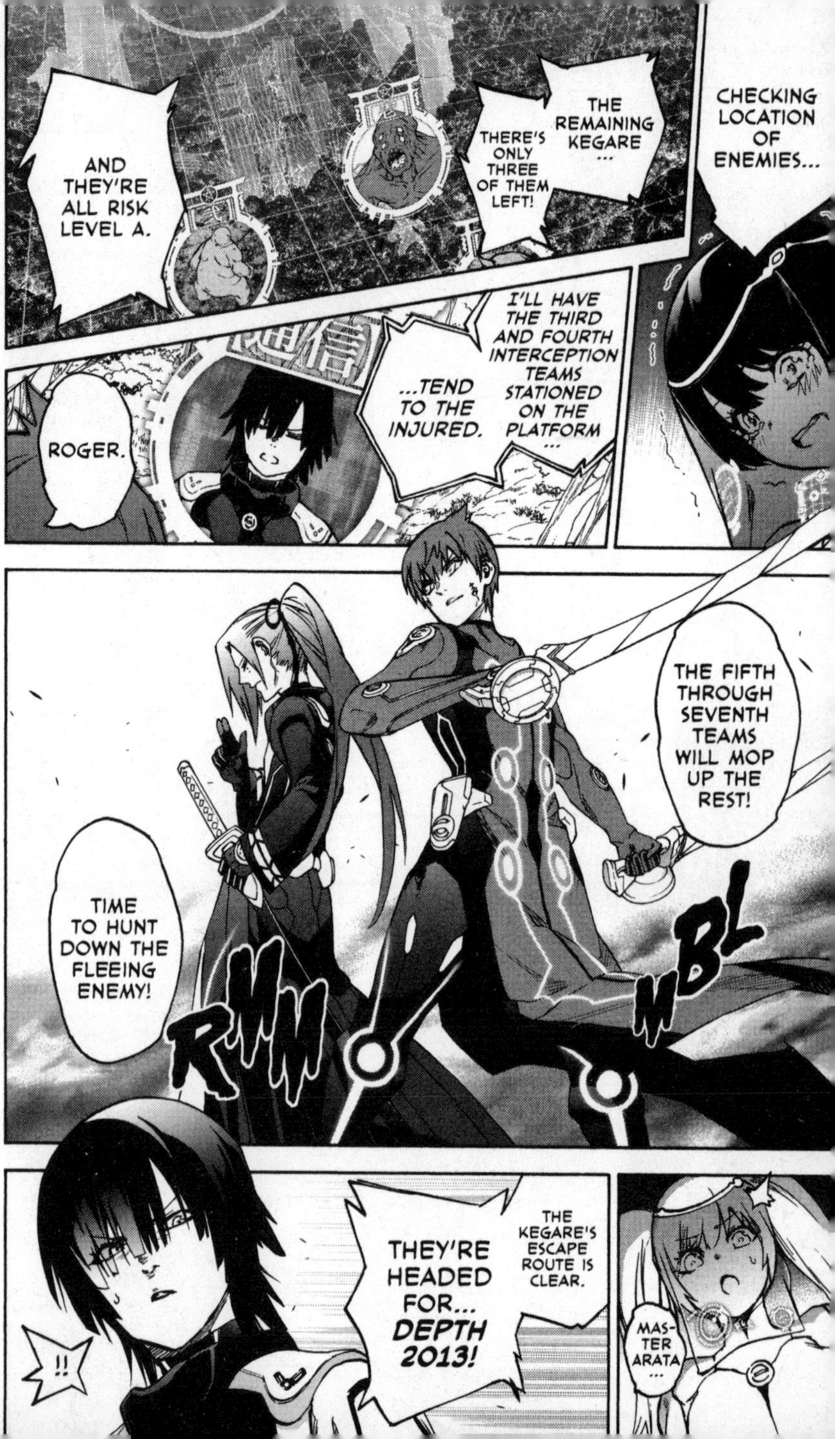
CHECKING LOCATION OF ENEMIES...
THE REMAINING KEGARE...
THERE'S ONLY THREE OF THEM LEFT!
AND THEY'RE ALL RISK LEVEL A.
I'LL HAVE THE THIRD AND FOURTH INTERCEPTION TEAMS STATIONED ON THE PLATFORM...
...TEND TO THE INJURED.
ROGER.
THE FIFTH THROUGH SEVENTH TEAMS WILL MOP UP THE REST!
MBL
RMM
TIME TO HUNT DOWN THE FLEEING ENEMY!
MASTER ARATA...
THE KEGARE'S ESCAPE ROUTE IS CLEAR.
THEY'RE HEADED FOR... *DEPTH 2013!*
!!

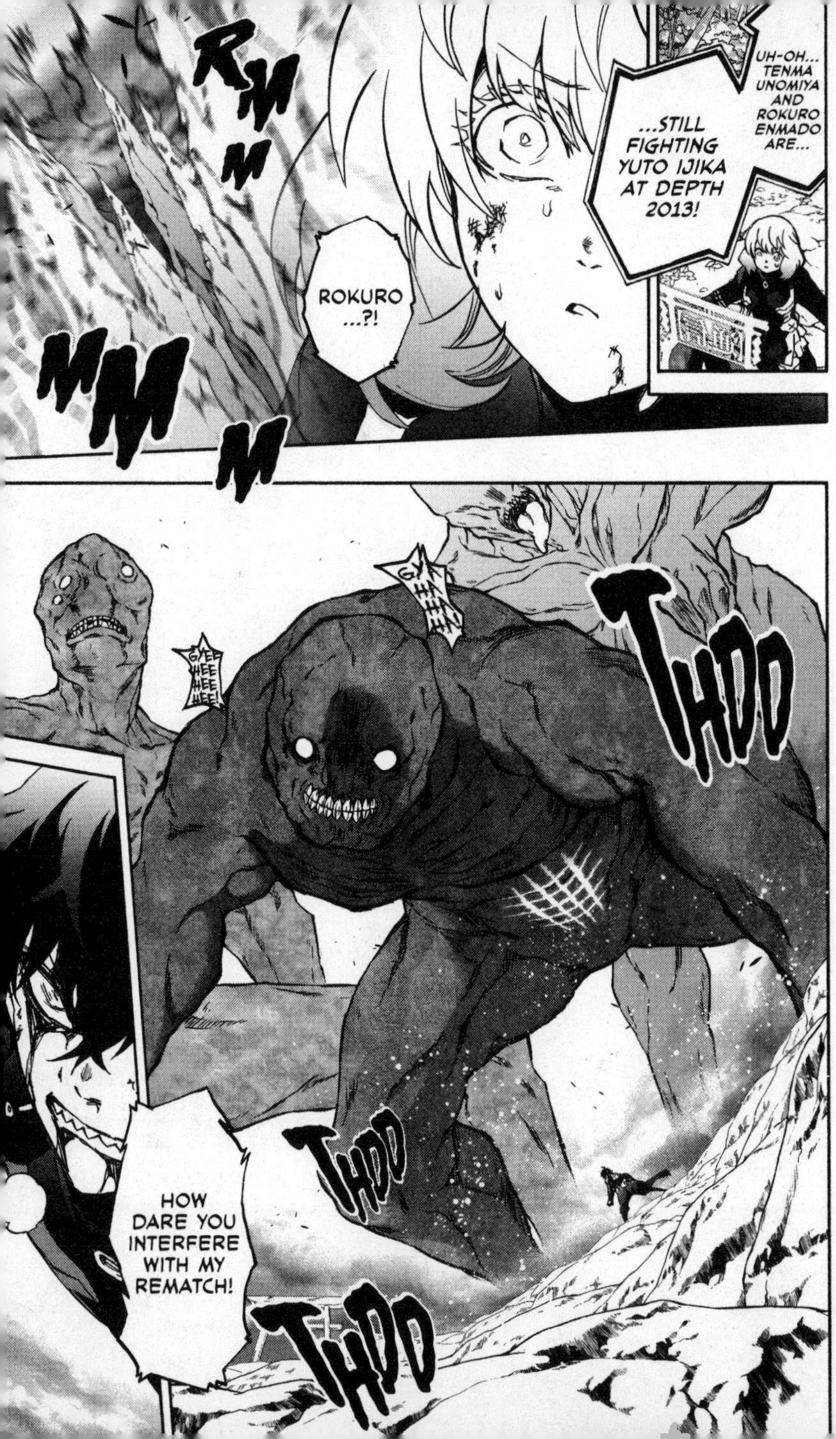
UH-OH... TENMA UNOMIYA AND ROKURO ENMADO ARE...
...STILL FIGHTING YUTO IJIKA AT DEPTH 2013!
RMMMMMM
ROKURO ...?!
GYAHAHAHAHA
GYEE HEE HEE HEE!
THDD
THDD
HOW DARE YOU INTERFERE WITH MY REMATCH!
THDD

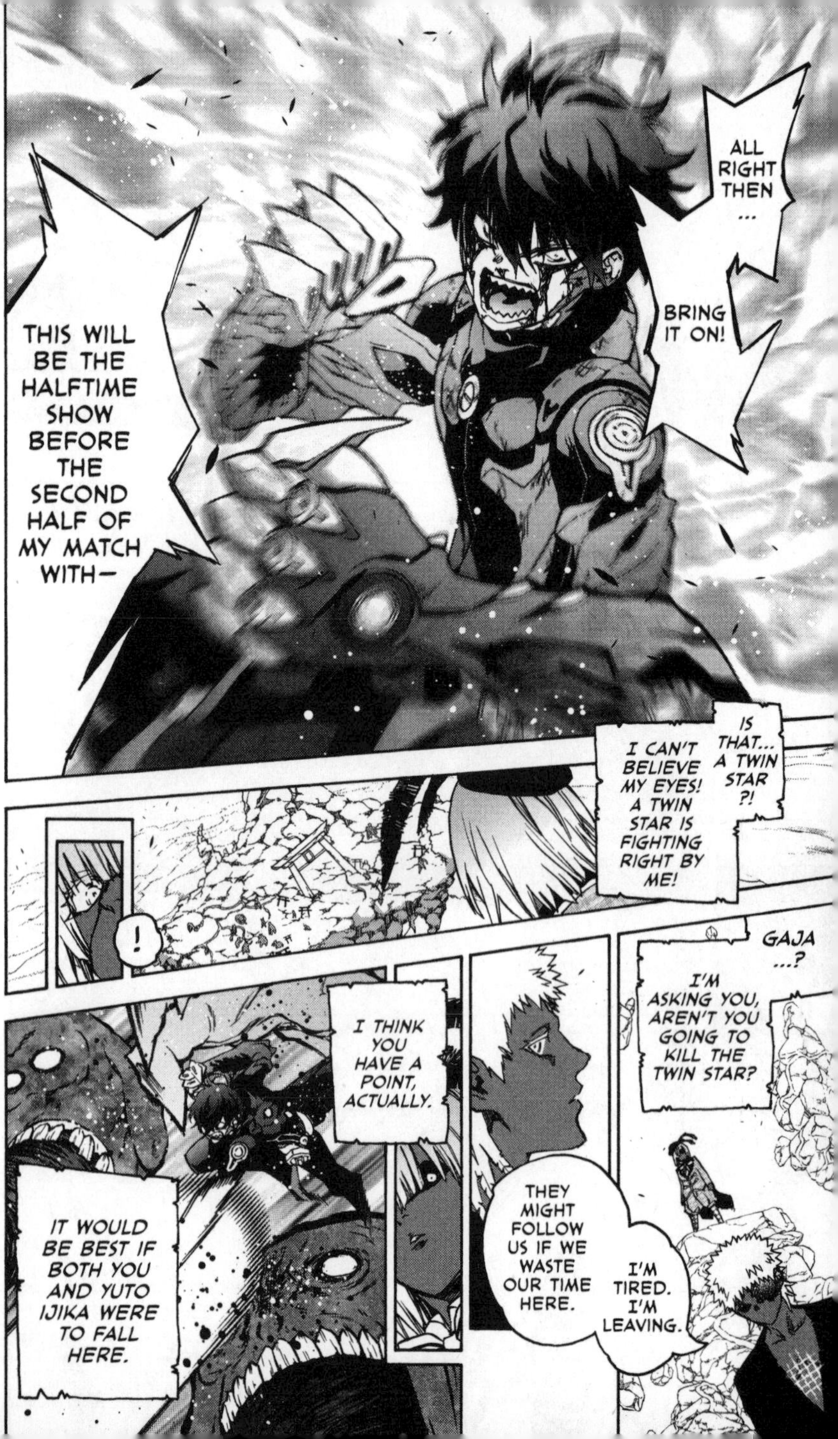
ALL RIGHT THEN ...
BRING IT ON!
THIS WILL BE THE HALFTIME SHOW BEFORE THE SECOND HALF OF MY MATCH WITH—
IS THAT... A TWIN STAR ?!
I CAN'T BELIEVE MY EYES! A TWIN STAR IS FIGHTING RIGHT BY ME!
!
GAJA ...?
I'M ASKING YOU, AREN'T YOU GOING TO KILL THE TWIN STAR?
I'M TIRED. I'M LEAVING.
THEY MIGHT FOLLOW US IF WE WASTE OUR TIME HERE.
I THINK YOU HAVE A POINT, ACTUALLY.
IT WOULD BE BEST IF BOTH YOU AND YUTO IJIKA WERE TO FALL HERE.

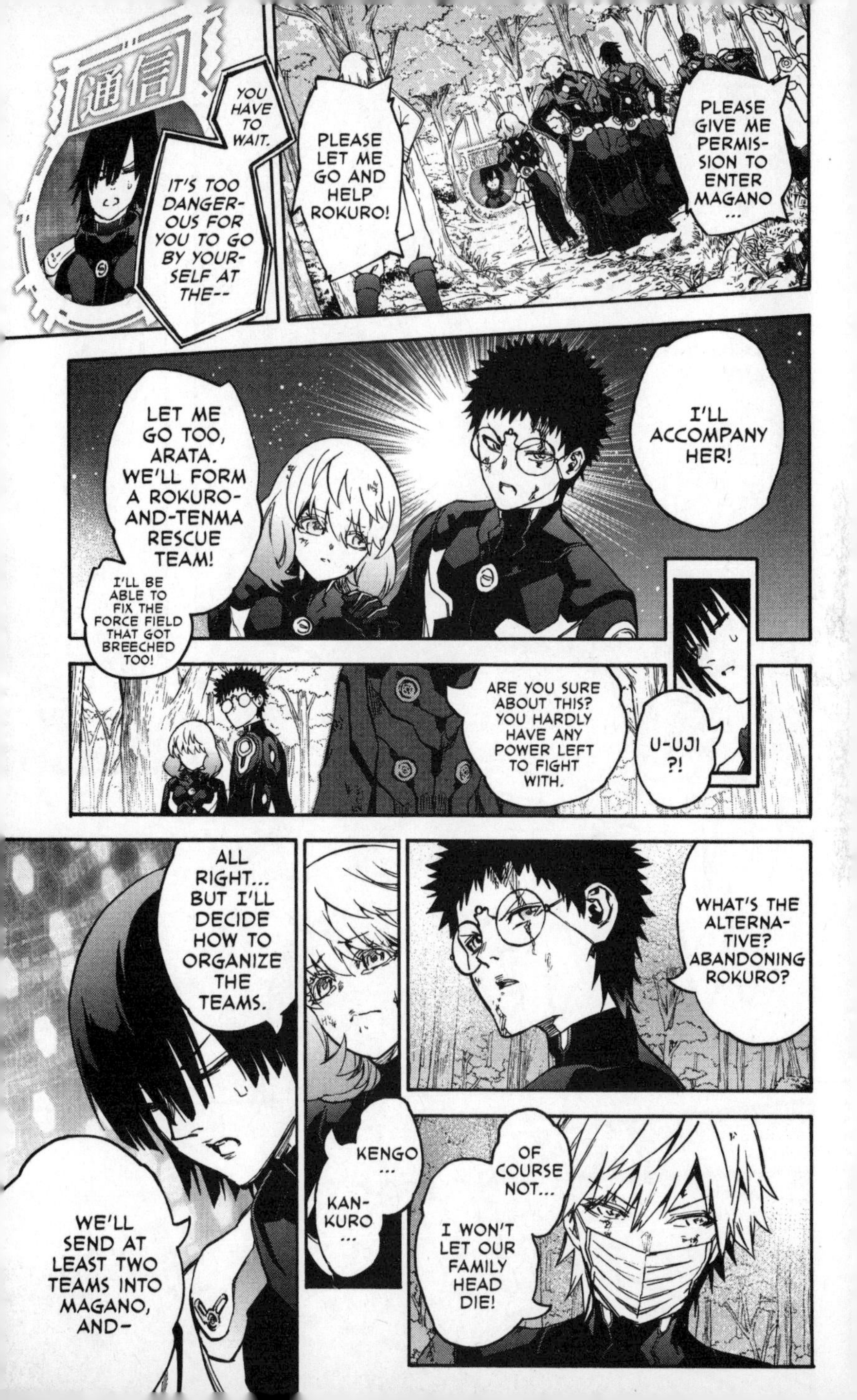
PLEASE GIVE ME PERMISSION TO ENTER MAGANO...
PLEASE LET ME GO AND HELP ROKURO!
通信
YOU HAVE TO WAIT.
IT'S TOO DANGEROUS FOR YOU TO GO BY YOURSELF AT THE--
I'LL ACCOMPANY HER!
LET ME GO TOO, ARATA. WE'LL FORM A ROKURO-AND-TENMA RESCUE TEAM!
I'LL BE ABLE TO FIX THE FORCE FIELD THAT GOT BREECHED TOO!
U-UJI?!
ARE YOU SURE ABOUT THIS? YOU HARDLY HAVE ANY POWER LEFT TO FIGHT WITH.
WHAT'S THE ALTERNATIVE? ABANDONING ROKURO?
OF COURSE NOT...
I WON'T LET OUR FAMILY HEAD DIE!
KENGO...
KANKURO...
ALL RIGHT... BUT I'LL DECIDE HOW TO ORGANIZE THE TEAMS.
WE'LL SEND AT LEAST TWO TEAMS INTO MAGANO, AND-

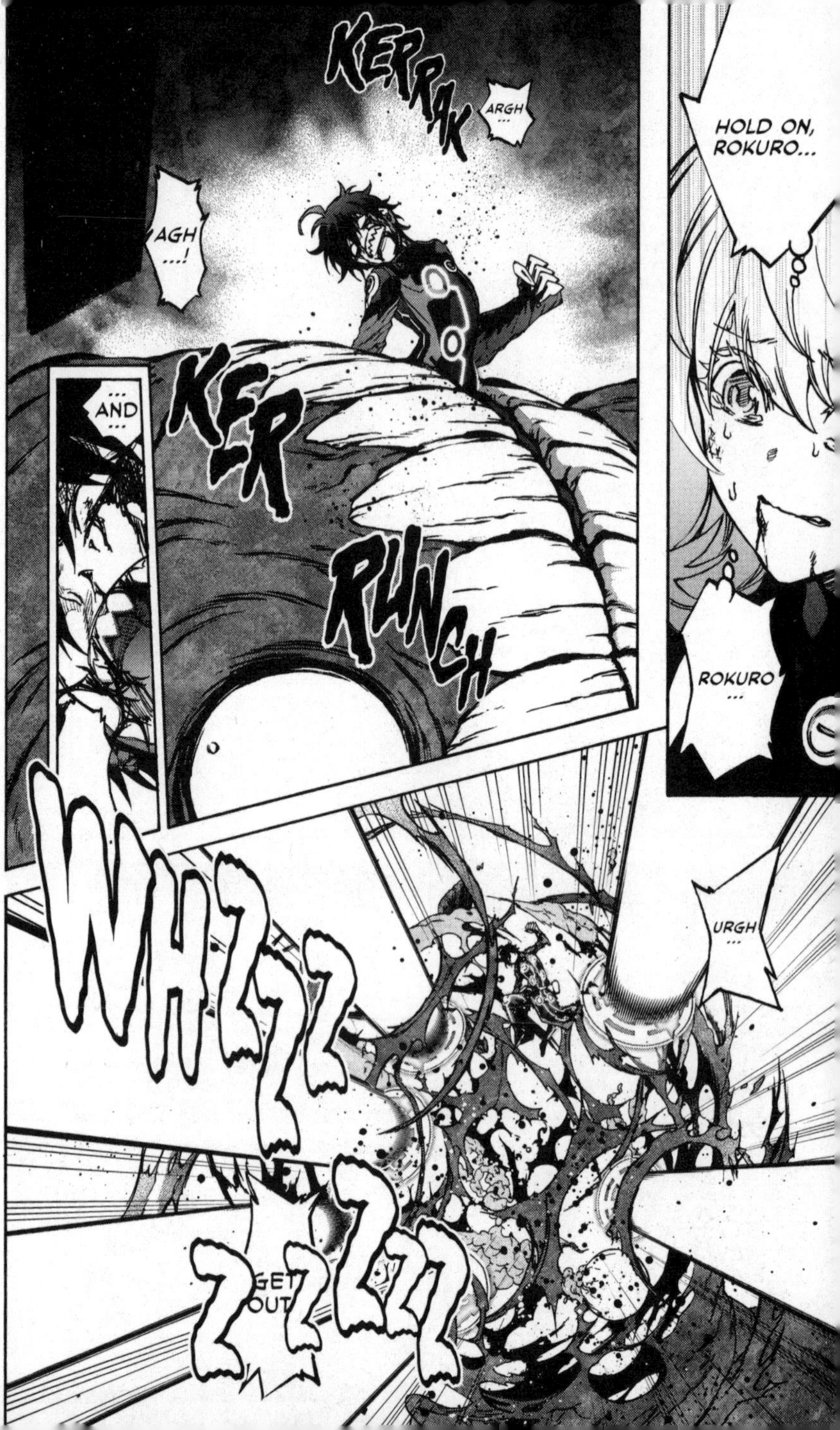
HOLD ON, ROKURO...
ROKURO...
KERRAK
ARGH...
AGH...!
KERCRUNCH
...AND...
URGH...
WHZZZZZZZZ
GET OUT

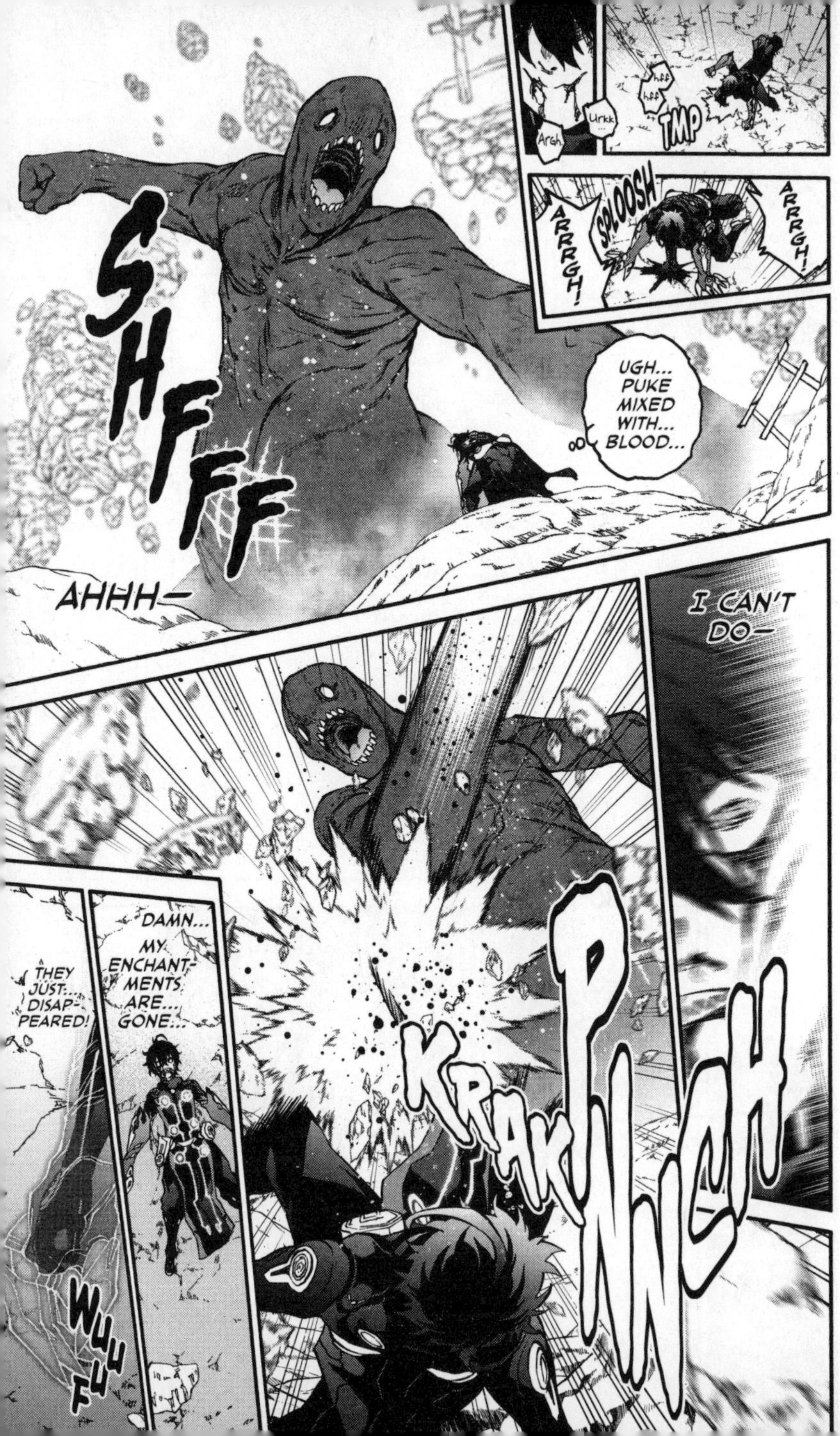
Urkk...
Argh.
hff
hff
TMP
ARRRGH!
SPLOOSH
ARRRGH!
SHFFFF
UGH... PUKE MIXED WITH... BLOOD...
AHHH—
I CAN'T DO—
KRAKUNCH
PWNCH
DAMN... MY ENCHANT-MENTS ARE... GONE...
THEY JUST... DISAP-PEARED!
WUUUFF

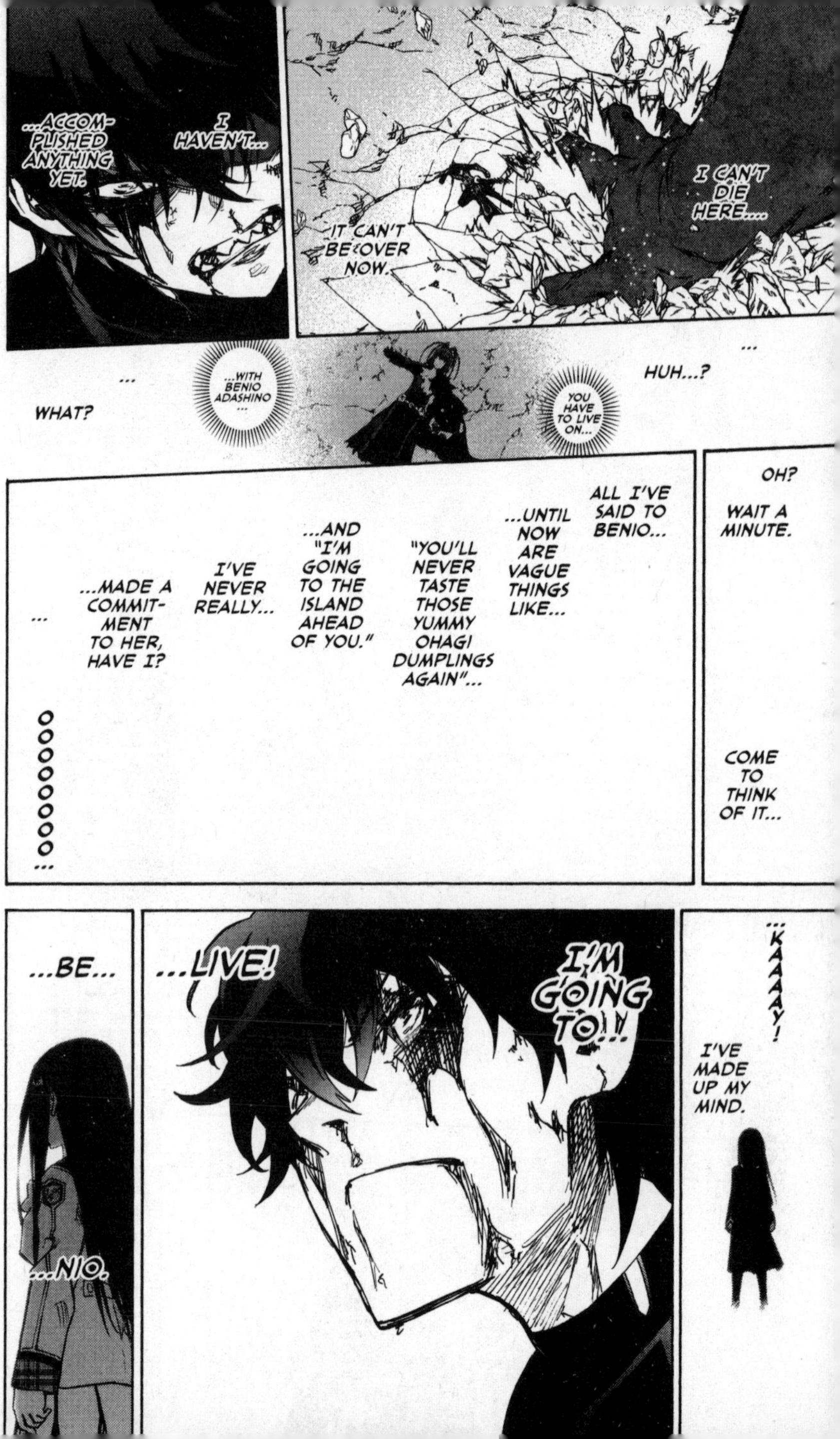
I CAN'T DIE HERE....
IT CAN'T BE OVER NOW.
I HAVEN'T...
...ACCOMPLISHED ANYTHING YET.
...
HUH...?
YOU HAVE TO LIVE ON...
...WITH BENIO ADASHINO ...
...
WHAT?
OH?
WAIT A MINUTE.
COME TO THINK OF IT...
ALL I'VE SAID TO BENIO...
...UNTIL NOW ARE VAGUE THINGS LIKE...
"YOU'LL NEVER TASTE THOSE YUMMY OHAGI DUMPLINGS AGAIN"...
...AND "I'M GOING TO THE ISLAND AHEAD OF YOU."
I'VE NEVER REALLY...
...MADE A COMMITMENT TO HER, HAVE I?
...
OOOOOOOO...
...KAAAAY!
I'VE MADE UP MY MIND.
I'M GOING TO!!
...LIVE!
...BE...
...NIO.

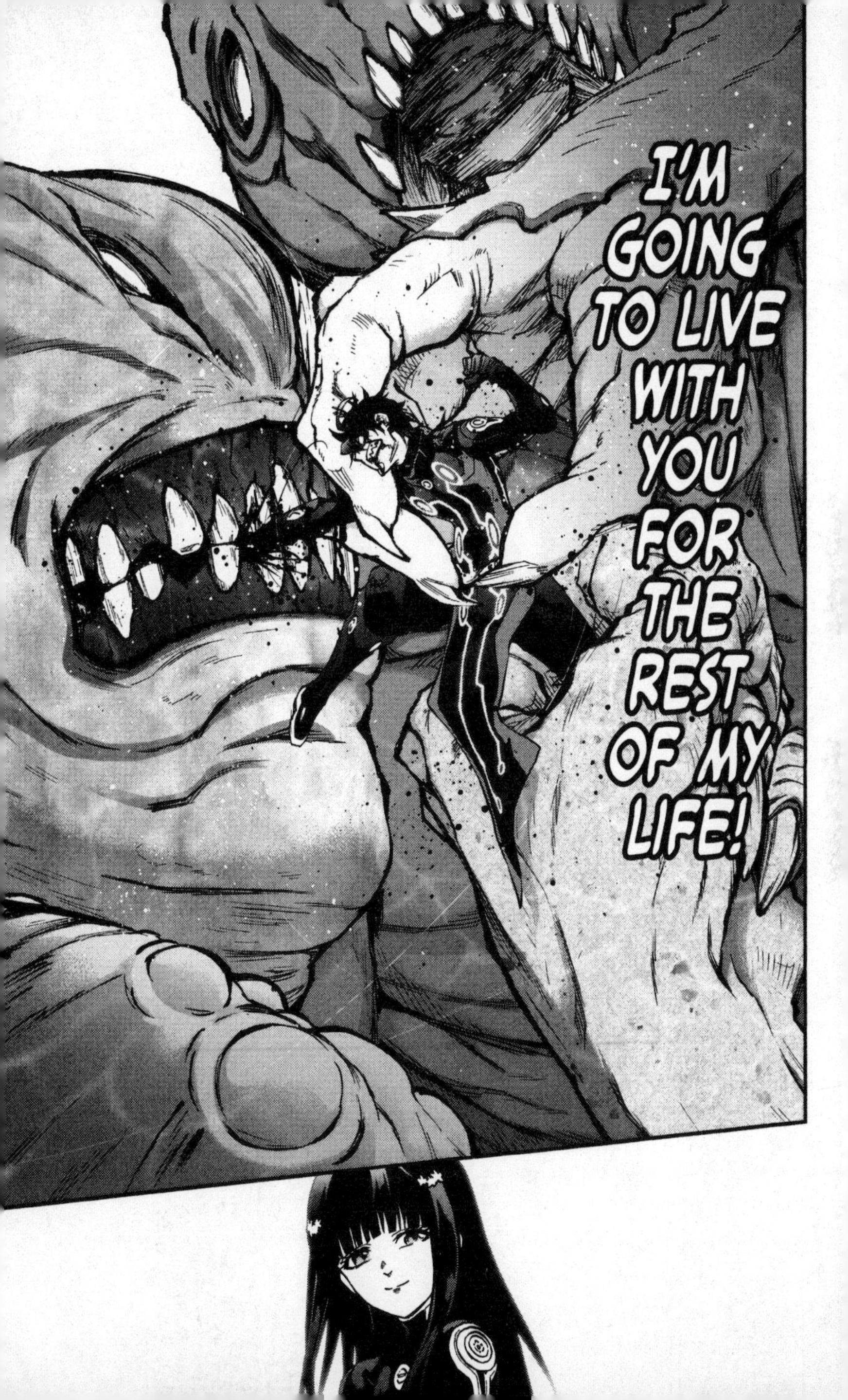
I'M GOING TO LIVE WITH YOU FOR THE REST OF MY LIFE!

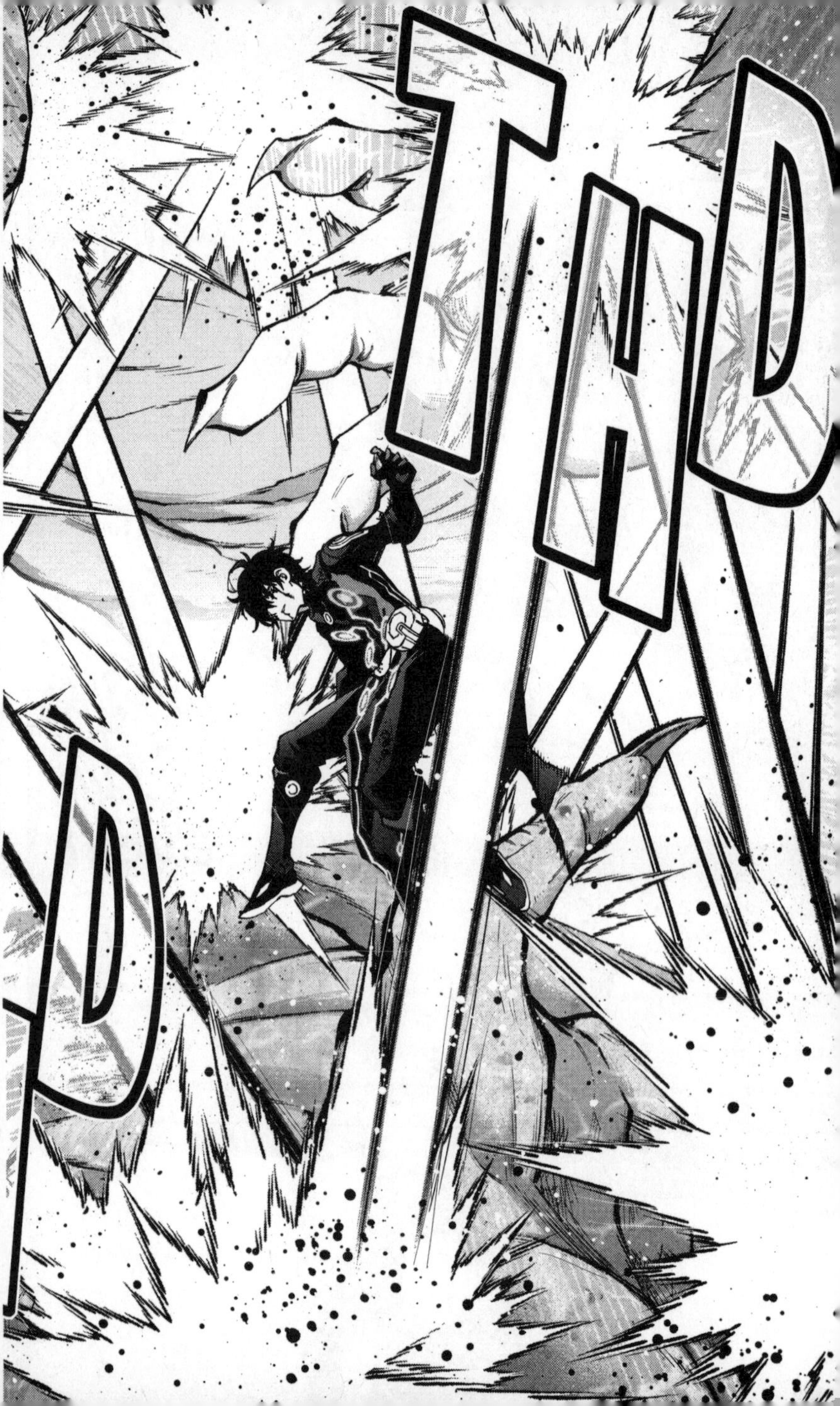
THUD

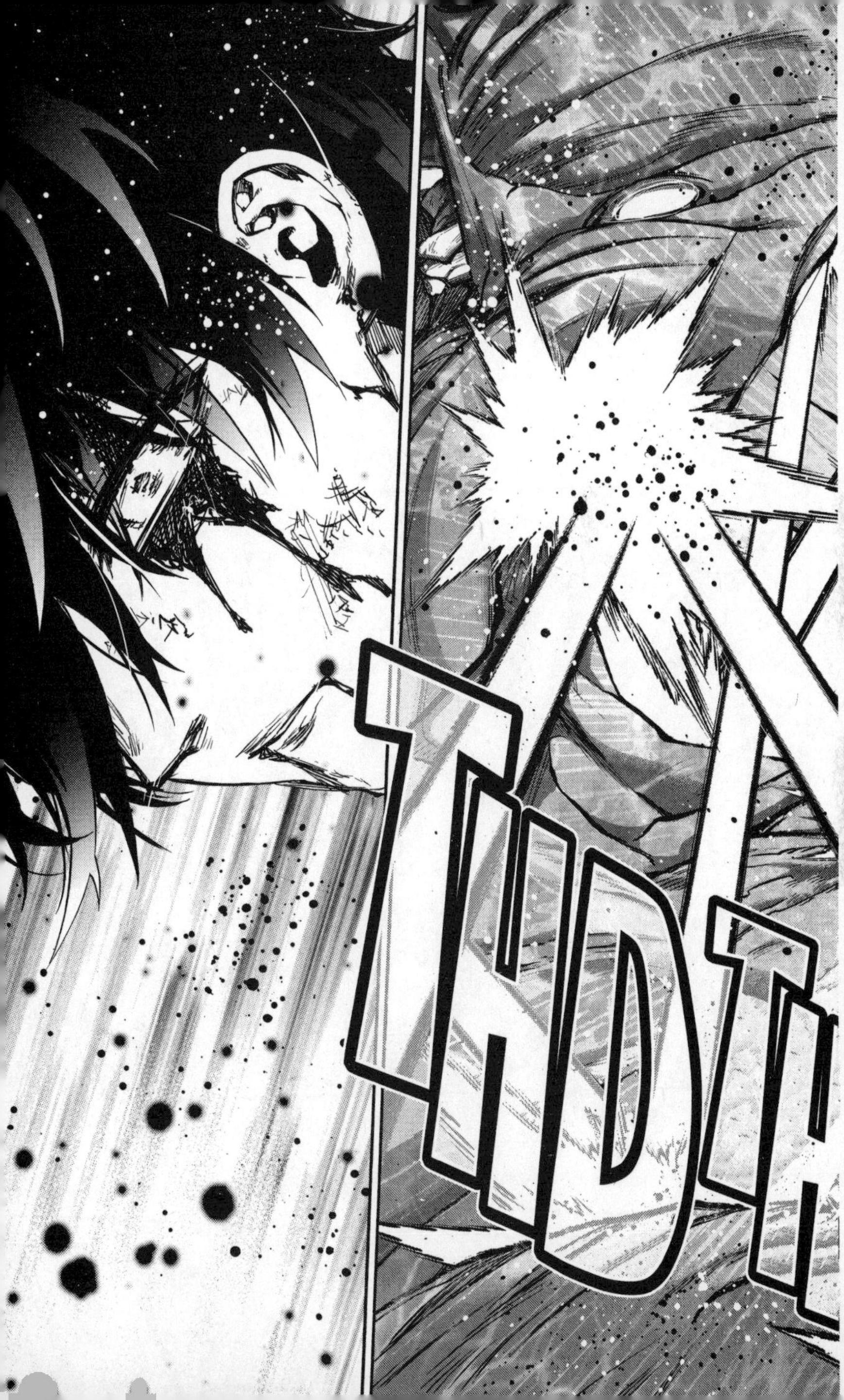
THDTH

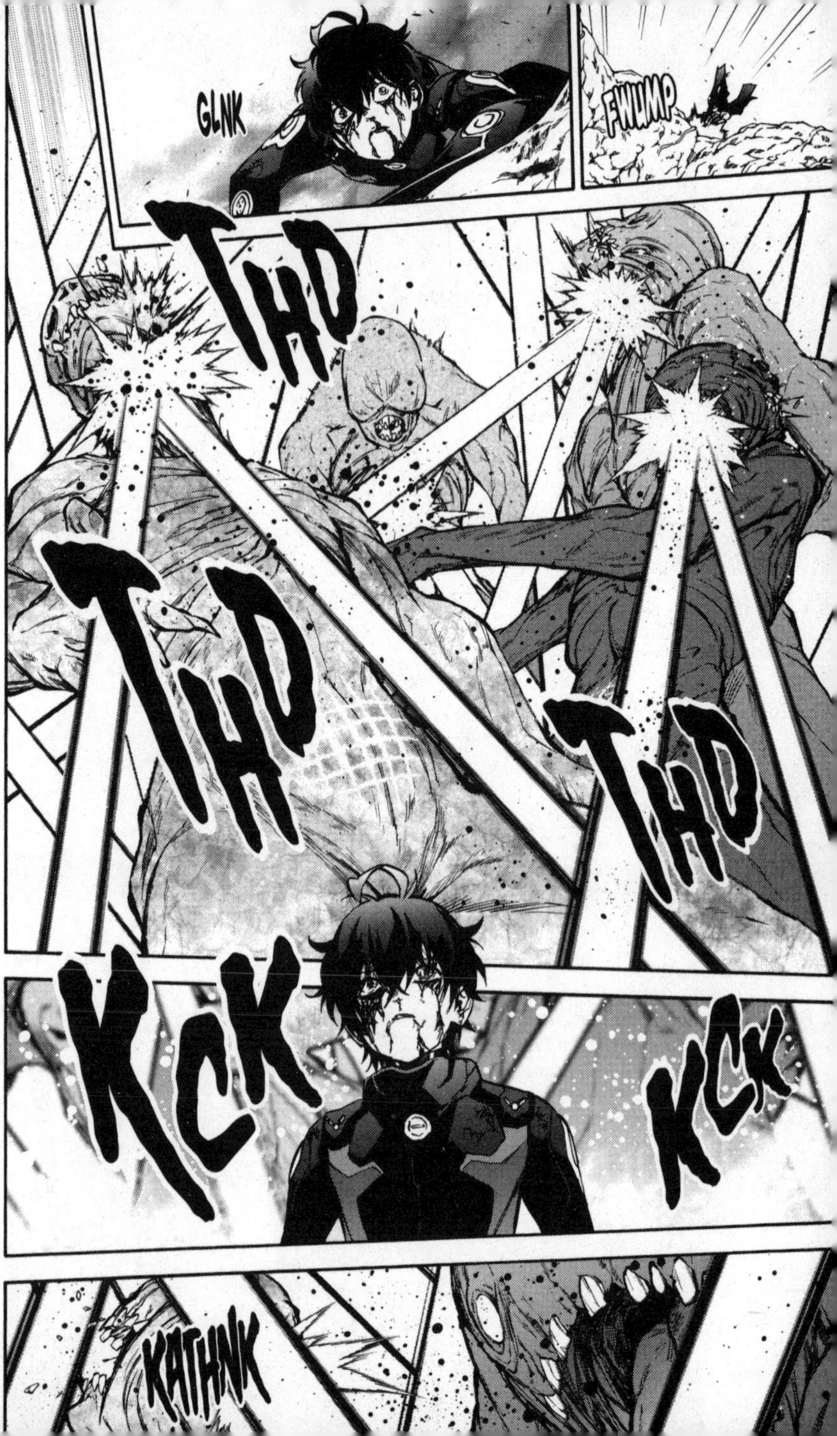
FWUMP
GLNK
THD
THD
THD
KCK
KCK
KATHNK

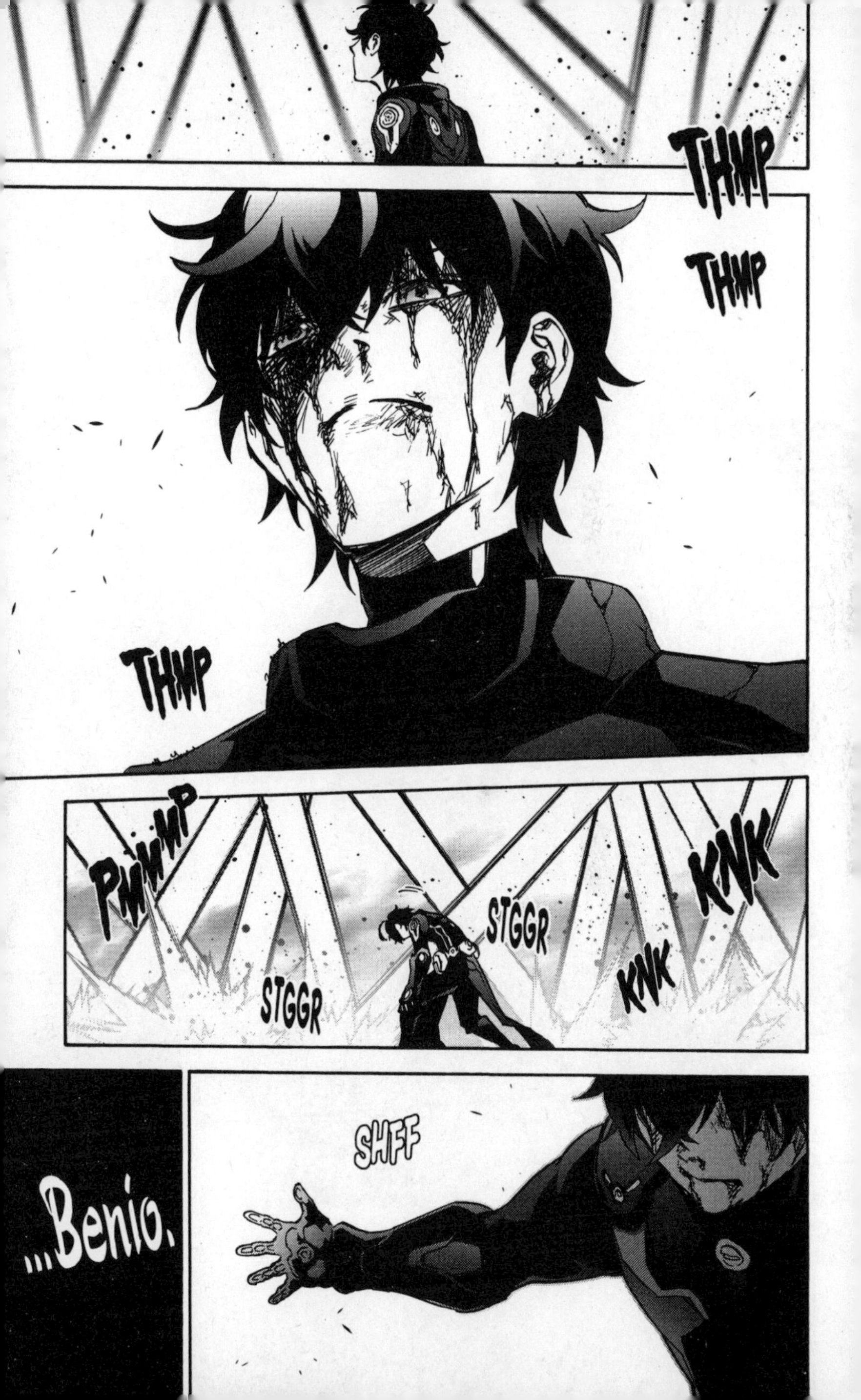
THMP
THMP
THMP
KNK
STGGR
PWMMP
KNK
STGGR
SHFF
...Benio.

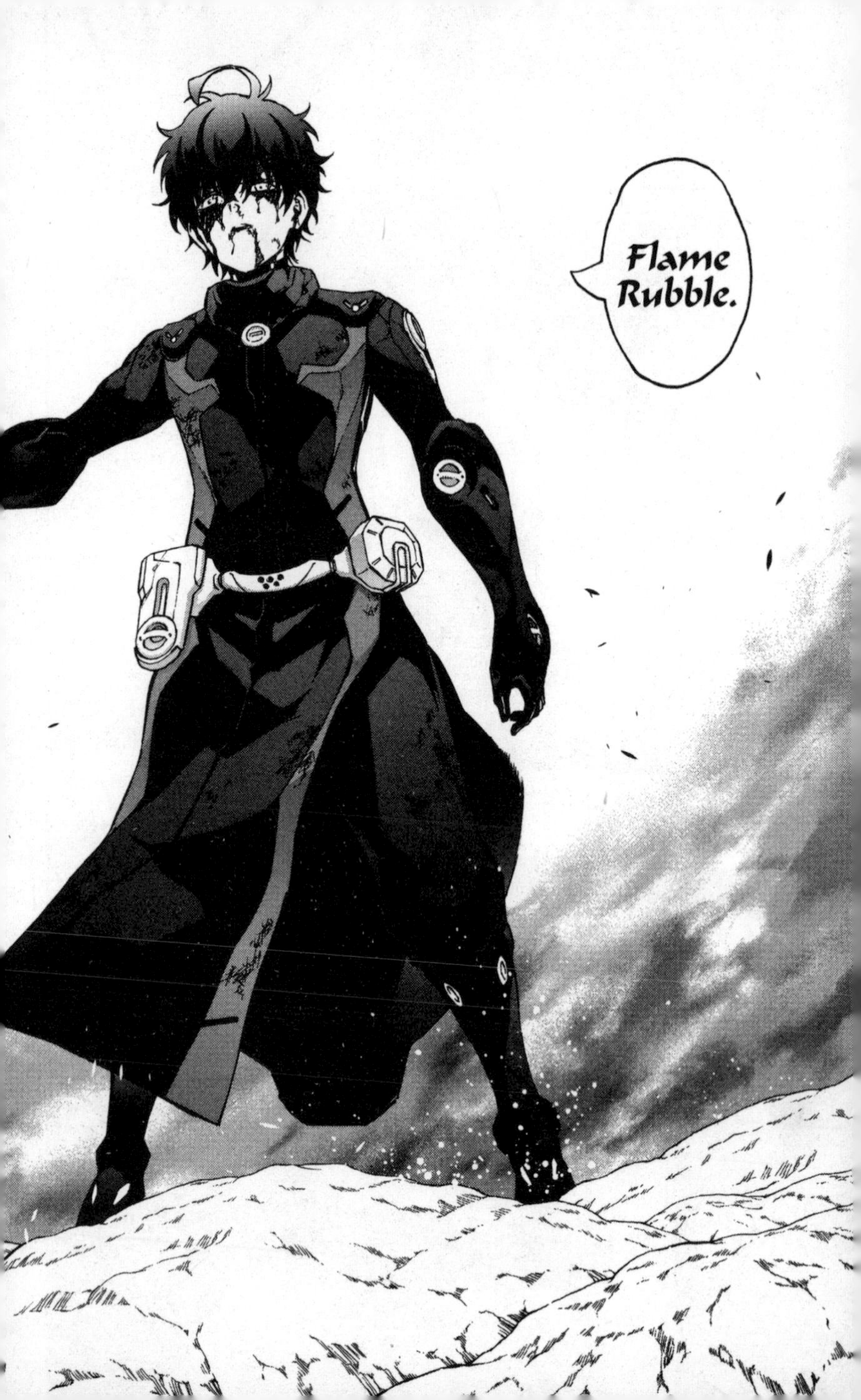
Flame Rubble.

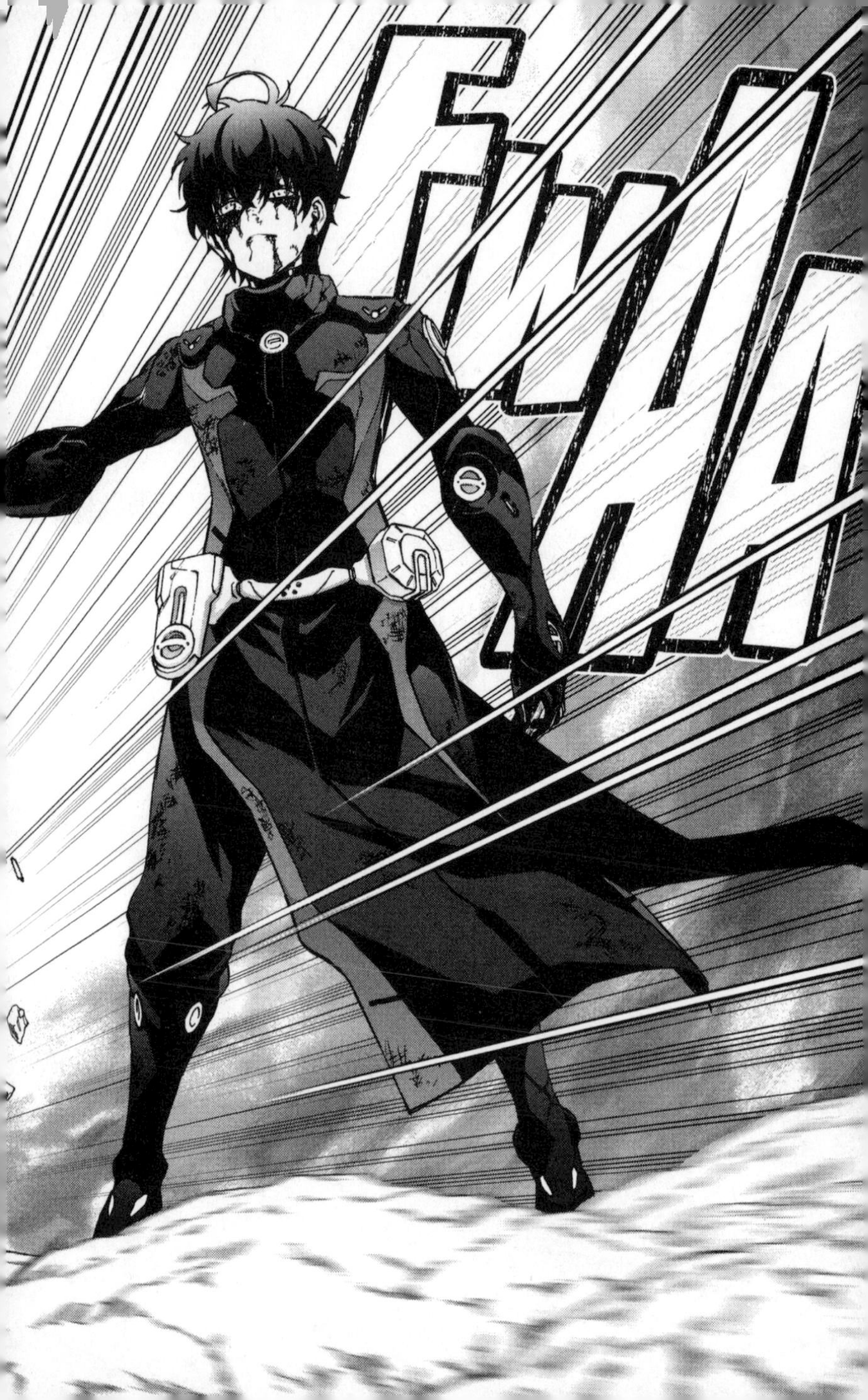
FWAA

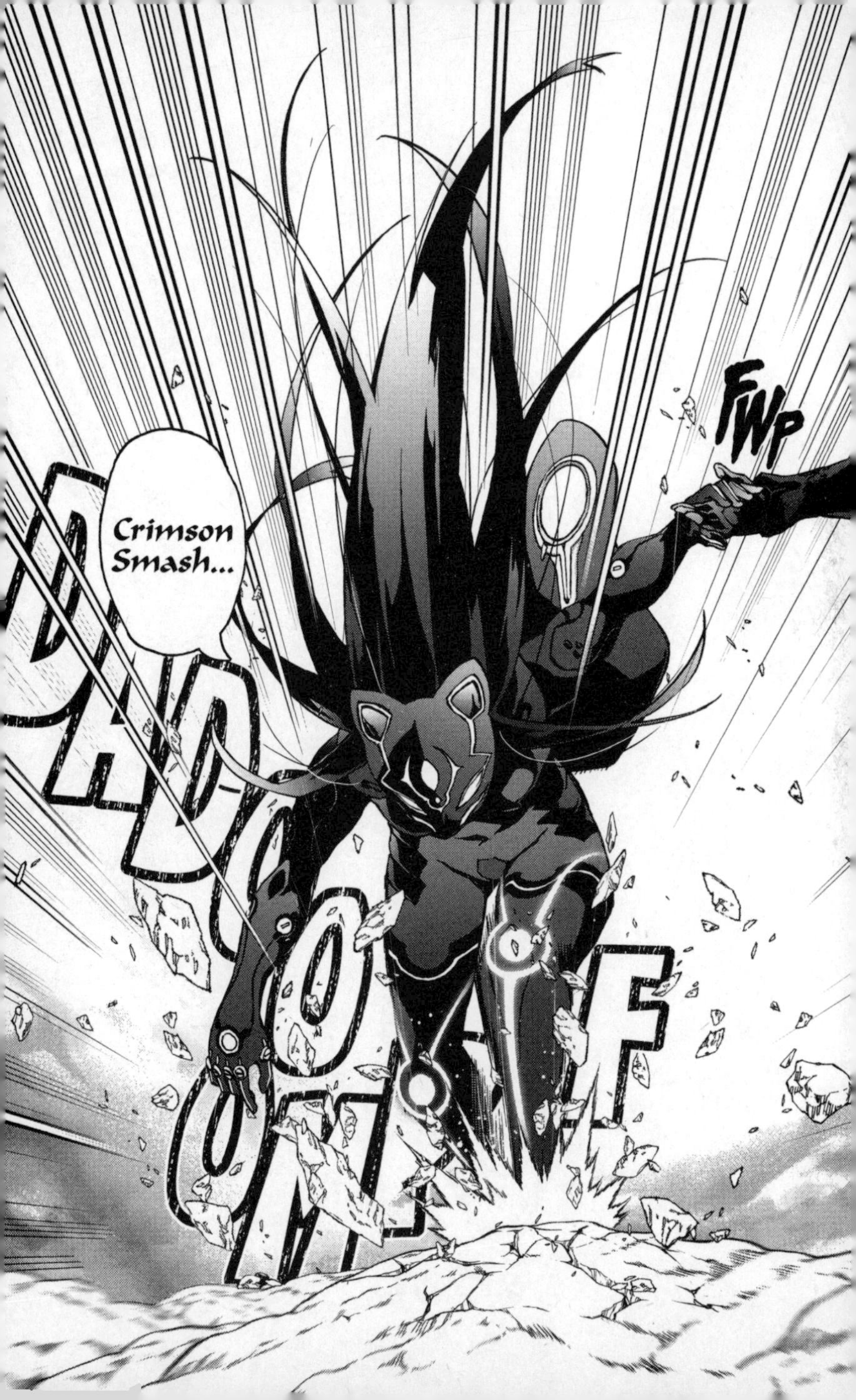
FWP
Crimson Smash...

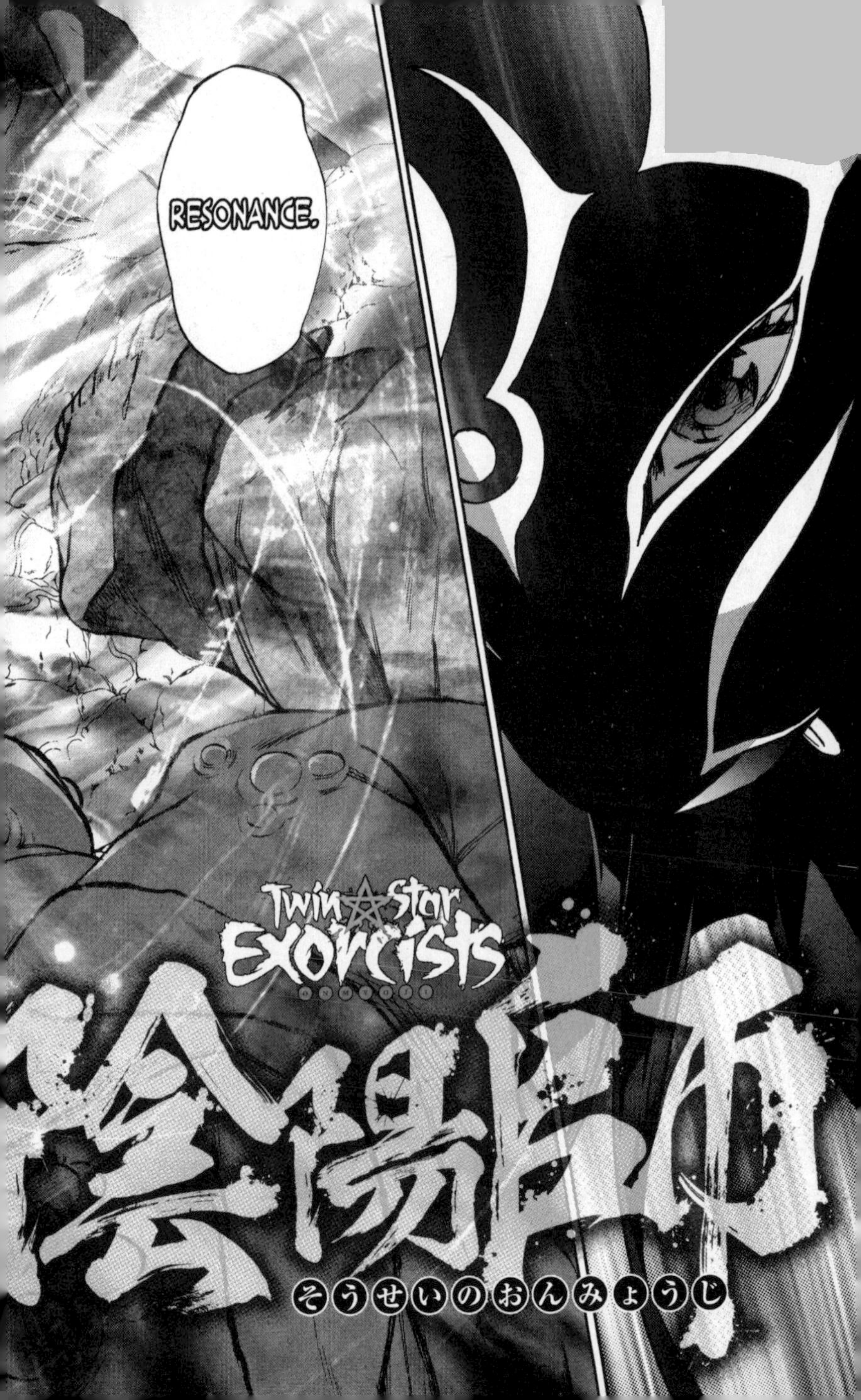
RESONANCE.
Twin Star Exorcists
ONMYOJI
双星の陰陽師
そうせいのおんみょうじ

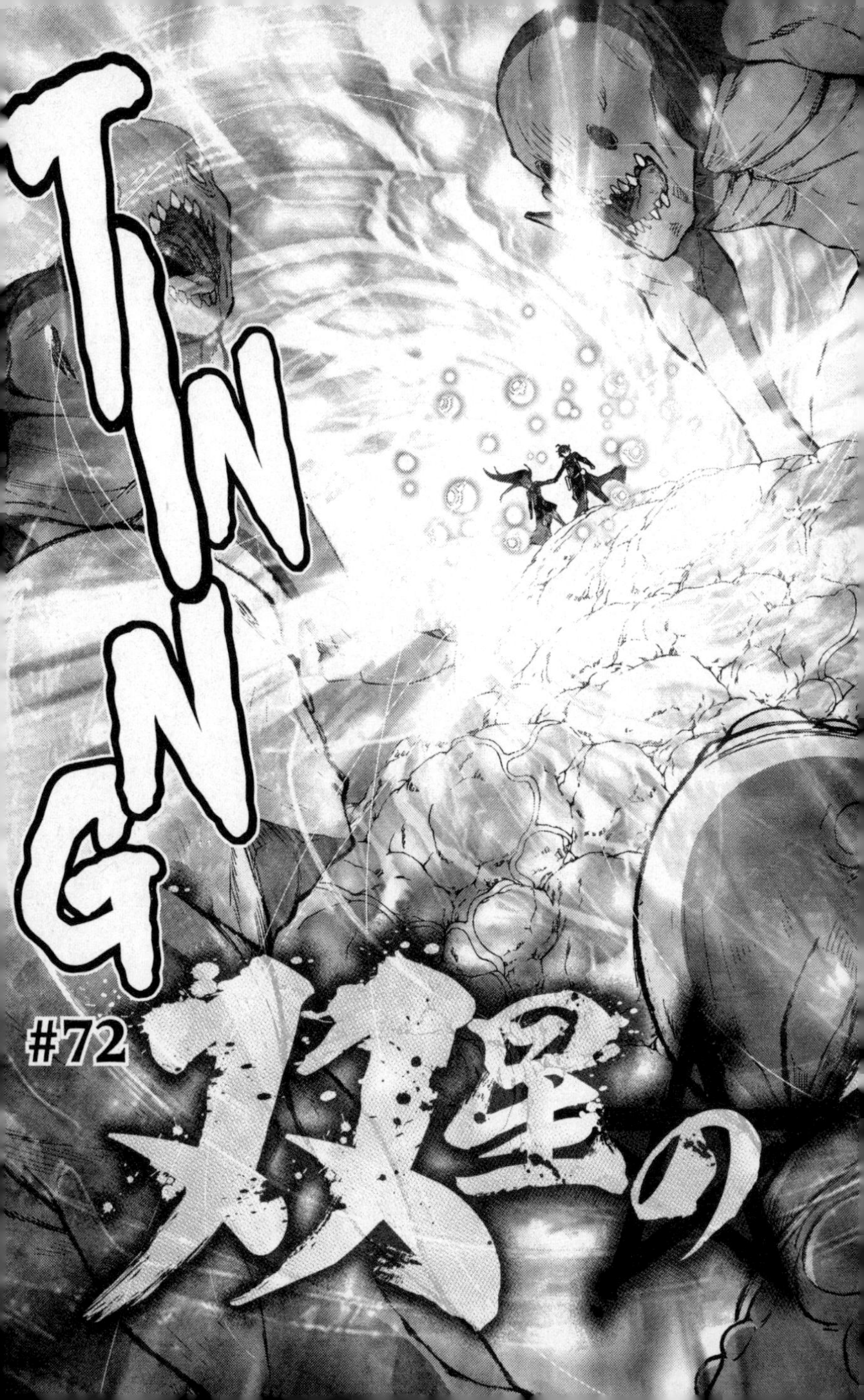
TINNG
#72
双星の

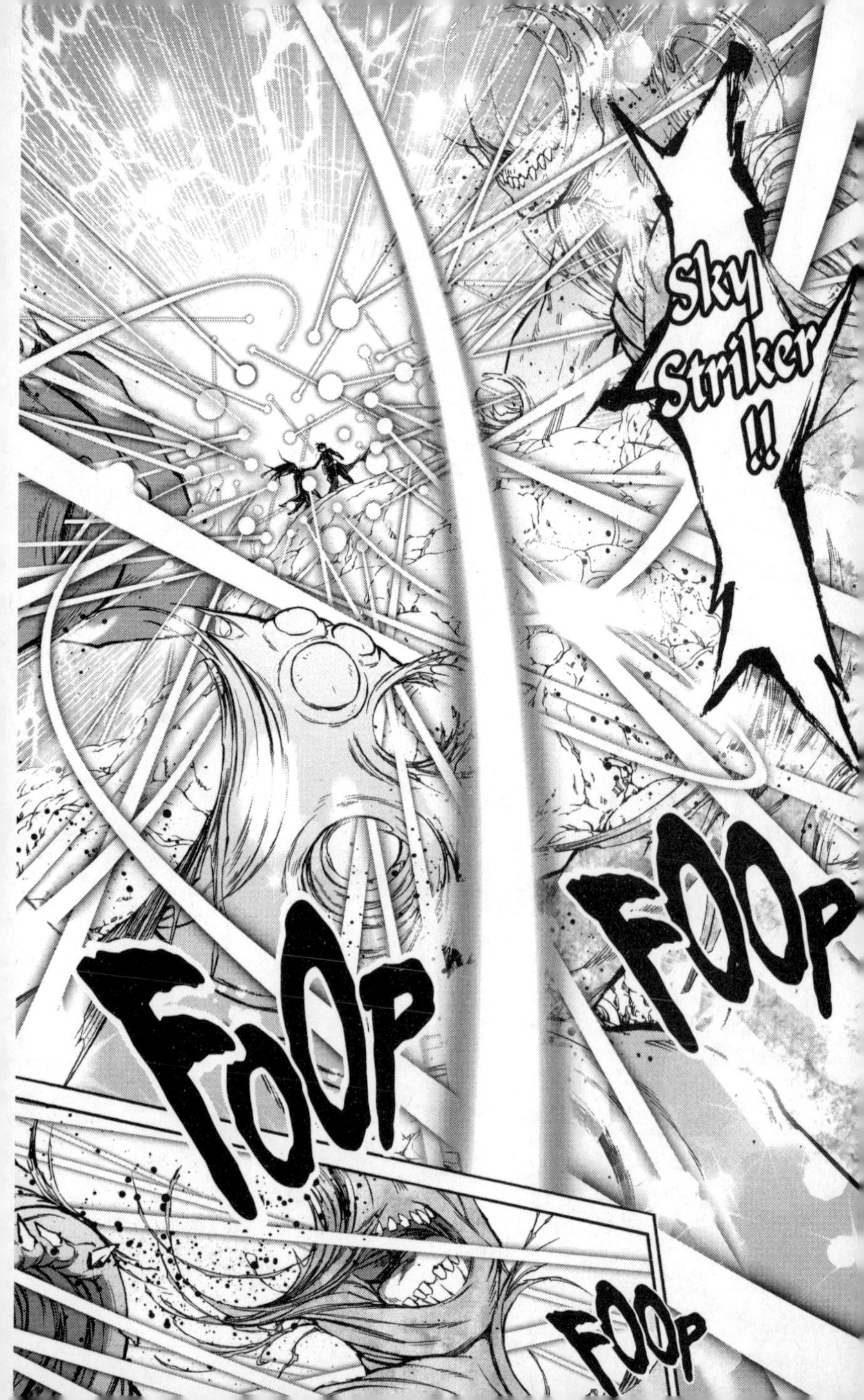

Sky Striker!!
FOOP
FOOP
FOOP

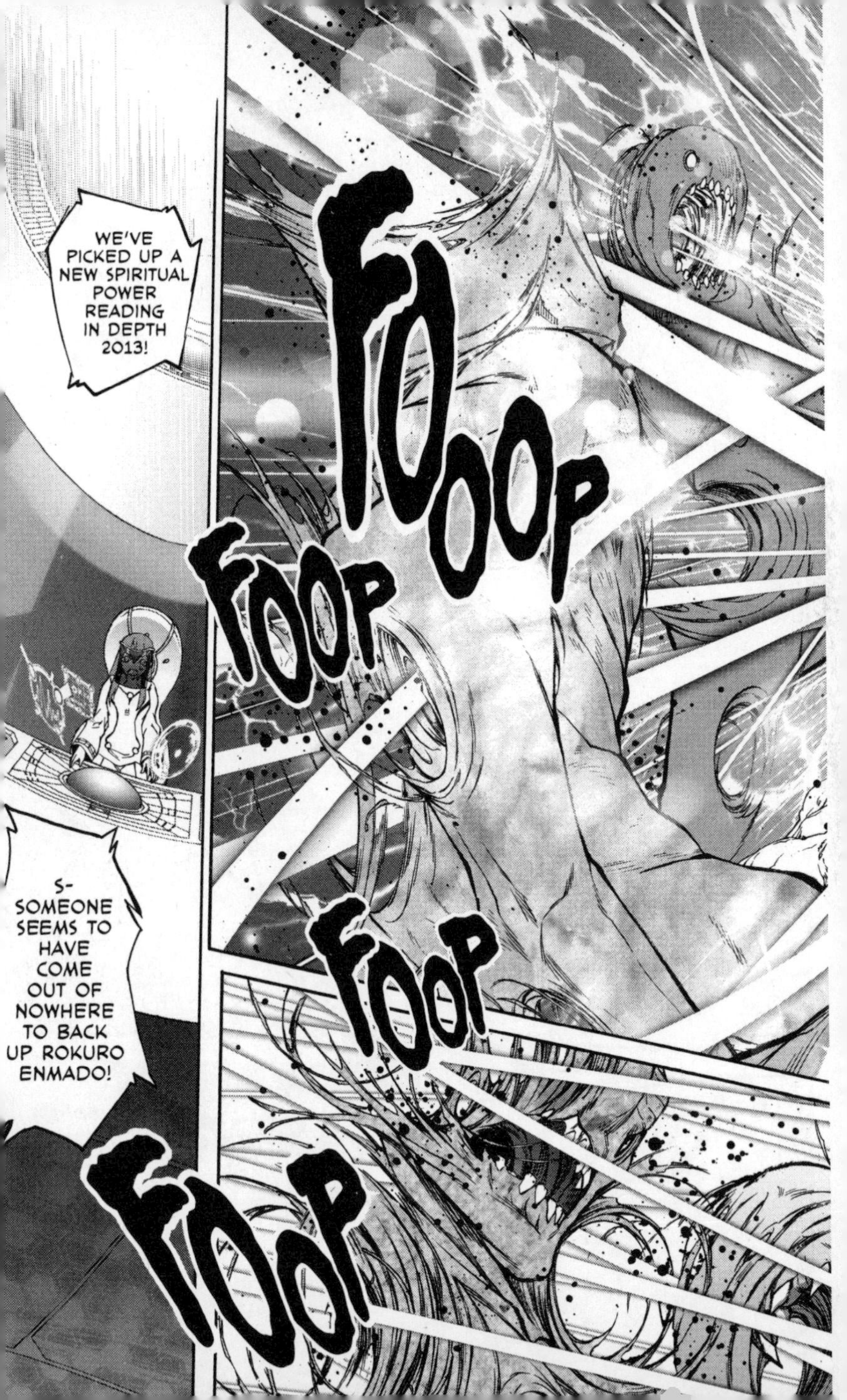
FOOOP
FOOP
FOOP
FOOP
WE'VE PICKED UP A NEW SPIRITUAL POWER READING IN DEPTH 2013!
S-SOMEONE SEEMS TO HAVE COME OUT OF NOWHERE TO BACK UP ROKURO ENMADO!

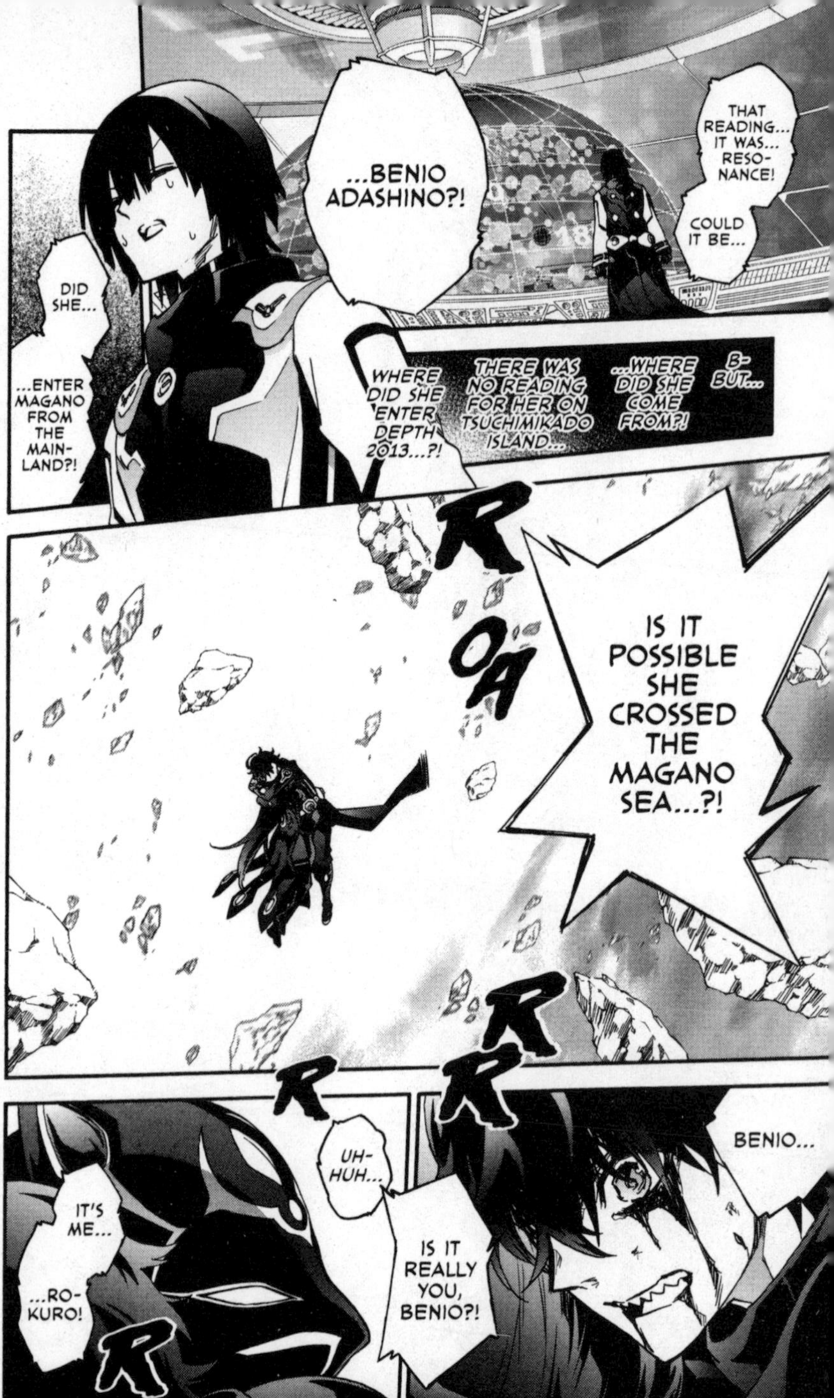
THAT READING... IT WAS... RESO-NANCE!
COULD IT BE...
...BENIO ADASHINO?!
B-BUT...
...WHERE DID SHE COME FROM?!
THERE WAS NO READING FOR HER ON TSUCHIMIKADO ISLAND...
WHERE DID SHE ENTER DEPTH 2013...?!
DID SHE...
...ENTER MAGANO FROM THE MAIN-LAND?!
ROA
IS IT POSSIBLE SHE CROSSED THE MAGANO SEA...?!
RRRR
BENIO...
IS IT REALLY YOU, BENIO?!
UH-HUH...
IT'S ME...
...RO-KURO!
R

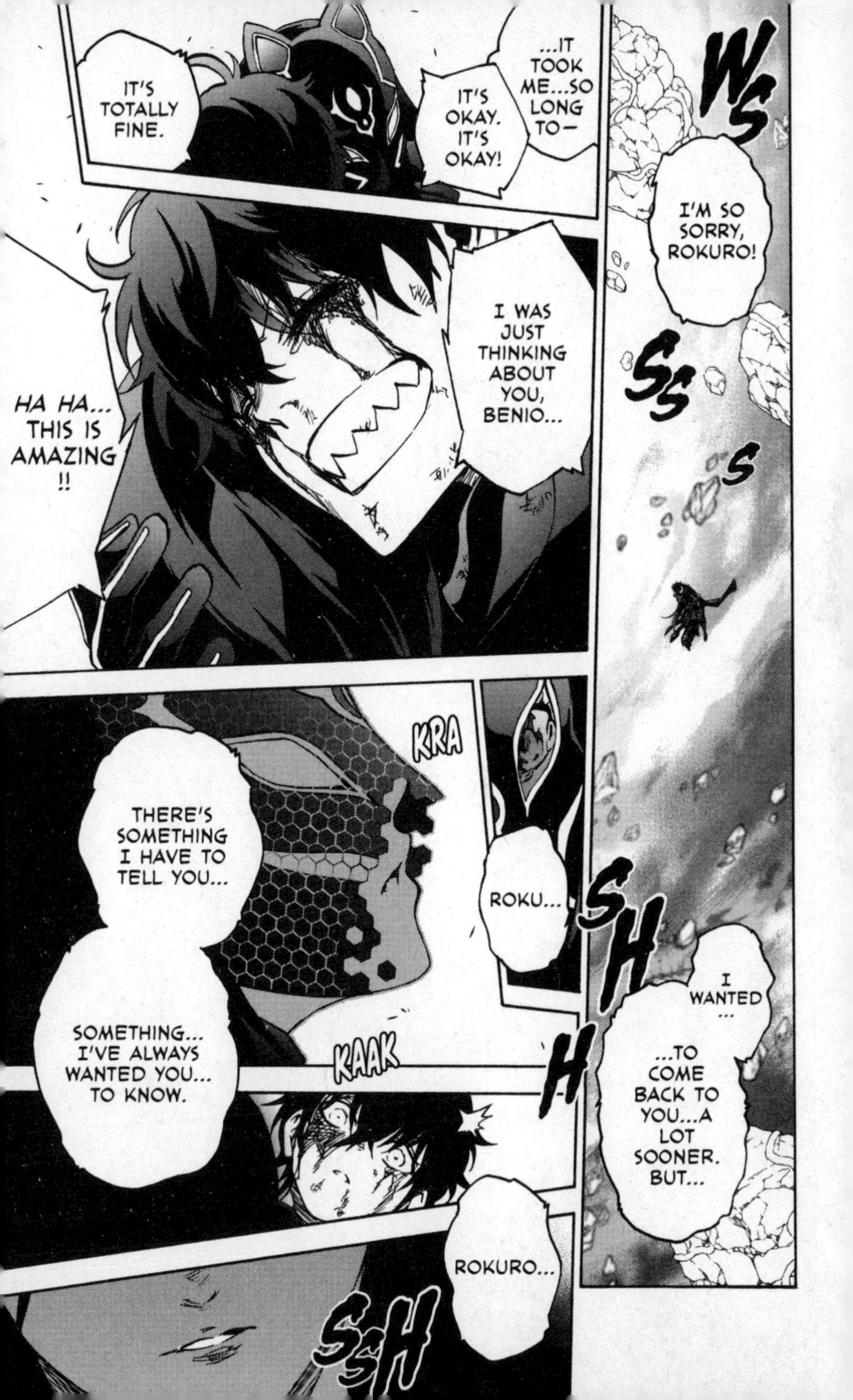
WS
I'M SO SORRY, ROKURO!
SS
S
SH
H
I WANTED...
...TO COME BACK TO YOU...A LOT SOONER. BUT...
...IT TOOK ME...SO LONG TO—
IT'S OKAY. IT'S OKAY!
IT'S TOTALLY FINE.
I WAS JUST THINKING ABOUT YOU, BENIO...
HA HA... THIS IS AMAZING!!
ROKU...
KRA
THERE'S SOMETHING I HAVE TO TELL YOU...
SOMETHING... I'VE ALWAYS WANTED YOU... TO KNOW.
KAAK
H
ROKURO...
SSH

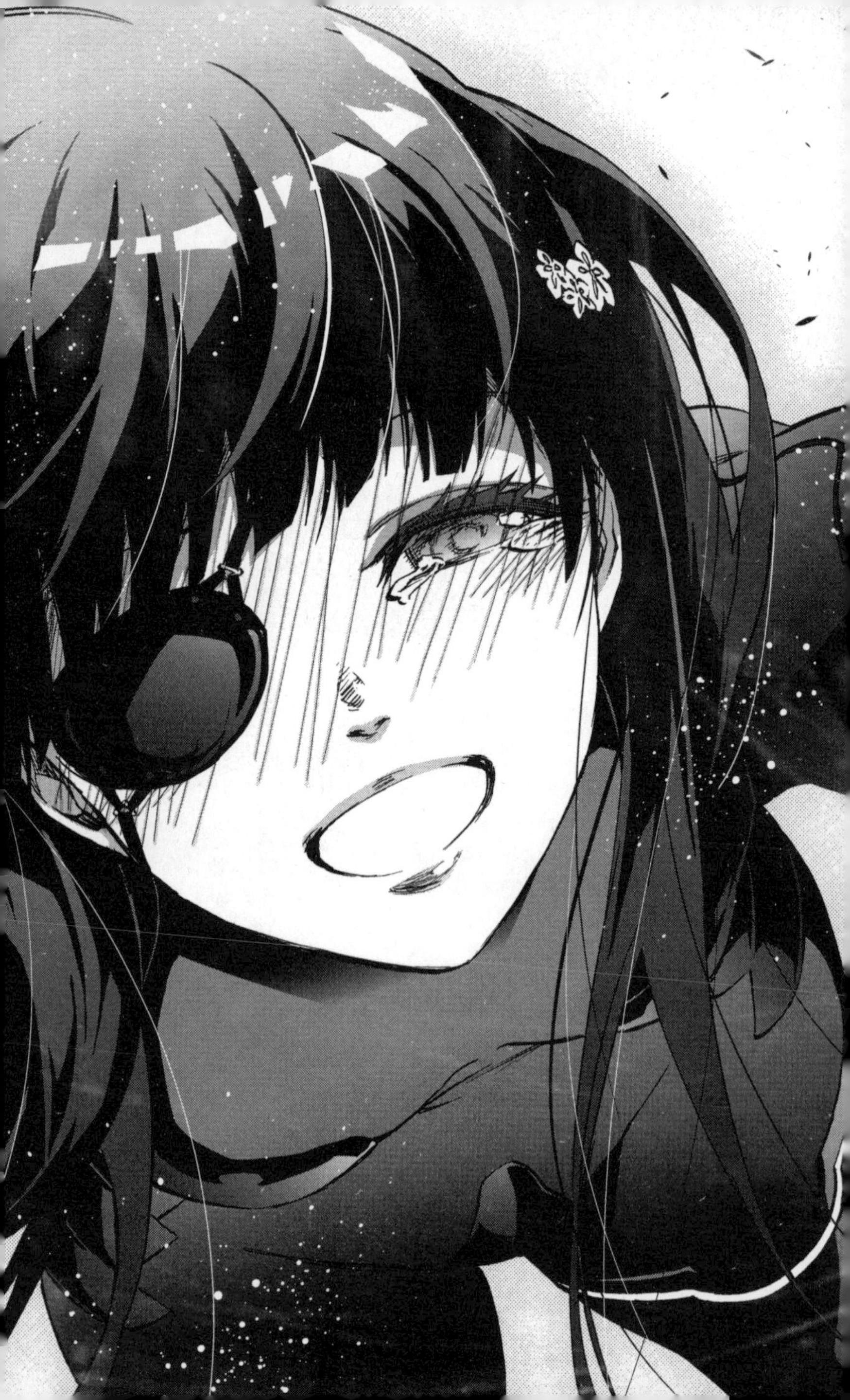

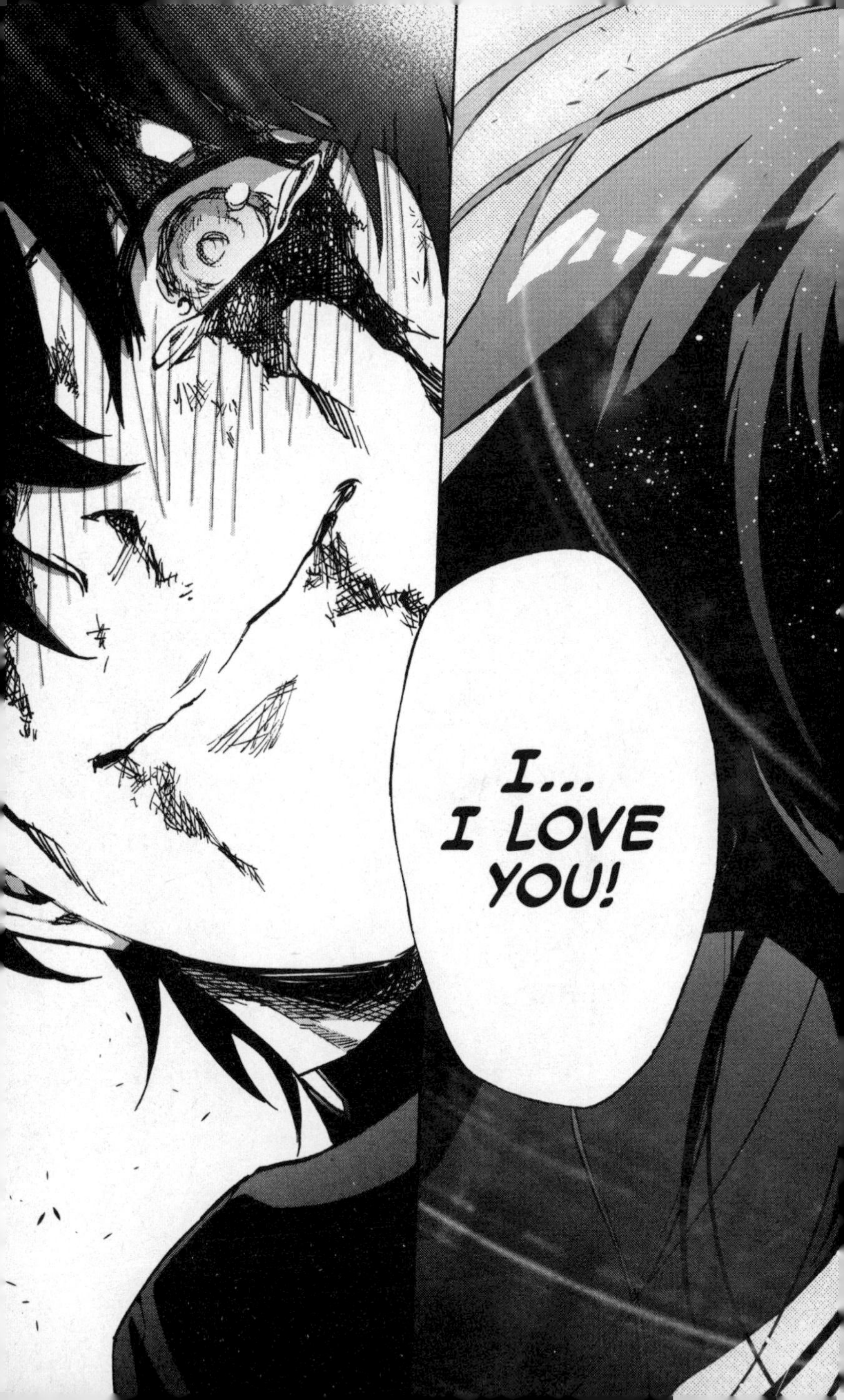
I... I LOVE YOU!

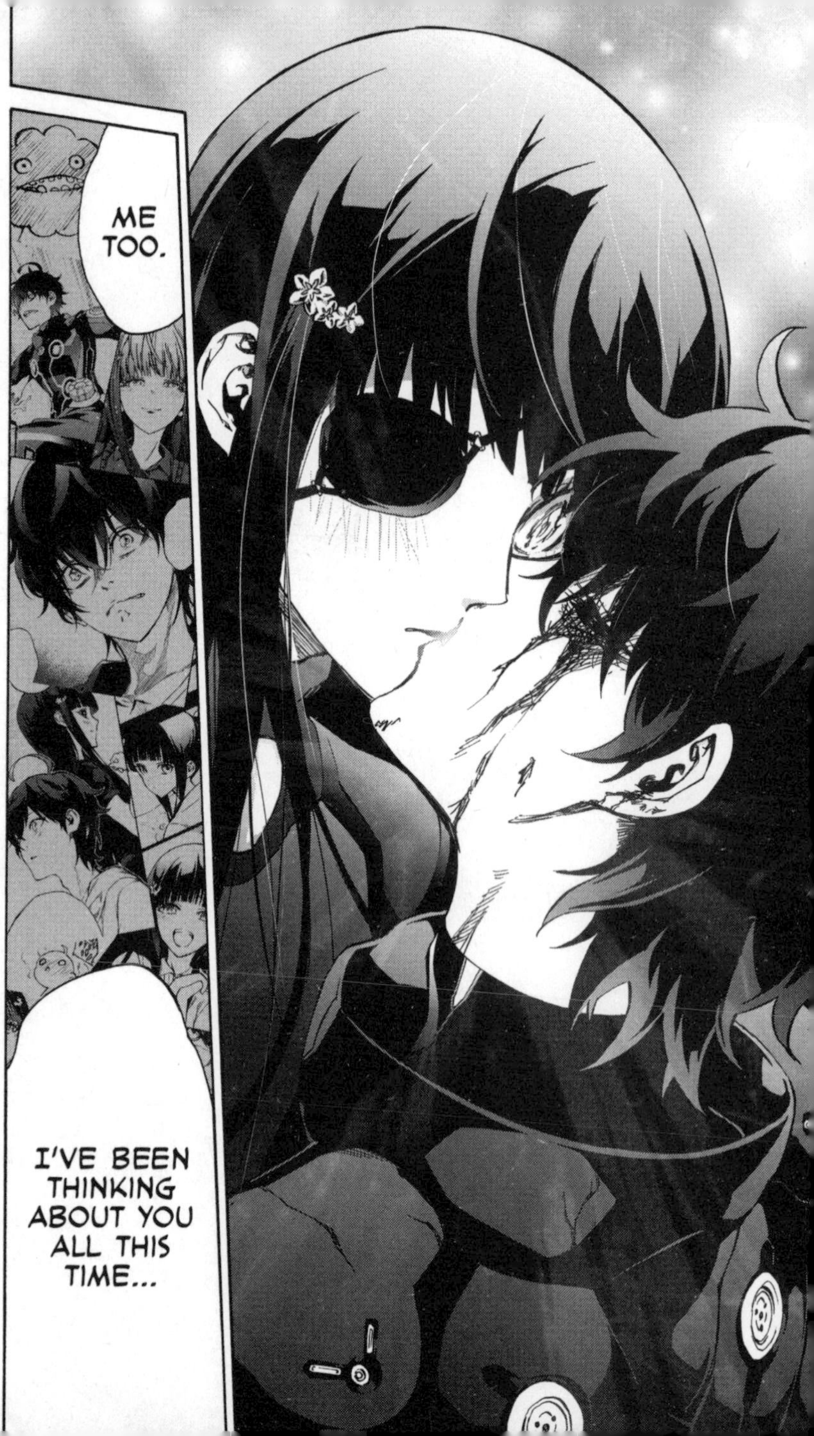
ME TOO.
I'VE BEEN THINKING ABOUT YOU ALL THIS TIME...

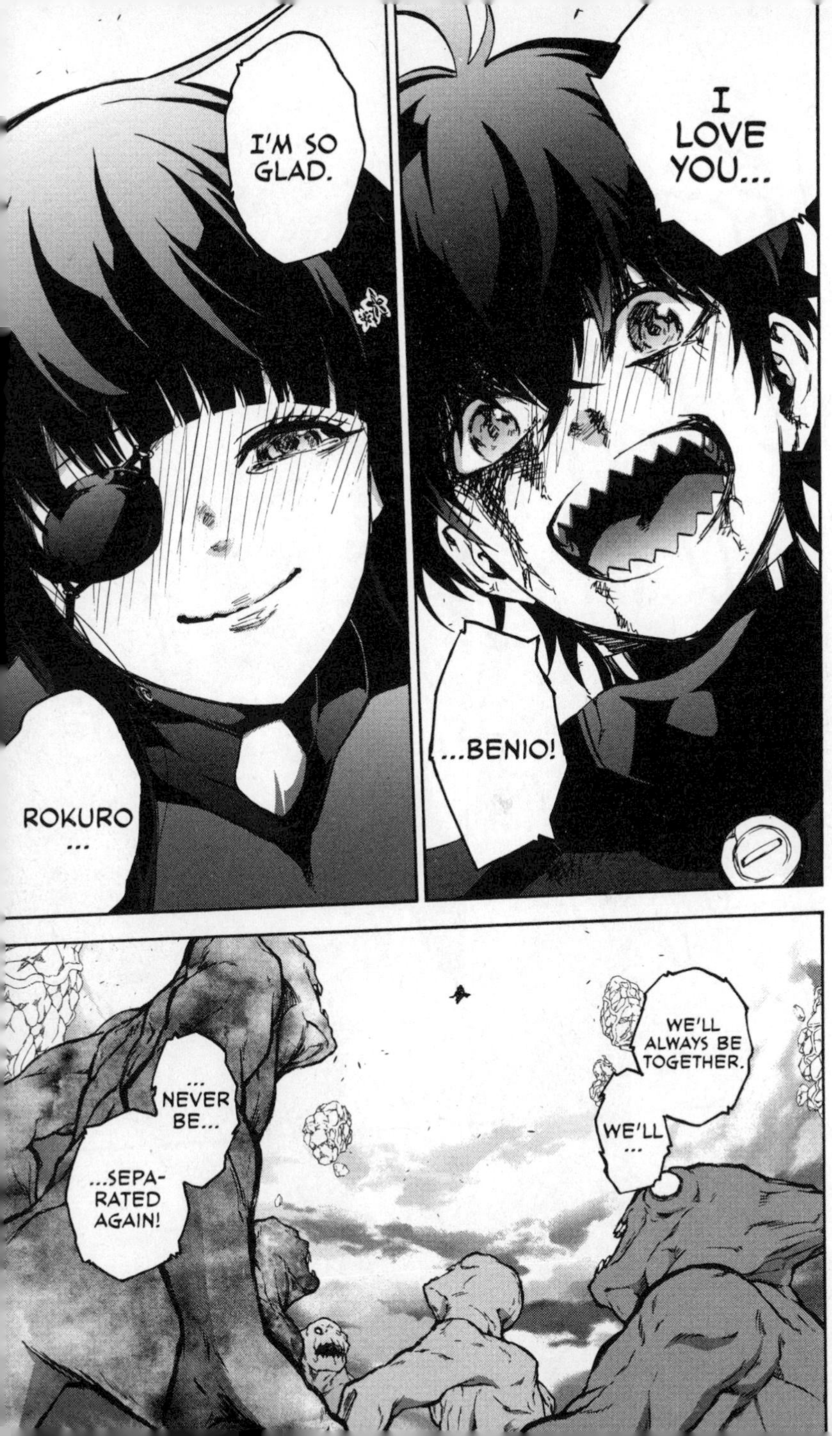
I LOVE YOU...
...BENIO!
I'M SO GLAD.
ROKURO ...
WE'LL ALWAYS BE TOGETHER.
WE'LL ...
... NEVER BE...
...SEPA-RATED AGAIN!

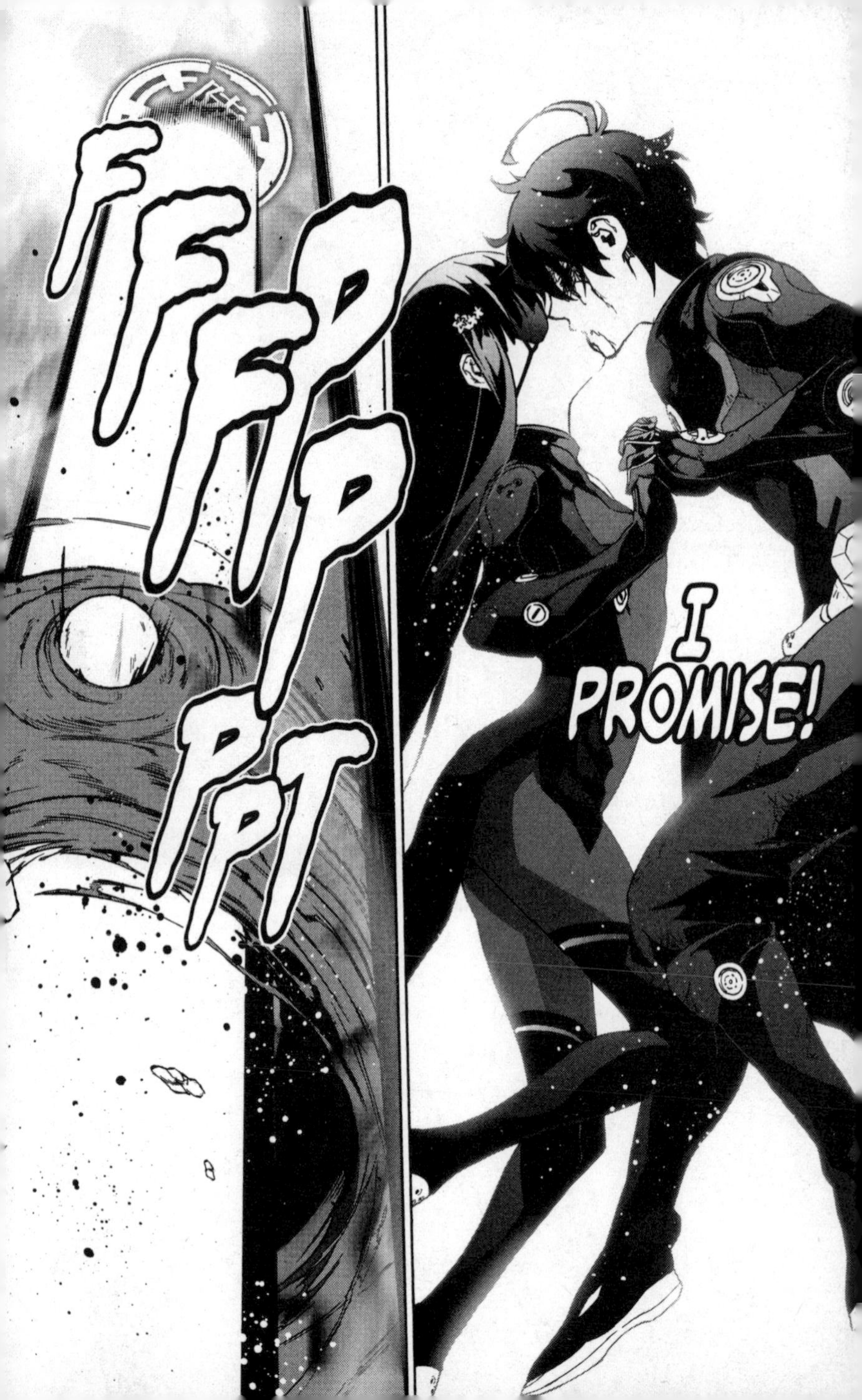
I PROMISE!

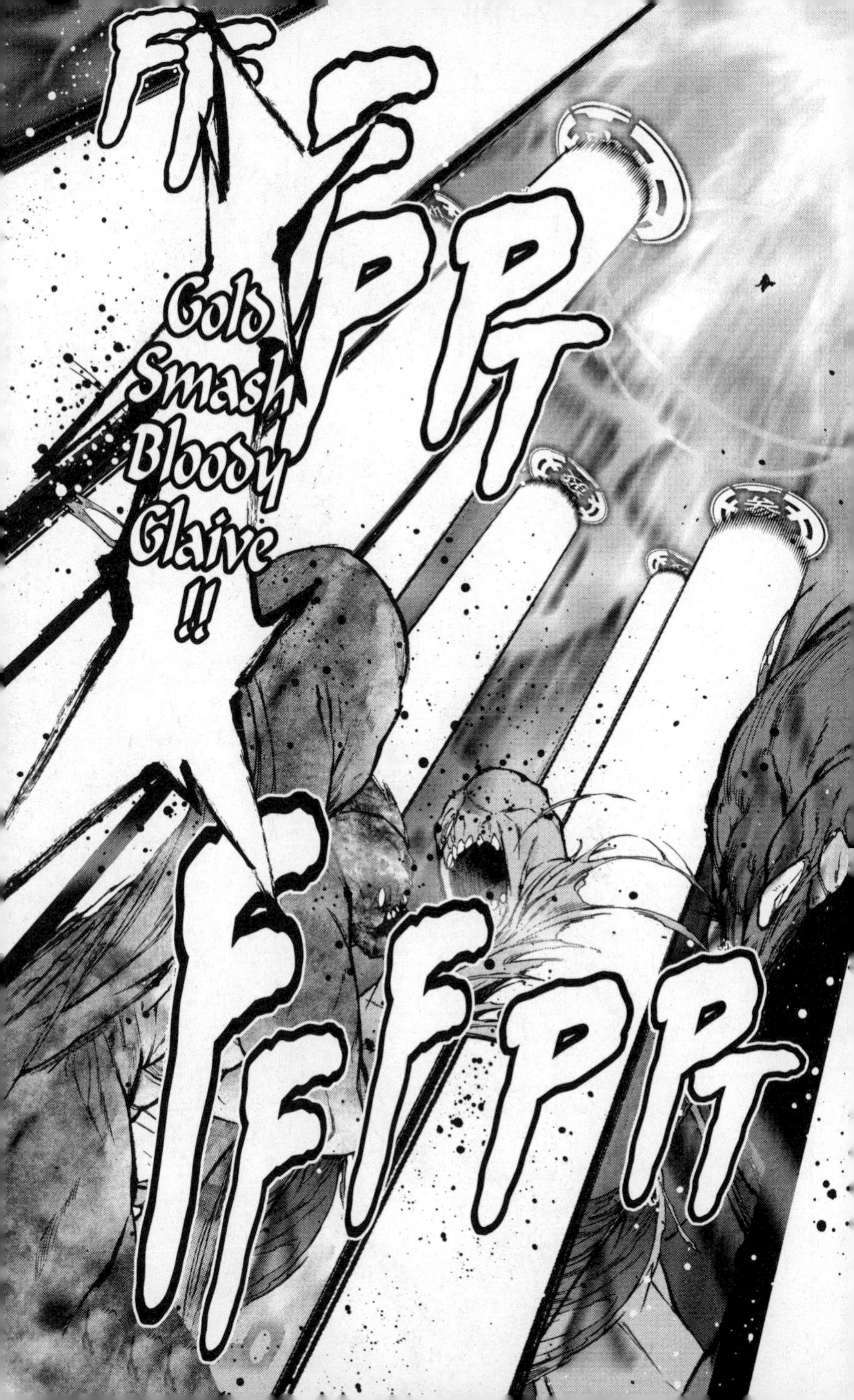
Gold Smash Bloody Glaive !!

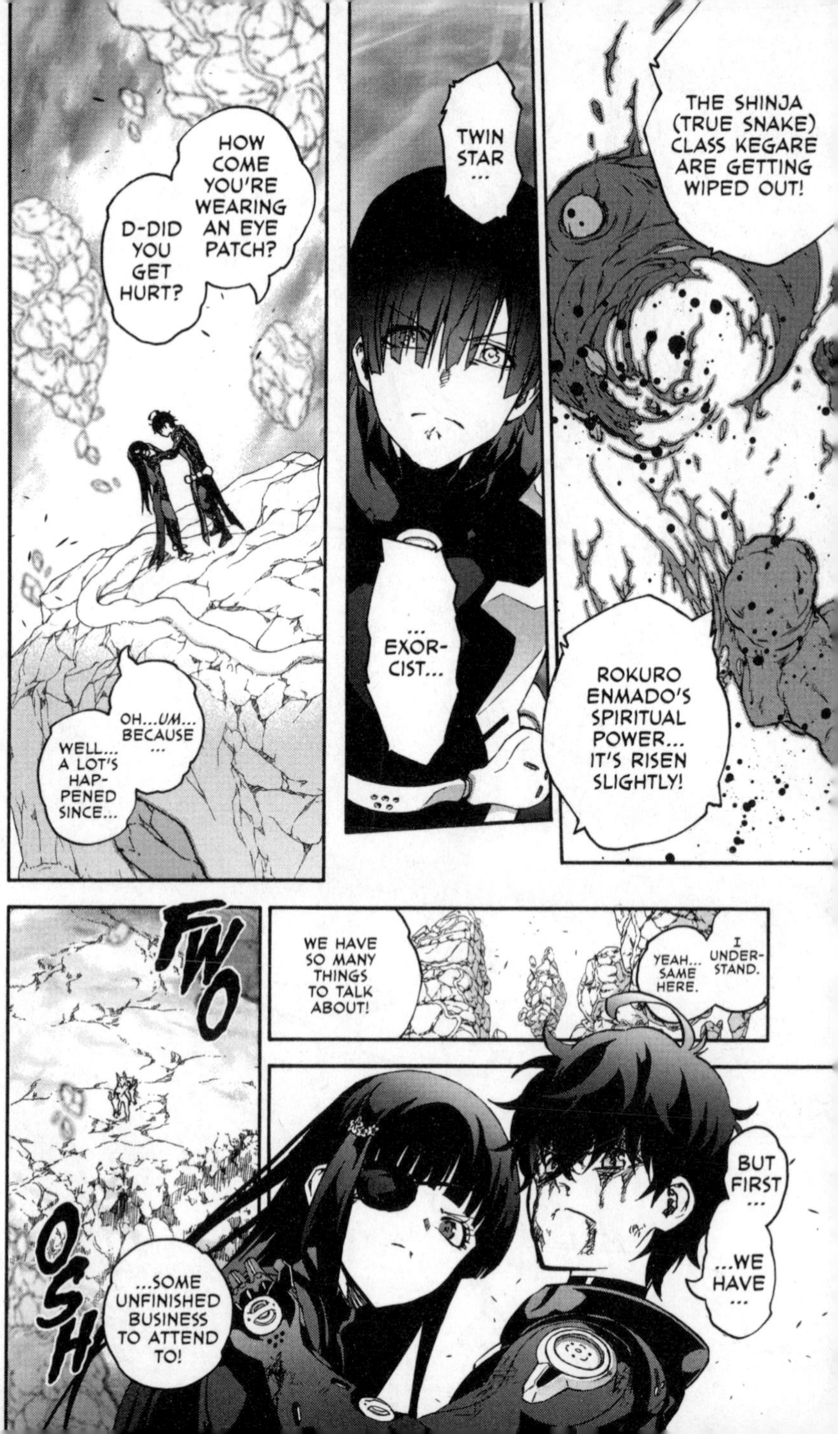
THE SHINJA (TRUE SNAKE) CLASS KEGARE ARE GETTING WIPED OUT!
ROKURO ENMADO'S SPIRITUAL POWER... IT'S RISEN SLIGHTLY!
TWIN STAR ...
... EXORCIST...
HOW COME YOU'RE WEARING AN EYE PATCH?
D-DID YOU GET HURT?
OH...*UM*... BECAUSE ...
WELL... A LOT'S HAPPENED SINCE...
I UNDERSTAND.
YEAH... SAME HERE.
WE HAVE SO MANY THINGS TO TALK ABOUT!
BUT FIRST ...
...WE HAVE ...
...SOME UNFINISHED BUSINESS TO ATTEND TO!
FWO
OSH

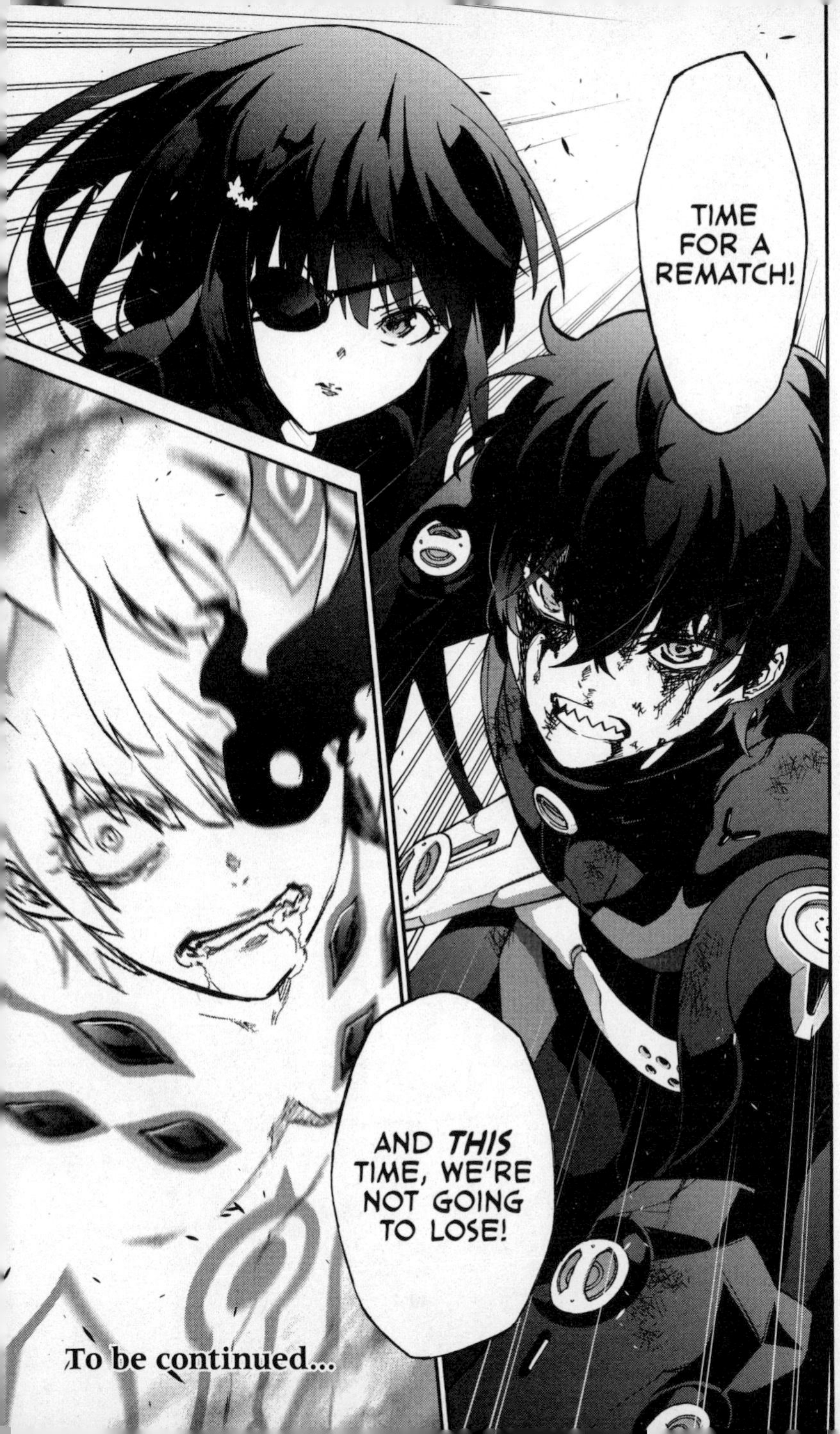
TIME FOR A REMATCH!
AND THIS TIME, WE'RE NOT GOING TO LOSE!
To be continued...

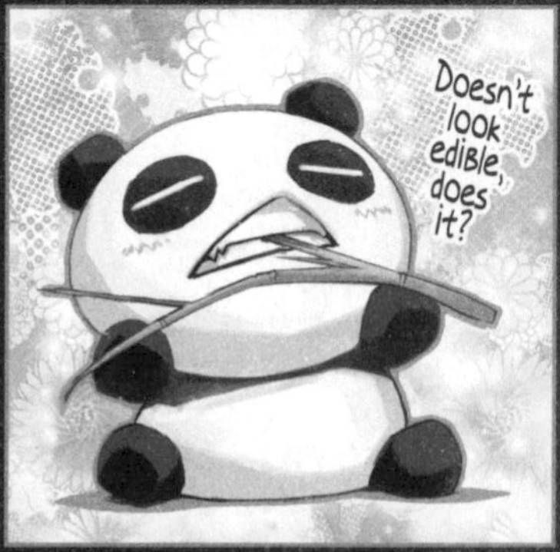
Doesn't look edible, does it?

I don't know what to create when I'm told, "Don't think about sales—just write what you want." Creating manga is fun. I enjoy everything about my work. However, in the back of my mind, because the manga runs in a commercial magazine, I always want it to be popular so it will continue to get published. Besides, it's difficult to completely ignore what people think of your work. Manga making sure is intense...and wonderful!

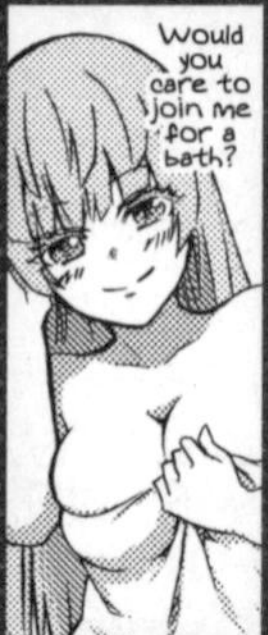
Would you care to join me for a bath?

YOSHIAKI SUKENO was born July 23, 1981, in Wakayama, Japan. He graduated from Kyoto Seika University, where he studied manga. In 2006, he won the Tezuka Award for Best Newcomer Shonen Manga Artist. In 2008, he began his previous work, the supernatural comedy *Binbougami ga!*, which was adapted into the anime *Good Luck Girl!* in 2012.

Birthday Manga

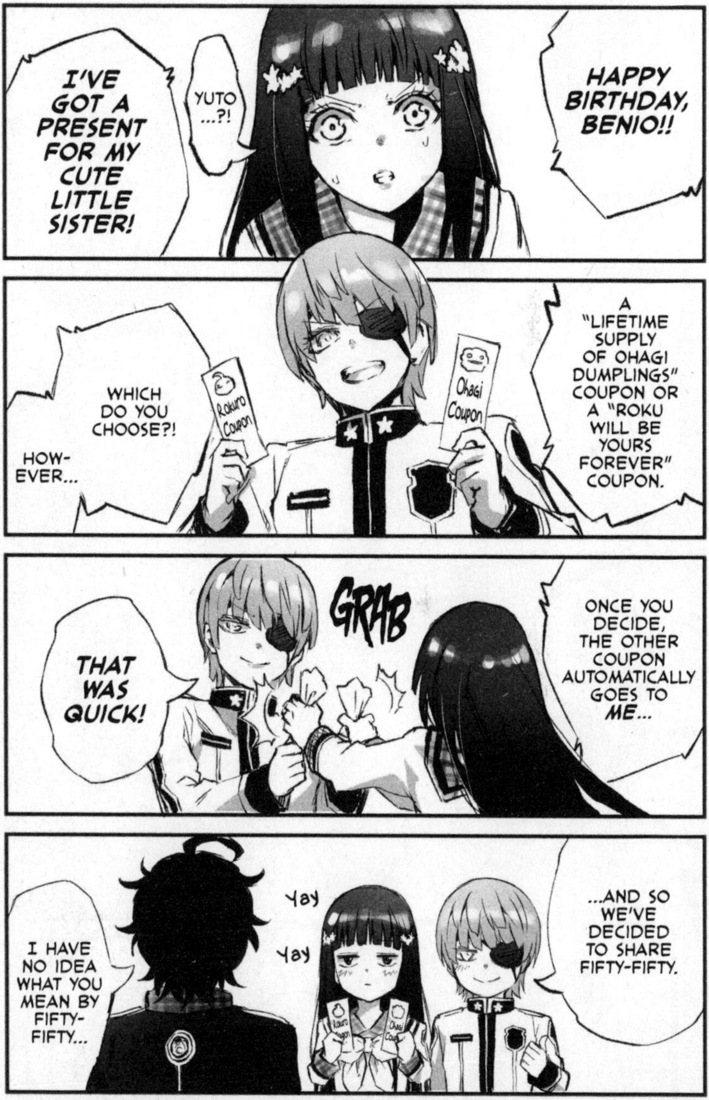
HAPPY BIRTHDAY, BENIO!!
YUTO ...?!
I'VE GOT A PRESENT FOR MY CUTE LITTLE SISTER!
A "LIFETIME SUPPLY OF OHAGI DUMPLINGS" COUPON OR A "ROKU WILL BE YOURS FOREVER" COUPON.
Ohagi Coupon
Rokuro Coupon
WHICH DO YOU CHOOSE?!
HOW-EVER...
ONCE YOU DECIDE, THE OTHER COUPON AUTOMATICALLY GOES TO ME...
GRAB
THAT WAS QUICK!
...AND SO WE'VE DECIDED TO SHARE FIFTY-FIFTY.
Yay
Yay
I HAVE NO IDEA WHAT YOU MEAN BY FIFTY-FIFTY...

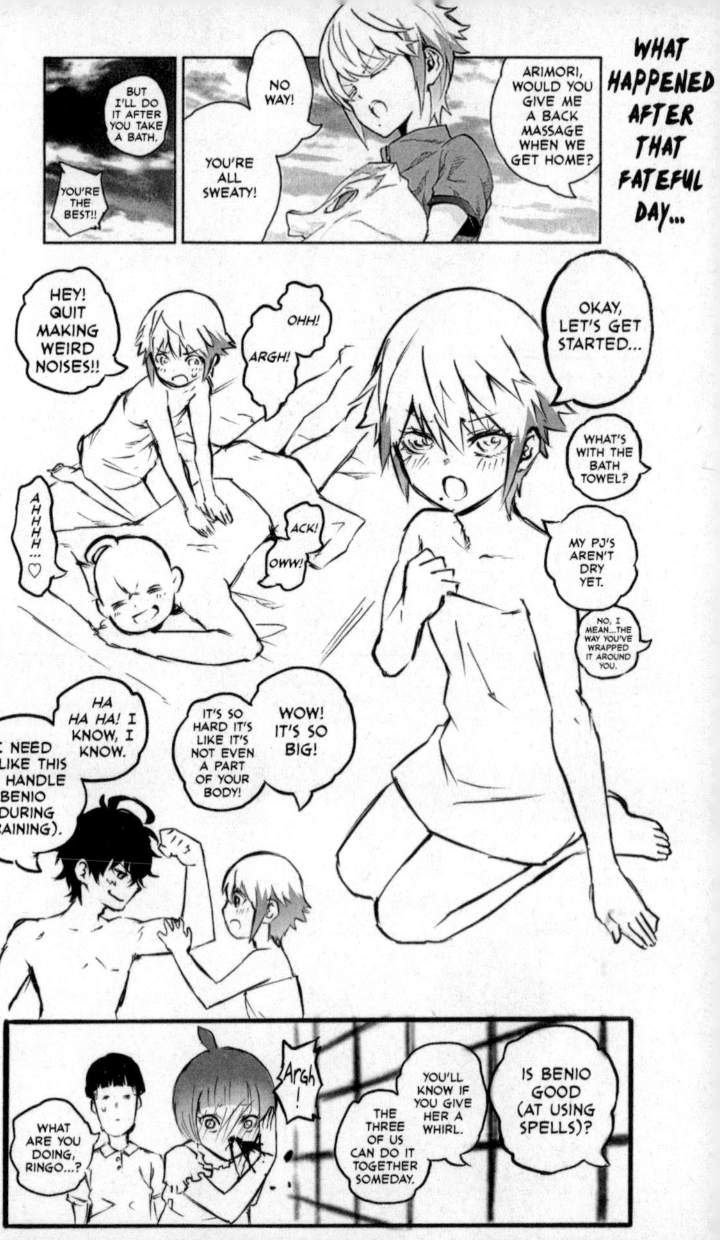
WHAT HAPPENED AFTER THAT FATEFUL DAY...
ARIMORI, WOULD YOU GIVE ME A BACK MASSAGE WHEN WE GET HOME?
NO WAY!
YOU'RE ALL SWEATY!
BUT I'LL DO IT AFTER YOU TAKE A BATH.
YOU'RE THE BEST!!
OKAY, LET'S GET STARTED...
WHAT'S WITH THE BATH TOWEL?
MY PJ'S AREN'T DRY YET.
NO, I MEAN...THE WAY YOU'VE WRAPPED IT AROUND YOU.
OHH!
ARGH!
HEY! QUIT MAKING WEIRD NOISES!!
ACK!
OWW!
AHHHH...♡
WOW! IT'S SO BIG!
IT'S SO HARD IT'S LIKE IT'S NOT EVEN A PART OF YOUR BODY!
HA HA HA! I KNOW, I KNOW.
I NEED IT LIKE THIS TO HANDLE BENIO (DURING TRAINING).
IS BENIO GOOD (AT USING SPELLS)?
YOU'LL KNOW IF YOU GIVE HER A WHIRL.
THE THREE OF US CAN DO IT TOGETHER SOMEDAY.
Argh!
WHAT ARE YOU DOING, RINGO...?

 19

SHONEN JUMP Manga Edition

STORY & ART **Yoshiaki Sukeno**

TRANSLATION **Tetsuichiro Miyaki**
ENGLISH ADAPTATION **Bryant Turnage**
TOUCH-UP ART & LETTERING **Stephen Dutro**
DESIGN **Shawn Carrico**
EDITOR **Annette Roman**

SOUSEI NO ONMYOJI © 2013 by Yoshiaki Sukeno
All rights reserved.
First published in Japan in 2013 by SHUEISHA Inc., Tokyo.
English translation rights arranged by SHUEISHA Inc.

The stories, characters and incidents mentioned in this
publication are entirely fictional.

Printed in the U.S.A.

Published by VIZ Media, LLC
P.O. Box 77010
San Francisco, CA 94107

10 9 8 7 6 5 4 3 2 1
First printing, August 2020

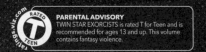

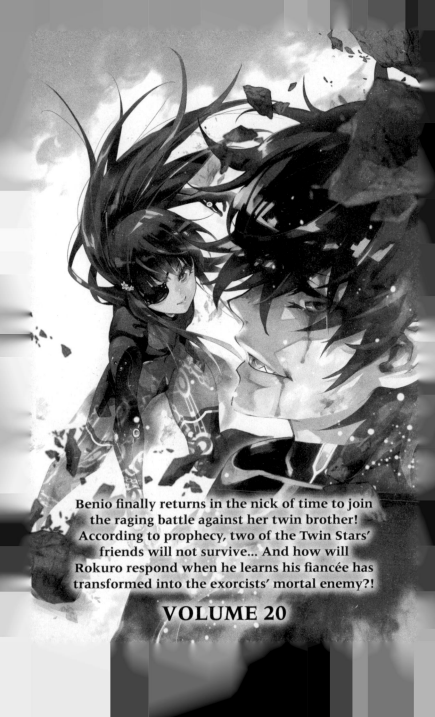

Benio finally returns in the nick of time to join the raging battle against her twin brother! According to prophecy, two of the Twin Stars' friends will not survive... And how will Rokuro respond when he learns his fiancée has transformed into the exorcists' mortal enemy?!

VOLUME 20

Dr.STONE

STORY BY
RIICHIRO INAGAKI

ART BY
BOICHI

One fateful day, all of humanity turned to stone. Many mille
later, Taiju frees himself from petrification and finds him
surrounded by statues. The situation looks grim—until he
into his science-loving friend Senku! Together they plan to res
civilization with the power of science!

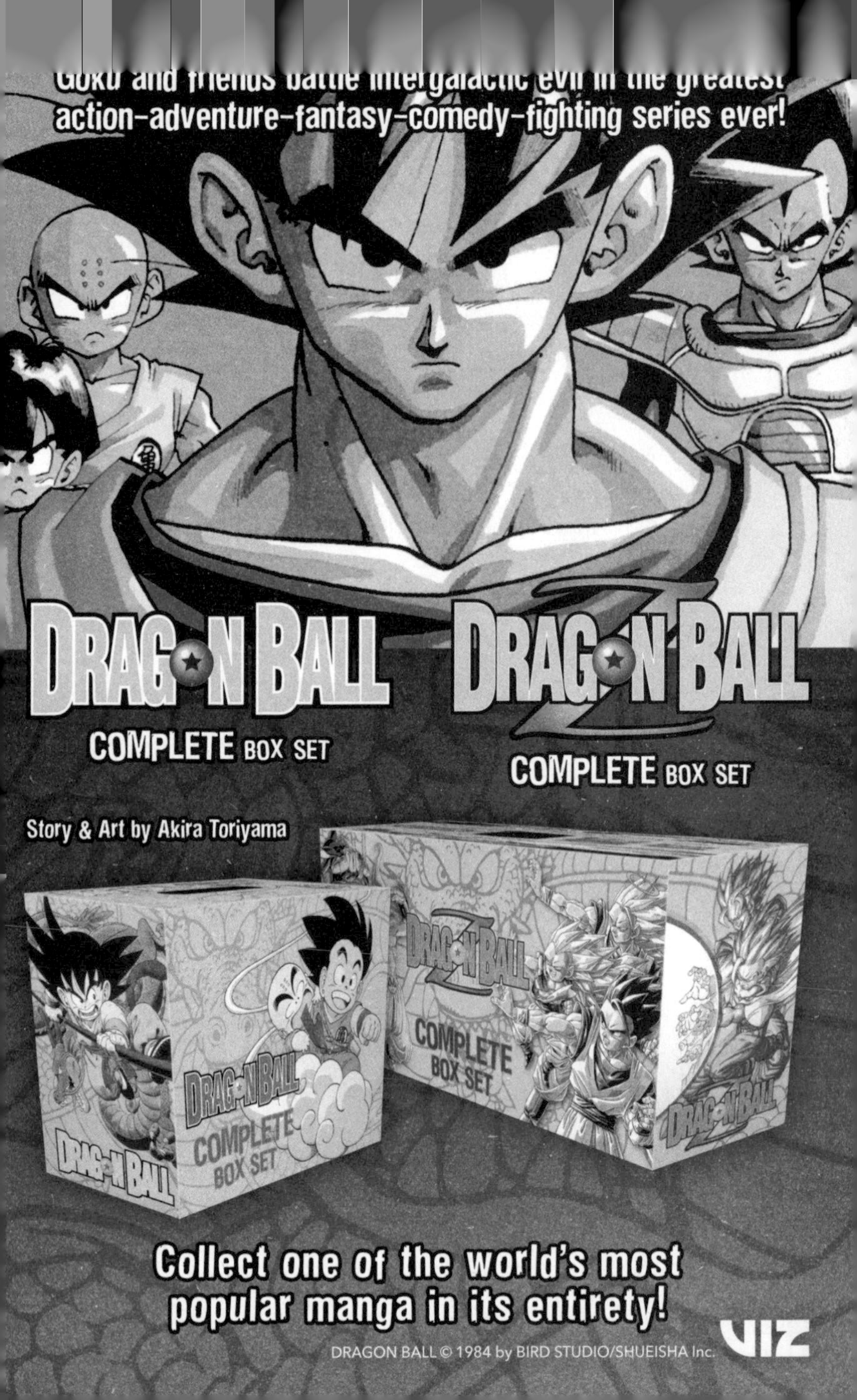

Goku and friends battle intergalactic evil in the greatest
action-adventure-fantasy-comedy-fighting series ever!
DRAGON BALL
COMPLETE BOX SET
DRAGON BALL Z
COMPLETE BOX SET
Story & Art by Akira Toriyama
DRAGON BALL Z
COMPLETE BOX SET
DRAGON BALL Z
DRAGON BALL
DRAGON BALL
COMPLETE BOX SET
Collect one of the world's most popular manga in its entirety!
VIZ
DRAGON BALL © 1984 by BIRD STUDIO/SHUEISHA Inc.

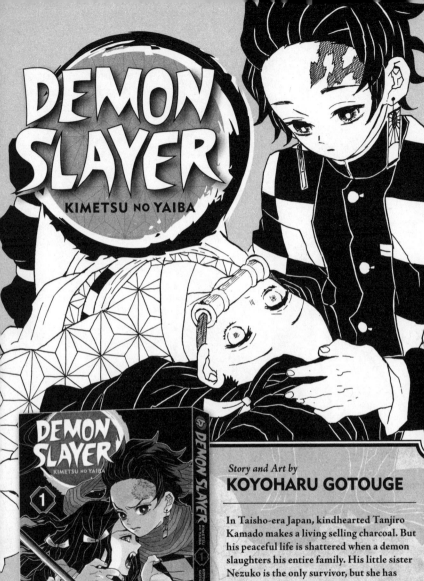

Story and Art by
KOYOHARU GOTOUGE

In Taisho-era Japan, kindhearted Tanjiro Kamado makes a living selling charcoal. But his peaceful life is shattered when a demon slaughters his entire family. His little sister Nezuko is the only survivor, but she has been transformed into a demon herself! Tanjiro sets out on a dangerous journey to find a way to return his sister to normal and destroy the demon who ruined his life.

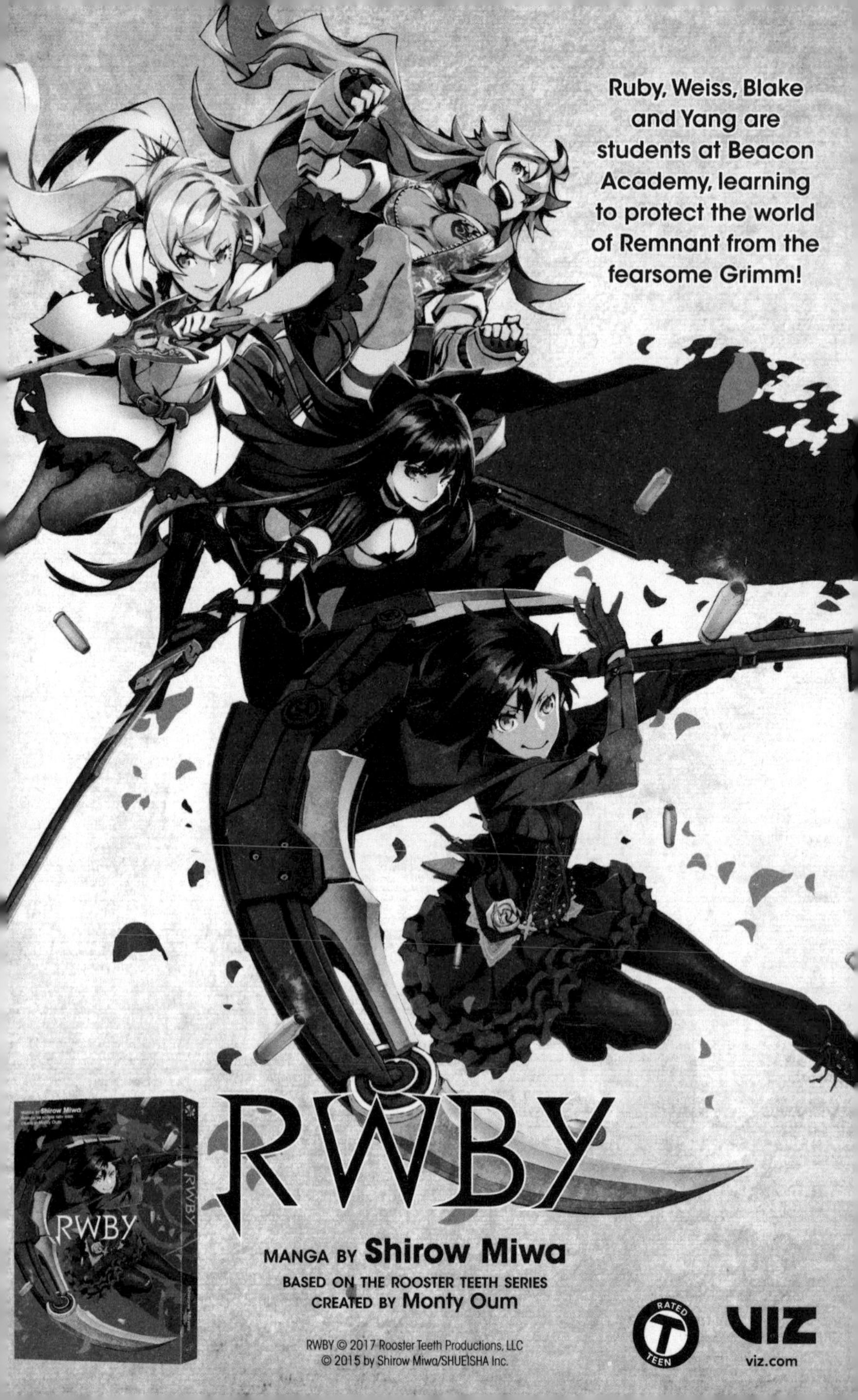
Ruby, Weiss, Blake and Yang are students at Beacon Academy, learning to protect the world of Remnant from the fearsome Grimm!
RWBY
MANGA BY Shirow Miwa
BASED ON THE ROOSTER TEETH SERIES
CREATED BY Monty Oum
RWBY © 2017 Rooster Teeth Productions, LLC
© 2015 by Shirow Miwa/SHUEISHA Inc.
RATED T TEEN
VIZ
viz.com